SCARLET RIBBON

A Personal History of
Manchester United

JOHN LUDDEN

ALL RIGHTS RESERVED

'ABIDE WITH ME'

Scarlet Ribbon: If you're properly cursed everyone's relationship with their football team has moments that will live with you forever. They don't have to be fantastic wins or great goals. It could be one almighty fine day out with friends or a memory of watching a match with your dad when you got absolutely hammered 5-0. But he might have said something that made you laugh and forever more will be there when you think of your team's colours.
And your dad.
Football is an addiction, don't let anyone kid you. Whether it be Morecambe, Mansfield or Manchester United. I became a red through family, late seventies, I picked my games! The first, West Bromwich Albion at home when we got beat 5-3. However, at the time in complete young anorak mode just to score three goals under Dave Sexton was today akin to winning the Champion's league. So, began a lifetime love affair. The 1979 FA Cup semi-final replay at Goodison Park against Liverpool. Listening with my mum and gran whilst my dad was at the match. The crackling tones emerging through the transistor radio and then Jimmy scored! My gran one of the great United fans and I miss her so.
A first trophy in 1983, Big Ron's team, Robbo, Whiteside and the lads, a thirteen-year-old watching United running round Wembley with the FA Cup. The eighties though, my season ticket should have been issued with a health warning stamped Liverpool. Come the nineties and Ferguson. Night turned to day. The Anfield mob were not just put in their place but evicted.

I experienced United winning the league after twenty-six years. I saw the European cup ripped from Bayern Munich in Barcelona like a thief in the night. Under Moscow red skies in a Mancunian downpour we drank and danced till dawn and more as my team took on and beat Abramovich's Chelsea in his own back yard. This as he watched on a throne. Priceless.

Life, kids, work, spark and shine, they break your heart and can make you cry, smile, laugh and scream at the moon, but one thing remains constant. Through love and despair Manchester United football club have always been there. My favourite moment as a red? Listening to 'Abide with Me' before kick-off at the 1994 FA Cup final against Chelsea and soaked to the skin as the rain came down. Then, with twenty minutes to go and 4-0 up the double won, United fans broke into a rendition of 'She wore a scarlet ribbon.'

Hope you enjoy the read. A selection of articles, stage plays and books.

You get one team,

and Manchester United were mine.

"She wore, she wore,
she wore a scarlet ribbon,
She wore a scarlet ribbon
in the merry month of May,
And when I asked why she wore that ribbon,
She said it's for United
and we're going to Wembley,
Wembley, Wembley,
We're the famous Man Utd
and we're goin' to Wembley,
Wembley, Wembley..."

The First time:
December 1978: The first you see is the floodlights from the 112 bus. We pile off, a sea of red. My Dad grabs my hand. The police horses, ticket touts…a man with 'THE END IS NIGH' sign. Walking down the Warwick Road. So proud of my scarf. 'Glory, Glory Man United' roars out, fists in the air. The smells of burgers and chips. It's freezing and starts to snow! 'Zip your coat up' says Dad' We reach the forecourt and I catch my breath and grab Dad's hand tighter. So,
this is Old Trafford. Wow!

CONTENTS

Introduction:
The Coachbuilders

Chapter One
The Coming of Busby

Chapter Two
If I hadn't seen such Riches: Jimmy Murphy

Chapter Three
A Certain Vintage: Duncan Edwards

Chapter Four
Miracles and Wonder: Duncan Edwards: The Eighth Day

Chapter Five
The Eighth Day: Munich

Chapter Six
Scarlet Ribbon: A United obsession with the European cup 1956-58 (Part One) (Book)

Chapter Seven
Blood in the Snow: Sir Matt Busby

Chapter Eight
Keep the Red Flag Flying: FA Cup Fifth Round: Wednesday 19th February 1958: Manchester United v Sheffield Wednesday

Chapter Nine
Once Upon a Time in Munich: Jimmy Murphy:(Book)

Chapter Ten
Champions of Honour

Chapter Eleven
THE 1963 FA Cup Final: Manchester United v Leicester City

Chapter Twelve
The Coming of Georgie Boy: Benfica v Manchester United: European Cup Quarter Final: Second leg: 1965

Chapter Thirteen
Bad Tidings from Belgrade: Manchester United v Partizan Belgrade: European Cup Semi Final: 1966

Chapter Fourteen
Strictly Business: Real Madrid v Manchester United: European Cup Semi-Final: Second Leg: 1968

Chapter Fifteen
The Boys of 68: Manchester United v Benfica: The European Cup Final: 1968

Chapter Sixteen
Fallen Angels: Matt and Jimmy:(Stage-Play)

Chapter Seventeen
Wilf (Part One): Novena

Chapter Eighteen
Twisted Blood: Georgie at Chelsea

Chapter Nineteen
What the Hell: George

Chapter Twenty
Wilf: (Part Two) Let It Be

Chapter Twenty-one
When the Lights Went Out: Manchester United v Manchester City: 1974

Chapter Twenty-Two
One Night in Manchester: Barcelona: 1984

Chapter Twenty-Three
The Scotsman: 1986: (Stage-Play)

Unpublished chapters From Cantona: When the Seagull Flew

Chapter Twenty-Four
Welcome to Manchester: Sheffield Wednesday v Manchester United: 1993

Chapter Twenty-Five
A Sense of Wonder: Sheffield Wednesday v Manchester United: 1993

Chapter Twenty-Six
Never Again: Manchester City v Manchester United: 1993

Chapter Twenty-Seven
Red Rain: Norwich City v Manchester United: 1993

Chapter Twenty-Eight
United South: Crystal Palace Manchester United: 1993

Chapter Twenty-Nine
When the Seagull Flew: Eric Cantona: (Book)

Chapter Thirty
Dancing with Tears in Red Eyes: Barcelona 1999

Chapter Thirty-One
The Man who can't be moved: Sir Alex Ferguson

Chapter Thirty-Two
The Ginger Prince: Paul Scholes goal against Barcelona: 2008

Chapter Thirty-Three
Priceless: John Terry's penalty: Moscow: 2008

Chapter Thirty-Four
Flares of Manchester: 2010:

Chapter Thirty-Five
Murder on the Dance Floor: United in Madrid: 2013

Chapter Thirty-Six
One Night Only: Cristiano Ronaldo: 2013

Chapter Thirty-Seven
There is a light that will never go out: Manchester/Madrid: 2013

Chapter Thirty-Eight
Fergie's Way: Sir Alex Ferguson

Chapter Thirty-Nine
Silver Bullet: David Moyes: 2014

Chapter Forty
Kingdom for a Horse: Sir Alex Ferguson

Introduction
THE BEGINNING

The year of 1878 sees the birth of the 'Galveston Giant' Jack Johnson, the first black heavyweight champion. It's also witness to British soldiers embroiled in bloody battle against a ferocious enemy in the mountains of Afghanistan. No change there. A flash of inspiration enables inventor Thomas Edison to begin work on the light bulb. Whilst in the American Wild-West, the murderous Lincoln County War begins and introduces to a fascinated American audience a certain William H Bonney. Better known as 'Billy the kid.'

Meanwhile, faraway in mid-Victorian Manchester, England, in a place called Newton Heath, the age of the Industrial Revolution is at hand. Tall, grimy chimneys poke their miserable noses into permanently murky skies. This is the terminus for the Manchester to Leeds railway and against a deafening backdrop of thunderous, rattling freight trains, a group of young men whose faces are still blackened by working in a depot yard are busy kicking a ball about.

These lads are employees of the Lancashire and Yorkshire Railway company and have recently been granted permission to form a works team by the grand gentlemen of the Dining Room Committee and wagon Works. Such is the enthusiasm for this new venture the railwaymen happily agree to pay a subscription for the right to play, but still they require a pitch

Luckily, in a rare show of generosity the Dining Committee are also providing them with a plot of company wasteland and goalposts in nearby North Road for matches. Sat alongside a railway line the surface is a pitiable sight, resembling a stone strewn, clay-scarred pit. A jagged, rock-hard death trap in summer and a mud-splattered swamp during winter. Adding further insult is the constant irritant of thick swirling mists of steam that engulfs all every time a train passes. But it's a 'home' and here amidst such splendour Newton Heath LYR football team are formed.

Match day preparations starts half a mile away at the Three Crowns pub on Oldham Road. Courtesy of a good-hearted landlord they are allowed to change, then a ten-minute dash to North Road for kick off. Playing in vivid colours of green and gold shirts, LYR challenge fellow inter-departmentals and excel against all. Rail yard teams further along the line from Middleton, Earlestown and Oldham come to North Road and are handed a beating. However, there is one side that due to local pride and Newton Heath bragging rights never lies down. Contests versus the neighbouring Company's Motive Power Division or 'Newton Heath Loco' are never for the faint hearted.

Loco play home matches a stone's throw away from North Bank at Ceylon Street. With their team made up from engine drivers and maintenance men weekday quarrels and fall outs are settled on a Saturday afternoon as the two local rivals fly at each other with a passion. But Loco apart, there is a serious lack of opponents good enough within the company to give Newton Heath L&YR a decent game. With crowds rising weekly and a growing reputation for tough, but good attacking play reaching beyond their own works set up, it's time to spread wings. Invitations are sent further afield for others to try their hand against the mighty 'Heathens!' Or as they are also becoming known. The 'Coachbuilders.' Letters are posted to such potentially exalted opponents as Manchester Arcadians, Hurst Brook Rovers, Dalton Hall and Blackburn Olympic amongst others. At the Three Crowns pub amidst the beery laughter, chit-chat and pipe smoke they await with anticipation whether their challenges will be accepted. Small acorns….

C1
THE COMING OF BUSBY

On 11th March 1941, the air raid sirens scream out in the city of Manchester. Dancing shafts of light illuminate the night sky searching for invaders. The ferocious crackle of anti-aircraft fire roars up at an invisible but deadly foe. The decision has been taken by German high command to destroy the munitions factories in Trafford Park. Also, the Park is home to Metropolitan Vickers whom make the Avro Lancaster bombers. This along with Ford who build the Rolls-Royce engines to power the planes make it a much sought-after target for the Germans. For three hours the bombs rain down as throughout the evening fierce battles rage to stem the fires that blaze across the city.

Leaping flames emblazoned against a red horizon. An inferno. It's a relieved Manchester that watches the sun rise above the River Irwell the next morning. One unexpected victim of the carnage is the home of Manchester United football club. A stray incendiary device fell setting it alight. Behind one goal an entire grandstand lies gutted, whilst the remainders of the terraces are reduced to rubble. Come the war's end Old Trafford cuts a pitiful sight. It appears only divine intervention can revive this ailing-seemingly dying club. A man arrives by train clutching onto a suitcase, wearing a trilby hat and smoking burnt-down cigarettes. Company Sergeant Major Matt Busby is home from the war and has come to Manchester.

C2
IF I HADN'T SEEN SUCH RICHES
JIMMY MURPHY

The Welsh Rhondda valleys have always bred a special type of person. Poets, fighters, singers and politicians. True leaders of men. Plenty have emerged from those grim black hills. An upbringing harsh but one that defined a certain kind of personality when growing up. You never moaned. Tears only shed in solitary silence and nothing ever stood in the way of getting the job done. Jimmy Murphy was of such stock and never were these traits required more than in the immediate aftermath of the Munich Air disaster. Murphy should have been on the Elizabethan aircraft that crashed through the end of that runway perimeter before finally coming amid raging fire and leaping flames, to a deathly, shuddering halt.
So much blood in the snow.
It was only at the insistence of Busby that he travelled to Cardiff instead of Belgrade, in his capacity as team coach to manage Wales against Israel, in a vital world cup qualifier that saved his life. The seat where Murphy would almost inevitably have sat, next to Busby was taken by Bert Whalley, who was killed outright.
Fate taking a helping if dark hand in the lives of men whom awoke that long gone Thursday morning sixty years ago, not knowing come the end of the day their lives would either have been ended or changed inextricably forever.
It was a joyful Murphy who returned to Manchester wholly unaware of what had occurred in Southern Germany. It was only on arrival at Old Trafford clutching a box of oranges, courtesy of the Israelis, that he was informed of the horrific events. One cannot even imagine

the thoughts of this man who along with Matt Busby had reared this team of boys into arguably one of the two or three top sides in European football at that time.
And, with an average age of just twenty-one they were only ever going to improve.
But, more importantly the babes were like sons to Murphy. His tools were a curse and a kind word. A bark and a smile. He hammered them, he praised them. He made them laugh, he made them cry. He made them rage with a grim determination to prove to him they were good enough for the United first team. They loved him and it must be said at times must have loathed and hated Murphy.
For their own good he taught them how to fight the good fight.
And he made them listen.
The poet and the fighter from the grim hills installed into them the basics of professional football. He also preached something infinitely more important. The Manchester United way of playing football.
You give the ball to a red shirt, help your mate. You pass and move and never stop running. You never give up.
With a passion and a clenched fist Murphy drummed home his message that to succeed at Old Trafford you needed so much more than just simple talent.
Heart, guts and the desire to die for the cause.
But, not on airplane in a far-off country returning home from a football match.
Not on a plane in a raging snowstorm where a third take-off should never have been attempted.
Not on a plane.
Not at Munich…...

Once he had downed a bottle of whisky and shed the needed heart-breaking, initial tears Murphy got on with the job of keeping Manchester United alive. A visit to the Rechts Der Isar hospital where a still gravely injured Busby pleaded with him to, 'Keep the flag flying to till I get back Jimmy,' was almost too much for the emotional Welshman to take. He promised to do so whilst clutching his old friend's hand.

And then he saw Duncan Edwards. His prodigy and favourite son amongst the babes. Duncan's body badly broken and beyond repair, but his spirit raging on. The thirst for one last battle was still there in the boy from Dudley.

'What time's kick off Jimmy?' It was all too much. A breaking down alone on a hospital stairway when he thought no one was listening, but secretly witnessed by United goalkeeper and hero of Munich, Harry Gregg. 'Jimmy cried and wailed. I could feel his great huge Welsh heart breaking.'

In his efforts to keep United going amid the unfathomable weight of sadness and depression that had engulfed Manchester, Murphy achieved miracles and wonder to honour his promise to Busby.

The flag was kept flying and Jimmy Murphy, the most undervalued man in the history of Manchester United scraped, argued, fought, cursed and battled to keep his beloved club afloat. So many funerals were attended. Devastated husbands, wives, fathers, mothers, daughters and sons. All handled with dignity and tenderness. Rare in Rhondda, but a trait Murphy possessed in abundance as he hugged, embraced and wiped away tears on the faces of the grieving.

Jimmy cried along, they were his boys too.

All of them.

To this day I'm not sure people are fully aware of just what Jimmy Murphy achieved in ensuring Manchester United did not die in the immediate aftermath of Munich. The idea of closure and winding up the club was discussed at board level, but swiftly knocked down by Murphy who raged at such an idea.

And, so, ranting furiously against the dying of the light and led by Murphy, United stood their ground, but for a time it was close.

So very close.

"If I hadn't seen such riches" goes the line in the James song *Sit Down*. Well, it was through Jimmy Murphy that ultimately, they did.

That there is no statue of him amidst the many that now stand at Old Trafford could simply be because of an embarrassment of when Jimmy was all but forced out of the club in the early seventies. Quietly retired. Hints were dropped that he was no longer wanted around the place. They took his taxi away?

That a man who saved this football club from extinction was treated with such indignity is a disgrace. At Manchester United never mix the myth and the legend with the reality. Never truer than in Jimmy Murphy's case.

The man from the Rhondda valleys who loved to tinker on the piano is the greatest of red heroes in my opinion and should never be forgotten.

C3
A CERTAIN VINTAGE
DUNCAN EDWARDS

Ask any Manchester United supporter of a certain vintage about Duncan Edwards, and almost inevitably the eyes will moist over and there will be a lump in the throat. Of all the great players whom have worn the red shirt with distinction over past decades, none have inspired more debate or devotion than the boy from Dudley who became not just an adopted citizen of the rainy city, but one of Manchester's most beloved sons. Though every soul lost in the Munich disaster was a spear through the heart, the loss of Edwards at the time was perhaps felt most profusely. More so because his injuries it was claimed would have felled lesser mortals. Not so Duncan, who battled on against all earthly odds to amaze and astonish the German doctors and nurses at the Rechts Der Isar hospital in Munich, whom all fought with grim determination to save him. When ultimately Edwards lost his fight for life fifteen days after the initial crash, their tears fell equally long and hard as those that were shed in the houses, shops and factories across Manchester.

That even now Edwards possesses the power to reduce grown men to emotional wrecks can only be due to the effect of what they witnessed him performing on a field. A powerhouse of a footballer and who today would be considered utterly priceless. Blessed with a thunderous shot, two great feet, strong and fast, great balance, a devil in the tackle and the ability to hit teammates with thirty yards passes. And, as Jimmy Murphy once so famous said, 'When we knock the rough edges off Duncan he'll be quite a player.'

For Edwards was only twenty-one years old when the heavens fell on Manchester United football club and the airplane bringing them home from Belgrade erupted into fire and flames in the Munich snow.

Twelve months previous United's 'Busby Babes' had run the imperious Real Madrid close in the European cup semi-final. In the second leg at Old Trafford, a 2-2 draw was sufficient to see Real go through 5-3 on aggregate, but the visitors, none more than the great Alfredo di Stefano were hugely impressed by the ferocity and skill of Edwards. On hearing news of the dreadful events in southern Germany, Di Stefano, as were all at Madrid, left devastated at such a tragic loss of life, 'No one deserved more than Duncan, a fullness of a great career.'

As this Munich anniversary arrives once more and the truly heartfelt accolades are spoken. As flowers are laid and songs sung. Older supporters will close their eyes and remember what must surely now feel like a different lifetime ago, that bunch of bouncing Busby Babes. And, if you really want to know about the magic of those times, those special young players. Duncan Edwards especially, well ask them. Then, look into their eyes and you will have your answer. A certain vintage. Born in Dudley, but ultimately, one of ours.

C4
MIRACLES AND WONDER
DUNCAN EDWARDS

If you believe the legends Duncan Edwards was seven-foot tall, spat thunder and unleashed lightning bolts from both feet. Others whom actually witnessed him play will tell you he was better than that.

No player in the history of Manchester United has attracted such love and interest than the devastatingly talented and hugely charismatic, handsome Dudley born Edwards, who at just twenty-one was lost to the world in the Munich air disaster.

That Edwards fought with such courage against injuries sustained in the crash for a further fifteen days only increased the pain and heartache felt across Manchester, and indeed the world when he finally took his last breath just after midnight, on 21st February, 1958.

Those many supporters who had prayed for Duncan to somehow be the catalyst for a United revival were crushed as news broke from southern Germany that Munich had claimed its final victim. As a footballer Duncan Edwards was a phenomenon. Powerful, fast, two footed, a thunderous shot, could see a pass and possessed the discipline and know how to play in any number of positions. Both for Manchester United and England he had already become irreplaceable.

Not just the heartbeat of the teams but the cornerstone. With Edwards, no matter how hopeless the situation there was always hope. Even at such a tender age supporters and fellow players had the attitude, 'If Big Dunc is playing everything is going to be all right.

Everything is going to be fine.'

The season previous with United going for a treble, generations before the miracle of Barcelona, they came up against a magnificent Real Madrid team in the European cup semi-final. Over two legs an Alfredo Di Stefano inspired Real simply proved too much, but in the return game at Old Trafford, Edwards made a profound effect on the Madrilenos and especially on Di Stefano. Not known for showering praise and quick to dampen any whom he feels may dance precariously in his shadow and take away the glory from himself, the 'Blond Arrow' spoke to his president after the match and informed him, 'If there is one player that could improve us it is Duncan Edwards.'

Then, a year on, as news of Edwards passing reached Madrid, an emotional Di Stefano spoke movingly to say, 'Today my heart is broken. None deserved more than the fullness of a great career.'

After the first game in the Spanish capital their president, Don Santiago Bernabeu, presented all the United players with a solid gold watch. None cherished this gift more than Edwards, who even when lay dying in his Munich hospital bed cried out for it. At first there was confusion but a taxi was sent to the crash site where luckily it was found and returned to Duncan.

For a while it was said the watch helped inspire a minor revival in Edwards. As ever with this young footballer hope sprung eternal, but sadly time ran out and the boy they fought invincible passed away. Such had been the brave fight to cling for life German doctors and nurses were left in floods of tears.

Legend also says that on his last breath the watch also stopped. Probably an urban myth, but one you would really like to believe was true.

I've published a book called The Promise. It's best described as a Mancunian 'Field of Dreams' featuring the Busby Babes coming back, albeit momentarily to help a grieving family. (It's a long story!) In it Edwards is united once more with his beloved watch.
There is a line in the Promise that features heavily.
'These are the days of miracles and wonder.'
But the true times of such magic were back in the mid to late fifties when Edwards and his fellow team mates were lighting up Manchester from black and white into technicolour. The great man may not have been seven-foot tall, spat thunder or indeed unleash lightning bolts from both feet, but do you know something?
I like to believe he was better than that.
R.I.P Duncan.

C5
THE EIGHTH DAY
MUNICH

Because so much has been written about the dreadful events of that horrific Munich afternoon of 6th February 1958, it is easy to forget that a true miracle did actually occur that gruesome day. This calamity in southern Germany rocked not only Manchester,
but indeed, the entire world.

A football team that in such a short space of time had captured not just more than their fair share of trophies, but maybe equally as important countless hearts. The Busby Babes, young boys reared in a style of playing the game by Sir Matt Busby and his assistant Jimmy Murphy. One so simple it was brilliant and when put to use on a football pitch utterly devastating, 'Give the ball to a red shirt. Pass and move.' They were a phenomenon. Nothing it appeared would be able to stand in the path of this outstanding team from beneath the billowing Mancunian smog and smoke. United were coming. Edwards, Colman, Pegg, Whelan, Taylor and so many more. An array of exciting young British and Irish talent that had been unearthed, nurtured and when deemed ready by Busby and Murphy, let loose on their first division rivals.

And, for a short but unforgettable period Europe's elite. But then came Munich,
and as dark clouds gathered over Manchester and news began to filter through from Germany of the ever-rising list of the dead, then what was once a dream turned overnight into a living nightmare. The Babes were no more.

Eight players in time were lost with Duncan Edwards fighting ferociously for fifteen days following the crash. Sadly, even his gigantic efforts would prove in vain for Edwards's injuries were just too great.

Old Trafford became a home of ghosts. Of torment and bitter, sad memories. Every corridor haunted with voices of the dead players. Distant laughter but when you looked there was nobody there?

It appeared Manchester United football club had reached its dying embers.

Step forward Jimmy Murphy, who as if possessed took control of this fallen giant and ensured that on the eighth day, United would start to rise from the ashes. What happened next and the following decade was a footballing and indeed human miracle.

For only ten years later on an unforgettable night at Wembley stadium, Manchester United became champions of Europe and it was one of the survivors of that dreadful day who staggered out of the felled aircraft, Bobby Charlton, who raised the trophy.

It is a tale if played out on a Hollywood big screen you would feel inclined to think, absolutely no chance. But it happened, it was real. The pain, horror and ultimate ecstasy. A journey's end that began when it was felt everything was lost. For truly the miracle of Munich was that amidst the shooting fire and flames of that burning aircraft, men such as Charlton, Bill Foulkes, Harry Gregg and of course the manager Sir Matt Busby were somehow spared the fate of so many others.

As the 60th anniversary dawns, when candles are lit, songs are sung and accolades are spoken, let it be remembered that the above lived to see the memories of those lost honoured against Benfica. And, when the great goalscorer Eusebio raced clear with only minutes to go, maybe it was a heavenly nudge from Duncan Edwards that caused the 'Black Panther' to fire untypically into Alex Stepney's stomach and leave an everlasting tread mark. Written in the stars?

Who knows for it really was that kind of story.

When times get rough once more let us recall that Manchester United football club, our team have lived through infinitely worst times. For thanks to men such as Busby and Murphy, United are still around, this alone is a miracle. And that is the eighth day.

C6
SCARLET RIBBON 1956-58
(part one)
A UNITED OBSESSION WITH
THE EUROPEAN CUP

Wembley Stadium: Champions League Final: Saturday 28th May 2011: It occurs in the 34rd minute, a slide pass from Ryan Giggs for Wayne Rooney to take aim and curl a delightful shot into the top corner past diving keeper Victor Valdez. 1-1! Suddenly, after being toyed with by a Barcelona team that treated possession like a spoilt child holds onto their favourite toy Manchester United are level.

And, for me this is a great place to begin.

As the scarlet ribbon song roars out from the United fans to salute Rooney's wonderful goal it comes laced with a history and a passion few clubs can claim to possess when it comes to this wonderful competition. An enduring love affair of heart-rending emotion. Of magnificent victories and gut-wrenching defeats. Of triumph and despair.

This will be a journey from beginning to end. From 1957 to the present day. It will be unpredictable and I hope interesting as we tell what is an astonishing tale of a football club that was almost wiped out in an air crash. We'll be meeting characters and revisiting matches from both sides. United against giants. The greats of Di Stefano, Gento, Eusebio, Ronaldo, Eusebio and the inestimable Messi.

It will be emotional, but for this book alone here is the first act. 1956-1958

1956: It begins with a terse phone call from the head of the English Football Association Alan Hardaker, to Manchester United manager Matt Busby. Hardaker tells Busby that under no circumstances, like Chelsea before them will United be allowed to enter this newly formed so-called European Champions Cup. Deeming it a nuisance, a pestilence and only for 'bloody foreigners.' Hardaker went so far as claiming to a Times Journalist, 'A competition with too many wogs and dagoes.' Whereas Chelsea had succumbed to the Football League's (bullying) pressure, Manchester United refuse totally to bow down. He is told in no uncertain terms by Busby to stay out of his club's business. Hardaker is left fuming and bitter, but ultimately helpless.

The United manager and his assistant coach Jimmy Murphy believe that the foreign fields of Europe are the next logical step for their boys to ply their illustrious trade. These lads reared through the United youth system. Impressive 'young apples' the best of the barrel. Products of a pass and move style of play that is already mesmerising much more experienced opponents in the First Division. The genie is out of the lamp.

It is just a question of how much better they will get. Busby and Murphy had watched like so many in stunned awe three years earlier when Ferenc Puskas and his magnificent cherry-shirted Magyars arrived almost unknown on these shores and rewrote not just the history books, but the coaching manuals also. The Hungarian's 6-3 dismantling of the previously unbeaten English at Wembley proving almost a religious experience for the football romantics.

These were strangers to the Western eye. Red dervishes, whom on that never to be forgotten date of 25th

November 1953, flitted in and out of the London fog and mist like ghosts. Phantom-like from behind the hidden menace of the foreboding Communist bloc. But there was so much more. A beauty and a magic dust about them. For as Puskas, Hidegkuti, Bozsik and Czibor toyed, tore and terrorised the home team to an inglorious surrender, a million eyes were opened.

The United management duo devise a plan. Taking the best of the Magyar philosophy and adding their own particular style they produce under northern grim, murky skies, a wonderful concoction of devil blood red. One that lights up this Mancunian outpost and captures neutral hearts with almost the same ease it wins trophies. The 'Busby Babes' are born and with Busby envisaging that this competition, though still in its infancy has the potential to be truly something special he wants Manchester United to be in there fighting for it.

And, so, after winning the first division title in 1956-57 Manchester United take flight. They are fledgling first steps, ones ultimately in such a short tragic time will be fatal also. But, for a while before they fall from the Munich sky it will indeed be enchanting, enthralling and utterly unforgettable. As Scarlet Ribbon begins we now tell of Roger Byrne, David Pegg, Eddie Colman, Tommy Taylor, Dennis Viollet, Liam 'Billy' Whelan and Duncan Edwards. We tell of the Busby Babes.

Maine Road: European Cup Qualifying First Round: Wednesday 26th September 1956: Manchester United don't just walk through the door and enter the European Cup, they knock it down with a sledgehammer. Forced to share Manchester City's Maine Road ground due to the Old Trafford floodlights still being in the process of being erected, United illuminate their neighbour's home by hitting an astonishing ten goals past the poor, devastated, unsuspecting Belgian champions of RSC Anderlecht.

With the prodigious Duncan Edwards away on National Service, he is the only change from an impressive 2-0 win in Brussels, earned with goals from Dennis Viollet and Tommy Taylor. But it is here back on Mancunian home turf that the reds go into overdrive and produce a simply jaw-dropping performance. One reminiscent of Puskas and his Magyars back in 53. On a mud swamp of a pitch flooded with pools of water, the Babes run riot; their football lightning fast, balletic, electric and bewildering. The ball not so much passed around the Anderlecht shirts, but struck like a pinball. Though also caressed and cajoled to torture the hapless Belgians in a manner they could never have dreamt up in their worst nightmares.

They are stools to magicians.

Despite Tommy Taylor's hat-trick and Dennis Viollet's four goal haul the undoubted star of the evening, the one who has tortured the beleaguered Anderlecht defenders to create the vast majority of the goals is left-winger David Pegg. It has been the type of night when everything Pegg attempted has come off as he effortlessly switches wings causing equal havoc on each. Indeed, such has been his contribution, the final moments have been spent with grateful team mates trying desperately to gift him a much-deserved goal, only for the ball seemingly tired of hitting the Belgian net refusing to comply.

The final whistle resonates and on an amazing 12-0 aggregate Manchester United have arrived to the soundtrack of thundering hooves in the European cup.

This savage mauling will now reverberate across Europe for Anderlecht are no easy touch. This is an outstanding team and their Captain Jeff Mermans speaks of his total shock. He is still reeling at what has befallen them when interviewed, 'We have played against the best teams of Germany, Hungary and Russia and no one has ever beaten us like that, no one.'

An exuberant and extremely proud Matt Busby fails to hide his excitement at seeing his young side play in such fashion, 'It was the finest exhibition of teamwork from any side I have ever managed. It was near perfection.' Near perfection? The boss sets a high standard. The Babes have shown their hand and word will now spread like wildfire of this working progress currently underway in Manchester. In a Mancunian downpour United have announced their arrival in the European cup in irrepressible manner.

Bilbao: European Cup Quarter-final, First leg:
Wednesday 17th January 1957: Matt Busby is fearful for Athletic Bilbao are a class apart from anything his lads have ever faced and in a torrid first half so it proves. In driving rain, amid a lashing snow fall of almost biblical proportions, with 45,000 screaming, fanatical supporters yelling for their heads United are slaughtered. A 3-0 scoreline, but in all truth, it could be double figures as Bilbao rip them apart.

A team that plays for the Basque nation, whom have toppled the might of Real Madrid and Barcelona to reign supreme in Spain are showing no mercy to their Mancunian visitors. An audience baying for blood sees their appetites sated three times in an opening period as the rapier-like Artiche and his equally dangerous partner in crime, Ignacio Uribe cause mayhem. It is no contest.

The second half begins and with their pride stinging and ears equally so after a rollicking from Jimmy Murphy, United come out blazing. None more than Duncan Edwards.

Murphy's favourite adopted son ploughs through the Basque mud and for the first time in the tie United play like the devils on their shirts. They hit back three minutes after the break when the tenacious Taylor momentarily escapes his shadow Jesus Garay to finish off Dennis Viollet's pass and rekindle Mancunian hopes. As the Basques rock Viollet swoops in typical manner to add a second from close range as he flicks out a foot to divert the ball past Carmelo making it 3-2.

The game becomes stretched and Bilbao hit back from a corner when their left-winger Merodio crashes home a fourth for the home team. Then, as a fraught United defence watch on in despair Arteche shoots past Wood from six yards to restore their three-goal lead. At 5-2 this quarter-final appears over.

United are all but done.

Five minutes remain when Manchester United's unassuming quiet, if beguiling Irishman Liam 'Billy' Whelan carves himself a notch in the short, tragic but glorious history of the Busby Babes.

The Dublin born Whelan, a devout Roman Catholic whose faith remains important to him above everything is a young man who can count many priests amongst his closest friends and who once told off United apprentice Nobby Stiles for swearing in a five a side game.

Now receiving a pass in his silky stride from Duncan Edwards, the tall, wiry figure of Whelan heads with deadly intent towards the Basque penalty area. On the side-lines with nerves exhausted and hearts racing, Busby and the entire United bench are screaming at him to pass to an unmarked Tommy Taylor, only for Whelan, ankle-deep in mud to take a different path. Suddenly, as if he could read his player's mind, Busby whispers within earshot of Jimmy Murphy, 'Go on Bill hit it.' Taking aim Whelan spots an opening and let's fly a swerving shot that hurtles past Carmelo into the top corner. A lifeline, one grasped by the boy from Dublin who with a moment of instinctive brilliance has dragged his club back into the European Cup. At 5-3 the game ends with both reasonably satisfied and knowing all is still to play for when battle resumes in Manchester.

Maine Road: European Cup Quarter-final Second Leg: Wednesday 6th February 1957: The Athletic Bilbao coach, fifty-seven-year-old Ferdinand Daucik lands in Manchester loudly declaring, 'No team on the planet can beat the Basque nation by three goals.'

We shall see. In a ferocious opening period both teams go hell for leather. Duncan Edwards surges into Basque territory and let's fly from the edge of Bilbao's penalty area. A ferocious effort which Carmelo fails to hold and ghosting in comes Dennis Viollet to smash home and unleash a Mancunian roar that splits the heavens!

From the re-start battle immediately resumes and tackles fly hard and high, but fair. An hour passes of this pulsating contest and United are still like a red rash all over Bilbao, but failing to convert opportunities when they arise. Tommy Taylor hits the woodwork with a thumping header, Johnny Berry hit the outside of an upright and suddenly now only twenty minutes remain. Athletic goalkeeper Carmelo is performing heroically; brave, agile and seemingly attracted like a magnet to the ball as it flashes endlessly across his area.

Amongst the crowd are many local priests given free tickets by Matt Busby. No doubt heavenly bribes. All favours now being called in. On it goes as David Pegg tears away down the left-hand touchline. Turning and twisting, desperate to give himself an inch, Pegg sends a cross into the penalty area where arriving like an express train is the magnificent Tommy Taylor. Roaring free of his flailing Bilbao shackles, the 'Smiling Executioner' takes the ball in his stride and flashes a splendid shot low past Carmelo into his far corner. Manchester explodes! An evening that has threatened to tug at the heartstrings becomes something quite extraordinary. Manchester United have fought, scrapped and clawed their way back into the European Cup. The Basques are bleeding, ripe for the taking and now United go in search of a killer third. The Athletic coach Daucik can barely watch as his beleaguered defence verge on the edge of collapse. Five minutes remain and 70,000 peoples are producing a volume of noise deafening to the ear and chilling to the bone.

Playing like a man possessed Taylor powers past an exhausted Athletic full-back Canito. On he charges into the penalty area. With the crowd screaming for their hero to let fly, Taylor instead keeps his calm and plays the ball to an unmarked Johnny Berry in a better position. At full speed Berry hits a scorching drive that roars into the top corner past Carmelo to win the tie and cause unadulterated madness to engulf Maine Road. As one the Athletic players fall to the turf, their resistance broken and shattered. 3-0.

This is Tommy's night and Ferdinand Daucik has the look of a broken man. His team have been ravaged. Welcome to Manchester!

It is twelve months to the day until Munich….
Madrid: Estadio Bernabeu: European Cup Semi Final: First Leg: Thursday 7th April 1957: Drawn against champions Real Madrid, Matt Busby now realises his boys face their greatest challenge to date. This is footballing Hollywood where the greatest players in the world have gathered to entertain and enthrall the regular 100,000 crowds in the Bernabeu. Foremost amongst them their Prince of the city. The 'Blond Arrow' Spain's other Generalissimo. The arrogant, strutting and utterly outrageously talented Argentine Alfredo Di Stefano. A player already recognised by Busby as 'The finest he has ever set eyes on.' A born leader blessed with sublime ball control, devastating passing, a leopard's acceleration and a deadly finisher. However, 'Los Chicos' 'The Lads' as they have been christened by the Madrid press are being treated themselves like visiting movie stars. Constantly mobbed whenever setting foot out of their hotel. This match is the biggest thing to ever hit Madrid with touts asking up for an extraordinary 1000 pesetas. United are already being deemed the greatest challenge to Real's fledgling European dominance. Everybody in the city wants to check out their heroes' competition.
Situated in one of the more lavish palatial quarters of Madrid, the Chamartin district, the Estadio Bernabéu soars high into the heavens. Built from white concrete, this is a majestic, awe-inspiring sporting cathedral fit for the footballing Gods.
As the game draws near thousand gather outside the stadium, many without tickets. There is a mad to rush to charge the barriers only to be forced back by mounted police. For a while carnage ensues before order is restored and in they come. Over 130,000 spectators

demanding a rout. For hours before kick-off the terraces are packed. The expectations high that the home team will put these English upstarts in their rightful place. United also will not be without support in the stadium with five chartered aircraft full of supporters having travelled over to cheer their boys on. Whether they will be heard in such a vast arena when up against such fanatical backing is debatable.

In the mid-afternoon of Thursday 11th April 1957, Real Madrid and Manchester United step out into the Spanish sunshine to do battle. The arrival of the two teams is greeted by a magical shower of white roses thrown from the highest bastions of this magnificent stadium. The United players look on in astonishment as this cascade of flowers floats down onto the pitch. The Real Captain Miguel Munoz applauds his supporters for their remarkable display. A truly epic and moving spectacle. Flashbulbs glitter across the terrace like a million fireflies as the Bernabéu explodes in a glorious, deafening symphony of rockets and cheering. A huge posse of photographers' scuttle like ants across the turf as both sides pose for their team photos. It is to be an afternoon they will talk about in Madrid for generations to come. So, it begins…

For an hour Manchester United fight tooth and nail to stem an endless array of Madrileño attacks. On the left side the Guarnizo born flying-machine Francisco Gento. The other touchline, the son of a polish mineworker and French mother. A beguiling right winger called Raymonde Kopa. Both combining to fire the bullets for their Argentine centre-forward hitman Hector Rial. Together with Di Stefano prompting and delivering his winger's thirty or forty-yard passes with their names ensconced, Real Madrid wreaked plague and pestilence on all their visitor's houses. Manchester United are no exception for they find themselves in the centre of a white storm. Penned back into their own penalty area, unable to break out and being run ragged.

United's full-backs are keeping manfully to the given tasks. On the left their Gorton born Captain Roger Byrne is in a battle royal with the explosive Kopa. Byrne's intelligence and pace being tested like never before in trying to halt the rampaging Frenchman's marauding runs down the flank.

However, on the other side the former miner from Saint Helens Bill Foulkes, is in the midst of a living nightmare against the flying-machine Francisco Gento. Time and again Gento feints to go one way then changes direction, switches instantaneously to over drive with a blistering turn of speed to leave Foulkes gasping for breath in the Spaniard's wake.

Like chasing the wind.

Half time is well gone now and the Mancunians though creaking and at times sliced wide open are still holding Di Stefano's magical orchestra. But ninety minutes is an awful long time to test your mettle against wizards and magicians. One master stroke from Di Stefano's baton and all hell could yet be let loose upon them. Hard work and discipline are worthy attributes but there remains much work to achieve before returning home with satisfaction to Manchester. For there is a whiff of the unearthly that abounds here in the Bernabeu.

Watching from a high a promising United youngster nineteen-year old Bobby Charlton watches on with a mixture of bewilderment and enchantment. He feels his team mates are up against white ghosts.

With an hour gone the European champions so relentless in their pursuit of an opening goal come again. Driven relentlessly forward by their Blonde Arrow and determined to unlock the red vault. Gento teases and jinks poor Bill Foulkes to distraction before tearing past him. Without even glancing up he delivers a superb cross onto the head of Rial, who powers a fierce stooping header from close blank range past a helpless United goalkeeper Ray Wood - the Bernabéu erupts! Across the huge terraces that stretch forever upwards into the heavens, thousands of white handkerchiefs wave in delight. Madrid is on fire! The deadlock broken. Now, think the home supporters, it is just a matter of how many?

Matt Busby's tactical ploy to keep Di Stefano on a leash has held for an hour. His every step shadowed by a most unlikely man-marker. The boy from Lowry's city in Archie Street. The wonderfully elusive and dynamic twenty-year-old Eddie Colman. With Colman harassing his every move, like an alley cat nipping at his ankles, Di Stefano found his aim stunted and touch unsure. The great man became increasingly rattled as Colman followed his every move, a red shadow etched onto a white knight. Whenever it appeared Alfredo's blistering acceleration would take him clear of his Salford nemesis, Irishman Jackie Blanchflower, intercepted to tighten the noose further and upset the Blond Arrow's regal state of mind even more so.

Finally, the fuming Di Stefano's snapped and he launched a sickening lunge on Blanchflower to scythe him down. This alone should have been enough to see him sent off, for the foul was committed only yards away from the referee. But how do you send off the leading man in his own personal theatre? Probably not wishing to face a local hate mob after the match the referee allowed the Argentine to stay on the field. This undeserved slice of luck did not save Di Stefano from the wrath of an outraged Bill Foulkes, who seeing his best friend Blanchflower almost decapitated, grabbed the Blonde Arrow by the shirt and was threatening to do much worse before being wrestled away by team-mates.

But now after Rial's breakthrough the genie is out of the lamp and with the crowd baying for blood, Real move in for the kill. After enduring a frustrating match Alfredo Di Stefano finally rids himself of a badly tiring Eddie Colman. Attached like a limpet throughout with seventeen minutes remaining Colman's chains have fallen away and Di Stefano breaks free.

With fearful speed and purpose, he roars past a ragged bevy of bedraggled red shirts to race dangerously clear into United's half.

Leading the chase to catch him the immaculate Roger Byrne, but Di Stefano is in no mood to be caught and with heavenly precision he executes a perfect chip over Ray Wood that lands perfectly under the crossbar to double Real's lead. Two goals down and the roof is now caving in on Matt Busby courageous young team. They now face the serious prospect of being massacred. The Madrileño crowd roar their approval, expectant and demanding more.

'Olés' rings across this grand stadium. Every Madrid touch cheered to the rafters. It is fiesta time as they taunt their exhausted opponents with keep ball. Never have Busby's team experienced this level of football. Played with such infinite precision and touch by masters of their art.

Men against boys. It is back to school.
The handkerchiefs wave. It is a bullfight and Manchester United are on the ropes. The footballers of Real Madrid are now putting on a show and theirs' is a command performance. This is a foreign game for many of the United players. Alien to all they have ever witnessed. Outclassed and outthought, their truly outstanding players such as Duncan Edwards, David Pegg and Liam Whelan now realising that they remained mere pupils compared to these white shirted figures that swarm amongst them. The ball being moved around at hellish speed, angelic technique and with devastating results. This is the world of Di Stefano's Madrilenos.
From the touchline Busby urges his players to keep on going and showing incredible spirit the Babes rally and finally start making inroads up the other end of the pitch. The visitor's own pass and move and swift interchanging suddenly has Madrid defenders on the back foot. David Pegg is making life horribly uncomfortable for the defender Jose Becerril. Time and again Pegg now leads Becerril a merry dance. They press on and with just eight minutes remaining Tommy Taylor escapes the clutches of Real's own hatchet man Marquitos. (A concoction of the devil with white horns) to head a Liam Whelan cross past the goalkeeper Alonso into the net. An unexpected lifeline has been grasped!
Back in Manchester packed households and workplaces erupts as radios crackle with the glad tidings from Madrid. It is now game on once more. United have somehow dragged themselves back into a contest that in reality should already be over. As the ball crosses the line a deafening silence falls across the Bernabéu. Taylor is

mobbed by teammates Dennis Viollet and Johnny Berry, whom both leap on top of the United striker.
Yet instead of settling for a 2-1 deficit United continue to go forward in search of a sensational equaliser. Viollet takes aim and from twenty yards smashes a low drive onto the Madrid post. Tommy Taylor is hacked down in the penalty area by Marquitos, only for the referee to ignore Mancunian claims. Never have Real Madrid experienced such pressure on home soil. Typically, brash and cocky the Busby Babes carry on attacking. They are growing up before Matt Busby's and Jimmy Murphy's eyes, but it is surely like rushing to the scene of your own execution. For taking Real Madrid on in a next goal wins free-for-all is never recommended. This is footballing roulette being played out at the highest level. If you light a match in front of a dragon it will surely retaliate by breathing fire into your face……..

  As the clock winds increasingly down in this Bernabeu shootout, a blinding fast interchange between Gento and Rial frees the brilliant young Madrid born striker Enrique Mateos, to fire in off the post past a diving Wood, and win the game 3-1 for the Madrilenos. Mateos stands tall before the roaring crowd. He slowly raises his arms to the heavens and remains in this pose to receive the adulation of the frenzied Madrid supporters.
It is a heartbreak of a goal for Manchester United to concede and leaves them now a mountain to climb. Come the final whistle the home players and supporters celebrate as if they have already won the European Cup itself. This victory in the end though much deserved, came not without a few scares along the way. A relieved Alfredo Di Stefano and his team gather in the centre-circle to take the acclaim of an adoring Bernabéu

audience. Mateos' third goal now handing them breathing space for when they travel to Manchester for the second leg.

All at Real Madrid know that although a fine victory has been achieved this semi-final was not yet won. For their great rivals and Spanish champions, the Basque of Athletic Bilbao assumed job done after taking a two-goal lead to England and they received a 3-0 drubbing. Crushed and broken in an atmosphere unlike none had ever witnessed. A thunder that came not from the sky but from a crowd seemingly possessed and determined not to be beaten. The Bilbao players spoke of a roar that resembled a plane taking off. Of a raw passion that resonated down from the terraces onto the pitch causing the United players to lift their game to unparalleled heights. Of a magic in the Mancunian air, that there was something special in that northern city. Murky and grey, hidden by smoke and fog and rain sodden maybe, but every so often illuminated by a startling red dash capable of lifting hearts and achieving footballing miracles. They called it Manchester United.

As is their way Real Madrid serve up a sumptuous post-match banquet for the English visitors. This is a club not just teeming with class on the pitch but also off it. Every United player and member of the coaching staff are presented with a gold watch in lasting memory of this memorable encounter at the Bernabéu. One United footballer particularly taken with his memento is Duncan Edwards.

Their grand President Don Santiago Bernabéu makes a heartfelt speech pledging the importance of friendship between these two great clubs. One man particularly taken by Bernabéu's words is Matt Busby. As the

evening goes on Busby finds himself cornered by two Madrid players. One says to him, 'Please come and manage us? With you at our helm we would win every trophy in the world.' The United manager though flattered and wondering if Don Santiago is behind this charming mugging replied with an honesty and class that left his Spanish inquisitors disappointed but still smiling. 'Listen my dear friends, if you were to give me Di Stefano, United would win every trophy in the world!' With baited breath Manchester now awaits the arrival of the Madrileños. There was a storm coming.
A white storm.
Manchester: European Cup Semi Final: Second Leg: Wednesday April 24th 1957: It is time once more to do battle. On a balmy April evening at Old Trafford, Madrileño captain Miguel Munoz leads out the legendary Real Madrid. Alongside Munoz strides Manchester United fronted by Roger Byrne. The heavenly white shirts of Real against the devil red of United. Though hardly statuesque when compared to the grandiose surroundings of the Bernabéu, for atmosphere and noise Old Trafford takes some beating. It throbs and heaves in frantic expectation. The packed terraces, 65,000 roaring their support for the home team.
United kick off and immediately step onto the attack. Early stages are all red as from a Liam Whelan cross into the Madrid penalty area, Alonso rushed out to punch the ball off Tommy Taylor's head. As the home side pin back their esteemed visitors and put them under intense pressure it appears that Madrid could well go the same way as Bilbao. But with Manuel Marquitos and his compadres competing for every ball as if their lives depended on the outcome they hold firm.

Suddenly, a loose ball from a United shirt is latched onto by Francisco Gento, whose fiendish acceleration sees him hurtle clear into the home half before finally being brought to earth by a last-ditch Roger Byrne tackle. This lightning burst by Gento brings a collective gasp from the crowd, his sheer speed off the mark causing disbelief. Madrid are now on the move. Rial's incisive through pass finds Di Stefano on the edge of the box who turns and cracks a fierce drive that Wood is forced to tip over the bar. Real are coming again and with United retreating, Gento explodes into the penalty area, but just when readying to pull the trigger he finds himself caught by a thunderous Edwards challenge.

Busby is watched anxiously as all eyes fall on one figure expecting the worst. The Blond Arrow has bided his time, but now on twenty-three minutes he swoops onto the ball and his swift pass releases Raymonde Kopa to shoot low past Wood from seven-yards to give the visitors a three-goal aggregate lead. Old Trafford is stunned.

From the restart Madrid immediately win back possession and turn on the style. Not simply passing the ball but cajoling and caressing it. Their arrogance and worrying ease suggests total confidence in being able to put United away whenever the mood arises. Gento careers once more down the wing before crossing for Hector Rial to smash home from close range past Wood and surely book Real Madrid's second consecutive European cup final appearance.

In later years records would show Rial was actually forty-years old that night and not the stated thirty as Madrid officials when they originally signed him were informed. But the hitman has done his job and the realisation that United's dream is over lies etched on Matt Busby's face. His boys although still bravely battling away are been hopelessly outclassed by a team from another planet.

As the Madrilenos now strut, pose and pass the ball around as if it was on a string Di Stefano is at their very heart. The Blonde Arrow is conducting his illustrious orchestra. It is showtime and Real Madrid are putting on a grand performance for their Mancunian hosts. In doing so each flick and backheel sending a message to let them know in no uncertain terms that they who ply their sumptuous talents in the Estadio Bernabéu. Who adorn the white shirt still rule the roost and that there remains a chasm in terms of class between the two sides. It is a lesson to watch both cruel and unforgiving, but also quite beautiful.

Tiring of the circus tricks Real go in search of a killer third to end United's challenge once and for all. Di Stefano demands possession off his defenders and away he soars. A rapier one-two with Rial before a pass inside to Gento, who skips away from Bill Foulkes, before returning the ball back to the grand Argentine. Alone he stands in the centre-circle, statuesque. His foot on the ball. As if to suggest, 'Here I am. You have read the stories seen the pictures and been told of the rumours. I am Alfredo Di Stefano, and I have come to Manchester.' Half time arrives like water for a man dying of thirst for United. Huge applause drifts down from the terraces for the efforts of their own team, but also the audacious display of these men in white and for one in particular. The Blonde Arrow. The Mancunians have now witnessed in the flesh this wonder called Real Madrid and they realise that it is both terrifying and spellbinding. They have come expecting something special and Di Stefano, Gento, Kopa and Rial have not let them down.

In the dressing room Busby wishes only for his boys to save the match and give the Madrileños a reminder that come the following season Manchester United will again be a threat. Taking their manager's words to heed the Babes re-appear a team inspired. Suddenly it is Real Madrid who are on the back-foot as Eddie Colman, Liam Whelan and David Pegg begin to stretch them from wide positions. In order to stem the attacks another side of the Madrileno. White shirts lash out to stem the red tide. Now it is the Spaniards who are rattled, boots fly high. Marquitos, Munoz and Zarraga take no prisoners though even such a mean and combative trio of hatchet men are finding it hard to deal with an on-fire Tommy Taylor. With the crowd reaching fever pitch Taylor races between two defenders and, under huge pressure bundles a low shot onto the Madrid post. As groans engulf the stadium the ball falls loose and as Old Trafford holds a collective breath, good fortune shines on Irishman Liam Whelan, who from three yards can't miss.

Now three down on aggregate and with thirty minutes left to play echoes of Bilbao come flooding back into the minds of the home faithful. Manchester is rocking; surely their heroes can't do it again? Real are frantic, their first half poise and beauty long vanished to be replaced by a grim determination and when necessary an utter ruthlessness to survive this Mancunian onslaught. As the crowd bay for an equaliser white shirts begin falling to the turf with alarming regularity. Zarraga, though immense throughout blots his copybook when he collapses in a heap after an alleged foul from Tommy Taylor. The lad from Barnsley looks on in disgust at the

Spaniard's play-acting, whilst an outraged home support scream in derision.

All good feelings towards the Real Players have now vanished as a Madrileño huddle surrounded the referee demanding Taylor's expulsion. Tempers are running high. With the final to be played in the Estadio Bernabéu the stakes for the Real Players are huge. Their desire not to succumb means they feel all foul methods are justified, but it hardly dignifies their reputation. Howls continue from the terraces as the Spaniards lash out at anything in red that dares to go by. The clock for United seemed to be on fast forward, for Madrid time has almost froze. The battle rages on as from fully twenty-five yards Duncan Edwards thunders in a shot only to see Alonso save magnificently with a flying leap. Tempers flare again when on a rare foray forward Rial attempts to stop Ray Wood taking a quick kick and is barged to the floor for his troubles by an angry United goalkeeper.

With five minutes left to play Bobby Charlton levels with a close-range effort to set up a torrid climax. Intent on just surviving the remaining moments Real attempt to play keep-ball, but now thirsting for a monumental winner, Manchester United attack once more.

The bitter memory of waging a losing fight against insurmountable waves of blurry white shadows swarming around him in the Bernabéu has left Duncan Edwards frustrated. Now, on home soil with Real again proving to have just too much for United the opportunity to show his true worth and see United into the final appears over. It has been Edwards who during the second half fightback has wrestled control almost single-handedly back of the contest from Alfredo Di Stefano and his seemingly impregnable Madrileños. Time and again he has powered across the halfway line, leaving in his wake tumbling white shirted bodies. Di Stefano himself stares in awe at this youngster whose power and sheer will to win refuses to wane, even when the battle is surely lost. Intent on just surviving the remaining moments Real are attempting to play keep-ball, but now thirsting for a monumental winner, United, inspired by the still rampaging Edwards, repeatedly win the ball back and continue attacking. Though requiring two more goals the Babes are refusing to give up and when the Madrid players attempt to time waste tempers flare up again on both sides. David Pegg cuts in in with the ball but clashes with Real defender Torres, who then in Oscar winning style collapses as if shot by a sniper from the stand. Players from both sides crowd around the apparently assassinated player. The Spaniards intent on keeping him lying on the ground, whilst the United players try in vain to push Torres off the pitch and carry on the game. Knowing time is horribly short, home captain Roger Byrne is in no mood for such antics and takes it upon himself to drag Torres back to his feet. However, he swiftly finds himself confronted by irate Madrid players who lift their fallen compadre away to lie him back on the pitch.

Enter Duncan Edwards-angered by the cheating tactics of his opponents, Edwards storms through a host of Madrileños pushing them aside and picks up Torres, before placing him over the touchline. A melee follows before calm is restored and the final seconds are played out with United still going for glory at the final whistle. Honours ended even but the war won overall by a relieved and spent Real Madrid. A splendid match.

As in Madrid a wonderful banquet is held afterwards in which both teams put aside all animosity to enjoy a fine evening of toasts and goodwill speeches. Later in the night when the party is in full swing, Don Santiago Bernabéu approaches the United manager with an offer the President is convinced he simply cannot refuse, 'If you come to Spain I will make it heaven on earth for you. You will have untold riches you can only dream of.' Busby listens and promises the Real President he will write soon with an answer. Two weeks later a letter arrives on Bernabéu's desk from Matt Busby thanking him for the kind offer but 'His heaven on earth exists right here in Manchester.'

The President was wrong for with players such as Duncan Edwards, Eddie Colman, Liam Whelan and Tommy Taylor and so many more Busby felt he was already in Paradise.

Belgrade: European cup Quarter Final: Second Leg: Wednesday 5th February 1958: Leading 2-1 from the first leg against crack Yugoslav champions Red Star Belgrade, Manchester United are now behind the Iron Curtain. Not so much a wall but a state of mind. Female soldiers shove the paths clear of snow. Army tanks are parked along the roadside. Their occupants sit abreast, smoking and watching - menacing. On being taken by coach to the Hotel Metropole which sits on the magnificent banks of the Blue Danube, everywhere the players look they see evidence of poverty. People dressed in rags in queues so long they disappear from view. A beautiful city strangled by an ideology that demands total obedience.

In the dressing room beforehand Matt Busby is in a smart raincoat and sharp fitting trilby and composed as ever.

Busby is alone as he gathers the players. For Jimmy Murphy is away managing Wales in a vital world cup qualifier. Even though Murphy was desperate to come, Busby insisted his loyalty on this occasion lay with the national team. He keeps it simple as kick off draws nears, 'There are no terrors on that pitch for you boys. You are Manchester United. We have beaten them once now do it again.'

And so, on a pitch laden with the last remnants of snow still visible but melting fast in the afternoon Belgrade sunshine, spring seems close, the two sides line up. The United players show signs of being pensive but grimly determined to get the job done. Today they are playing in traditional kit of red shirts, white shorts and black socks. The Captain Roger Byrne looks down the row of his team mates and there seems nothing to worry about. They are ready. Duncan Edwards is tucking his shirt into shorts. A sure sign he is set for battle. Eddie Colman, Similar. Harry Gregg looks deep in concentration. As does Bill Foulkes. Whereas Mark Jones appears lost in thought. The others stare straight ahead. Ken Morgans, Bobby Charlton, Dennis Violett, Tommy Taylor and Albert Scanlon. This is the last line up as the photographers click and snap away. A picture set to become a final testament to the team that was and will forever be known as *The Busby Babes*....

The Battle of Belgrade: A last encore: Within ninety seconds a rampaging Tommy Taylor sets up his striking partner Dennis Viollet, to fire past the legendary black shirted goalkeeper Vladimir Beara. With the home side stunned the visitors go for an early kill. Matters turn much worse for the Yugoslavs when the magnificent Bobby Charlton wins the ball before taking aim and hitting a glorious, rasping twenty-five-yard drive low past Beara. Two minutes later with Belgrade aghast Bobby is gifted a second when Beara saves a typically explosive Duncan Edwards thunderbolt, only for a clumsy kick out to fall at Charlton's feet. Faced with an open goal the young Geordie puts it away. Just thirty minutes gone and United look to have already sealed a semi-final spot.

Half time comes and goes and whatever was said or threatened in the Red Star changing room has the desired effect, for they have returned a team transformed. Two minutes in centre-forward Bora Kostic chances his luck with a twenty-yard effort that sneaks past Harry Gregg into the far corner to ignite the stadium and rekindle Belgrade hopes. Their playmaker Sekularac, blessed with the ability to create and dazzle is leading the comeback and causing mayhem. The Gypsy. An artist painting pictures.

The visitors cause is hardly helped by the constant barrage of snowballs launched by spectators behind the goal at United's defenders and goalkeeper. The air filled with unwanted missiles as with deadly intent the Belgrade crowd pick out their targets in red! Such intense home pressure finally tells when Red Star are awarded a soft penalty. As the Crvena Zveda holds its collective breath, Tasic remains calm to thrash a precise spot kick high past Gregg. Suddenly, Manchester United are in big trouble and with an injured Duncan Edwards reduced to mere nuisance value and Harry Gregg lying hopeless on the turf, Red Star's Cokic somehow contrives to miss an open goal from five yards. Cokic punches the floor and behind the net hordes of supporters surge down from the terraces onto the running track, many tumbling and

collapsing en masse. Dazed and staggering they are helped to their feet by Yugoslav soldiers.
Meanwhile, back on the pitch the siege continues as Sekularac's unerring talent to pick holes in the Mancunian rearguard is at times uncanny. Only by sheer dogged determination and willingness to throw their bodies into the line of fire are United surviving. His goal under siege, Harry Gregg is ranting and performing heroics to keep the Belgrade forwards at bay. Two minutes remain when Red Star win a free kick just outside the penalty box.
A dubious decision awarded against Harry Gregg, as he dives at the feet of tricky winger Branko Zebec, only then to slide outside the area on the treacherously surface. Up comes Kostic to let fly and see his shot deflect off Dennis Viollet's head before slipping agonisingly through Gregg's grasping fingers and into the United goal to level at 3-3.
5-4 on aggregate. Red Star needed one more to take the tie to a replay on neutral territory. A limping, bedraggled United are all but done. One last time the Gypsy sets off, alluring and deadly only to be stopped in his stride as Herr Kainer blew for full time. An epic clash ends with both sides exhausted. Dropping to their knees the home side receive a magnificent ovation from their supporters as do the much-relieved visitors. An unforgettable last encore for a doomed football team.

 The Ballad of Miro Radojcic: It is a joyous bunch of Mancunians who are celebrating into the early hours at a post-match party laid on wonderfully by Red Star. Replicas of Soviet Sputniks circled the banquet room, speeches of goodwill are heard, endured mostly by the footballers and applauded by all. Presents are handed out as each visiting player receives a tea pot and a bottle of gin! Hostilities forgotten, bad tackles forgiven and for some, those fortunate few life-long friendships are struck on both sides. Vast quantities of Yugoslavia's finest wine downed, toasts made and songs sung. Captain Roger Byrne leads a rousing version by his team mates in tribute to their Yugoslav hosts, "We'll meet again, don't know where, don't know when. But I know we'll meet again some sunny day."

Later, when official duties have been performed Roger Byrne passes a scribbled note to Matt Busby, asking permission for the players to be allowed a few hours grace. Aware he can trust them not to start World War Three, Busby agrees and to hushed cheers they make their plans. Most disappear into the dark and intrigue of the Belgrade evening to enjoy the mysterious delights of Eastern European nightlife where away from prying eyes they can truly celebrate reaching the semi-final.

For one Yugoslav journalist Miro Radojcic, a writer from Politika, the night's events unknown to him at this time are to prove life changing. After chatting and drinking with Tommy Taylor and Duncan Edwards he is left alone with his thoughts and is thinking on flying back to Manchester with the team and write a story from the United angle. A look at England's top team seen through the eyes of one of Yugoslavia's most celebrated journalists.

It is near dawn when an excited Radojcic finally decides to go and he prepares to pack a bag. Outside the Belgrade sky is thick with snow falling like huge confetti onto the city. Soon for Manchester United it will be time to go home and Miro Radojcic is going with them. On reaching the airport a horrified Radojcic realises he has forgotten his passport. Radojcic pleads with the airport authorities to hold the aircraft for as long as possible whilst he takes a taxi trip back to his home. By the time he returns the twin-engine Elizabethan has taken off, bound for England via Munich where it will stop to re-fuel. This is the luckiest day of Miro Radojcic's life....

Munich: A sorry looking group of players, officials and reporters are gathered at Marshall Tito airport to board the plane taking them home to Manchester, via Munich. Hungover, bleary-eyed but relieved at qualifying against a fine Red Star team. Fate appears to be transpiring for another clash with Real Madrid and one which now holds no fear for the Babes.

At around 180 miles per hour the Elizabethan flight G-ALZU A857 makes its wary path over the Alps towards Germany. As they finally descend a huge blizzard is sweeping across Munich airport. A short spell in the departure lounge follows whilst the aircraft is refuelled. A call then goes out over the tannoy for all passengers to begin re-boarding.

At 2-30 pm the Elizabethan sets off again down the runway. Slowly gathering speed and with the engines at full power it suddenly comes to an ominous, shuddering halt scaring all on board. Permission is sought from the air traffic control tower to try once more, only again to falter. Finally, take-off is aborted and it's a worrying band who make their way back across the tarmac in a blizzard to reach the terminal building.

For the third time at 3-03pm flight G-ALZU A857 accelerates into the darkness of Munich runway. At reaching a speed of 117 mph, Captain James Thain notices a surge in the boost control. The air indicator drops dramatically and as the runway's end draws ever closer panic fills the cockpit. As the slush and sleet from the wheels hurls against the portholes the plane speed towards its tragic end. Back amongst the passengers many have their eyes shut. Fear etched on faces as the reality that something has gone dreadfully wrong takes hold. A frantic Thain tries to retract the undercarriage to get them airborne but the fuselage refuses to lift. From that moment on they are out of control. Sparks all around, a hellish rollercoaster. The aircraft crashes into a nearby house slashing off its roof, then skids into an empty army barracks. Forty yards away lies a fuel dump and part of the wing careers into it causing huge plumes of flames to shoot into the sky. Spinning round and round in ever maddening circles the hulking Elizabethan finally comes to a sickening halt ripping it in two. A ghastly, twisted mess that any time threatens to explode.

Carnage has ensued, seven of the United players amongst many more of the passengers are killed outright; Roger Byrne, Tommy Taylor, David Pegg, Mark Jones, Geoff Bent, Eddie Colman and Liam Whelan. Dazed, confused and disbelieving survivors stagger through the wreckage. Bodies lie scattered, some burned beyond recognition. A shocking silence is broken only by a hissing noise emanating from the downed aircraft. Like a death knell. The blood runs red in the Munich snow.

Old Trafford: European cup Semi-final: First Leg: Thursday 8th May 1958: A now infamous tournament for Mancunians that has become etched with the blood of those who perished on that wretched German runway. But the show must go on and in front of 45,000 spectators, Manchester United and AC Milan do battle. Showing no mercy, the Milanese so outclass a makeshift home side that it appears only a matter of time before the

Italians go ahead. Arguably Milan's greatest ever player, the alluring Uruguayan maestro, inside-forward Juan Schiaffino. So pale and slender he dominates the ball as his snake-charming left-foot ripped the home defence apart at will.

On twenty-four minutes the Rossoneri deservedly take the lead as Schiaffino, with an artist's precision places his shot beyond Harry Gregg into the goal.

A turkey shoot threatens to ensue as the Italian champions press but duly squander a host of opportunities to finish off United. An impassioned Jimmy Murphy rages on the touchline, infuriated and helpless as his side are toyed with. Playing in white United are hardly angelic as they tear into tackles, some legal, others fraught with desperation in an attempt to repel Milan dominance.

Whipped into a fury at the sheer injustice and cruel circumstance of the last three months the home crowd erupt in grim defiance. With the recently signed playmaker from Blackpool Ernie Taylor beginning to dictate more of the ball, the decibel level goes even higher. Five minutes before half time the normally impeccable defender Cesare Maldini misdirects a back pass and is forced to watch in horror as Munich survivor Dennis Viollet intercepts. As Old Trafford holds its collective breath, he races clear before dispatching with typical aplomb past goalkeeper Lorenzo Buffon to level. United return after the interval in a blaze of fury and a second half blitz orchestrated by the guile of Ernie Taylor has the Italians hanging on. This scheming thirty-three-year-old ex- submariner has proved an inspired signing by Murphy and is swiftly earning himself cult status at Manchester United. Knowing another goal is essential to have any hope for the second-leg in Northern Italy, United throw caution to the wind and with just eleven minutes remaining they received just reward.

Again, the impressive Dennis Viollet creating trouble for Cesare Maldini as he outpaces the Italian to race clear into the penalty area. Struggling to keep up Maldini cuts across United's number ten causing the two men to go down. As Old Trafford screams for a penalty the Danish referee Leo Helge points to the spot and AC Milan to a man go mad!

Maldini collapses to the turf in mock grief, team mates confront and surrounded the referee whilst officials race from the stands to join in and demand Mr Helge reverse his decision. Finally, calmer heads prevail and order is restored. Away from the madness United's penalty taker Ernie Taylor simply stands, watches and waits for his moment. Once Helge has forced all the irate Italian players back beyond the eighteen-yard line he motions Taylor forward. With a stadium uproarious and teeming with emotion, up he comes to lash the ball off the underside of the bar with such ferocity past Buffon that it almost breaks the stanchion! Ernie Taylor's position in the annals of United folklore now secured.

Despite a cup run littered with bodies, burning wreckage and scarred images of survivors, somehow United remain alive and have earned themselves a fighting chance of reaching the final when battle recommences in the San Siro.

San Siro: European Cup Semi Final: Second leg: Wednesday 4th May 1958: Milan. A dynamic city of grace and style and a football team determined to put right what they deemed at Old Trafford to be a severe injustice. Manchester United are staying at the Hotel

Principe e Savoia where they are being treated with great respect by their Italian hosts. However, now as match day dawns everything changes. As 80,000 Milanese gather at the San Siro with the mindset of a baying mob the Italians in a blatant act of gamesmanship refuse United's coach entry at the stadium and the players only make it to the dressing rooms twenty minutes before kick-off.

The entrance of the two teams sparks a deafening fervour of flares and fireworks, some thrown directly at the visitors. The vitriol and animosity towards the Mancunians is overwhelming and as they come into view rotten fruit, cups filled with urine and coins rains down upon their heads. Benevento Milano!

On the pitch matters are not much different as the German referee Albert Deutsch turns a blind eye to the scandalous off the ball antics of the home side. When Herr Deutsch dares give a decision in United's favour the entire Milan bench invade the pitch to remonstrate! Four times this occurs as play is held up much to Jimmy Murphy's disgust on the touchline.

Carnage ensues.

Shirts are tugged, elbows fly and punches thrown as United players are hacked down and spat at. Then there is the overacting when any Milan player is tackled that would shame a circus clown. As thunder rolls across grey Milanese skies Manchester United are hammered 4-0 and dumped unceremoniously out of the European cup. For amid all the thuggery and cheating AC Milan produce football that glitters. None more than Juan Schiaffino, who back on home turf tortures the English. It is his precise, low strike from twelve-yards past Harry Gregg that begins the rout after just two minutes.

On the half hour Herr Deutsch blows his whistle and stops play for a minute's silence. The United players look staggered for they have not been informed this was to occur? At first the English contingency in the stadium presume it is for the Munich victims only later to be told it was in honour of an Italian FA official who died earlier that week. United hold on grimly in the first half, but shortly after the interval Milan score again when a glorious Schiaffino chip beats Gregg, only for a defender to handball on the line. Up steps 'Il Barone' the wonderfully sublime, blond Swedish attacking midfielder Nils Liedholm, to fire past Harry Gregg and open the floodgates. As the Rossoneri cut lose a badly outclassed and much intimidated United are being given a thrashing. Further goals from Milan right-winger Giancarlo Danova twenty minutes from time and a last encore from the devilish Schiaffino puts paid to Jimmy Murphy's brave but limited side. Ironically at the post-match banquet the Milan President gives a speech lauding the merits of 'sportsmanship!' One can only imagine the thoughts of Murphy as he listens on?

And so, the most horrific season in United's history ends. Murphy has worked miracles since the crash but defeat at Wembley in the FA Cup final to Bolton and the massacre in the San Siro proves the road back from Munich will be long and arduous. In that miserable, early summer of 1958, Manchester United have descended into football hell. It will be seven long years before they again qualify for the European cup…

To Be Continued:

C7
SIR MATT BUSBY
BLOOD IN THE SNOW (Thursday 6th February 1958)

Through Sir Matt's eyes:

The roar of the engine grows deafening as ice and snow flies against the porthole. I clasp hold of my seat. Something is terribly wrong. Then an almighty bang, like an explosion. We've gone through a perimeter fence. I brace myself. For what, I've no idea.

'Please God save us!' I hear a voice shout.

We start to spin round and round. Like a rollercoaster in hell. Then everything goes black, the terrifying sound of tearing metal. Something hits my head. There are sparks, my chest is cracked and I can't breathe.

So, this is how it ends. On a snow bound runway in Southern Germany.

In Munich.

The plane is spinning, there are sparks igniting. There is fire and smoke. Round and round, we are upside down. Everything is going slower now. There is silence. I'm drifting, I can see the sky and the snow is coming down.

I think I'm dying.

I regain consciousness; I'm lying flat in the freezing snow. I open my eyes to scenes no mortals should have to witness. This is the pits of hell. I see friends bleeding, open wounds, pleading for life, screaming for loved ones.

Others lying dead. This isn't fair. You say you're a rightful god, a peaceful god? We survived a world war, your war. You invented that. And we served and survived. We kissed our loved ones on return in joy and hope that we could live simple, peaceful lives. But oh no, you just had to twist the blade a little deeper.

Has Manchester not suffered enough?

Fire and flames, I'm so very cold. My chest feels like it is set to explode. It is so hard to breathe.

There is blood coming from my mouth. I prop myself up on one arm. I can see the aeroplane fuselage still smoking, it lies twisted and smouldering. I see bodies in the snow. 'Are you okay boss?' I hear a voice. It is Bill Foulkes. Bill leans down.

'It's my chest son, I can't breathe.'

'You hang on in there,' says Bill, 'I'm going to get help.' And then he is gone. I wake up once more. I'm in a vehicle; the pain is agonising. We seem to hit every bump on the road. I hear a familiar voice. It is young Bobby Charlton. His face covered in cuts, his eyes watering. He is holding my hand, 'We're going to the hospital boss. Hold on, everything is going to be alright.'

Then another voice. It is Big Bill. He is shouting. I see him hit the driver over the head, not once but twice. He is close to tears with shock and anger, 'Slow down you German bastard, slow down. And watch your driving. He is dying back there, dying back there…'

I can hear screams and crying and loud voices. Men shouting. I'm on a hospital stretcher being taken down a corridor. It is brightly lit. Lights that blind my eyes. There are faces unknown staring down at me. White figures, blurred white figures. Angels maybe? They are chattering in German. They appear concerned over somebody or something. I see one make the sign of the cross. Then I hear somebody speak in English. He is whispering. It is like he does not want me to hear, 'Many dead, it is a disaster,' he says. 'They are all but wiped out.'

What is he talking about?

I can't feel my legs. My chest is heavy like a dead weight. My breathing is slowing. I close my eyes and don't expect to open them again. I'm so tired. Is this heaven?

I'm in the hospital bed. I can feel no pain, but something tells me I must not sleep for I'll never wake up. I can make out a man in a white collar. A priest is stood over me. He takes hold of my hand and starts to speak in English.

'Through this holy anointing may the Lord in his love and mercy help you with the grace of the Holy Spirit.'

I recognise these words. This is the Holy sacrament of the Last Rites. The Priest has a kind voice. His fingers are cold as he anoints the top of my forehead.

'May the Lord who frees you from sin save you and raise you up.'

So be it. But it appears my body is strong where my will is weak, for I'm refusing to die. As I drift in and out of consciousness this hazy mist in front of my eyes doesn't lift. And yet through the fog I can make out a familiar face. My old friend the Priest has returned. Once was not enough for I'm still around and I'm to be given the Last Rites again.

My collapsed lungs and chest prove to be too badly damaged and so I feel his cold, kind hands on my forehead once more. This time I shall gladly go. I want to go. It does no good to keep the Good Lord waiting. The Good Lord? I must remember to ask him one question when I walk through those big white gates. One that I feel deserves an answer.

Why?

I was born into a loving family on 26th May 1909, in Orbiston, Bellshill. A tiny mining village near

Motherwell, east of Glasgow. I lost my father to a German sniper, curse him, in the First World War, leaving my mother to raise four children in a two-room cottage. Come my early teenage years we almost ended up immigrating to America. Fate decided otherwise and now aged forty-eight, in the early days of 1958, I lie here in a German hospital bed. By all reckoning after twice being given the last rites I should be dead, but for a reason known only to the almighty he has spared me.

Still, I have no idea who has been lost in the crash. Father forgive me for my sins. I never meant it to be like this.

Now, who has perished, I must know. Tell me the cost of a fallen dream?
I would recognise that Welsh growl anywhere. Jimmy Murphy is here. I open my eyes. He's gripping my hand tight. I try to talk but find the words won't come. I have so many questions - Who is alive? Who is dead? Am I the only one? Jimmy notices, 'Save your energy old pal.'

He strokes my forehead. What does he know that I don't?

I look into his eyes hoping they may give me a clue but they are empty. He appears tired, so very tired. I try to push myself up on the bed, I must talk and I have to tell him. Somehow, I have to find the willpower to make the words come out of my mouth. Jimmy leans close and I whisper into his ear, 'Keep the flag flying until I get back Jimmy.'
To know or not to know. The realisation, the pain of loss. The guilt, all measured up against the terror and sheer frustration of not knowing. I fear for my sanity and so I ask Jean. I tell her, 'I will say a name and you either nod if they are alive. Shake your head if they are not.' I've

heard whispered names already in hushed German conversations. Jean has tears in her eyes, but I must insist. I have to know

'Okay Matt' she replies.

Who do I mention first? Who do I wish to have lived more? This is evil, cruel and unfair. I begin and decide to go from the goalkeeper onwards.

'Ray Wood?' Jean Nods. 'Roger Byrne?' Jean shakes her head. 'Mark Jones?' Jean shakes her head… we go on.

I'm on the hospital balcony looking out over the grounds. It is a beautiful clear blue German sky. The birds are singing, it is early morning. Yesterday I was told Duncan has gone. His was a truly courageous struggle for life that left doctors and nurses heartbroken and in tears. So typical of the boy. Sadly, this is one battle Duncan has lost. That takes the total of the boys lost to eight. Eight mother's sons. Then there are Bert Whalley and Tom Curry and the poor journalists.

It's my fault. I could have said we are not getting on that damned plane. I should have done something.

I should have done something. I should……
The radio man hands me my speech, 'When you are ready Matt. 3, 2, 1.'

'Ladies and Gentlemen, I am speaking to you from my bed in the Rechts Der Isar hospital in Germany, where I have been since the tragic accident at Munich, just over a month ago. You will be glad I'm sure to know that the remaining players here and myself are now considered out of danger. And this can only be attributed to the wonderful treatment and attention given us by professor Maurer and his fine staff.

'I am obliged to Empire News for giving me this opportunity to speak to you. For it is only in this last two or three days that I have been able to be told anything about football. And I'm delighted to hear that the club have reached the semi-finals of the FA Cup. And I enclose my best wishes to everyone. And finally, may I just say. God bless you all.'

'Well done Matt' says the radio man with tears falling down his cheeks.

The German surgeon Doctor Georg Maurer has been invited by the club as guest of honour for a forthcoming home match. The very least we can offer for a man whose surgical skills have saved and healed so many of our people. I swear this man has not slept since the crash. He is taking over to Manchester a tape recording I made earlier today to be played over the tannoy at the stadium. But also in my absence performing a most terrible service.

'Matt, I just wanted to say thank you for this wonderful if sad honour. It will be my privilege on your behalf to visit these people and express condolences.'

Earlier today with Jean's help I had written for him a list of the bereaved families and their addresses.

'Doctor Maurer, you are a wonderful man and truly sent to us from God.'

He shakes his head, 'What we did to try and save all your boys was nothing to do with God. In what I witnessed during the war and again this last month. Young men suffering so called God's will? No.' He smiles, 'I prefer my Scottish friend to think our actions were just common human decency.' This man raged against all the carnage, hell and furore wreaked by Munich.

Myself and Manchester United will owe him forever more.

In the early afternoon of Sunday 18th April 1958, I arrive home in Kings Road, Chorlton. Alongside me in the back of the car is Jean. She holds my hand tight. A large crowd has gathered to welcome us back. Well-wishers along with pressmen and photographers mill around.

How normal everything looks?

I have been to hell and this place has not changed at all. I can see our two children Sandy and Sheena stood at the door. I have to hold it together. I'm home now.

'Everything is going to be okay now Mattha,' says Jean, whispering into my ear. People are waving, shiny happy faces. I slowly manoeuvre a way out with my sticks. I smile wide to our audience. A little girl steps forward and hands me flowers. I bend down and kiss her on the cheek,

'Thank you young lady' I say. I turn to the reception committee, 'Are you alright ladies and gentlemen. How have you all been whilst I have been away?'

In the pits of hell….

Saturday 3rd May 1958: Manchester United have against all unholy odds made it to the FA Cup Final against Bolton Wanderers. There are simply no words for what Jimmy Murphy has done. 'Murphy's Marvels' I've seen them referred to. More like 'Murphy's Miracle.'

I'm here on sticks but in all honesty, I wish I was a thousand miles away. I simply cannot face this. Jimmy has asked if I wished to say a few words to the boys before kick-off. I'm stood outside the dressing room waiting for him to come out and say they are ready. What do I say, what do I do? They are not my lads. My boys are shadows and dust. Jimmy appears, he smiles, 'The boys are ready Matt.' I enter and look around at faces. Some I don't even recognise. I blink and my boys are back. They are staring at me: Duncan, Roger, Tommy, Eddie, Liam, Mark, David and Geoff. I have to leave. I break down. I turn to Jimmy,

'I'm sorry but I can't stay.'

I so miss my boys.

With a glass of fine Spanish wine in hand I'm sat on Don Santiago Bernabeu's spacious balcony overlooking the city of Madrid. Santiago is sat opposite. He has generously invited me and the other survivors to his beautiful city to recuperate and to use the club's magnificent facilities. The man will not accept a penny, 'You are our friends Matt. It is the least we can do.'

His kindness touches my soul and must never be forgotten. Once we were genuine rivals, friends but sporting adversaries, now I fear his majestic Real Madrid are too far beyond the stars for us to even dream of competing with them for many years. Then I have an idea.

'Santiago, your kindness has already been overwhelming. But may I be so bold as to offer you a proposition. We cannot afford your match fee but can pay in instalments over time. Would you be willing to accept such an offer?'

Don Santiago smiles and raises his glass, 'My dear friend, you pay us only what you can afford. Ours is a shared bond. A Tale of Two Cities shall we say.'

We raise our glasses, 'To Champions of Honour' he toasts, 'to Manchester United.'

There are no words.

If there is such a thing as a footballing visitation then 60,000 have experienced it here at Old Trafford. With a sense of wonder and through the number of tears I see flowing amid grown men, I fear blind despair, we watch as Real Madrid destroy Manchester United 6-1 with the natural ease of someone swatting an annoying fly with a newspaper. Tonight, we have witnessed football from the heavens: Di Stefano, Puskas, Gento and Didi have cast white scorch marks on our pitch. I like others surely cannot help but think what if? These wonderful boys from Madrid would have found themselves in a battle royal tonight. For we were close, so damn close before hell overtook us and now we start again. But will there ever be enough time? Do I possess the strength and will to carry the fight on? These magnificent Madrileños gather in the centre circle and salute the crowd and the reception they receive from the Mancunians is as if these lads were our own. A reminder of happier times. Of paradise.

We were close. So very close.

A late February morning in 1960 and on a rain lashed Old Trafford forecourt we stand as the Munich memorial clock is officially unveiled. Jean is next to me and grips my hand tight. Words are said, kind words about those we lost. But words mean nothing. I look in the eyes of the bereaved families. I can still see the pain. Time, they say is a good healer. It ebbs away over the years until the grief is just numbness in the heart. Always there but you can live with it. It has been two years since and I'm still on the plane.

In my dreams I still feel the cold of the ice and snow. But it is a beautiful clock and there is polite applause as the curtain draws back. I tell myself I must not cry.

For one day I swear we will win the European Cup.'

C8
KEEP THE RED FLAG FLYING HIGH:
FA Cup Fifth Round: Wednesday 19th February 1958:
Manchester United v Sheffield Wednesday

'Everybody lost something at the end of that runway.'
Matt Busby:

  A football club founded in Newton Heath in 1878 and all but wiped out on a German runway eighty-years on had reached the lowest point in its history. With a future uncertain and spirit broken it was a question of tossing a coin and calling either salvation or disaster. For in time-honoured tradition, despite untold grief at the loss of so many broken hearts and unhealed wounds, the show went on and just thirteen days after the catastrophic air crash Manchester United prepared to host Sheffield Wednesday in an FA Cup fifth round clash. With their flag flying at half-mast over the ground as a mark of respect for the victims, those left behind prepared for a game that would go down in the folklore of Manchester United football club.
  'Keep the flag flying Jimmy until I get back.' These impassioned comments of an ailing Matt Busby still battling for his life in an oxygen tent in Southern Germany to his assistant and friend Jimmy Murphy, who had flown over to the scene of the disaster. Busby lay gravely ill. The wall of his chest had been savagely crushed, severely endangering his lungs. What Murphy witnessed, heard and felt in Munich at the Rechts der Isar hospital almost broke him. His boys lay dead and dying, some injured so badly they would never play again, but it

was the sight of one he deemed invincible, Duncan Edwards, that almost drove him to despair.
'What time is kick off Jimmy?"

Suddenly, Murphy realised that the gods had no favourites after all, that they gave and took as they pleased. For to take one so special as Duncan Edwards, to destroy everything he and Matt Busby had strove to create would test anyone's faith. A devout catholic, this firebrand Welshman from the Rhondda valley had seen his own life spared by an act of fate that would haunt him forever. Only Matt Busby 's insistence that Murphy did not travel to Belgrade saved his life. Busby successfully convinced him it was his duty to remain behind in his other capacity of managing Wales. This meant that Murphy's normal seat next to the manager on the plane was taken by United trainer Bert Whalley, who was killed outright in the crash. But it was Busby's haunting words that gave Jimmy the necessary courage to carry on. "Keep the flag flying Jimmy till I get back. Keep the flag flying, keep the flag…

Manchester was a city in mourning. Numb with shook, shattered and in despair. In order to escape such a doom-laden atmosphere, the decimated United squad disembarked to their normal refuge of the Norbreck hotel. Its huge glass-fronted windows overlooked the rough waters of the Irish Sea. There Jimmy Murphy gazed at the far horizon and planned for an uncertain future. A welcome helping hand arrived when an old friend of Murphy's, former Manchester United goalkeeper Jack Crompton, left Luton Town to rejoin his former club as temporary assistant trainer taking the place of the much-lamented Tom Curry.

And so, to Wednesday 19th February 1958. Four hours before kick-off bedlam reigned outside Old Trafford with thousands of supporters desperately on the lookout for match tickets. It was an insatiable desire that could never be met and with passions running high, what should have been a solemn occasion threatened at times to spiral out of control with extra police drafted in to help keep the huge crowds in order.

The scenes were bizarre - most simply stood milling around, uncertain of what to do, say or feel while others looked to cash in. Ticket touts found rich pickings as they made a quick killing by demanding treble face value. But in doing so they risked life and limb with some supporters regarding them as vultures picking the bones of their dead players. As emotions overflowed trouble inevitably flared around the ground with many touts given a good hiding and relieved of their tickets.

Such was the dire extent of United's plight, Jimmy Murphy found himself unable to name any semblance of a team when asked by the programme editor. Left with no option as the minutes slipped by, the programme went to press with the home team blank.

Since the grim Reaper had ripped the heart out of the Red Devils Murphy had begged, borrowed, bought and stolen to ensure United remained in business on the pitch. He worked endlessly to bring in reinforcements for those whom had perished. Then there were the funerals to attend, each soul destroying, harrowing and causing Murphy untold heartache. But amid all the deaths, tears and sadness it was essential that albeit if only slight, a sense of normality carried on.

At 5-30, two hours before the match began and with thousands still searching desperately for tickets, the decision was taken to lock the gates. This meant there would be no full house for, such was the chaos caused by the crowds, those with tickets could not get near the entrance turnstiles. The official attendance was later given as 59,848, 7000 below capacity. Meanwhile, those lucky enough to be inside the stadium paid 4d for their match program - The United Review. On its front cover club Chairman Harold P Hardman penned the following: "Although we mourn our dead and grieve for our wounded, we believe that great days are not done for us. The sympathy and encouragement of the football world and particularly of our supporters will justify and inspire us. The road back may be long and hard but with the memory of those who died at Munich, of their stirring achievements and wonderful sportsmanship ever with us, Manchester United will rise again."

  For United supporters there followed the harsh reality of reading the team sheets. On the bottom of the centre pages the Sheffield Wednesday players were as listed: United's? A poignancy beyond mere words, just eleven empty spaces. To honour those who died many supporters came dressed in black overcoats whilst adorning red/white scarves around their wrist or necks. It was like a funeral without a burial service. The constant cheers of 'United' thundering out from the packed terraces gave the impression of this being just another game. But then those who sang did so with tears streaming down their faces for a football club that had been brought to its knees.
A dreadful silence greeted the naming of Manchester United's team over the loudspeaker, broken only by sobbing or the screaming out loud of a dead player's

name. In a voice shaking with emotion the tannoy announcer carried out his painful task, firstly asking for spectators to write in the names on the program sheet left blank. But few did, simply preferring to listen and weep. He continued:
"Manchester United: Gregg, Foulkes, Greaves, Goodwin, Cope, Crowther, Webster, Taylor E, Dawson, Pearson, Brennan."

Of those named only two were survivors of the plane crash; goalkeeper Harry Gregg and defender Bill Foulkes. Accompanied by Jimmy Murphy they had arrived back in England the previous Friday to be met by a barrage of pressmen and photographers as they stepped off the train. Neither player would comment on their horrific experience, instead it was Murphy who, to satisfy the constant questioning by reporters said, "I am pleased we left our injured players and Matt Busby much better and it cheered us up on our long journey from Germany." The reality was both men were in a state of bewilderment after the crash and in no mental state to partake in what was sure to be a traumatic occasion. But the monumental scale of United's dilemma meant that Jimmy Murphy was left with little option but to ask Gregg and Foulkes to help keep the red flag flying, if not high then at least half-mast. The rest of the side was a hotchpotch concoction of promising youth and reserve players, allied together with those who had been brought in to see the club through the eye of the storm.

Beyond that infamous Munich runway lay a new red dawn. A fearful place, one certain to be beset with trauma and worry. For those chosen to carry on, it would sadly be a case of drown or cover yourself in glory. Jimmy Murphy had few options with what he had left. Twenty-six-year-old Ian Greaves came in at left-back for United Captain Roger Byrne and his usual deputy Geoff Bent, both dead.

Greaves, now one of the most experienced players left alive at Old Trafford, recalled the horror and sadness of those terrible days for Manchester United: 'Having lost so many friends, it was hard to take; those first two or three weeks we were training and going to our friends' funerals, too. Geoff Bent, the left back, was my best friend. I should have been on that trip myself, but because of an injury situation Geoff went instead. But that was the thing about Munich – we all lost a best friend.'

Reserve Freddie Goodwin played at right-half instead of Eddie Colman, dead. Twenty-four-year-old former amateur footballer Ronnie Cope was at centre-half for Mark Jones also killed and Jackie Blanchflower, so seriously hurt that his career was over. The highly rated Colin Webster was on the right-wing for Johnny Berry who, like Blanchflower, was soon forced into injury-related retirement.

At centre-forward the prodigious battering ram Alex Dawson led the attack as he bravely attempted to follow in the footsteps of the late, much-lamented Tommy Taylor. Another talented reservist was Irishman Shay Brennan and potentially the best of the surviving United youngsters, along with Bobby Charlton was twenty-year old Mark Pearson. He filled in for the severely injured Dennis Viollet and the lost David Pegg. Alongside the home bred players were two newcomers. Blackpool's inside-forward Ernie Taylor and finally, Aston Villa's, hard tackling, twenty-three-year-old wing-half Stan Crowther signed only an hour and sixteen minutes before kick-off for £32,000.

Greaves again on United's late arrival: 'We were in the dressing-room and, at ten past seven Stan Crowther arrived in a taxi. We didn't know him – we just went out on the pitch and we didn't even know what he could do. We just got on with it. We had to. While you were playing, it just went from your mind, you were chasing a ball again and you didn't feel sorry for yourself any more. You were playing a game of football and not for your friends or the Munich disaster. Against Sheffield Wednesday, you just couldn't allow your mind to go.' Crowther was handed the ominous task of replacing Duncan Edwards, who at that time was still fighting for his life in a Munich ward, oblivious to the goodwill and prayers being said for his recovery. Having already played for Aston Villa in the FA Cup previously, Crowther received special dispensation from the football Association to play for United in their darkest hour. It was a rare show of humanity from the authorities towards United and one which would not be repeated in the desperate weeks and months to follow.

At first Stan Crowther was dubious about the move to Manchester, claiming he was happily settled in the Midlands. Tough and blond, he was not known for his sensitive side. Crowther resisted until the very end, only finally relenting to the sheer fervour of the crazy Welshman whose passion for Manchester United knew no bounds. Crowther was also wary that in turning Murphy down, he would have earned himself a lifelong enemy.

It was in Jimmy Murphy's' pre-match speech before kick-off that all the pain and anger stored up from the horrors of Munich was released and those present claimed it could have scorched the paint on the dressing room walls. '
Play hard for yourselves, for the players who are dead and for the great name of Manchester United.' Then he broke down and wept, unable to carry on. Murphy's assistant trainer Jack Crompton took over and simply told those now representing Manchester United, 'let's go lads.'

  The appearance of Munich survivors Harry Gregg and Bill Foulkes as the first two United players out of the tunnel into full view of the crowd brought the atmosphere inside Old Trafford, which was already bordering close to boiling point, beyond the point of no return. The others followed, so many new faces in red shirts, these strangers in the night.
The referee Mr A Bond from London called the two Captains together, Bill Foulkes and Albert Quixall. Foulkes later recalled the moment, 'We shook hands and I looked at Albert and he looked at me and neither of us wanted to play. It was like what are we doing here?' There followed a one-minute silence in honour of those killed. The atmosphere was unnerving and unnatural, a communal grief. Even hard nose policemen told by superiors to always keep a stiff upper lip, were seen with tears rolling down their faces. Old Trafford has witnessed many nights both before and since that have left unforgettable scenes of drama but none ever came remotely close to matching what occurred on that fateful evening.

Earlier in the season Sheffield Wednesday had gone to Old Trafford and given the Busby's Babes an almighty fright before going down in a close fought match 2-1. On paper, all things considered, the visitors from across the Pennines had been handed a great opportunity to beat United and earn themselves a place in the FA cup quarter-finals. Unfortunately for Sheffield Wednesday they were up against not merely eleven players in red but a sheer tidal wave of human emotion that ultimately overwhelmed them. Some spectators were halfway up the floodlight pylons, holding on for dear life with one hand whilst whirling their red scarves with the other. In a furious opening, Murphy's patched up Manchester United tore into the Yorkshiremen.

The visitors were a fine side, tough but fair and in no way deserving the intolerable pressure placed upon them as Manchester let loose all the sadness, anger and despair of the past fortnight upon their heads. A simple cruel twist of fate that left them the bad guys to those whom had refused to go gently into the murderous Munich night. Wednesday had walked into a cacophony of breaking hearts.

Albert Quixall, who signed for United the following September, would later say, 'We were playing more than just eleven players, we were playing 60,000 fans as well.' With Stan Crowther crashing into tackles and Ernie Taylor the playmaker, constantly encouraging the youngsters around him, United played as if lives were at stake, and in a cruel manner out of their skins. In the stands sat next to Jimmy Murphy was Bobby Charlton. Driven from his family home in the north-east to be present as United attempted to fight back from the edge, Charlton had considered quitting the game. His mind was in turmoil after the crash but after much soul searching and speaking once more to Murphy he realised life, and the club he so proudly represented, had to go on. Otherwise what meaning would those whose lives were lost have?

On fifteen minutes new signing Taylor so nearly became an instant Old Trafford legend when his fierce drive from twenty yards smashed against the Wednesday post. The noise from the crowd greeting the near miss was unworldly and deafening, what did this club have to do to get a break, had they not suffered enough? Still the blood red shirts pressed forward, on twenty-seven minutes the heavens cupped their ears as a goal arrived from a most unlikely source. Deputising as a left-winger, it was one of the new boys, twenty-year old Shay Brennan, that scored direct from a corner after goalkeeper Ryalls fumbled the ball on his goal line. The affable young Irishman had only been informed that same morning he would be playing and as his team mates celebrated with him, as Jimmy Murphy punched the air. As Old Trafford exploded like never before, Shay Brennan became immortalised in Manchester United history.

As the game wore on it became blatantly obvious to neutrals that the Sheffield players were clearly not up to spoiling what was a cruel contest. Who would ever wish to cause upset at a wake? Throughout United's football was full of fire and heart; thrilling at times if sometimes lacking the quality the fans were used to. Murphy's scratch team gave everything but a lack of understanding and class was obvious in certain positions. Yet still they defied all logic by playing well above themselves. United hammered away endlessly at the Sheffield Wednesday goal, shots rained in but it wasn't until twenty minutes from time that they finally made another count, when once more the unlikely Shay Brennan seized onto a rebound from close-range to flash a shot past Ryalls. Five minutes from the end it was 3-0 when Alex Dawson, the son of a Grimsby trawlerman, capped an unforgettable night of drama by crashing a third low and hard into a besieged Ryall's net to confirm United's place in the FA Cup quarter-finals. They called it the 'Murphy Miracle' but no one at Old Trafford believed in miracles any longer.

It had been a remarkable performance by Murphy's boys as they ran and fought like dervishes, the searing pain of Munich slightly easing, only to surface instantly once more in the cold light of the final whistle. At the finish most of the United youngsters were in tears with the overwhelming emotion of the evening taking a heavy toll. Back in the sacred surroundings of the dressing room, Jimmy Murphy addressed his team and told them how proud the lads whom had died would have been of them. Then he broke down again, to be consoled by all. Both Harry Gregg and Bill Foulkes simply sat quietly remembering dead friends, their hearts and minds still languishing amid the snow and ice of that far away German runway.

A Pathè news crew arrived armed with a bottle of bubbly to present to the players to celebrate a great victory, though when the pictures are viewed there are few smiles to be seen. Nevertheless, it was perhaps the most important game in the club's history. This rag tag team of youth players, reserves and sequestered veterans had combined to ensure that Harold Hardman's evocative words 'Manchester United would rise again' was made

flesh. Most importantly, United had proved they were not yet willing to go gently into the night, the Red Devils had given themselves priceless breathing space and the veiled curtains that lay drawn across the city were opened ever so slightly to reveal the merest chink of light.
Yet two days later the sky fell in on Manchester when Duncan Edwards lost his fight for life. He was the eighth player to perish in the crash. Sometimes words are simply insufficient. For those of a United persuasion it had become hard to breathe.

'Had we lost that match I think Manchester would have died from a broken heart.' Bobby Charlton

C9
JIMMY MURPHY
ONCE UPON A TIME IN MUNICH
'Just keep my dad humble and
you'll catch him.' Nicky Murphy

INTRODUCTION
Manchester United v Bolton Wanderers. FA cup final. Wembley stadium. Saturday 3rd May 1958.
By God's grace I've survived a world war, missed an air crash by a twist of fate but I'm quite certain I'll not live through Abide with Me. I'm forty-seven years old and feel a hundred. My broken heart and every bone in my body is telling me I've lived a full life.
I feel shattered, worn out and done in. I'm so, so tired. I can't remember the last time I had a peaceful night's sleep. I don't sleep because I daren't dream. Sometimes I'm scared to close my eyes just in case I accidentally slip off into the darkness and hear the boy's voices again. Maybe even see their faces once more. Duncan, Eddie, Tommy, Roger, please god don't take me there,
I couldn't bare it.
I swear to god I couldn't stand that. Not now, not ever.

It's a beautiful early summer's May Day. I'm stood in the Wembley tunnel looking out onto the pitch. It's an hour before kick-off and the massed bands of the Grenadier Guards Division are heading past me. All brass, braid and splendour. I'm thinking on what to say to the boys in the dressing room when suddenly a dark suited Wembley official walks past eating an orange. I catch the man's eyes and he smiles, 'Hello there Mr Murphy, a wonderful job you've done. To get your boys to the final after what happened? Extraordinary. Good luck today old chum.' I don't reply. I just nod in thanks and stare and watch until the man has disappeared from sight.

My mind is racing, the sweet-smelling odour of the orange still fresh in my nostrils. I hold my nose and try desperately to rid myself of the pungent smell. I don't want the memories back. Not yet, not ever. Just keep going forward, don't look back, too painful. Open wounds. Just empty seats in the cliff dressing room and canteen. Echoes of lost voices drifting in the Mancunian air.

Red ghosts-Salford, Manchester, Dudley, Yorkshire and a gentle Irish accent. Laughter in the corridor and the clack, clack of football boots. Yet, when I go to look there's nobody there?

I turn and head back to the dressing room. Matt is here and is going to say a few words to the boys before kick-off. He's still on crutches and in dreadful pain but determined to do it. I can only imagine the demons in his head. If they are like mine then we're both cursed. This I know Matt is dreading but then so am I. Twelve months ago the boys we spoke to in that same room. Most are dead now.

Three United supporters from Manchester in flat caps and wearing huge red rosettes have managed to wrangle themselves past a policeman guarding the tunnel and they approach me. They're all smiling wide, for them this day also a release from the constant pain. They surround and put out their hands for me to shake, 'Good luck Jimmy.' 'All the best Jimmy lad.' 'God bless Jimmy, you've done bloody miracles! A miracle man you are.'

I just stare and the smiles disappear from their faces. 'You okay Jimmy?'

I walk off leaving the three supporters stood staring blankly.

'Bloody ell' lads,' I hear one of them say. 'Our Jimmy is feeling it today.'

The policeman whom they originally avoided appears. 'Right you three sod off back in the stands otherwise you won't see the game. I'll stick you all in a bloody cell. Bleedin' northerners. Go on, hop it!'

The supporters walk off. Suddenly forlorn. One turns around and spots me stood watching them from far back. He waves but I don't respond.

'Hello Jimmy.' I turn around and it's Matt. He's smiling, leaning on his crutches but I can tell how nervous he is about going in to see the players.

'Hello old pal' I reply. Trying to sound upbeat but failing miserably. 'Are you ready to go in? It'll be great for the boys to hear a few words.'

'I'm not sure I can do it Jimmy. I don't think I have the courage.'

'It's not a question of courage Matt. You need to walk through that dressing room door and see the shirt not the faces. These are our boy's now. They're more nervous of seeing you than you them. You need to do this old pal.'

He nods, 'I miss paradise Jimmy. I miss my boys.'

Matt enters and I just stare….

My mind and thoughts now back in a time before the air crash. Before the darkness…. I'm back in paradise.

Act One
ORANGES AND BOWLER HATS
Highbury. Arsenal v Manchester United. Saturday 1st February 1958. 'I take it back Jimmy,' said the smiling Arsenal fan with a broad cockney accent as we stood up

off the bench at the final whistle. 'He's not bad is that Edwards!' I smile as does Matt. The same man who shouted out as we took our seats at the beginning, 'Hey Busby, where's this Duncan Edwards then? Where's Superman? I'd looked around angrily and caught his eye but as ever, the calming influence of Matt restrained me from giving him back a mouthful. We both sat down nervously chain smoking. The lads always used to joke it looked like smoke signals coming from the bench. Secret messages! Well after just ten minutes when young Kenny Morgans sped past two chasing Arsenal defenders, before crossing perfectly for Duncan to take the ball in his stride and smash gloriously past the Arsenal goalkeeper Jack Kelsey. I couldn't help it! With both myself and Matt on our feet celebrating, I turned again to face the Arsenal fan from previous and caught his eye, 'That's him,' I shouted. 'The big fellow. That's superman! That's Duncan Edwards!'

It's been a hell of a game today. The boys have really put on a show and the boss is delighted. The crazy 5-4 scoreline and our defending has I have to be honest given me a dozen heart attacks this afternoon, but to look around now at this packed Highbury crowd. To see them all on their feet giving our lads and their own a standing ovation. It's enough to bring a tear to a glass Welsh eye and even touch the heart of a grizzled, hard-bitten old cynic like me. Matt always says playing Arsenal here with their grand marble statues and wonderful history is like performing at the London Palladium. Well we've been top of the bill today and brought the house down in true Manchester United style. As the boys leave the pitch, our all white strips with a red dash caked in mud, they're all smiling and acknowledging the applause.

'Bloody hell Dunc' I hear Tommy Taylor say to Edwards. 'I think they like us mate!' Another Arsenal fan leans down towards me, 'Hey Jimmy.' I look up. 'We've scored four goals today. What have we got to do to beat your lot?'

'Just keep praying son.' He laughs, not knowing I was serious. There always seems an extra bounce in the lad's stride when they come to London. We sense it on the train south. 'They're up for putting on a show Jimmy,' Matt would say. 'God help these cockneys!' United are now treated by the press hacks like movies stars. There was a time not so long ago a team from Manchester coming here when the mention of flat caps, ferret, pigeons and billowing chimneys spewing black smoke forever upwards was simply inevitable. A miserable northern outpost christened 'Cottonoplis'. The rainy city where no one smiles and is grey and drab. Well not anymore for it is now the home of the finest young football team this country has ever witnessed. And they're ours. One we've raised from the crèche. Taught them the basics, pass to a red shirt, keep moving, play hard, play fair and attack! A dash of red angel dust now covets the Mancunian sky. Matt no longer bothers trying to play down our boys to outsiders. But woe betide any of them getting too big for their boots. Oh, I'm on them like a wolf I am. But I love them all. I love them all I do and today they've done their city, themselves, myself and Matt proud. The Londoners will never forget this day when Manchester United came south and rocked their world.

We're on the night train travelling back north to Manchester. I'm sat in the dining carriage with Matt opposite and also a journalist sharing more than a few drinks with us. For we are celebrating conquering London see! The Evening chronicles' Alf Clarke. A United fanatic from well before the war and one of Matt's favourites. The two not necessarily going together but the fact when the reds are beat Alf always finds a way to make it sound like the biggest injustice ever to hit this wonderful game of ours always helped! But make no mistake Matt can play all these press boys like I play a piano. As we're chatting away about the Arsenal match Matt looks up. He's spotted his old Captain and Manchester United great Johnny Carey stood over us smiling wide. Johnny is now manager of Blackburn Rovers and he and Matt have remained close. A good lad is Johnny. Will always be United.

'Johnny, you rascal' smiles Matt. 'What's brought you on this train?'

Carey laughs, 'Looking for players boss. Not a problem you have!'

'Oh, you never know,' teases Matt. 'We might have the odd one going spare for the right good fellow.'

'That left half of your looks tidy,' smiles Carey. 'Is it Edwards his name? I shall happily take him off your hands if he's going spare?'

We all laugh.

'He scored a great goal today Johnny,' I add. 'Duncan is getting better each game.'

'The best I've ever seen Jimmy' replies Carey. 'You and Matt have created a masterpiece with that boy. The penalty he scored a few weeks ago against Bolton's little Eddie Hopkinson when you hammered them 7-2 at Old Trafford? Eddie was determined to save that shot, full of determination he was. Then, suddenly Duncan hit it and bang! Past him like a rocket! Eddie hadn't moved a

bloody inch! Tommy Banks the full-back, a funny fellow is Tommy. He said to Eddie as the ball lay in the back of the net, 'You can move now Eddie. It's all over!'
We all laugh loud. Eddie Colman is walking past and is immediately clocked by Matt, 'Everything alright there young Colman?'
'Not too sure boss.' Eddie looks around at the carriage and all the different after-hours characters on the tables having meals, 'This train is a bit Agatha Christie if you ask me.'
Matt scratches his head quizzically, 'That sounds as if it needs a deal of explaining. Go get a drink son and stay out of trouble. That goes for the rest of you. Pass it on. No adventures is that understood?'
He salutes and smiles, 'Yes boss.' Off he saunters. Salford's finest but a cheeky little beggar.
'I'll leave you gentlemen in peace,' says Carey. He shakes all our hands.
'Good luck in Belgrade boys. Stay safe.' We watch him go.
Alf refills all our glasses. I sense a question coming on from the old hack, 'Matt, the first interview you ever gave me thirteen years ago, you said you were determined to attract the best youngsters around into Manchester United.'
'Aye I remember it well Alf,' smiles Matt.
'Well-then, you have a day like today. Seeing these lads put Arsenal away like that. It's all falling into place. I have to say they are bloody world-beaters. And here's to them.' Alf raises his glass and we toast.
'I could never have hoped they'd develop as fast as they have,' replies Matt. 'But they're good Alf. The way we're going, I'll have nothing to do except polish an

office chair for the next ten years and speak to Jimmy here!'

I smile, 'Aye Matt, keep the bar well stocked for when I join you!'

Again, we're laughing. These are good days. Paradise.

It's Matt who insists I stay behind in Manchester in my other role as manager of Wales and not travel to Belgrade. But I'm in two minds see. He's recently had an operation for the veins in his leg and I know the man better than himself. That despite saying little he's in some terrible pain. I constantly catch him wincing. When I ask it's always the same, 'Ah don't fret Jimmy; it's just a wee twinge.' The long arduous journey to Belgrade by stopover at Munich is the last thing Matt needs. After all the hassle and aggravation of getting home from Bilbao last season, this time we've hired our own plane for the 2000-mile round trip back from Belgrade. Via Munich. It's a beauty; a true aristocrat of the skies. It's bigger and so much more comfortable for the lads and press boys who'll be travelling with them. A moaning bunch of buggers but all good lads. Also, it's been used by her Majesty the queen on previous occasions, so if it was good enough for that lady, then equally so for Manchester United.

As for me going along?

Well Matt is adamant that I should be in Cardiff for the second leg of our world cup qualifier against Israel. We won 2-0 over there and barring a disaster have all but qualified for the summer's world cup in Sweden.

'Your heart is Welsh Jim,' he says. 'You're a Rhondda man and you've been with these boys for two years, if it was to go wrong and you weren't there you'd never

forgive yourself. Go to Cardiff man. Get Wales to the finals. Don't worry about Belgrade. We'll be fine.'
We'll be fine. His words. How can I not believe him? The thought that one of my best pals in the world, Bert Whalley, will be sat in my normal spot alongside him on the airplane and also be sleeping in the next hotel room calms my fears a little over Matt's health. Bert will watch him like a hawk. Indeed, I told him as much, 'Keep an eye on the boss Bert. He isn't well,' I say. 'But he won't say anything to nobody. Stubborn as a mule see.'
'Don't worry Jimmy old pal, he's in good hands.'
But I'm still uneasy. It doesn't sit well with me not going. It just doesn't feel right. Like a dereliction of duty see. But what can I do? Matt has all but ordered me to go to Cardiff and he's right. If it was to go wrong I'd never forgive myself. No, United are in good hands. My boys will be back before I know it and then life can go on as normal.

I say my farewell for a day or so at the Cliff training ground on the Monday before they head off to Ringway. I call them together. I clap my hands, 'Now you lot c'mon now, I've something important I want to say.' Suddenly the fooling around and the chatting ceases and every eye falls upon me. Duncan winks. That grin so wide and generous, 'What's going on Jimmy?'
The finest player of his age I've ever seen. He's my favourite see, but I'm always careful not to show it. In a manner they're all family but Duncan is my adopted son. I love them all I do.
'Well played on Saturday Duncan but it means nothing now. The match in Belgrade will be tough and they'll be gunning for you lad so be ready. You'll need eyes in the back of your head. Play hard but fair Dunc lad. Show that

lot stuck behind the Iron Curtain just what you're made of.'

'I will Jimmy' smiles Duncan. 'Don't worry about me chief.'

'Oh, I don't son' I say smiling. 'You keep improving and you'll nearly be good enough to play for Wales. Now I'll see you all in a couple of days. I 've business in Cardiff with the greatest country in the world! And when I get them to the world cup finals, I'll be coming back to Manchester on Thursday to meet up again with you ugly lot. And also with the glorious news that Manchester United have made it through to the semi-finals of the European Cup. Am I right!'

They all cheer, 'We won't let you down,' say Duncan. 'You just get the Taffs to Sweden and I'll see you there!'

I smile, 'I know you won't Duncan lad but it's not me, its Manchester United, the fans and the boss you have to think about. And most importantly yourselves. You boys show the world that we're ready now to take on Real Madrid this time around and beat them.'

'Hey Jimmy,' It's Eddie Colman. The rascal from Salford. But my rascal with the huge cheeky grin that lets him get away with murder. And the most wonderful inside left with a body swerve that could send a charging army in the wrong direction. 'Yes Colman' I reply, trying not to smile and keep a serious face.

'I've got my beans and tomato soup packed in the suitcase Jimmy. They won't shoot me these commies if they find them at customs, will they?'

'They might try to Eddie' I reply. 'But you drop that shoulder of yours, take a swerve son and those bullets will hit anyone but you.'

'Remind me not to stand next to you at the airport Eddie,' shouts out Tommy Taylor. They all laugh.
'We've got this Jimmy,' said the Captain Roger Byrne. 'I'll make sure of that.'
Roger smiles at me. This is a man, a man amongst our babes. Whenever the press boys dare criticise any of the lads in front of Roger he'd tear a strip of them, 'You can criticise me, but not the team' he'd rage. A true leader. You can see in the eyes. The way Roger holds himself. Never afraid to stand his corner against me and even Matt. Which at times annoys the boss no end but I know deep down he respects Roger for it. Matt knows the young lads could not be in better hands on the pitch.
'And I promise you something,' I tell them. 'You get through and come Friday morning I'll go easy on you in training.' They all cheer. 'Just a little though' I add. To the soundtrack of a few groans. I smile wide.
'Well you wouldn't have me going soft now would you lads!'

And so, with my usual routine I wake early to make the breakfast for the kids. I kiss Winnie goodbye and leave my adopted home of Manchester and travel by train from Piccadilly's London Road to Cardiff. The lads working on the platform much to my embarrassment all recognise me,
'Good luck With Wales Jimmy,' one shouts out.
'Thanks son' I reply.
'Let's hope you Taffs win, United get through against Red Star and that we smash the Wolves at Old Trafford on Saturday.' He gives me the big thumbs up, 'Thanks for all you and Matt are doing Jimmy. Making us proud. You're making Manchester proud.'

I wave and get on the train. My mind is racing. After beating Red Star Belgrade only 2-1 at Old Trafford, I know it's set to be a battle royal behind the Iron Curtain but with Matt and my good pals Bert Whalley and Tom Curry looking after the boys, I try not to worry too much. But still I find myself fidgeting and fretting all the way to Cardiff on this damn bloody train.
How fit is Roger after taking a bad knock at Arsenal?
Will Duncan be able to boss their midfield?
Will the referee be swayed by what's going to be a hostile, frenzied home crowd?
Will Matt's legs hold up with all the travelling?
And on and on…
There are only two of us in the carriage. I'm sat opposite a man in a bowler hat reading a Times newspaper and smoking his pipe who keeps peaking over the top of it to stare at me. Three times he does this before finally lowering the newspaper and staring me straight in the face.
'You're Jimmy Murphy?'
I smile and nod and just continue smoking my cigarette. I look out the window but can still feel his eyes upon me.
'How come you're not going to Belgrade with Manchester United?'
I turn around and look at him. His is a posh Cheshire accent and he's speaking with a tone that irks, 'Business away, 'I tell him. Before continuing to stare out.
'What kind of business?'
'My country's' I reply. In a manner I hope will make him go quiet.
'Very well then, be it on your conscience if anything goes wrong.'

That said he disappears back behind the paper. I count to ten and decide to ignore his crass remark.
But god help him if he opens his bloody big mouth again…

Ninian Park. Wales v Israel: World cup qualification play off: Wednesday 5th February 1958. It's great to meet up again with my old friend John Charles. We'd managed to persuade Juventus to release him for the two games against Israel. Already 2-0 up after winning in Tel Aviv it's now just a question of keeping our nerve. What a trip that turned out to be, the reception we had from the Israeli supporters was unbelievably friendly. As to the game over there big John took some stick early on but his brother Mel shown brotherly love and swiftly sorted out the offenders. At the start my Captain and Arsenal's also, Dave Bowen exchanged flowers, only to see ours confiscated at Customs on return. Health risk they called it. I bloody ask you.
On a side-note, immediately arriving in Cardiff I made a bee-line to Dave and thanked him for his actions the previous Saturday. Our Duncan had gone a little crazy in the 5-4 win at Highbury after we'd first blown a 3-1 lead. Dunc was going around tearing into Arsenal players and wreaking carnage. It was Dave who had a quiet word in his ear, 'Stop taking liberties big fella or we'll gang up and make sure you finish the game on a fuckin' stretcher.' With Belgrade coming up this calmed Dunc down. It was a huge favour and much appreciated by myself and Mr Busby. We need him out in Yugoslavia, not back at Old Trafford on a damned treatment table.
At half time in Israel four large cart loads of oranges arrived in the stadium and were passed amongst all the spectators. It was an amazing sight to see the stands turn

bright orange. Altogether it was a great time although the whiff of war which I'd experienced not so long ago was forever in the air. As a passing note after the game at night, we let the boys go for a drink. Most of the girls they chatted to carried rifles over their shoulders. So, all behaved!

John Charles is a really good pal. A son of Cwmbrwla, Swansea. A magnificent footballer, six feet two and equally majestic as both a centre half and centre forward. In Turin they adore him equally as they did at Leeds. The supporters bow before 'Il Buono Gigante!' The 'Gentle Giant.' This lad has a heart bigger than a football. He greets me with a massive grin and huge bearhug at training that almost lifts me off my feet, 'Jimmy how are you old son?'

'Put me down you crazy Swansea man!'

'So, Jimmy how's things in paradise with Mr Busby and those apples of yours?'

'He's not too clever John. A leg operation has left him in agony, typical Matt, he says nothing to nobody, but I know its driving him mad. As for Belgrade? They're a good team with some special players. We've a real fight on our hands but it'll be okay.'

'You've some special boys at United too Jimmy. That Edwards lad? A monster of a talent. I read about his goal at Arsenal. It had the Highbury Clock End applauding. What are you feeding him?'

I laugh, 'Welsh beef! Big Dunc? Ah he's still growing John. You just wait, by the time myself and Matt have polished off the rough edges he'll be even better.'

A smiling John shakes his head, 'What time do they kick off in Belgrade?'

'Roughly the same time as we do. So, screaming at you lot should keep my mind occupied until their score comes through!'

'I bet' he says laughing. 'Not one to keep your feelings to yourself on that touchline are you Jimmy. But don't worry old mate. Be a nice red double for you tomorrow. I promise.'

A last friendly tap on my shoulder, a huge smile and John runs off to join the other lads training. Would be a handy addition at United but more chance of us selling Juventus Duncan than the Italians letting their gentle giant wear a red shirt. Come the end of training an Israeli delegation arrives and a beautiful exotic lady with dark hair and huge almond eyes presents me with a large basket of oranges. The Israelis are wonderfully friendly people. But I sense a fierceness in them that gives away their constant battle against all who surround and want to throw them back into the sea. Therefore, I know that despite our two-goal lead the second-leg is no foregone conclusion. As my United boys in Belgrade will have to fight for all they earn tomorrow afternoon then so will we against this brave new nation.

In the end Wales have won 2-0 with late goals from Cliff Jones and Ivor Allchurch. It's a tough game, the Israelis scrapping hard. Making up for any lack of real class with a willingness to fight and scrap for every ball. But with John again outstanding we have far too much. For the first time Wales are going to the world cup and I'll be at their helm. Once back in the dressing room, amidst the celebrations I seek news of United's result. A few phone calls to various newspaper pals and they confirmed the boys have fought out a breath-taking 3-3 draw to quality for the European cup semi-finals.

My day is complete.
I seek out John and embrace him, 'I got my red double John. United went through as well. Well played today son, we're going to that world cup and not just to make up the numbers.' I clench my fist, 'We're going over to win the bloody thing.'
He smiles, 'Take some team to stop us Jimmy. Take one to stop us!'
I look around at the players; I clap my hands and shout loud, 'All right lads, give me a minute eh!'
Immediately silence falls across the jubilant dressing room and I feel all eyes on me.
'Been waiting for this Jimmy,' calls out Ivor Allchurch. Everybody laughs, including me.
'Okay boys I'm going to keep this short and sweet.'
'You're never sweet Jimmy,' calls out a voice! I smile, I love these boys, 'You've done your country and me proud today. You kept your nerve and done your jobs and now this little nation of ours, small in size but huge in heart.'
I point to mine and smile, 'Well we've got ourselves a little summer's break see!' They all cheer.
'We've got ourselves a working holiday in Sweden at the world cup! 'They cheer once more but louder.
'And you know boys; we're not going there to just make up the numbers.' I point at John Charles, 'What country on earth could possibly give birth to a man and a footballer like this?' John smiles whilst the others pat him on the back. 'Now I have urgent business back in Manchester. My other sons have done me proud too.' Again, all the Welsh players cheer and applaud. 'I'm off now to be there at Old Trafford when they get home to tell them how proud I am and to keep their bloody young

feet on the ground! Only one thing we miss at Old Trafford lads is a few more bloody Welshmen.' I point again at John Charles and everybody laughs, 'So, if you ever get bored of all that Italian sunshine John and fancy a little Mancunian rain, you let myself and Mr Busby know instantly?'
'Yes Jimmy' he replies smiling. 'Straight away Jimmy!'
'Good lad' I reply. 'You know it makes sense son. You and Duncan would be quite a tidy pair I can imagine!'

I'm walking fast through my hotel foyer in Cardiff, carrying a suitcase, bag of oranges and rushing for the train taking me back to Manchester. Two suited Welsh officials with glasses of beer in their hands suddenly appear. I don't need this now. 'What's going on Jimmy?' says one, who's obviously already put a few drinks away. 'Not slipping away are you? Bloody hero of the hour you are man.'
I smile, 'No time boys. Got to get home for the day job.'
'Oh, come on Jimmy,' replies the other one. Also, quite happily plastered! 'A little drink for the road? What do you say?'
'Celebrate a great day,' adds the other.
'Not happening see. My lads are flying home as we speak and I want to be there when they arrive home and hear all about it.'
'Can't even tempt you for a quick one then Jim?'
I grab an orange from the bag and show it them, 'I'll have one of these in victory on the train. Now goodbye boys!'
BBC Radio Newsflash:
"We interrupt this broadcast of Mrs Dale's diary for a news flash. Reuters reports that a British European Airways Elizabethan aircraft carrying the Manchester

United football team has crashed on take-off at Munich airport. Some casualties are feared. We will interrupt programmes with more details as soon as possible…"

SILENT NIGHT: Thursday 6 February 1958. I look at my watch; it's twenty-five minutes to four in the afternoon. I'm back home at London Road railway station. It's bitterly cold. There are mountains of snow in a dark and miserable Manchester sky as I walk out the station towards the black taxi rank. As well as my suitcase, I'm carrying these damned oranges off the Israelis. Suddenly a blond petite lady with huge blue eyes, well dressed, pretty in her teens, grabs my arm. She's showing me an apple whilst smiling wide and pointing at the oranges, 'Oranges are not the only fruit Mr Murphy,' she says. 'We blues like these!'
I laugh, 'Ah yes that maybe true my love but your apple is red!'
'Ha!' She offers me her hand and we shake, 'Fair do's Mr Murphy. Mind how you go now and up the blues!'
I smile and head for the leading taxi. The driver recognises me, 'Hey Jimmy, you going to paradise?'
'Yes, mate if you don't mind.'
'My pleasure squire. Hop in.'
Off we drive. I look out the window and the streets are filled with people heading home from work. The traffic is thick. I notice hordes stood around newspaper vendors. A lady crying on the pavement. Another man catches my eyes as we pass him. He has a look of incredulity. All very strange.
High above the skies are a foreboding dark, almost hellish colour in its gloom. Like a black veil over the city. Small snowflakes are falling. I catch the taxi driver looking at me through his mirror. He's smiling wide,

'What a performance by the lads Jimmy. Let's hope we avoid Real Madrid and save them for the final eh.' My mind is already racing ahead to Saturday's match against our great rivals Wolverhampton Wonderers. A top of the table clash neither of us can afford to lose. Stan Cullis will have his mob ready to go. We're going to need to be at our very best to beat them. From the little I've heard the boys were kicked from pillar to post and heaven knows what the situation is regarding injuries. Duncan was supposedly a passenger in the Belgrade snow in the second half. Matt leaving him on the pitch for nuisance and numbers purposes only.

'Well done with the taffs as well Jimmy,' continues the taxi driver. 'Some job that. Wish you all the best of luck old pal, so long as you don't draw England!'

We both laugh, 'Thank you' I reply. 'Me too.'

Secretly I'd love to play the English in Sweden and thrash them. But I'm being polite here whilst inside already bursting to see the lads and Matt again. Also, Bert and Tom, both salt of the earth types. My pals. Good old boys. Tomorrow I'll grab them and over a cuppa get the full story of what went on. Who played well, who's tired. Who needs a kick up the backside or an arm around their shoulder. Let the boss get on with the paperwork. The journos and contracts. I'll tell him what he needs to know. The final word as ever lay with Matt but we supplied the main ingredients in the cake whilst he placed the iced toppings. It may be the Busby babes to our supporters and outsiders but these are our lads. Mine, Bert's and Tom's. We know what makes them tick both on the pitch and off. Who's not getting on with the girlfriend, wife or mother-in-law. Who's hitting the bottle. Who's enjoying himself too much with the ladies.

Or dancing with the devil at the bookies. Who needs a kind word or a rollicking. I can do both, tough love you see.
They always thank me in the end.
Matt is the politician, the face of Manchester United. Undoubtedly the boss but we're the heartbeat. We make our boys tick and when he enters the dressing room they're ready to run through walls for him and this club.

Finally, we turn into the Old Trafford forecourt. I pay the driver and climb out of the cab into the icy cold once more. 'Tell the boys well done from me Jimmy. Little Eddie is my favourite. I live in Archie Street opposite him. I love Eddie, my two little boys love Eddie.'
I smile and hand him an orange from the bag,
'Everybody loves Eddie son. Look after yourself.'
'I will do Jimmy and thanks for the orange! The name is Billy by the way. Billy Mac.' He puts out a hand and we shake, 'It's been a pleasure Jimmy. A bloody pleasure.'
'The pleasures all mine Billy lad.' I wave and off he goes. Inside, despite my painted smile thank goodness he's gone. It may have cost me an orange but well worth it. So much to do. Wolves will be upon us in no time. Now to go and see Alma George, Matt's secretary. Alma runs this club. Without her we'd all be whistling in the wind. The woman is incredible. No matter how busy she copes. Always a smile and forever in good humour. She also knows when to ignore the language which you can imagine in a football club can at times, shall I say, be a little coarse. But around her everybody watches their language. Or tries too!

I enter through a staff door into the ground and up the stairs to the offices. Nobody is around. Me still clutching the oranges, 'Alma are you there?'

Suddenly she appears from an adjoining room with tears falling down her face. It's clear she's been sobbing, holding tight onto a handkerchief.

'My god girl' I exclaim. 'What on earth's wrong?'

'Has no one told you Jimmy?'

'Told me what girl. What are you on about?'

'There's been a terrible accident. A crash.'

'What do you mean Alma, what kind of crash?'

'The airplane Jimmy, it's crashed at Munich. We don't know who's dead or alive.' On hearing these words my heart doesn't so much sink but crash through the chest. I drop the bag of oranges and they roll all over the floor.

I hold a devastated Alma tight as she falls into my arms. I'm trying so hard to register what Alma has just told me. Her words don't sound real, 'We don't know who's dead or alive,' striking me like a bullet. I gently move her face from my shoulder. I wait as she dries the tears.

I look in her eyes, 'Contact the British embassy in Germany. Found out as much as you can. People are going to expect us to know exactly what's gone on.' Alma is shaking. 'Whilst you do that I'll ring around. The newspapers, the police, the BBC.' Alma wipes her eyes clear of tears, 'I'll get on it Jimmy.' I watch her go and try desperately to clear my head. I walk into a small office and sit down at a table. Alma reappears with a list of numbers. Suddenly the phone in front of me starts to ring. I look at Alma, it deafens. The silence of the room is unbearable but this just shrieks. It stings my ears, I pick it up.

'Jimmy Murphy.'

'Oh, Jimmy thank god, have you heard the news?'
I recognise the voice. It's Paddy McGrath. A close friend of Matts' and owner of the Cromford club. The top club in town, 'Paddy I know nothing yet. I'm just about to make some calls old pal.'
'All kinds of rumours Jimmy. Not good. Terrible really.'
Suddenly, another phone rings and Norma rushes to answer it. She shouts back in, 'Jimmy its Bill Fryer from the Daily Express. They need to speak to you.'
'Paddy I've got to go.' I put the down the receiver and head over to Alma who hands me the phone.
'Hello Bill, Jimmy speaking.'
'Hello Jimmy its bad news. We're receiving names of those killed. I'm so sorry. Do you want to write these down?' I close my eyes. I simply can't take this in.
'You mean there are survivors?'
'We believe so Jimmy. Some are severely injured, others have just walked out of the wreck, but everything is so murky. The plane was on its third take off. They overran the runway, the pilot lost control and the airplane was lost. The Germans are saying it's a catastrophe. It's still mad over there. Utter carnage. But…'
I hear the line go quiet, 'Go on Bill.'
'We can tell you,' Bill's voice is choking. 'First Jimmy nothing has come through on Matt but we can confirm through the Reuters newswire that the following people have been confirmed dead…Are you ready?'
My hand is shaking as I hold a pencil and get ready to write down the names, 'Go on Bill.'
'I'll give you the players first…Roger Byrne.'
Oh, Christ no, I think…. this can't be happening.
'Tommy Taylor…David Pegg…Billy Whelan…Geoff Bent.'

Each name is a nail in my fucking heart. Our Father who art in heaven hallowed be your name. What the fuck have you done?

'Eddie Colman.'

Oh, not Eddie…please god no.

'Mark Jones.'…. the line goes quiet as I scribble down the names with tears falling on my face. I can hear Bill crying,

'C'mon Bill Mate' I say. 'We need to do this. Who else?'

'Sorry Jimmy. There's more....'

'Go on Bill.'

'Tom Curry and Bert Whalley are on the list. I'm so sorry mate.'

I close my eyes, I'm in hell. During the war I saw action in North Africa and Italy. I saw terrible, terrible things but this is too much to take in. I try and compose myself.

'Bill can you tell me with a hundred per cent confidence that these names you've given me. All have died. There's no error? It's so important. I'm going to have family members ringing soon. They're going to be coming to the ground. I need to know for certain.'

'They're all dead Jimmy. God rest their souls. Our boys are gone.'

The line goes off. I put the phone down and notice a bottle of whisky on the shelf. I stand, take a glass and pour myself a large drink. It's gone in one go, I pour another and another…I need to clear my head. So much to do. I take a deep breath.

I need some air and head outside. Already groups of people have started to mill around. A police car has pulled up and two officers are walking towards me on the forecourt. 'Thought you may need our help Mr Murphy,' one says. 'I'm Sergeant Thomas and we're here as long

as you need us. There's bound to be an awful lot more people arriving soon. Not going to be nice around here. Awful lot of upset and frustrated people.'
'Thanks lads' I say.
'We're so sorry Jimmy' replies the other. 'I can't believe it.' The young policeman is in tears. The Sergeant punches him on the arm, 'Oi Constable Potter pull yourself together lad. We've got work to do.'
'Sorry Sarge,' he wipes his eyes clear.
'Right I best get back inside. Thanks lads.' Suddenly I'm surrounded by hordes of supporters. I feel like I can't breathe, I can't talk.
'What's happening Jimmy?'
'Any news Jimmy?'
'Are they all dead Jimmy?'
'Is Matt alive Jimmy?'
'Is big Dunc okay Jimmy?'
'Please tell me Eddie isn't dead Jimmy?'
'Why Jimmy, why the fuck why?'...
The Sergeant and the constable swiftly grab me away, 'Get inside Jimmy, we'll mind things out here.'
In I go and Alma is waiting, 'There are more names Jimmy. 'Walter is gone. Also, the newspaper boys. Eight have been killed. The BBC are reporting twenty-one dead in total but that's likely to rise.'
Poor Walter Crickmer, our club secretary and no nicer and gentler soul will you find. Alma hands me a list of names. I recognise and class them all as pals. Alf Clarke from the Manchester Chronicle. So biased through ted tinted eyes that the other press lads would joke when a United player got kicked Alf limped. But a damned good journalist. Don Davies of The Manchester Guardian. 'Old International.' A word poet. As was Eric Thompson of

The Daily Mail. George Fellows. The Daily Herald. The Manchester Evening News' Tom Jackson. Smiling, good old Tom, always smiling. Archie Ledbrooke of The Daily Mirror. Formidable but always fair in his match reports I found. And Dear old Henry Rose of the Daily Express. A supreme showman, bloody outspoken and at times I could've strangled the beggar, but a true gent. And a good friend. And big Swifty. Oh Christ. Frank Swift who was working for the News of the Word also killed. Cheerful, my good pal. Lost forever. We survived a war together only for him to die like this? In fucking Germany? The irony is to be so painful as can only be ordained by a higher power. But I'll speak to that bastard later.
I sit back down at the desk and stare at the list of Journalists killed. The paper is stained with Alma's tears. I take another drink and another. I'm just numb, I simply can't take this all in. The phone rings and I pick it up.
'Jimmy Murphy speaking.'
Jimmy its Sandy Busby, we've just had a telephone call, my Dad's alive. He's been taken to a nearby hospital but thank God he's alive Jimmy!'
'That's wonderful news son.'
'I prayed Jimmy. I was convinced my dad was dead but I said a prayer on my knees in the bedroom and my uncle John came running in shouting 'Sandy he's alive. He's alive!'
'God is good Jimmy.'
God is good he says, 'Well you go and help your mum son. There's been many of our people killed today. Their families are going to need you. Not your prayers, but you.'

I put the receiver down. I need to ring the families of the players who've been killed. They need to hear it from me. It's only right. The least I owe them. I look over and see Alma picking the oranges up off the floor and putting them back in the bag. I go over to help. I bend down alongside her, 'I'm going to ring the boy's families,' I say quietly. She nods in recognition, 'I'll get you their numbers Jimmy. Why has this had to happen? Why us Jimmy? It's not fair, they were all so young. So much to live for.'

Alma again has tears rolling down her cheeks. I take the bag of oranges off her, 'I've no idea love. Nothing is set girl. We're born, we live and when the good lord decides to take us.' The good lord? The words stick in my own throat, 'Well our time ends. Now c'mon dry those eyes again, we've got work to do.'

'I'll get you those numbers Jimmy.' She stands and I watch her go…

This will be the longest night. The longest and most silent night.

It's just gone nine o'clock in the evening. The whisky is almost gone. I've just come off speaking to the last of the player's families. I went through Alma's list. Ticking as I go. My heart breaking each time I dialed the numbers. Roger Byrne. I spoke to his wife Joy. She sounded in shock and spoke almost in sniffling joking terms but I could hear her heart breaking over the phone.

'I've only known him three February's Jimmy. The first he crashed our car into a lamp post. The second into Matt Busby's neighbour's garden and now the third he's gone and got himself killed in a damn plane crash.' She let slip also they were expecting a baby and Roger didn't know. She was going to tell him on returning. I cried with her.

Tommy Taylor, Barnsley's finest. I cried with both his mother and father, Viollet and Charlie. 'He loved you Jimmy' said Viollet. 'And he loved Manchester United.' David Pegg's mother Jessie sobbed through tears and I sobbed too.

Liam 'Billy' Whelan. A boy who wanted to be a priest but only the love of a ball saw him put on a red shirt and not a cassock. I had no number but I knew the name of the Dublin road: St Attracta, so I found out through the operator a neighbour's phone number. I rang them and asked if they could possible go and put Liam's mother on the phone. She already suspected, 'I knew Jimmy' she said. 'I could feel my Liam's spirit soar. He was ready for Heaven and I'm sure god will be only be too happy to see him. Liam is with the angels.'

Mark Jones' pregnant wife June screaming in despair. Geoff Bent's wife Marion weeping till there was no tears left to fall, 'What do we do now Jimmy. I already have one five-month-old baby and another on the way.'

Eddie Colman's dad Dickie said little but I could hear his heart breaking in nearby Salford across the river. Eddie was their life, His grandfather Dickie Senior whom all the players adored. Young Bobby Charlton and Wilf McGuiness in particular. They'd gather in Eddie's living room and the old man would enthrall them with tall and terrible and wonderful tales of his past escapades. There'd be singsongs and joy and laughter in Archie Street.

Not anymore.... My apples, my golden, golden apples. And I hadn't even thought about Duncan. He wasn't on the list but has been confirmed as critical. But where there's life hope remains and in Big Dunc's case he's bigger than life itself. So, let anyone try to take him before he's conquered the world. A colossus and such a wonderful lad. They all are, were…god give me strength to face this coming darkness.

Trying so hard to hold it together Alma re-enters, 'Jimmy I've got Alan Hardaker on the line.' Hardaker is the head of the Football League. We've been at war with this bastard ever since Matt took us into the European cup. The Football League were against this from the start. Matt asked Hardaker for a postponement of the Wolves match but oh no, not him. Threatened us with a point's deduction if we failed to, his words, 'Fulfil our commitments to the Football League.' He stopped Chelsea going in as champions and thought he'd just had to click his fingers and Manchester United would do similar. Well he thought wrong. He said to Matt 'Why do you want to play in a competition full of wogs and dagoes that means absolutely nothing?' The man is a pompous arrogant fool and god help him now for he will feel my wrath if he dared cometh the line I told you so.

I pick the phone up and Alma puts him through.

'Mr Murphy.'

'Mr Hardaker sir.'

'May I on behalf of the Football League offer our deepest sympathies on your loss.'

'Thank you.'

'Obviously in light of what's occurred, the crash, erm, terrible loss of life we will certainly be postponing the game against Wolverhampton Wonderers.'

Hardaker's voice is cracking.

'We appreciate that sir.'

'Well, if we can help in any other way please let us know Mr Murphy. Good luck.'

…. 'Goodnight Mr Hardaker sir.' The line goes dead.

I'd fallen asleep at the table but woken from my slumber by Alma. She gently shakes my shoulder, 'Jimmy I've some good news. Bill Foulkes, Harry Gregg and young Bobby Charlton have all been confirmed as survivors.' She's almost smiling, almost. I rub my eyes, 'Any news of the others?'
She shakes her head, 'No more fatalities. But they're saying Mr Busby is critical, Duncan also is 50/50. The others…'
BEA have also been on. They are putting on an airplane tomorrow morning at nine o'clock to take yourself and family members over to Munich.'
I look at my watch. Its three-thirty in the morning, 'Get your coat Alma I'm going to arrange a car to get you home.'
'No' she insists, 'I'm staying here with you. I go when you go.'
'No, I'm heading off also. I need a change of clothing and to make arrangements for travelling to Germany. I go to get her coat, 'We can't do nothing more here for now.' Alma looks me in the eyes, 'Are we all that's left Jimmy?' I smile and try to think of words to reassure. At the moment I'm not sure, 'No Alma love, it just feels like it.' I point at the door, 'Out there everyone will be suffering like us tonight. And tomorrow? Well tomorrow will be worse. And the day after that. But we won't be crying alone Alma. Believe me there's a red army out there that will dry your tears and hopefully give us the strength to go on. Now, c'mon girl.'
We go outside and the two policemen are all who are left around. It's a bitter cold starless night. 'Any chance of a lift home for the lady Sergeant?' I ask.

'Of course, Mr Murphy.' He looks across to the Constable, 'Get this lady home lad and drop Mr Murphy off too.'
'Yes Sarge.'
'Thank you, Sergeant, but I'd much prefer to get some air. Think I'll walk.'
The Sergeant smiles. He looks at his watch, 'Jimmy it's nearly four in the morning. You live in Whalley Range. Now there's not a cat in hell's chance you're doing anything else but getting in that police car over there with Constable Potter. Is that clear old son?'
I nod and don't argue, 'I'll come quietly.' I look at the Constable, '100 College Road please lad.'
He smiles, 'No problem Jimmy.'
We drop off Alma first and continue on. The Constable invites me to sit in the front which I do. We don't talk. Every now and again I can feel his eyes turn to me but I keep looking forward through the window. Manchester is black, silent and still. Dawn is an hour away.
'Jimmy do you mind if I ask you something?'
'Go on son' I reply. Knowing he's been desperate to speak since I changed seats. 'Is that it Jimmy. Are United finished?' I turn to stare at him. He catches my glance before returning his eyes to the road.
I'm not tired see, I'm simply numb. I'm angry, I'm so fucking angry. Why us? Why, why fucking why? Hasn't the almighty already had his fill of blood lust with the war? What, he fancied more barrels of blood and jugs of tears to satisfy? Sat on his big white throne behind his big white pearly gates demanding complete absolution of sin of fathers, sons and brothers past by hurting us even more. Well he can fuck right off see. My faith is not important tonight. I'm close to losing my sanity, my heart

is broken and no amount of praying. Our Lord's prayers and Hail Mary's. Hail Mary for what? For not killing everybody? Nothing will bring my boys back. No, I think best I don't' linger on my feelings towards the good lord tonight. God is good they claim. Well today he's had a fucking day off.
I snap back to reality and remember the constable's question. Are United finished? 'No, we're not finished son. We're grieving and the pain and loss is horrendous but so long as I've got a breath in my body United will carry on. I promise you that.'
We finally pull up outside my house. The downstairs light is on in the living room and I see Winnie poke her head through the curtains. 'Well thanks for the lift home.' I put my hand out and the constable shakes it. I get out the car and go to walk off. 'Hey Jimmy' I hear him shout. I turn around and he's stood outside the police car holding the bag of oranges, 'You've forgot something.' I go to take them off him. 'You look after yourself Jimmy. God bless.'
That said he gets back in the car and drives off. Winnie appears at the door. She walks down the garden path and links my arm, 'Come inside my love.' Under a black Mancunian sky where even the stars are refusing to shine as a mark of respect to our lost we go inside.
In the living room I hand over the oranges to Winnie, 'Can you put these in a place where I don't ever have to look at them again.'
'Of course,' she replies. 'I'll put them in the cellar.' We sit down on the sofa. With tears streaming down her face she takes my hand, 'When I first heard I thought you was on the plane. For a split second I'd forgotten you'd gone to Cardiff. Oh, Jim I just wish I could make things right.'

Suddenly I hear a noise. A shuffling of feet outside the door. 'Come in' I shout. Jimmy Jnr, Nicky and Stephen and my two lovely girls Pat and Anne. All have red shot eyes. It's clear they've no tears left, 'Come here you lot.' They run over and fall into my arms. I hold them tight, 'We've all got to be strong. I'm going to be away for a while looking after things. I need you to be strong for your mum and those lads we've lost okay?' None of them speak, they simply all nod and hold me tight and tighter…. I never wanted them to let go.

  I'm lying in bed as morning breaks and a new day dawns over my adopted city. Winnie is asleep, no doubt exhausted after waiting up for me. I rise from my bed and formality takes over. I stand, fall to my knees, make the sign of the cross and begin my daily, Dear lord in heaven, give me the strength and then reality hits. I stand back up, straighten my hair and head for the bathroom. Myself and the almighty are still not talking. I go check on the kids. They are deep in slumber. Looking at them so peaceful, naïve of the true horrors of this world. Up until now. I stare at their faces and almost forget what has just occurred. Almost, but then the darkness descends and the despair hits me once more like a brick in the face. Munich. I get dressed and pack a few clothes. I go downstairs. I want to be gone before anybody wakes. I ring a taxi to take me to the airport.

'With you in ten minutes Jimmy. So sorry Jimmy,' says a man's voice. 'So very sorry.' The phone line goes dead. Winnie appears, she rubs her eyes, 'Why didn't you wake me Jim?'

'You need your rest girl' I say. 'It's going to be hard for you Winnie. People are going to call on you and you'll have to be strong for them. Hug the kids from me, tell them the same. Our family has been lucky, others have lost so much. We hug and I kiss her gently on the head. A car horn beeps and I look out the window. My taxi for the airport. The driver is familiar. He opens the door and stands looking towards the house. Our eyes meet through the window. It's Billy Mac from yesterday. The man who drove me from London Road to the ground. That now feels like a different time. Another world. One full of hope and joy. Far as inhumanly possible from these dark days and nights now and what are sure to follow.

It's bitterly cold and I pull up the collar on my coat. I'm already on my fourth cigarette. I walk down the garden path and Billy comes to greet me. He puts out his hand and we shake. I can tell by his face that tears have only recently dried up, 'I haven't slept Jimmy. It isn't fuckin' fair, they were just kids.' He takes my suitcase and walks off to the taxi. I follow him slowly. In the back of the car I see Winnie watching. As I look up all the children are also at the window waving. As we move away I raise my hand to say farewell. They watch until we disappear around a corner. It starts to rain. A gentle splatter that soon turns into a torrent. I remembered Billy lived opposite Eddie Colman's house on Archie Street, Salford. I lean forward and Billy catches sight of me in his mirror. He must have read my mind, 'They're just all in total shock Jimmy. After you rang Dickie to confirm that Eddie was dead he left the house and walked into town. We found him in Piccadilly about an hour later in his slippers simply sobbing on a bench. Dickie snr is trying to hold it together for the rest of the family but….' Billy goes to dry his eyes.

'It's bloody awful son' I reply and put my hand on his shoulder. Not being able to find the right words to describe such horror. Awful hardly doing what has gone on justice.

We arrive at the airport. I go to pay Billy but he waives it away, 'No chance Jimmy. Please give all the boys my thought and prayers. Those who are left anyway.' We shake hands once more.

'I will do Billy lad.'

'And those that are gone Jimmy, when you bring them home we'll be waiting to say our goodbyes. One last round of applause eh.' I'm choking on hearing these words but attempt to nod and feel what I hope is a half-smile on my face, 'Will do son.'

Inside the airport I'm immediately approached by a man in a dark suit and long moustache who appears more like a funeral director, 'Mr Murphy, my name is Charles Hobbs. I work for BEA. We shake hands. He's another who appears not to have slept since Paradise ended just after four o'clock yesterday. 'Firstly, may I offer on behalf of BEA my deepest sympathies to all the lost one's families, to yourself and Manchester United for what has occurred.'

I light up another cigarette and look in his eyes. I sense an aura of guilt. This man is obviously waiting for some kind of response off me. What does he want me to say? It couldn't be helped, just one of those things. God decided we'd too much light in our lives and decided to darken the rare fucking Mancunian sun? I've yet to know the full details. The newspaper boys told me of two aborted take offs so why attempt a third? I can't let my mind go there yet. Hobbs takes my arm, 'If you'll come with me Mr Murphy. Mr Busby's wife, son and daughter and others are waiting for you.'

We enter a sparse room but with a large single window overlooking the runway. There sits a single plane. Sat in small unspeaking groups are Matt's wife Jean, his son Sandy, daughter Sheena. Duncan Edward's fiancée, Molly Leach. Other relatives of the injured also. Stood and sat milling around. All are ashen faced. Pots of tea and coffee and plates of toast lies untouched on a serving table.

On seeing me Sandy rushes across and shakes my hand, 'So very glad to see you Jimmy. It's been horrific.' Jean and young Molly who I know well come over and they both embrace me together. I can feel their hearts breaking. Neither yet knows if their loved one are going to live but at least they're blessed with that wonderful sense of a modicum of hope. Something that others in Manchester at this moment have already had snuffed out. We come apart.

I grab Sandy's arm but address all eyes in the room now on me, 'We've all got to be strong. When we get on that plane and land in Germany you're all going to see and hear things that are beyond your worst nightmares. But for the sake of those lost we cannot show our pain and must think only now of those living and fighting to stay alive. There will be a time to grieve but not just yet. Okay?'

All are silent but seem to be in agreement. It has sounded and felt like a team talk from the bowels of hell.

Act Two
ONCE UPON A TIME IN MUNICH

The pilot makes his announcement that we are getting ready to land and to put on our safety belts. Nobody has spoken much throughout the flight. We've flown via

Paris but few hardly noticed. Everybody so wrapped in their own private fears that have to be overcome. I look through the window porthole and the swirling clouds and can just make out Munich coming into view. A most elegant place they tell me. Full of art galleries, museums and beer halls. But a place I'd always associated with Hitler and his bastard Nazis. A beautiful city but etched with a sense of everlasting evil. And now, every time I hear the name of Munich it will make me wince even and forever more.

A very pretty air hostess approaches me and leans down to check my belt. She appears close to tears, 'Mr Murphy, on landing there will be a coach waiting to take you and your party direct to the Rechts Der Isar hospital. I'm so very, very sorry. United are my team and I still can't believe what has happened. Please god don't let anybody else die.'

The girl has a Manchester accent. I reach into my jacket pocket and hand her a handkerchief, 'Dry your eyes girl. United will go on. Now you go and look after these other nice people here.' She wipes away the tears, smiles sadly and nods, 'I will do Mr Murphy. Thank you.' I watch her go. There must have been enough tears in Manchester spilt since yesterday to engulf a damned ocean.

As the airplane doors open cold air jolts me and the snow falling is only a light shower. What greets could well be a Christmas card scene if it wasn't one drenched in the blood of my boys. Munich is coveted in a white sprinkling of snow that appears to me to be hiding the hideous events of yesterday. On walking down the steps I notice smoke from what must be the crash site still rising in the distance at the far runway's end. I stop for a moment.

'Oh my god' I hear behind me. It's Sandy staring towards the billowing smoke. 'It's real. It's all bloody real.'
Jean puts a hand on his shoulder, 'Come on son, remember what Jimmy said, we have to be strong.'
I notice waiting at the bottom of the steps a man in a dark suit. Behind him is a coach with a driver stood to attention next to it. Baggage staff are already busy unloading our cases and putting them on board. The man is a handsome fellow, smartly dressed but whose features are sombre and grim. He steps towards me and we shake hands, 'Welcome to Munich Mr Murphy, my name is Doctor Hans Baumann. I work for the hospital's chief surgeon Professor Georg Maurer. Herr Maurer is amongst Germany's finest and sends his regards and also deepest sympathies for such a tragic occurrence on our soil.' Baumann points towards the coach and then addresses us all, 'Please all follow me and we shall take you direct to the hospital. Do not worry about your belongings. They will be taken to the Starthus hotel in the city where you shall be staying tonight.'
Baumann turns back towards me as everybody starts to board the coach, 'I would be grateful if you would sit next to me Mr Murphy. There is much we need to discuss.' I nod and take one last lingering look at the smoke in the distance. I can also make out what has to be the large bulk of the crashed plane. Now nothing more than a tomb. A sudden chill cut me to the bone as an icy cold breeze blows from the far runway's direction and into my face. Baumann smiles and places a hand on my shoulder, 'Come Mr Murphy, let us get aboard.'
As the coach starts up I go to light a cigarette but my hand is shaking. Baumann produces a lighter and does so for me. I nod in thanks.

'Mr Murphy let me begin by saying the list of fatalities remains as when you left England. We are doing all that is humanly possible to keep alive those of your people still in danger. There are five surgeons. All specialists now working around the clock. Some of the best we have and all under Herr Maurer. You will meet him when we arrive.'

'What is the latest on Mr Busby?'

Baumann shakes his head, 'Your friend is strong but I must stress his injuries are stronger. I fear Herr Busby's fate is in the hands of someone higher now?'

'And Duncan, er Duncan Edwards. It was said he was 50-50 when we left England?'

Baumann pulled a packet of cigarettes from his own suit jacket and lit up. He inhaled then looked me straight in the face, 'Duncan's will to live is incredible but like Herr Busby we can only hope and pray that all we are doing is enough. He was admitted with severely damaged kidneys, a collapsed lung, broken pelvis and multiple fractures of the right thigh. Remarkably from the neck up Duncan has not got a mark on him but such is the damage overall?'

He sighs, 'Sadly, Mr Murphy we are only doctors and not magicians I'm afraid.'

Slowly Baumann takes me through the other survivors.

'Johnny Berry-In a deep coma with a fractured skull and other fractures.

Albert Scanlon-left leg badly injured and his scalp gashed.

Dennis Viollet-Head injuries and shock.

Bobby Charlton-Head injury and shock.

Jackie Blanchflower-Fractured arm and pelvis.

Ray Wood-Leg and arm injuries.

Ken Morgans-Head injury and severe shock
The seven confirmed dead are Geoff Bent: Roger Byrne: Eddie Colman: Mark Jones: Billy Whelan: Tommy Taylor: David Pegg. The other two players Harry Gregg and Bill Foulkes were allowed to leave the hospital late last night and we put them up in a Munich hotel. You and your party will be staying there also.'
Baumann spoke in such matter of fact terms I feel a momentarily flash of anger coming over me. Then I look at this man and realise that without him and his colleagues, even though United is all but wiped out, our situation could've been even worse, 'Thank you and to all your colleagues for what you've done so far doctor.'
'Mr Murphy your thanks are duly noted and welcome but hardly necessary. Our doctors and nurses are refusing to go home and insisting carrying on working.' A slight and very kind smile appears on his face, 'We are all Manchester United at the Recht Der Isar now my friend. You've become our family. Please believe me, I promise you we shall do all that is earthly possible and in our power to save those still in our hands.'
I turn to look through the window so Baumann doesn't see the tears welt up in my eyes. No time for tears. So easy for me to tell everyone they have to be strong whilst inside my heart continues to break into a thousand pieces. The time is drawing on. The snow again begins to fall heavy as day slips into night and we finally arrive at the Recht Der Isar hospital. The coach pulls up at the main entrance. A huddle of photographers stands waiting. I'm in no fucking mood to see these people put through a barrage of flashing lights and painful inquisition from men whom should know better after seeing how many of their own were killed in the crash. Baumann appears to

read my mind and is first off the coach. He shouts instructions in German and two policemen appear to push the press hacks back. We all head swiftly towards the hospital main doors and into the foyer. Baumann follows us in. He goes to reception and speaks to the lady working.

He walks back over, 'Please everybody, Professor Maurer and his party are on their way down now. You will shortly be reunited with your loved ones.'

Suddenly, a lift door springs open and a small rotund balding figure in glasses but walking with real vigour approaches. Behind him a host of white coated doctors, nurses and a holy sister. The man in front is obviously Professor Maurer, 'Please everybody my staff here will now come amongst you. Tell them of your immediate kin and you shall be escorted to be by their side.' That said he motions to his staff and armed with clip boards they start to mix. Maurer, himself of that rare ilk blessed with the ability to produce calm in the midst of a terrible storm places his hand on Jean Busby's arm, 'Madam, you and your family please come with me.' That said Jean, Sandy and Sheena follow the professor into the lift. I watch them go. Baumann links Molly, 'Come Jimmy let us go see Duncan.' Molly looks frightened, 'Now girl' I say. 'We've got to stay strong.' I link her other arm and we enter the second lift and Baumann presses for the fourth floor. Once done he let's go of Molly and stands facing us both, 'Now Duncan is gravely ill but is still fighting hard. He is in a coma and it's too early to say what may yet happen. All I can say is that already we are amazed with Duncan's sheer will to survive. He is a remarkable young man.'

The doors re-open and we walk into a frenzy of white coated doctors and nurses scuttling around. Baumann leads the way then stops outside a door. He turns to Molly. I spot out the corner of my eye Professor Maurer with Jean and her family entering what must be Matt's room. This floor must be for the most seriously ill patients.

'You must still talk to him young lady,' says Baumann. 'There is a slight possibility that he may be able to hear you.' That said Bauman opens the door and in we walk. Immediately, Molly lets out a gasp and covers her mouth at the sight awaiting us. A nurse is sat at the side of Duncan's bed. My boy is wired up to so many machines I find it hard to believe he's still alive.

A distraught Molly is led by Baumann over to the bed. The nurse stands to let her sit. I stay back. The sight of Duncan almost broken is simply too much too bare. I saw this boy as invincible see, a colossus. Bigger than life and to see him reduced to this? Kept alive by the beeps of a fucking kidney machine. Never in all my life did I fear losing my religion but looking at Duncan here. Where is the sense in it all? It has no rhyme and even less reason. This lad was a footballer coming home to his girl. They were going to get married. They were pure and innocent. Duncan lived only for his football, his family and Molly. She lived only for Duncan.

What does any god get to gain by bringing the girl's world crashing to earth? And elsewhere in this place the same thing being repeated over and over. An endless stream of tears. Did the almighty not let his son die on the cross to take away our sins? He's experienced mortal pain so why do unto others what he's felt himself? God is good they say? Well this is not the acts of a good god.

There are people crying and mourning lost ones in this hospital. Some taken before they've experienced hardly anything of life. Now I promised myself I'd hold it together. I wouldn't get mad. I wouldn't cry even. And listening to Molly sobbing hysterically at the sight of the boy she loved more than anything in the world fighting for every breath…. Well if there is a bible in the hotel room where I'm staying tonight, I swear at this moment in time I'm going to throw it out of the fucking window see.

'Come and say something Mr Murphy,' says Molly in floods of tears, 'Please come and say something to my Duncan.' How can I refuse? I walk across. I take her hand and try so hard to smile at Duncan's, I like to think only sleeping face, 'How are you doing Duncan lad. I know you can hear me son. Just sleeping see. Now you get some rest because when you're back on your feet we've got a lot of work to do. Maybe I never told you enough but I'm so proud of you lad. I'm proud of all of you. Eddie, Billy, Roger, Jeff, Tommy, David, Mark. I know I've been hard on you all at times but it was for your own good. It's just I love you all like my own son's and only ever wanted the best for you. From the bottom of my heart and deepest part of my soul you're all part of me. My apples. And you son, well I'm not supposed to have favourites. But I suppose you more than any captured what myself and Matt wanted Manchester United to be about. So, you sleep now. Sleep sound and when you wake we'll go back to work.'

I leave the room to give Molly time alone with Duncan. Baumann follows me out, 'Can I go and see Matt?' I ask. 'Of course,' he replies.

As we walk towards Matt's room Jean, Sheena and Sandy are huddled deep in conversation with Professor Maurer outside his door. Maurer spots me coming and a slight smile crosses his face, 'Mr Murphy, please join us. Jean grabs my hand. 'Now I must tell you all,' continues Maurer. 'Matt is very, very poorly. He has been given a Tracheotomy operation to enable him to breathe. But his chest and lungs have been severely affected. There is massive internal and external damage. My prognosis is not good but he is strong and god is always good.'
…That damned line again.
'Now is your husband a religious man Mrs Busby?'
'Yes very, why?'
'I would suggest he is offered the Last Rites this evening.'
Jean's features visibly crumble whilst Sheena shrieks and Sandy swiftly puts an arm around her. Jean composes herself, 'Very well Professor.'
She looks across to me. Tears once more falling down her face, 'Would you like to go in and see Matt Jimmy?'
I nod grimly and like a zombie I enter.
Matt is unconscious in an oxygen tent. I don't recognise him, who is this stranger before my eyes? A nurse sat at his bedside stands and smiles and points to the seat.
'Bitte,' she says. I try and smile back.
'Thank you, lass.' I sit down and place my hand on Matt's. He appears forty-nine going on eighty, 'Alright boss, bloody mess eh. Remember when we first met all those years ago in Bari? I was mouthing off at a bunch of soldiers who were fooling around and not taking the game seriously. Well you know how that gets me. I went mad I did. You pulled me afterwards and offered me the job at Old Trafford. You told me we'd not just take

United into the heavens but beyond the stars. Well we're not there yet so I need you back see. It isn't time to say goodbye Matt. So much more to do. Got to knock that bloody Real Madrid off their damn pedestal. I can't do it on my own. I need you by my side. Matt and Jimmy together. Our red devils. I stoke the fires and light the flame in their bellies and you supply the gold dust. The magic. A bunch of bouncing Busby boys…So you stay away from that light old pal.'

Suddenly, I feel movement in Matt's hand. The eyes flicker and open. He recognises me and a pained smile comes across his face. He tries to speak but it is nothing more than a strained whisper. I lean in close and can just about make out Matt's words, 'Keep the flag flying till I get back Jimmy. Keep the flag flying.'

Then, seemingly spent of all energy the boss's eyes close once more and he drifts off back into unconsciousness. But I had my orders and something told me Matt was going nowhere fast.

Desperate to see the other lads I asked Baumann if he'd take me but was clearly reluctant, 'Mr Murphy, it is too much of a burden for you to see them all tonight. There is only so much pain one man can take. Please go and get some sleep and come back fresh early tomorrow morning.'

This is a good man, 'Please call me Jimmy' I say. 'But really I must insist. I won't leave this hospital tonight until I've spoken too or at least seen all the lads. They're my boys Doctor Baumann. They're all my sons.'

Baumann smiles, 'And you Jimmy, you must call me Hans. Come my friend.' He takes my arm, 'Come let us go and see the rest of your Manchester United family.'

And this I did. My heart breaking at the sight of each and every one. Jackie Blanchflower, Kenny Morgans, Ray Woods, Johnny Berry. Denis Viollet and Albert Scanlon. Finally, twenty-year-old Bobby Charlton. Baumann explained that by some miracle Bobby received only minor head injuries. Miracles were in short supply yesterday and for this we can be truly thankful. He was given a sedative after the crash but after waking remained in a state of shock.

'Jimmy, the poor boy must have witnessed scenes of sheer horror but only discovered this afternoon the full extent of the tragedy. A patient in the bed next to him was reading out loud the names of those killed. At first Bobby thought these were survivors, only to be told they'd actually died. Since then he's not spoken.'

I enter the room and Bobby on seeing me immediately sits up on his bed, 'Hello Bobby lad how you holding up?'

'They're all dead Jimmy,' Bobby blurts outs. His face and voice crushed with grief, 'They're all gone. Why Jimmy, why us. We just went to play a football match for god's sake. It doesn't make any sense.'

I sit down beside him, 'I don't know Bobby. Nobody does. There are no answers son. When you're allowed out I want you to go home to your mum and dad in Newcastle. Stay there, forget about football. You concentrate on getting better. That's what is important for you now.'

'I saw my friends dead Jimmy. Burnt, twisted, crushed. Roger looked like he was just sleeping but was gone. I woke up still in my chair but thrown from the airplane. I looked down to the floor and there was just a drop of blood in the snow. I climbed out looked around and I saw hell Jimmy. I witnessed hell on earth. And Duncan, they won't let me see Dunc. How is he Jimmy, please god let him be alive?'

'He's alive Bobby.'

'And is he going to be alright Jimmy?'

I smile, 'Yes son. Duncan is going to be fine.' Bobby visibly relaxes. He puts his head back down on the pillow. 'Thank god for that,' he continues, but almost in a whisper. 'I can just about handle it Jimmy but if anything happens to Dunc. Not Duncan….' Bobby's eyes close and he falls asleep.

Watching this young man's heart break reminded me so much of what I'd seen in the war. Men driven to the edge after witnessing scenes from the depths of hell. I remember tough-battle hardened Eight Army soldiers in North Africa after months of merciless fighting against Rommel's Afrika Korps in the blazing desert just breaking down in tears on seeing the ocean. No, all I can do is be here for young Bobby. Listen until he's all cried out and pray that what he witnessed yesterday does not leave a burning scar on his soul.

Baumann is driving me to the hotel. It has just gone ten in the evening as we make our through the dark Munich roads lit by the magical, blurry-haze of bright street lamps. This man has helped me so much tonight, 'Thank you for everything Hans.' A smile crosses his face, 'Jimmy, you must not even think such things. Myself and everybody at the Rechts Der Isar are committed to doing everything we can to help your people.'

'Well we do appreciate it Hans and the many acts of kindness will not be forgotten. Never, you are our family now also. Professor Maurer reminded me of Matt in the way everybody appears to look up to him. A true leader but with real warmth.'

'The professor was a war hero. The holder of an Iron Cross but he was no Nazi. He saved many lives and on both sides Jimmy. It was at places like Dunkirk where his experience of dealing with mass casualties meant that when word reached us yesterday of the crash we were already drilled to perfection on our emergency procedures. Even to the point where the professor had stationed an engineer at the hospital in case the lifts broke down. He left, as you English say. No stone unturned!'

'I'll forgive you this once Hans, I'm Welsh son!' Baumann looks at me with a mixture of mirth and shock. Then we both smile. For a second I forget that life was once, only a short time ago nothing short of paradise. We pull up outside the hotel and enter inside. Baumann goes to reception and returns back to me with the room key, 'Come Jimmy, we've put your people on the top floor, away from prying eyes of the press and photographers.' Also at the hotel are Harry Gregg and Bill Foulkes. I have been hearing all day small snippets that these two shown tremendous bravery during yesterdays' catastrophe. Exiting the lift on the top floor Baumann points out my room, 'Next to you is Gregg and then Foulkes. I've arranged for a bottle of whisky and sandwiches. They are waiting for you. I will pick you up at nine tomorrow my friend. Try and get some sleep.' We shake hands and Baumann heads back to the lift. 'Hans,' I shout after him. He turns around, 'I don't think I will ever sleep again.'

He smiles but it is one touched by real sadness, 'I was at Stalingrad Jimmy. Men like me and you we simply have to survive the darkness of the night and pray the days bring enough solace to block out the sadness. Take care my new Welsh friend.' That said Baumann enters the lift, it shuts and he disappears. Leaving me alone outside my room. I unlock the door, switch on the light and true to Baumann's word the whisky and sandwiches lie in wait. I go to pour myself a drink.

'Alright Jimmy.'

I turn around and Harry Gregg is stood facing me at the open door. Himself clutching a bottle of whisky and glass. This son of Ireland is as tough a character as you'll find but there's a look on his face of a man who's walked through hell. His eyes have clearly seen enough horror and despair in the past twenty-four hours to last a lifetime. I go across and embrace him. Finally, after a moment or so we come apart. I stand facing Harry. He appears a broken man.

'C'mon son let's sit down.' He follows me and we settle by the window. Outside the snow is falling from black skies onto the Munich Street down below. What began as a small sprinkling is turning heavy and cars and buildings are swiftly turning white. A minute passes and neither of us speak. Harry seems content to simply watch the snow. I take a drink and do the same.

'I should be dead Jimmy.' Still he continues to stare out and doesn't look at me, 'I've been told you was a bloody hero Harry. That without you it could've been so much worse.'

He laughs but in a disbelieving manner, 'Worse? Fucking hell Jimmy, we've been wiped out. How could it possibly be worse?'

'I'm not letting this club die Harry. The story does not end at the end of that damned runway. I, we owe it to the boys who've died to carry on.'
'Jimmy its football, it's not important. It's not life or death. It doesn't matter.'
'Aye' I reply, 'Well try telling that to our seven lads in the hospital mortuary Harry. Plus, the journalists who've lost their lives.'
'And how do you suppose we carry on Jimmy? There's no team anymore. It would be like fighting a war without any weapons. It's over. Manchester United died in that fucking plane yesterday.' Harry refills a glass and downs it in one. He shuts his eyes, 'I can't get the images out of my head Jimmy.'
'I don't want to ask this but feel it only right to do so, 'Do you want to tell me what happened Harry? Try and get some stuff off your chest son?'
Harry nods. He smiles, 'A trouble shared is a trouble halved eh Jimmy.' He wipes a tear from his eye, 'I think it will do me good to talk it through.'
'In your own time Harry lad,' I say, 'In your own time.' I'm absolutely dreading what's to follow.
He refills his glass, downs it again in one and wipes his mouth, 'We should never have got back on that fucking airplane a third time Jimmy. Never. I watched through the windows of that damned Munich airport lounge the snow falling and the airplane disappearing in front of my eyes. I looked at the boss and he appeared at a loose end. We all knew he had to get us home otherwise United would have to forfeit the Wolves games and lose points. But at what cost? In the end we got the nod to embark. We looked at each other. We were uneasy…It was touching four o'clock. I boarded and sat myself down; I

loosened my shirt and unfastened my belt to get comfortable. I was sweating and this amid a raging snow blizzard. The likes I'd never seen. The engines roared up only then to stop because they realised we were one passenger short.'

Bill smiles, 'It was the journalist Alf Clark. He was still in the airport lounge phoning in his bloody story. Anyway, Alf appears at the door to a hail of friendly abuse. 'Scoop' the lads were singing at him. Typically, he bows and tells us under his breath exactly where to go. He was a good lad Alf. Was…This for a few moments eased tensions but they soon returned Jimmy. Once we'd buckled in again. I looked around and saw nothing but worried faces.'

Harry takes another drink then continues, 'Roger Byrne was sat opposite me. He looked terrified. The engines started up again, there was nervous coughs, muttering, bad jokes to cover the fear but little Johnny Berry wasn't laughing, 'I don't know what you're all laughing at,' he said, in that brummie accent of his. 'We're all going to get fucking killed here.' Billy Whelan called out he was prepared to die. Billy said this whilst praying with his eyes closed. I know this, I saw him. When I get home, I'll tell his Mother this Jimmy. Hopefully it will bring her some peace. Billy should've been a bloody priest after all. But it was at this time somebody should've said something because the plane wasn't right, you could feel it. Felt more like being on a fucking rollercoaster. Maybe if somebody had stood up and objected? Had shouted out to the boss, 'I'm not happy, this isn't fucking right. But it takes either a very brave man or a truly frightened coward to do so and none of us opened our mouths. We sat there like stuck pigs heading into a fucking slaughterhouse. Lads began to move around the plane. Young Bobby and David Pegg who'd been sitting near me at the front went and sat at the back where most of the press lads were. Old school, some war veterans whom were always told this was the safest place to be in case of a crash. Well that fucking worked out well didn't it. Dead.... Nearly all of them.

By this time, I was glued to my window porthole watching the huge mounds of slush flying into the air as we went ever faster. The airplane was now going past places that in the previous two aborted take offs we hadn't even reached. It was fucking mad Jimmy. What were they thinking of? I saw the wheels actually lift up off the runway and then…. And then the world turned upside. It was utter carnage. A shuddering crashing sound and debris began falling and flying. It was light, then darkness, then light again. As if some bastard's hand was turning a switch on, off, on, off. I was being bombarded on all sides. A terrible-ripping sound of metal breaking up. A screeching-soaring, deafening noise that I never want to hear again. We were being thrown round and round like a nightmarish carousel you can never get off. Now I'm no fool Jimmy, I'm not what they call a well-read man. But I was raised on fire and brimstone. As a kid my priest tried to put the fear of god into me and if there is a hell which I'm sure there is after yesterday…I was in it at that moment.

And yet all through this awful mayhem I heard no screaming, no voices. It was like everybody had simply vanished…There was sparks and small fires all around, I could feel the salty taste of blood in my mouth, I'd been cracked on the top of my skull and felt scared to touch it in case part of my head had been sliced off. And then

came the brief silence. I felt sick and dizzy. I remember thinking, although it sounds crazy now that I couldn't speak German? Then came the frightening fear that I'd never see my family again. That stirred me into action Jimmy. I noticed a shaft of light in front of me and knew I had to head for it. I went to unfasten the seat belt, only to realise I was already lying on my side. I crawled towards the light and stuck my head through the hole….'
Harry stops.
'Look son, if you don't'…
'No' he replies, 'I've got to do this Jimmy. I need to get this stuff out of my head. At least for tonight. Tomorrow is another day, I'll deal with that then. Yeah, I looked through the hole and down on the ground I saw Bert Whalley lying motionless. His eyes wide open and not a mark on him. But somehow Jimmy, I'm sorry, I know how close you two were. I knew Bert was dead…I kicked the hole bigger and managed to squeeze and jump down into the deep snow. For a second I felt like I was the only one left alive. All was ghostly quiet apart from a fucking hissing noise coming from the bulk. I looked around. That will stay with me forever. It was Dante's inferno Jimmy.
The snow was burning, small fires all around. One of the wings had gone then from the airplane cockpit Captain Thain appeared with a fire extinguisher in his hand, 'Run you stupid bastard,' he screamed at me, 'It's going to explode!' As he disappeared from sight I heard a small cry back inside the airplane. Suddenly, I remembered a baby with its mother sat just behind me. Without thinking I began trying to crawl back in. Out of the corner of my eye I noticed four or five figures running clear of the airplane. 'Come back' I shouted, 'There are people still

alive in here!' But the bastards kept running so in I went Jimmy. I crawled back to where the cries where coming from and found the baby lying under a pile of debris. By some miracle the little lass had suffered only a bad cut above her eye. Once back outside, one of those who'd ran had returned. It was the radio operator. A man called George Rogers. I passed him the baby and went back in looking for more survivors. Then I found the baby's mother. A Yugoslav lady. She was in a terrible state but I managed to drag her clear also.
But there was so many dead. Words can't describe what I saw in that snow Jimmy. Roger, Eddie, Tommy, all the lads scattered around. Some thrown clear their bodies lying twisted and burnt. Others dead in their seats. So much blood in the fucking snow.'
Harry wipes his eyes clear. He takes another drink.
'Looking around me, I suddenly realised what'd gone on. There was a house about sixty yards away with half its roof torn off. Next to it was a compound that must have been a fuel dump. Now alight. We must have careered off the runway, broken up with part of the airplane resting at the house whilst the rest slid onwards. I watched as explosions lit up the black sky. Huge plumes of flames leaping high, shooting upwards. The heat melting the snow turning it into slush and water. Water and blood….
'I found Ray Wood but I couldn't move him because he was trapped under too much fuselage. As was Albert Scanlon. Scannie's injuries were so bad I was nearly sick. I couldn't budge either of them. I needed help Jimmy but there was nobody around. No police, no ambulances, no fire engines, nothing. I'd convinced myself both of those boys were done for. I stumbled upon young Bobby and

Denis both simply staring at the airplane. The crash had thrown them over twenty-yards clear still strapped in their seats and they appeared from a few bloodied scratches relatively unscathed.

Then I came across the boss lying propped up between the aircraft wreckage and remnants of a burning building. Compared to what I'd already witnessed he didn't appear too bad at first glance. A small trickle of blood behind an ear but he was also rubbing his chest and moaning, 'My legs, my legs.' I tried to make him comfortable as possible but couldn't stay too long. You see I felt like I was on my own. That it was all down to me to save as many people as possible. A few Germans had arrived to help but still no ambulances or fire engines. I came across Jackie Blanchflower. My best pal was crying out that he'd broken his back and was paralysed. The lower part of his right arm looked to have been severed and I tried making a tourniquet with my tie but snapped it. Looking desperately for something else to use a stewardess appeared from nowhere. I screamed at her like a madman for help. We found a rag and I stayed with Jackie and tried to calm him. By this time more people had arrived but it was still nothing organised Jimmy. There was screams coming from all around, explosions, melting snow and slush, pools of reddish water and yet still it fell from the sky and thick enough to blind your eyes. This is no horror story Jimmy, it was reality. No one will ever really know what it felt like once upon a time at the end of that fucking runway. In Munich.

A German with a hypodermic needle in his hand came towards us. I shouted for him to hurry only for an explosion to send him flying into the air. Happily, he landed on his backside with astonishingly the needle still in his hand pointing upwards. One lucky bastard. A local man who lived nearby turned up in a Volkswagen. Myself and Bill Foulkes loaded the boss and Jackie inside. Then two others placed a body in the back who was wearing a United blazer. I couldn't recognise him he was so badly burned. I only found out later it was Johnny Berry. We jumped in also, stopping only to pick up the Yugoslav girl who I pulled clear previous. I found out her name is Maria Mikla.

And finally, we arrived at the hospital. Soon the survivors and casualties began to arrive. They wanted to keep me and Bill in for the night but when I heard the words 'Herr Swift Kaput' over the tannoy I couldn't face it and they brought us here.

Myself and Bill both went back to the runway today. Oh, you couldn't move for fucking fire engines and ambulances. The airplane fuselage was still smouldering and smoke was still visibly rising from the fuel dumps. All that was missing was the bodies. Our bodies. When he found out who we were a German official asked us to explain what happened? Us? 'You tell me?' I said. We walked amongst the wreckage. Bill climbed back into the part of the plane where he'd sat. Jammed against the roof in the rack above the seat he found his case totally undamaged. Bill opened and remarkably inside a bottle of gin lay intact. We made short work of that before coming back here.

I wondered around and came across a cap with COLMAN written on it. The boys used to go in the Continental club back in Manchester where the owner as a gimmick had these made to hand out. Eddie always used to wear his. I found Eddie's scarf too. Red and white.

Bill also spotted a paper bag containing an apple, orange, some tea and sugar. Eddie's mum had packed them for him. That upset Bill so we came away. I did notice a policeman checking out a briefcase. I inquired whose and got told it was Walter Crickmer's. It contained nothing but traveller cheques and Walter's silver hip flask. A lovely man. Poor Walter.

They'd been tidying up Jimmy. Rushing to get back to some sort of fucking normality. Getting the slush off the runway. I wonder why? Fifteen flights took off from Munich yesterday afternoon, Fifteen. All with no problems. Something stinks to high heaven. The German authorities and BEA officials were all over the crash site today but don't let anyone ever tell you that it was all hands on when we crashed because it wasn't. We were on our own for what felt an eternity and until the day I die I will stand by these words.'

Harry is sitting with head in hands. I put my hand on his shoulders. He needed to talk, I needed to know but I wonder now if it has really done either of us too much good. Harry looks exhausted, 'Go try and get some sleep son.'

He lifts his head up, 'If you don't mind Jimmy, I think I'd rather stay here with you. Just drinking whisky and looking out this window at the snow.'

I smile and refill our glasses. On the sideboard I notice a holy bible. I walk over and put it in a draw. Harry's presence means it has been spared the long journey down from the window to the street. Because make no mistake after what I've just listened to I would've done it.

'Are you serious about keeping United going Jimmy?' I refill Bill's glass once more and mine also.

'What do you think?'

'Why is football so important to you Jimmy, even now after all this?'

'Because we've got nothing left son. At least for ninety minutes there's nowhere else to run see. Drink, women, aye, for some. But not us. Not me and you. The clack of the boots onto the pitch, the smell of the recently cut grass and the roar of the crowd. It's a poetry that Keats or Byron could not dream of aspiring to. A sliding tackle in a mud patch, Duncan charging over the halfway line, Eddie dropping his shoulder and sending half of Salford staring towards the Irwell as he runs the other way. Tommy leaping high and scoring, that glorious smile. Our boys Harry, a dip of magic dust when the whistle blows and our people who work like dogs all week enter through a magical door where we put right all wrongs. At least for a while. But think where they'd be without us? Now, I don't care about death defying odds, you can stick your grim reaper up his not welcome arse. Take it from me now, Manchester United are going nowhere so long as I have a breath left in my body. And let any bastard say otherwise.'

I look at Harry. He's smiling, 'You can count me in Jimmy.'

'I know son. I know.'

The next morning as he promised Baumann is waiting in the hotel foyer to take myself, Harry and Bill Foulkes back to the Rechts Der Isar hospital. Nobody speaks much in the car. I've made preparations to get the boys home by train and boat. No doubt it will be long and draining but neither are anywhere near ready to step on a plane again yet. I doubt if ever and who could blame them?

On arriving we're met by Professor Maurer. He's smiling, 'Good morning gentlemen. We all shake his hand.

'Any further news Herr professor?' I ask. Dreading his reply…. 'Edwards has regained consciousness.' My heart jumps a beat. 'He is very restless as can only be expected. But the boy is asking about a missing watch? He is very upset over it.' For me, Harry and Bill the penny immediately drops, 'Duncan is talking about his solid gold watch Herr Professor,' answers Bill. 'He loves it. We all got presented with one last year by the Real Madrid President Santiago Bernabeu. He's so proud of it. Constantly polishing and asking us if anybody wants to know the time? Wherever Dunc goes so does that bloody watch.' Maurer points towards the lift, 'Come, I suggest we go up now.'

Once in the lift Maurer has an altogether more serious expression, 'Gentlemen, I must tell you now. Even if your young friend does recover and at the moment that is far from certain then his days as a sportsman are over. Such are the injuries Duncan has sustained he will be in a wheelchair for the rest of his life.'

Hearing these words from such as Professor Maurer cuts me like a knife. It's clear they've had the same sledgehammer effect on Harry and Bill also. The doors open and we head for Duncan's room. Once outside Maurer gently puts an arm each on Harry and Bill, 'Why do I not take you around to see your team mates whilst Jimmy speaks to Duncan alone first? I fear if he sees the three of you together it could be a little overwhelming. Doctor Baumann please stay with Jimmy.' He nods and in we go. Sat besides Duncan is a nurse.

'Jimmy' says Baumann, 'This is Sister Solemnis.' She stands and we shake hands, 'Thank you for all you are doing Sister.'

She smiles, 'Duncan is upset about a watch. I keep telling him he was admitted in without it on his wrists. But he is insistent.'

'Let me have a word' I say. She leaves the room.

'Hello Duncan,' I sit down beside him. He slowly turns his head towards me and smiles, 'Hello chief.'

I grab his hand, 'How are you feeling son?'

'I'm so tired. I can't find my watch Jimmy. I keep telling them but they're not listening. Somebody has thieved it. It was solid gold. A present off Real Madrid. I need it Jimmy I really do need it.' I take off mine and fasten it onto his wrist, 'Here you go son. Have mine until we find out where yours is.' Baumann taps me on the shoulder, 'I am going to ring the airport. See if they have found anything resembling the watch from the plane.' He leaves the room.

'There you go Dunc,' I put it to his ear, 'You can hear it ticking. I'm going to have to go home soon. Sort matters out. But you're in great hands son. These are good people, they'll make you better.'

'I don't remember nothing Jimmy, they tell me we were in a crash?'

'Aye, you've had a bad time.'

'Is everybody else alright Jimmy?'

I grip Duncan's hand tight, 'You just concentrate on getting yourself well lad.'

'Will do. What time's kick off Saturday Jimmy?'

'It's three o'clock lad.'

Duncan smiles…. 'Get stuck in chief.'

His eyes starting to close until finally he's gone back into a deep sleep…

I stand to leave, 'Get stuck in chief.' I'd give everything to have this boy well again. Outside the room I notice a fire escape and head through it for I need to be alone for a few minutes. To compose myself before I go and see the rest of the boys. I sit on the stairwell and suddenly the pain, nerves, tension and sheer agony explodes. The tears begin to flow. From a trickle to a river and I can't help myself and pray nobody comes through that fire door now. They think I'm unbreakable but I'm not see. I break and fall like anybody else. Finally, I dry my eyes, blow my nose and head back upstairs. Seems I'm all cried out. At least for now.

I need to clear my head before going in to see Matt again. I spot a small side-waiting room along the corridor and head in there. It's empty thank god. I just need a couple of moments. I can feel every eye upon me. I'm not allowed to crack. I'm the tower of strength they tell me. I mustn't crumble. I mustn't fall. I sit down and light a cigarette. My hands are shaking but somehow, I manage to light it.

Outside the hospital I hear the blare of ambulance sirens. I hear raised voices in German. These people. Only thirteen years ago I hated the bastards. I was killing them. Now I'm embarrassed and ashamed at such thoughts after seeing the kindness and love they've shown us.

'Are you okay?'

A voice makes me jump and I turn around to see a chap sat in the corner that I never noticed on entering. A good looking young man. Mid-thirties, dressed in smart attire. My guess he works for the British embassy. Taking a

moment like me away from this choking veil of unrelenting grief that has engulfed the hospital.
'Yes, thank you,' I answer, 'Yourself?'
'Hiding' he replies, smiling.
'From who?'
The man has stood up and is moving towards me, 'You're Jimmy Murphy?'
Oh god, here we go, 'Yes son, don't tell me, you're a journalist who wants a piece of my soul and will pay heartily for it?'
'No not me Jimmy.'
He sits down next to me. Never have I seen a man with such a haunted look. As if the sins of the world are weighing on his tortured soul.
'Are you okay?' I ask him
The man looks at me and is clearly close to tears,
'We did everything right Jimmy. All was by the book but they'll come after me. It's already started. I don't care what anyone says. The fucking press, even my own people. What happened was out of our control. We did our job but they will need a scapegoat. They'll want to nail me to the fucking cross.'
I can only imagine this man was working at the airport yesterday in some sort of capacity and is suffering what can only be described now as shellshock. He's seen too much blood. I can only feel sorry for him, 'Listen old son, you were only doing your job. It wasn't your fault. You did your best and like you said it was out of your control. So, you mustn't feel guilty.'
Suddenly, the man starts to laugh. One more hysterical than comical, 'Oh Jimmy, Jimmy please forgive me. I never realised. I am so, so sorry sir.'

Now he's really starting to get under my skin. I'm thinking that drink has been taken and I'm losing patience fast, 'Okay then friend,' my voice giving ruse to my temper rising, 'Tell me. Just who are you?'
The man ruffles his hair back, shuffles uncomfortably and then he looks me right in the eyes, 'Jimmy, I'm James Thain. I was the Captain of the airplane and my heart is fucking broken.' I stare at the man. There is nothing I can say or do to make him feel better or worse. So, I think best to say nothing. I stand to go. I offer my hand and Thain accepts it. Tear falling down his face. I turn to go and I'm back in the corridor. I have my own people to see and comfort. I'm still far too raw to offer redemption. May god forgive me, for what he's worth at the moment, but amidst this continuing horror, Captain James Thain is not my priority. Let him deal with his own demons for I have enough of my own.

   I head off for Matt's room only to see Baumann coming towards me. He's smiling, 'I have good news Jimmy. I phoned the airport and they have the watch. It is being brought back now by taxi.'
'Thank you, Hans.' Suddenly, raised voices are heard coming from Matt's room. We head towards it and inside see a nurse arguing with a press photographer who somehow has managed to make it up to the fourth floor and was busy taking pictures of Matt in the oxygen ten. We charge in and I hear Matt groaning, 'The flashes are hurting my eyes.' Baumann grabs the photographer and quite literally drags him out. I watch as he slaps and pushes him towards the lift.
'Are you okay?' I ask the young nurse, 'Yes, thank you,' she replies. I go across to Matt, 'It's alright old pal, he's gone.' In all my years I've never seen a man look so grey

and drained of colour. I look up towards the nurse and her
face was already telling me everything. My friend is slipping away.
'What have I done Jimmy?' I turn back to Matt and he is crying, 'Eh you, take it easy. Come on now'
'I shouldn't have let our boys get back on that plane Jim. It wasn't right, it was just me being pig headed and…they, they were kids, boys. I should...'
'Hey now you stop that' I say, 'It was nobody's fault.'
'It was all my doing. I was rushing. How dare I play god with people's lives. This is all my doing.'
The sister comes across and puts a hand gently on my shoulder, 'I think we should let Herr Busby try and get some rest now.' Matt turns his head away, the tears falling down his face. I stand to leave. I can't find it in me to say goodbye or anything so final. The thought I would never see this man again is too painful to bare, so no goodbyes, long or short. We will meet again my friend; our club is not going to go gently into the night. I will attend to that. Any who dare to bring us down then god help the bastards for I will rage against all both human and from heavens above. No number of funerals or tears will stop me. I may fall, stumble, and drink to stupor at times to ease the pain but I vow this to myself and to those boys who'll not grace our shirt no more. We are not going away…

   I enter back into Duncan's room with Baumann alongside me. The sister sat beside him at the bed smiles when she sees me holding the watch that has just been brought back from the airport. 'When he next wakes,' I ask her, 'Please give him this.' I hand over Duncan's watch. It has been badly mangled in the wreckage but

miraculously is still working. The sister takes mine gently back off his wrist and hands it back to me. I'm choking with emotion but I daren't cry again. I daren't, 'Can you tell him sister that I'll be back to see him soon and to keep playing hard.'
She smiles, 'I will Mr Murphy, you are a good man. I wish you a safe journey home.' We leave the room and head off to see the others. Baumann appears deep in thought. 'Jimmy can I ask you something?'
'What's bothering you Hans?'
'You spoke about going home and carrying on. Have you seriously thought how you are going to do this? Most of your players are dead my friend.'
'They may be gone but their spirit will see us through the coming dark days Hans. I'll damn well make sure of that. I intend to buy, beg, steal, bribe and bloody kidnap if needed to ensure United have enough players to keep us going, until once more we can grow our own.'
Baumann stares at me like I'm mad then breaks into a small smile, 'My crazy Welsh friend. If I could play football I would put on a red shirt and join you in Manchester tomorrow.'

   That night I can't sleep so despite advice to the contrary with so many press boys around I go down to the hotel bar. I settle myself down in a spot where I can see all around and can't be bushwhacked. A smart looking young barman comes across to serve me, 'A large whisky please?'
He smiles, 'Of course Mr Murphy. I will put it on the Airlines bill.'
'Thank you.'

He quickly returns with a full bottle of Bushmills, a glass, a plate of cheeses and an ashtray, 'Enjoy Mr Murphy.'

'You're a good lad,' I say, smiling.

The whisky tastes good. Normally I like it with sugar and hot water but I don't want to further bother my new-found friend behind the bar. I look around and the room is quiet. I see one gent sat in the corner reading a book. Well-dressed but clearly not a hack. Though he seems somewhat familiar. He catches my eye looking over. He waves across. Oh no, my fault. Here we go.

'Jimmy, I thought it was you,' he says smiling, whilst holding a jug of beer. My vacant impression appears to be amusing him, 'Harry Jackson mate. Chief Inspector, Stretford Police.' Now I remember. I'd seen him many times at Old Trafford after matches having a natter with Matt. Our paths had crossed but it was never more than a fleeting nod. He offers me his hand and we shake, 'What brings you here Harry?'

'A horrible and sad state of affairs Jimmy. The RAF flew me over. Official business but I suppose I can tell you.'

The barman reappears, 'Can I have a jug of beer for my friend here please?'

'No problem Mr Murphy. Again, on the Airline bill.' He winks.

'Thank you. You're a man after my own heart son.' We all smile. Jackson clinks my whisky glass with his jug, 'To the boys we've lost Jimmy.' We toast and drink.

'So, you were about to tell me Harry. Your business here?'

'Not nice at all I'm afraid. It was to identify the bodies of the players.'

I look at this man's face and my heart sinks...

'They're in peace now old son,' he says, 'The suffering is for the living not the dead.'
Words I'll never forget…

Myself, Harry and Bill are on the train home via the hook of Holland, then ferry to Dover, train again to London and then taxi to Manchester. It's an uncomfortable time as every brake, screech and jolt in the line has the lads jumping out of their skin. I try desperately to keep minds off it but my attempts fail miserably. Like before when chatting about players that we were going to need. Positions to be filled and such when a Chinese gentleman entered our carriage and sat down. He smiled, politely removed his hat and nodded to us all, 'Hello my old china' I said to him, 'Can you play inside left?' He simply glowered in my direction, turned and left, leaving Harry and Bill staring at me like I'd gone mad!
We arrive in Dover port and coming off the ferry I notice a large crowd of pressmen and photographers waiting on the jetty. Including a BBC outside broadcast van. Why won't these people just leave us in peace. 'I'm going to punch some bastard on the nose Jimmy,' says Harry, 'I'm not in no mood for dealing with this lot.'
'Me neither' adds Bill.
'Leave it to me' I say, 'Just follow lads.' I lead them down the gantry towards our unwanted welcome back party. 'Right you lot,' I shout as they gather at the bottom, 'Piss off and let us through, otherwise someone is going to get a right hook off me. And don't bastard push me because I'm ready to drop all of you I am!'
'We reach them, 'Steady on Jimmy' one says who I don't recognise. 'Just a few lines eh for the people at home.' Cameras start to flash and click all round as the press

boys move in, 'Fucking leave us alone you bastards!' shouts Harry. I push a way through the melee as the reporters with their note books and pens in hand fire questions in our direction, 'Are United finished Jimmy?'
'How many people did you save Harry?'
'Did you see any of the dead bodies Bill?'
'Could you have done more Harry?'
'Why did you all get back on the plane?'
'Do both you boys blame Matt Busby for what happened?'
At that I snap! I turn and face them, 'I piss on all you bastards' I shout. Suddenly they're shocked into a momentarily silence, 'Steady on Jimmy' urges a voice from the back of the crowd, 'Bloody ell' calm down Jimmy,' says another, 'We're just doing our job.'
'What you're doing is dancing on our dead that's what this is. Now we're getting in that taxi over there to take us to the railway station.' I point across, 'And if any of you have the slightest spark of a conscience you'll stay well away.' Nobody moves or speaks.
'Good lads' I say, 'Play fair eh. You'll have your day with me but it's not now.' Harry and Bill are watching on. I feel even they have been shocked by my words. I place my arm around them, 'Come on boys we're going home.'

Act Three
THIRTEEN DAYS

I'd hired a taxi to get us the last part of the journey to Manchester. The closer we get to home the more pensive the atmosphere becomes in the car. I'm sat in the front with the driver but keeping a close eye on Harry and Bill. I've no doubt their minds still at the end of that damned runway in the wreckage of that damned plane. On that damned, infernal day. Both have agreed to play on. We're on a life support machine now and it's a race against time to stay alive. 'Bloody 'ell look at that!' exclaims the taxi driver, 'It's like a painting of the last day in the world.'

He could well be right. In front of us on the quiet road an apocalyptic black sky covets the city. Never in my life have I seen anything so grim and doom-laden. I can only feel the desperate mood below has affected the heavens above and the almighty has acted accordingly. We've still not spoken, my faith rocked like I never thought possible. But seeing this sight before me now. A broken city enveloped by what can only be a dark heavenly veil to shelter it from all prying eyes. The Mancunian's pain still so raw and hurting as not yet ready to open their broken hearts to good willing but unwanted outsiders. Well maybe he has a guilty conscience after all?

'Thank god you're home Jimmy.' The words that greeted me on arriving back at Old Trafford spoken by club secretary Les Olive. Salford born Les has been left holding the fort. His youthful features so much more haggard than I remember. Only thirty he appears to have aged ten years in just the short time I've been in Munich. His boss and my friend Water Crickmer now dead, Les has taken over his duties. Huge shoes to fill are Walter's. A more gentle, caring man you'd struggle to meet. Thirty-two years of wonderful service but I know of no man more capable. Les has been at Manchester United since he was fourteen. He started as a member of the ground staff and in the early years played twice for the first team as a goalkeeper. Les bleeds red for United and has never been needed more by his club now.

We walk up the tunnel and out into an empty stadium. It's getting dark and also bitterly cold. Les runs a hand through his hair and look around the stands, 'The old place just doesn't feel the same Jimmy. Since last Thursday I've felt the magic drain away.' I grab him and point to the centre circle on the pitch, 'Come on let's talk over there Les.' We head across.

'Listen Les, I want you to ring Mr Mitchell the Luton chairman. I need Jack Crompton back in the fold. He's a decent chap and he'll understand. Mitchell knows Jack is family. Make that your first call tomorrow old son.'

'Will do Jimmy.'

'So how are things?'

'Well most of my time has been spent organising funerals.' He pulls a piece of paper from his pocket, 'I've got the full list here. Young Nobby Stiles' dad is helping out. He owns a funeral service in Collyhurst and will be ferrying family members around for free. A lovely gesture. Well here we go….

Tuesday: Willie Satinoff and Henry Rose.

Wednesday: Roger Byrne, Frank Swift, Eric Thompson and Archie Ledbrook.

Thursday: Tommy Taylor, Geoff Bent, Bert Whalley, Tom Curry and Alf Clark,

Friday: Eddie Colman, Walter and Tom Jackson.'

Les takes a deep breath and rubs his eyes, 'I'm almost numb to the grief Jimmy. I've spoken to the families but the pain is still so raw. There's a lot of anger. Shock. And the one question I keep getting asked?'

I sigh, 'I can guess Les. Why did the boys get back on the plane?'

A wry but utterly sad smile comes over his face, 'Exactly.'

We arrive in the centre circle. I light a cigarette and pull up the collar on my jacket. I gaze around, 'They are going to want us to carry on Les and I intend to make sure we do.'
'There's a board meeting on Tuesday and they want you there Jimmy. I fear the worse.'
'I need players and I need them now. First thing tomorrow morning I want all the youth and reserve team players assembled at the Cliff. Nine o'clock sharp. Walking wounded, everybody. Let's see what we've got left. Also, I'll ring round the local clubs. Get them to send over their best players for trials.'
'I've had the Liverpool chairman Tom Williams on the phone. He's offering us some of his reserves. Also, Leeds and Nottingham forest have contacted us asking if they can help. Plus, there's something else Jimmy?'
'What is it?'
'It really is quite extraordinary. People are sending money and I'm not talking a pound here or there. It's arriving by the sackload. Thousands of pounds. Alma is sorting through it. Herself and four other ladies.'
'But we can't afford to pay anybody else Les.'
'No Jimmy you don't understand. They've volunteered. It's pouring in. Schoolboys are sending dinner money and spends. Old ladies their life savings. Weekly wage packets, charity donations, local business that've had collections. We've had half of Trafford Park queuing to drop off bags of cash. The Lord Mayor has set an appeal up. At the Plaza Ballroom people didn't dance, they just threw money onto the dance floor. We've even had twelve guineas brought in by a police officer from Strangeways. The prisoners have had a whip round. We

can't keep up. The girls are working all hours but more is coming each day.

'We're not alone Jimmy.'

'No, we're not but I need to start a forest fire Les. Build up a head of momentum because it will be too easy for the board to listen to outsiders and shut us down. Over my dead body son will I let that happen.'

'Les smiles, 'My Jimmy! Listen, what on earth are we doing here in the centre circle? Its bloody freezing. Let's go inside and grab a cup of tea. Maybe something stronger eh?' I look at him and point to the markings surrounding us, 'This circle here is the heartbeat of our football club. When we got those boys and trained them in the United way. Boys to men to red devils Les. This is where it led to.' I stand in the centre circle spot and point at it, 'From this here is where we go on. We use their strength, me and you because they'll be watching. Deal?' Les smiles and offers me his hand and we shake, 'It's a deal' he says.

'What say we stay here for twenty minutes and just remember our boys?'

'Fine by me Jimmy,' Les replies… 'Fine by me.'

And so, with a military salute and a holy blessing on the runway my boys leave Munich and come home. The flag draped coffins are brought through the streets of Munich before dawn and loaded onto a BEA Viscount. Later, through a guard of honour formed by the Munich city police, representatives of the civic authorities and West German football clubs take wreaths into the cabin. In the afternoon, following a service attended by the British consul, the aircraft takes off for England flying low over the silent wreckage of the crash site.

The Viscount arrives an hour late at Ringway airport just after 9-35pm.
One by one the coffins are carried from the plane to waiting hearses and in a single line they set off on a last journey to Old Trafford. Along the ten-mile route over a hundred thousand broken hearted people line the pavements to pay their last respects. They are wailing and screaming, others simply red-eyed, sniffing, hiding disbelieving faces behind handkerchiefs. Many are simply speechless and unable to believe what they are seeing. Finally, realisation kicking in. Surreal but true, the boys really are dead. The cortege make its way in a slow respectful single column. A morbid night. Nobody speaks, just a grief-stricken silence. Broken only by the sound of sobbing and the gentle hum of the hearses. Flowers are thrown onto their roofs and in the paths. And then, as if he could hold it in no more, the almighty weeps also and the heavens open and only apt the Mancunian rain comes down in torrents.
And a city cries…
Around Manchester, black drapes, wreaths, veiled curtains and heartfelt epic poems dedicated to them covet shops, schools and factories. On arrival at Old Trafford the column comes to a halt as the thousands of people on the forecourt blocks their path. And then like the parting of the red sea the crowds open and the hearses drive up to the south stand where the coffins are to be placed in the club gym. A Temporary chapel of rest. Two policemen will look after them. They are my friends now, Sergeant Thomas and Constable Potter. However, their only task appears to be handing out tissues for the tears of weeping family members.

It's just gone eleven o'clock in the evening when I summon up the courage to make my way from the office to the gym. I've a promise to keep see. One made on the day my lads set off to Belgrade. I told them then I'd go easy next time we meet up if they made it through. So, a promise made is a promise kept. I need that final chat. I have to say a last goodbye to my boys.

In my darkest and primitive thoughts, I could never have imagined what greets my eyes as I enter and gaze upon this sight.

'Would you like a few moments alone?' asks Sergeant Thomas. 'Yes, please boys, if you don't mind.'

'No worries Jimmy, we'll be outside if you need us. Come on Constable Potter; let's give Jimmy some time eh.'

The policemen step out and I'm left alone with my golden apples. My boys, my sons. I walk to the nearest coffin and it's Tommy Taylor's. I slowly run my hand over the top of it. All look beautiful. Sleek black with gold handles and a red white and black scarf tied upon them just in case the almighty forgets who would soon be calling upon him.

He better have a decent fucking pitch.

I move slowly amongst all of them: David Pegg, Roger Byrne, Geoff Bent, Liam Whelan, Eddie Colman, Mark Jones, Walter Crickmer, Bert Whalley and Tom Curry.

'Well done lads' I say. I'm trying so hard to hold it together, 'You did it see. A little close from what I heard, but you kept your nerve and you done us proud you did. Now, if I remember rightly I promised you all an easy time if you got through, so I won't keep you long. I will let you sleep. Just bear with me for a little longer eh, you lot? I know you always thought I was hard on you. That I was a tough taskmaster but it was only because I saw greatness in you boys. I just needed to sharpen down the rough edges and then you'd be ready to conquer the world. To spread your wings and fly. And you've done it see, you've soared beyond the heavens. Charmed the Gods, created a sense of wonder amongst all who saw you play. And even now when you've fallen from the stars, although my heart is broken and will never mend, I can promise you this. From the bottom of my soul you'll never really die boys. There will be songs and poems and flags, you will forever be in the hearts of every Manchester United supporter. From father to son, from generation to generation they'll tell tall tales of your brave deeds and you will live forever. You watch, it'll happen.

And Walter, Bert and Tom, you lads make sure they behave up there. You let me know if anyone slouches or fools around in training and they'll feel my boot they will.

One last thing, I can tell you all now I won't allow this club to wither and die. Munich will not be an end but a new beginning. That's the least I owe you. For you gave me everything and more. They call me the starmaker. Well you lot, you made dreams come true. Both young and old, so goodnight lads. Sleep well eh. For you shown me paradise and Paradise is now where you're going. And how blessed they will be to have you.'

Suddenly I'm on my knees. It's all too much and I cry out.

The policemen re-enter and help me up, 'Come on Jimmy mate' says Sergeant Thomas, 'Let's go get you a cup of tea eh.'

Right, now I've paid my debt it's time to get down to work. Manchester United may have crashed and burned in most people's eyes but trust me, there will be a phoenix rising that will shake this world. For red devils don't die you see, they live through fire and flames and they go on and on. You just wait and you just see.

The next morning I'm at the Cliff, 7-30 sharp. I head into Matt's office. I sit down in his chair. There's a picture of Jean and the family on the desk. I put it in a draw and slam it shut. Today the fightback begins. It's silent and still. I stare at the phone and then at the notepad and pen in front of me. I think of phoning the hospital in Munich. I pick up the receiver but change my mind and put it down again. I couldn't handle it if there's more bad news. More loss.

What the bloody hell am I doing? This is hopeless. I start to think of a speech to give to the boys arriving later on. One that will rock their world but my mind is numb. Oh God I'm missing Bert and Tom. Now that three has become one, maybe it wasn't me with the magic after all? Maybe I'm a fraud? What's the saying? The whole is greater than the sum of the parts? That's it then. I'm nothing without my two pals. I might as well be lying next to them in the Old Trafford gym. Or is this me just feeling sorry for myself?

I'm not going home. I daren't. Winnie, the kids, I love them all so much but I'm sleeping at the ground. I can't switch off, I mustn't switch off. If I even take half an eye off going forward then it's all over. All is lost. I pick up the notepad and hurl it across the office. Fuck it. Fuck it all!

'Morning Jimmy.'

I look up and stood at the door is a smiling Jack Crompton. Back from Luton.
He picks up the notepad and puts it back on the desk, 'How are you doing old pal?' I stand up and we shake hands, 'I'm sorry Jack its...'
'A terrible thing Jimmy but we'll get through this.'
'I didn't expect to see you back so soon.'
'Well Les rang the chairman yesterday evening and I travelled down overnight. I went straight to the ground, paid my respect to the boys and was told you'd be here. One thing though. They said you slept in Matt's office?'
'Well there's so much to keep an eye on Jack.' I rub my eyes, 'It's good to see you again though. I can't thank you enough. It means so much but I knew you'd come. Family see.'
'Family Jimmy. He points to the notepad, 'What was all that nonsense about?'
'I'm trying to think of some lines to inspire the lads. I've got everybody coming in at nine and can't think of anything to say to them.'
Jack shakes his head and smiles, 'Are you mad? Since when have you ever needed to write anything down? Do this from the heart because you and your passion are the fuel that's going to drive us on old pal. If you break down it's over. The grief and the sadness are the petrol so you rage and rant against it and we'll be okay. And when those boys come in today you shout and scream and laugh and you cry and make them believe that miracles are possible.'
It feels good to have my friend back.

I'm going through positions we're going to need to fill and one name keeps coming to mind. I'm going to need an experienced head. A ball player, someone to keep it moving quickly. Little Ernie Taylor at Blackpool. He's a good sort as well but whether we can afford him? There's a knock at the door.

'Come in' I shout. It's Jack.

'They're waiting for you Jimmy.' I look at my watch, its only half past eight. Jack smiles, 'Keen as mustard old pal. Everybody wants to play their part.'

I look out the window and see them all stood crowding around waiting for me. All so young, 'Well Jack lad,' I reply smiling whilst standing up, 'God loves a trier so they say. Let's go see what we've got.'

We walk out of the building towards the training pitch and immediately I feel all eyes fall upon me. I've been with most of these lads since they were knee high to a grasshopper and they've know nothing else except Manchester United and it's up to me that doesn't end any day soon. I look at their faces, it's clear many are traumatised. I see it in their eyes. Bewilderment. But I know how players think. Deep down even though none here will admit it they'll be thinking this could be my chance. We shall see.

Jack claps his hands together, 'All right listen up you lot. Jimmy's going to say a few words and then we'll crack on.' I step forward. I pray my eyes stay dry and my throat doesn't, 'This is our darkest hour boys. Our loss has been immense and whilst we continue to pray for the boss and Duncan and all the other lads still in that Munich hospital, United must go on. Now we've all shed tears and asked why us? But it's happened. Dreadful and shocking as it is we're on our knees. Now, I'm after not just players with ability, I need those with heart and courage. The type to play football the way Roger, Eddie

and Tommy did. The way all of them did. And Duncan who's lying in that hospital bed with a still never-say-die no matter what the odds. Well he's fighting his greatest battle now and do you know what he said to me before I came home? He said get stuck in chief. And that's now what I want you to do. All of you. In every training session you perform like it's the last time you'll ever kick a ball. And if you're picked to play then you do so with a desire and determination not to lose, but also to thrill and play hard. Though most of all, to win. And do so in the Manchester United way.
Alright boys?'
I notice some are close to tears but all look ready to run through walls for me and this club.
'Well let's get going then!' I shout, 'No time to lose.'
'C'mon boys,' adds Jack, 'You heard the boss.'
We head onto the training pitch. Now to find new heroes.
  I'm back in Matt's office at the cliff. It was a good start. Already some have shown they're ready for the fight. Lads like Alex Dawson, Freddie Goodwin, Shay Brennan, Colin Webster and Mark Pearson will give us a fighting chance.
The phone goes.
'Hello Jimmy Murphy.'
'Jimmy it's Alma.'
'Hello love, how are things there?'
'Jimmy we've just heard from Jean at the hospital in Germany. It's not good. Matt was given the Last Rites again last night. It's just a matter of time.'
'I close my eyes, 'Any more news on Duncan and the other lads?'
'Duncan remains fifty-fifty, the others no change.'

'Thanks for letting me know Alma.' I put down the receiver.

Jack enters, 'We've got a visitor Jimmy.'

I've no time to dwell on the grave news from Munich because appearing behind him dressed dapper in a beautiful hand-made suit with a handkerchief in his top pocket, sleeked black hair and a smile that could light a football ground is Don Raimondo Saporta. A representative and fixer extraordinaire for Real Madrid. I stand to greet him. I've nothing but good memories and nice feeling towards this man and his football team. In our clashes in the European cup semi-final last season they treated us like visiting royalty. Our boys given gold watches by the President Don Santiago Bernabeu. Sheer class both on the pitch and off.

Saporta comes towards me and I stand to greet him. We embrace. His unsmiling features not what I'm used to seeing, 'Jimmy, I had business in France but I've come here because our friendship is far more important. I bring from Madrid, from my city, my football club and my president. From the bottom of my heart our deepest sympathies for Manchester United and your loss. And a personal message from Don Santiago that whatever we can do to help, we shall. Already, Real have issued a pendant with the names of your lost footballers on and all profits well be sent direct to you. Also, when the time is right, any of the families involved in this tragedy we would like to invite to Madrid. As well as the injured players whom can have full use of our medical and rehab facilities. A break in the sun as you strange British call it!'

'That is so kind Raimondo. And it's good to see you old pal.'

'There's something else Jimmy that our President would like me to convey to you. It is clear you need help and not just money. Don Santiago would like to loan you two players for the rest of the season. He has spoken to both and they are prepared to travel to England at a moment's notice.'

I'm momentarily stunned at the sheer generosity of Saporta's and his President's offer. But realistically they're bound only to be reserve players and though undoubtedly talented would struggle to make any impact in the blood and thunder of our league.

'Raimondo, look, I deeply appreciate everything but the idea of young Spanish players from your reserves trying to survive in our first division...I'

Saporta puts his hand up to silence me, 'Oh, I don't think you understand Jimmy. We are not talking about inexperienced reserve players. I am talking about two first teamers.'

'Who exactly?' I ask. Now I'm truly curious. A smiling-wide Saporta is I suspect enjoying slightly teasing me, 'You may have heard of them Jimmy. It is Di Stefano and Puskas!'

'Oh my god!' Exclaims Jack.

I stare open-mouthed at Saporta, 'Raimondo did you just say Di Stefano and Puskas?'

'Yes Jimmy. Both Alfredo and Ferenc have been deeply touched by your loss and are ready if called upon to play in United red until the end of this season.'

He laughs, 'But then we want them back amigo!'

'I don't know what to say?'

'How about yes Raimondo, we would like to accept your offer?' I pull out a cigarette and light it. I look in Saporta's smiling eyes and offer him my hand. He accepts and we shake. I smile, 'Yes Raimondo we would like to accept your most wonderful offer.'

'Excellent,' he replies, 'Now I shall arrange for the paper work from Madrid. If you can deal with your authorities, I shall inform the players this evening. In the mean time I would appreciate if we kept this just between us Jimmy? Politically in Spain for our President this could ignite fires. Especially if Barcelona overtake us this season without Di Stefano and Puskas. But it is what he wants to do, so if Don Santiago wishes it, then it shall happen.'

'Of course. I understand Raimondo. Can you tell him from me he will never be forgotten by our supporters and club for this magnificent act of friendship?'

'Ours is a tale of two cities Jimmy. And shall be forever more.' Saporta shakes his head, 'Please forgive me, I almost forgot to ask. What is the latest news on Matt and your other boys?'

'Matt is gravely ill, Duncan is fighting. Fifty. The others, Johnny Berry and Ray Wood are out of danger.'

'There are no words to the depths of your loss my friend. I can only assure you that your friend's in Madrid will be forever by your side. Now, I must go. Business in Paris with a beautiful lady and then Brazil. We're hearing rumours of a young boy called Pele. They say he could be useful and would look good in the white of Real Madrid. May god go with you and your team Jimmy Murphy.
Adios'

  I'm back at Old Trafford speaking to Les Olive in his office and telling him of Madrid's marvellous offer.

'You're going to have to speak to Hardaker at the Football League yourself Jimmy. He's a stickler for the rules and even though public opinion is with us, something tells me this man carries a grudge beyond the grave. Especially in our case. Matt's defiance of him taking us in to Europe left Hardaker seething.'

'He wouldn't dare block it Les. He just wouldn't dare.'

Les looks at me with eyebrows raised, 'No? You don't think so? Ring him.'

Les writes down his number on a notepad and passes it over. I pick up the receiver and dial.

He answers:

'Hello.'

'Mr Hardaker sir, It's Jimmy Murphy.'

'Mr Murphy, how are things?'

'We're doing our best to keep going sir and actually in need of a big favour off yourself, if I'm being honest.'

'Go on Mr Murphy, I'm all ears.'

'Well our good friends in Madrid have offered us two players until the end of the season. They're no ordinary two bob reserves. It's Di Stefano and Puskas. It's just the boost we need sir. Also, we feel it would be good for the League to have wonderful talents such as these on show every week for the supporters to see live.'

'Oh, you do, do you Mr Murphy?'

'Yes sir.'

'Well I disagree. I look at it as taking jobs from our own boys. Why should the Football League give up two places for a pair of damn foreigners? What, are our own British born and bred players not good enough for you and your new team Mr Murphy? I see no reason why you have to go over shores. Manchester is a lot closer to the Midlands than Madrid don't you think? Why not there? I seem to remember Edwards did okay for you when you swept him away from Dudley under the nose of Wolverhampton Wonderers.'

'With due respect Mr Hardaker this is two of the greatest footballers in the world we are talking about? And yes, Duncan is a magnificent talent and may I remind you not to talk of him in the past tense.'
The bastard.
'Always been your trouble at United Mr Murphy. Got a little above your station a few years back. Fly the flag and all that. Thought you were better than anyone else and look where it has got you. Let me remind you Manchester United have been given plenty of help and goodwill off the Football League since the crash. We've postponed your two forthcoming fixtures, but this? Well it simply isn't on. My answer has to be no.'
I can feel my blood boiling. Les is watching me. I can tell by his eyes that he knows I'm going to blow, 'Where exactly has it got us Mr Hardaker sir?'
'I beg your pardon?'
'I asked you where do you think it has actually got us?'
'My personal opinion is that you should just call it a day Mr Murphy. You bit off more than you could chew with this European cup business and have paid a dreadful price as a result. It's over for you.'
'Well let me tell you something Mr Hardaker sir. With all due respect you're talking through your fucking arse see. Manchester United are not going anywhere. Especially out of business. Oh, I know you'd like that. Sweet revenge. Still sticks in your throat doesn't it that Matt had the courage and the vision to go against your wishes and take us into Europe. You bitter, twisted and small-minded fool.'
'Now look here Mr Murphy!'
'Don't you interrupt me sir. I will tell you now, United are going to be your biggest nightmare in the future. You

don't want to help us, well we shall look after ourselves. I'd like to wish you a good day but I'd only be lying. I'd suggest though that next time we are in close vicinity you stay well away from me. As for your crass remarks about Duncan and how we had this coming? They are so beneath contempt that they could only come from the mouth of a fucking moron.'

I slam the receiver down and Les is staring at me in utter disbelief. He smiles, 'I guess that's told him.'

I stand arms folded on the Old Trafford forecourt with Jack alongside me, as the ground-staff are going through the skip containing the player's kit and boots that's just arrived back from Munich. Two of the boys helping are young Nobby Stiles and Johnny Giles. Nobby from Collyhurst and Dublin born Johnny. We've high hopes for both. Nobby in particular looks upset.

I call him over, 'Nobby son!'

He stops and comes across. He wipes his eyes clear of tears or at least tries, 'You alright lad?'

'Yes boss, just I've come across Eddie's boots. I always use to clean them. He was my idol. I loved him. I loved them all, but Eddie, well he was different. Always had time for a laugh…. feels like I've lost an older brother.'

Again, Nobby goes to dry his eyes.

'Go and fetch Eddie's boots,' I tell him.

Nobby races over to the skip and carries the boots back under his arm. They're still caked in Belgrade mud…

'I want you to clean them until you can see your face, do you hear me Norbert Stiles?'

'Yes boss I will. I always did.'

'And when you've done that I want you to take them home and never let them out of your sight. Okay?'

Tears are now falling freely down Nobby's Face.

'Will do Jimmy, I promise.'
'Good lad, now get back over there with your mate. Go on.'
Nobby smiles and jogs back over.
'Keep your eye on him and young Giles Jack. They're both players. They are both Manchester United players.'

I enter Paddy McGrath's The Cromford club in Manchester city centre. Elegant, smooth and classy. Just like it's owner. Paddy greets me in the foyer with a warm handshake. He's closer to Matt than me, best pals really but we've always got on well. A big, tall, dark looking man. Always immaculately dressed, the sharpest suits with the shiniest shoes and splendid cufflinks. Paddy resembles one of Chicago's finest.
A lovely, kind man, though his business's interests mainly exists in that mysterious Mancunian shade between what's legal and not. A gangster I hear from many people. Paddy allegedly made his money in Blackpool during the war with a host of clubs and casinos. His town they call it. But I take as I find and since the crash this man could not do enough to help us and today has insisted I call in here because there's somebody he wished me to meet.
'Jimmy how are you holding up?'
I shrug my shoulders, 'Well as can be expected. You heard the latest bulletin on Matt?'
Paddy produces a silver cigarette case from his pocket, takes one out and lights up. He nods, 'I don't care what the reports or those bloody doctors say Jimmy. Matt is a tough old bird. He'll be okay. Just you wait and see.'
'I hope so Pat.'
Paddy takes my arm, 'Come with me.'

We enter into the inner sanctums of the Crompton. Dimly lit. An exclusive dining room area with a stage and a sumptuous thick red carpet. Only two people are present. A barman in a white shirt and black-tie cleaning glasses, and sat on a lounge suite, a diminutive little figure who on seeing us enter smiles and waves across. It's the Blackpool playmaker Ernie Taylor.
I look at Paddy, 'Please tell me you haven't kidnapped him Paddy?'
He laughs, 'Not exactly he came of his own accord. Come on let's go and say hello.'
Ernie stands to greet me and we shake hands. Only five feet four but a lovely little ball player and intelligent with it. He's also made of the right stuff. During the war Ernie was a sub mariner. Pressure to him was surviving under the North Atlantic whilst hunting and being hunted by the German navy. Anything that could occur on a football field faded into comparison to this.
'Ernie it's great to meet you,' I say.
Paddy motions to the barman and he brings over a tray with three beers on and puts them on the table. We sit down. Me facing Ernie and Paddy sat next to him.
'You too Jimmy. First my deepest sympathies for what's gone on. I loved playing against those boys. They had a magic, a gold dust about them.'
'Let's get down to business Ernie,' says Paddy.
'Tell Jimmy what you told me?'
Ernie smiles, 'I want to help Jimmy.'
'Blackpool want eight grand,' adds Paddy.
'I'm not sure we can afford or go to that figure,' I reply.
'Well offer what you can and don't worry about the rest.'

'I'm not so sure Paddy,' says Ernie. 'The Blackpool board run a tight ship. If they say eight grand they mean it. Not a penny less.'

Paddy smiles, 'Don't worry Ernie lad. They may run a tight ship but I run Blackpool.' He raises his beer glass and we all do similar, 'To Manchester United and the boys lost.'

We toast.

'Well I've now got three players lads. Harry, Bill and your goodself Ernie. Today is the 10th February, I have nine days to find a side to face Sheffield Wednesday in the FA cup at Old Trafford and I'm going to need more than a holy medal to kiss to pull this off.'

'Any new apples to come off the tree?' Asks Paddy

I smile, 'Oh, there's a couple and more chomping at the bit. Rough and ready boys. In normal circumstances I wouldn't dream of throwing them in, but? Well I'm swiftly finding goodwill is one thing but a real desire to help are in short supply. Obviously present company accepted and our good friends in Madrid, I'd say we're more or less on our own.'

Paddy smiles, 'That's still not bad odds Jimmy and they're not one's I'd back against.'

'Aye, well tomorrow Pat, there's a board meeting at Old Trafford and something tells me I'll be going to war again.'

11th February 1958: Afternoon. Earlier this morning I attended Matt's good friend Willie Satinoff funeral. Willie is the first of the crash victims to be buried. He'd gone to Belgrade as a guest of the club and especially Matt. The recent death of our club director George Whittaker only a few weeks ago meant a position on the board had become available. Willie and Matt's other great pal Louis Edwards were the major candidates. Now with there being just one seat left free on the airplane Matt met with both and said the only fair way would be to toss a coin for it. Satinoff won but ultimately lost. Such is the cruel, cruel hand of fate.

The Daily Express's poor Henry Rose has just been given a most amazing send off. The swashbuckling Henry. Dashing, charismatic, a larger than life character and one who I liked dearly. His thick portly figure. The brown trilby hat and of course, inevitable cigar. Oh, he's caused myself and Matt and the players some grief over the years, but you could never stay mad with our Henry for he acted, said and wrote everything I'm certain with a wonderful and teasing twinkle in his eye. Such was the fondness that existed in this city for Henry all the black cab taxi drivers had volunteered to transfer free anybody at the Express, or indeed anyone who wished to go to his funeral six miles away at Southern Cemetery in Chorlton. A huge fleet of black cabs stopped off at the Express offices in Great Ancoats street in town. And, then they headed off. A never-ending thin black line of wailing and weeping that broke the hearts of all who witnessed it. Munich was real as this scene proved. Henry was Jewish and so at his graveside we all wore headwear. A grieving-silent mass of Homborgs, fedoras, headscarves, bowler hats and berets. Then, the last blessing of the Rabbi. A final show of respect for a lovely man and scribe who was laid to rest under black skies and in the midst of a bitterly cold Mancunian afternoon.

Sleep well Henry son.

Now I have a date with the board at Old Trafford for what I'm sure they intend to make my third funeral of the day.

I get out the taxi on the Old Trafford forecourt and immediately head inside. Alma is stood waiting for me, 'More updates from Munich Jimmy.' Her face I can no longer read because it appears in a constant state of sadness.

'Go on girl.'

'Well it's so much better on Matt. A miracle really. Professor Maurer says he's making a remarkable recovery and can now be treated as a normal patient. He's going to be okay.' Her voice is cracking.

I remembered Paddy's words from last night, 'A tough old bird' and feel a smile coming on my face. Good news is a rare item these days. But another look at Alma and I suddenly realise there's worse to follow, 'Alma what is it?'

It's Duncan Jimmy. He's taken a sudden turn for the worse. The doctors are alarmed at the unusually high nitrogen levels in his blood. He's got six times more than is normal in a human. They say this isn't good and Duncan is in serious trouble again.'

'Aye well' I say smiling. Trying desperately to hide the pain, 'Duncan isn't a normal human being though is he love?' Norma tries to stifles the tears, 'No Jimmy. Oh, I almost forgot, they're waiting for you in the board room. Good luck.'

I enter and walk slowly across to the long boardroom table where waiting for me are the Chairman Harold Hardman, directors, Alan Gibson, William Petherbridge, newly appointed Louis Edwards and club secretary Les Olive. At least one friendly face and ally. This is one of my least favourite places in the world and I've always thanked god Matt dealt with all this, the business side of the football club. I've never been one to doff my cap to anybody and don't intend starting now. This just isn't me but today I'm ready and willing to rip the head off any bastard who dares to mention the idea of us giving up. Gentlemen of the board, do your worst.

'Afternoon Jimmy' says Les, 'Take a seat old pal.' I do so. I notice a whiskey bottle on the table that's half full. There's nervousness in the air. All are smiling towards me but I sense trouble in the air.

'Jimmy' says Hardman, 'May I begin by saying how much we all appreciate your huge efforts these last few days.'

'Hear, hear' the others reply in unison.

'Thank you gentlemen, well I've managed to acquire the services of Ernie Taylor from Blackpool for a small fee as I'm sure you're aware. I'm busy ringing round, plus some of the young lads are looking quite promising in training. I think with a bit of luck and a fair wind we should be able to put out eleven players against Sheffield Wednesday on the 19th. A rag tag bunch but…'

'Hold on a second Jimmy,' interrupts Hardman, 'It's not that simple. Now, I hear you but we have to be realistic. You must remember the players killed were not insured and there's simply no money in the kitty. Now we've talked about this as an option and feel it is best practical and indeed honourable. I'm sorry, but after much discussion and with huge regret myself and the board feel it is in the best interests of all concerned that for the time being we shut down Manchester United until further notice.'

'No, no you can't do that, we're needed more than ever now.'

'Jimmy, you're never going to get enough players to pull on a Manchester United shirt in just eight days. It's simply impossible.'

'I can do it.'

'It can't be done!' Snaps back Hardman.

Now I'm truly annoyed, 'Don't you tell me what can and can't be done. When Matt first brought me here after the war to a bombed-out shell of a ground they told me it couldn't be done. That Manchester United was finished. We'd never be a success. We'd never win the league playing with kids. That we'd never match the best sides in Europe. The Athletic Bilbao's and the Real Madrid's and every bloody time we proved them wrong. So, please. With respect sir. Don't tell me it can't be done. It can and I'll make sure of it.'

'Jimmy old friend,' says Alan Gibson, 'You're letting your grief dictate your actions.'

'Aye your damn right I am Alan, because what else have we got left? No players or money, no hope, grief is our fuel now. It has to be our lifeblood.'

'You're simply not being rational Jimmy,' adds Hardman. I…'

'Bloody rational!' I cut him short, 'Now I knew those lads that were killed better than anyone. I found and nurtured them, I studied them through dark, miserable, bitter and cold Mancunian mornings. In the pissin' wet through rain. In fogs and gales. On ice and snow. I flogged them on mud patches until they moved like ballerinas and stung like dervishes. Like red devils. They allowed me to mould their lives from the ground up. To make them the best this country has ever seen. And the most loved. And they repaid me with their skill, courage, passion and now…. Now at the end of that damned

runway with their lives. And you lot think I'm going to turn my back on them Mr Chairman by giving up and lowering the red flag? Never.'
Hardman looks crestfallen, 'Jimmy, we all want to honour the memory of those who've died…'
'No, no you don't understand' I say, 'It's not about their memories. Those boys are going to live forever. It's about those who are left behind showing who we are to the world. We cannot let this be the end. That we, this club cannot afford to be bowed by tragedy. Because how Manchester United are in the future will be founded on the way we behave today. Now, I'm putting out a team against Sheffield Wednesday and you are either with or against me. Am I understood?'
Around the table all heads are down except Les, who's smiling towards me, 'I have to say gentlemen, I'm with Jimmy.'
All eyes now fall upon him. Les shrugs his shoulders, 'Can you blame me?' He points in my direction, 'Is anyone at this table really going to bet against this man?'
Hardman smiles and also looks up towards me, 'Quite. Okay then best put it to the vote. All those in favour of carrying on raise your hand.'
They all do so, 'Well that appears quite unanimous,' quips Hardman.
'There's one other thing gentlemen. Before I have to get on with things.'
'Go on Jimmy,' replies Hardman.
'I need to get the boys out of Manchester and away to our normal spot in Blackpool. It's too stifling here. The atmosphere is overwhelming and we need to be able to breathe and to think straight. Especially Harry and Bill. Every time I look at them, their eyes are still on that

runway. They don't get a moment's peace here. Either from the press or supporters. A little sea air and change of scenery is needed I believe. Get us away from the tears and the grief on every street corner in the city. It's just too much.'

'Very well. When do you wish to go?'

'Tomorrow.'

Hardman glances around the table and is met by a host of nods.

'We'll contact the Norbreck. Send me a postcard Jimmy,' says Hardman.

I smile, nod and stand to leave, 'You need to stay strong gentlemen. We are in a battle for our very existence and cannot afford a moment's weakness. Now good day to you all.'

That said I walk out the door. But stay behind it just to listen.

'Has he just fucking bollocked us?' I hear Louis Edwards say. 'I believe so,' replies Hardman, 'And to be honest, I think we deserved it.'

I'm in my office. I look around. My new house. I miss Winnie and the kids so much but I can't go home yet. I can't even contemplate it. I already have a team in mind for the Sheffield game. Raw, inexperienced and a desperate gamble. But life now is nothing more than a game of poker. We're on a game of bluff. Outsiders looking in read the newspapers who write of bravery and a worldwide tidal wave of goodwill to ensure we carry on. Oh, sure there's goodwill but no one will give me what I really need. Decent players. I sense a slight reluctance, though well-hidden to not let United back in the game. Oh, they send wreaths, hold silences and speak

generous words but it feels to me like throwing a drowning man a brick.
Alma enters, 'Jimmy I've got John Charles on for you from Italy.'
Good old John. A friendly voice in this goddamn wilderness.
The phone rings and I answer.
'John, how are you old pal, thank you for ringing.'
'Jimmy I'm so sorry. When I heard my heart broke. How are things?'
'We're still fighting John. We need players like a flower needs rain. I think you know what I'm going to ask son?'
'Jimmy believe me I've already tried but Juve won't let me go.'
I close my eyes. My heart sinks.
'I'm with you in spirit my friend. You know I'd give anything to be in Manchester helping you out.'
'I appreciate your kindness John.'
'You keep the fires burning Jimmy. Those boys of yours will be in heaven now and they'll be saying the same thing. 'Play hard, but play fair, but most all you win. You win! Pob lwc fy ffrind. God bless Jimmy.'
'You take care also John. Pob lwc fy ffrind.'
The line goes dead.

  The grand old Norbreck hotel sits facing the Irish Sea. It's Manchester United's second home and the staff are like family to us now. Many times previous Matt brought the team here before huge games to escape the close intimacy of Manchester and relax along the wide sweeping beaches and enjoy the fresh Blackpool air. Our home city is broken with grief and has responded by throwing a protective if strangling arm around us. So overbearing that we can't breathe. I needed to get them away from the genuine do-gooders but also the curious and the morbid.

'What was Eddie like?'

'What was Roger like?'

'What was Tommy like?'

Bastard questions that helped no one. And then the national press, those jackals feeding on the bones of my lads and the grieving families. Parked on doorsteps, offering money to fathers, mothers, brothers, sisters and girlfriends for their stories. Shaming their own killed in that plane. A bloody disgrace they are.

But here on these sand dunes on a cold and bitter February morning away from prying eyes the boys can focus totally on what I'm telling them. It appears nobody else is coming in so we are going to stand or fall by our own and in many ways that suits me fine. The players are on a long-distance jog along the shoreline. The sea is so far off as to be almost invisible and can just about be made out. The boys are stick figures. Jack is stood alongside me as we watch them. Both almost hypnotised by the sight.

'Jack old pal do you know how many times in the last couple of days I've scribbled down a team for the Sheffield Wednesday game then ripped it up and started again?'

He smiles, 'I've seen your waste paper bin in the office. Hundreds.'

'I have five definite starters. Gregg, Foulkes, Taylor and two youngsters Alex Dawson and Mark Pearson. Both are tough beyond their years and made of the right sort. They'll be up for the fight ahead but that's me still six short. Others like Colin Webster, Ian Greaves, Freddie Goodwin, and Ron Cope have all played for the first team before, but they weren't good enough to hold down a place then. So why now? There's another kid, a young Manchester boy Shay Brennan. Cocky, confident, quick with a quip but not in a manner you'd find grating. There's something there Jack, I've got a good eye on him.'

'Shay is a good kid but what you say about the other lads? You can't think like that anymore Jimmy. They'd get in most first division teams. What's gone has gone and this…This place, this world we inhabit is where we are now. They are going to have to play and you're going to have to inspire them to perform in the red shirts of giant's past old pal.'

This is why I wanted my friend Jack back in the fold. Wise words from a decent man.

'How are you finding Harry and Bill Jimmy?'

'Both are quiet as a night sky Jack. Whatever they saw and heard will stay with them forever. We just have to keep an eye on them around the hotel. It's an awful thing to say but try not to let them have too much time to think. God knows there'll be enough of that in the years to come. But myself and you, for the time being we can try and nurse them through this with football, football and bloody football.'

'And they say it's just a game Jimmy?'

'Ah Jack, this thing of ours is a most wonderful and beautiful thing old pal. But it is just a game…. At least since last Thursday.'

Its night time and I'm sat in the hotel bar nursing a large whisky with hot water and sugar. I've just come off a phone call to Professor Maurer in Munich. For the first time in a while I feel the slightest modicum of hope. The news regarding Matt and Duncan is more positive as to

be bordering on the miraculous. Matt continues to improve dramatically and has been deemed well enough to even have a glass of beer, whilst Duncan?
I best let Professor Maurer take up the story.
'The struggle was nearly over and there was only one last thing that could save him now Jimmy. An artificial kidney to help filter the nitrogen out of his bloodstream. Unfortunately, the closest one to us in Munich was over 210 miles away. So, we arranged an urgent collection and could only pray Duncan could hold on until it arrived. For he is a fighter Jimmy. His will to live is incredible. Finally, it was brought into the hospital and rushed to his side. We attached and left it running and hoped the artificial kidney took the strain off his badly damaged ones. This allowing the blood to return to its normal circulating system.
So, we waited.
Twenty-four hours passed Jimmy and then with my nurses making the sign of the cross Duncan opened his eyes. 'Where am I?' he said. It was a miracle because his nitrogen intake was 500 when 45 was the figure for normal people. He should have been dead. The machine had worked and there were cheers and many tears amongst my staff. For your Duncan is also our Duncan now. At this moment we are pleased with his progress and have even allowed him a little milk. Alongside his girlfriend Molly, Duncan's mother and father are here now and constantly by the bedside. They are wonderful people and they too are now also our family. Goodnight Jimmy, I hope this good news greets you well. Duncan is far from safe but continues to battle on with the heart of a lion. I pray this miracle continues.'

Unexpectedly another whisky arrives in front of me that I hadn't ordered. A large one. The waiter points to a man at the bar. A smart suit, sleeked black hair, untrustworthy eyes. A slender, dapper moustache, mid-thirties and smiling over towards me. Being honest he resembles a spiv. A travelling salesman probably just wanting somebody to share a drink with. He's raising his glass in a toast. What the hell, I'm in a rare good mood after the news from Munich. I acknowledge by raising my own and then he starts to walk over.

'Ah the great Jimmy Murphy!'

Immediately he's getting under my skin. What have I done? The man sits himself down next to me.

'Thanks for the drink son?'

'A man like yourself Jimmy. You should be drinking champagne in the finest hotels in the country. Not slumming it in a miserable shithole like this.'

Alarm bells are already ringing in my head, 'Can you mind your language lad. The people who work here are friends of mine.'

He laughs, 'Oh Jimmy, Jimmy, you're a fine and wonderful fellow. Heaven will be such a better place when you arrive at those pearly gates old chum. But you're not there yet. Whilst still here on earth with us mere mortals why not enjoy life and embrace those who wish to make your life better?'

I'm losing patience with this fool, 'Just who are you?' The man motions to the waiter for two more whiskies. He looks back at me and smiles, 'Let's just say I represent very important and rich people whom would value your services and are prepared to pay well for them. Shall we say £5000 a year plus bonuses? Not forgetting a considerable signing on fee. A thank you sum of £2000?'

Keeping a poker face I nod as if in consideration.

The waiter arrives with our new drinks. I take a sip, 'And your team is?'

'Myself Jimmy, I'm a South London boy. Charlton Athletic for my sins but those who sent me north and what a damned miserable world it is here, they are over the river. North London.'

'So, let me get this straight,' I say. 'You're offering me a job?'

'I certainly am Jimmy and you would be mad to turn it down.'

'My lads not yet cold in their grave and you're offering me a job?'

'Jimmy look, what do you owe Manchester United? I know your wages and I know what Busby was earning. If they cared so much about you then they'd have paid you your true worth. Which is what the people I represent are willing to do. Get out of this Jimmy, this depressing fucking madness. United are finished, it's over. You have to look after yourself and your family. They are what matters now. You give me the nod tonight and I guarantee you money will be in your bank account tomorrow and come weekend, all this. This fucking about in a northern town that had one thing going for it. Lads who could kick a ball about? Well time to play with the big boys. Come south, the big smoke. Where men like you and their talents are truly rewarded. Don't let yourself get caught up in this nonsense that United are still alive, they're not, I've seen the bank statements Jimmy. It's over. It's all fucking over. Your dreams and hopes died at the end of that runway. Follow the money

Jimmy get real, this is what football is really about. Get your nose in the trough man before it's too late and your star has fallen too far through being tainted with all this United will go on claptrap. So, what do you say? Do I make the phone call to tell my bosses they have a new manager?'

In a way I needed this utter low-life bastard in here tonight to help cleanse the demons that lie dormant in my soul. This man sat next to me looking like the cat that's got the cream. Well…. here we go.

I smile. I take a large drink and slam down the glass. He jumps a little, 'I hear what you say. You know something boy, I always thought if I sat here long enough then someone like you would approach me with this kind of offer. Make no mistake I am a man of the world. I've seen stuff that would break lesser men but I am not of your kind, I am not even of your world. And I always knew that when your type turned up I'd know exactly what I was going to say...

Get the fucking hell out of my sight.'

'Jimmy look…'

'Don't you Jimmy me, you fucking parasite. Did you and the pond life you speak for seriously believe I'd walk away from United when we are on our knees? This is my club, my family and where I come from you just don't do that. I'm from the Rhondda son. Traits like loyalty matter to us, we wear it as a badge of pride. Whereas you and those like you consider it a goddamn ailment. So, you go running back south, to your big smoke and your rich overlords and you tell them thanks, but no thanks. Am I clear?'

My face only inches from his. He tries not to flinch but fails. The man puts down his glass, straightens back his hair and tries hard to smile whilst fixing his tie.
'Clear as day Jimmy, I'll be seeing you.'
He goes to walk off.
'Not if I see you first,' I shout after him.
The man turns and has a quizzical look on his face, 'Good old Jimmy walking bravely into oblivion. You can't win this one. But I wish you luck anyway.'
With that he leaves the bar…

'Who was that Jimmy?' I look up and its Harry Gregg and Bill Foulkes staring down at me, 'Nobody important lads,' I smile, 'Just a travelling salesman trying to sell me a pile of crap.'
'Jimmy, me and Bill have had an idea?'
'Bloody hell Harry, wonders never cease son. Must be the sea air!'
They both laugh, 'All the lads are in the hotel lounge waiting for you Jimmy,' adds Bill.
'The thing is' continues Harry, 'They've never heard you play the piano. We thought for some of the young ones it might, well you know, give them a taste of what's gone before.'
'Let them know that the band is playing on,' smiles Bill. 'Especially the piano man.'
'Boys I really appreciate this but I'm not sure I'm up to it.'
'Oh, Jimmy come on' says Harry, 'Show the lads there is so much more to the boss than what they see on the training pitch. You told us all many times of how you first started playing the church organ at fourteen in your home town of Ton Pentre. And that started your love affair with the piano. Come on old pal let them see

you're not all just growling and sandpaper voice. Play hard, play fair but win! Show them also the magic in your Welsh soul. The poet in the Celtic warrior. What do you say?'

'Harry Gregg!' I laugh, 'Have you swallowed a poetry book? Very well but you lot may well regret this. I've not done much tinkering lately.'

I stand to walk with them into the hotel lounge.

An old fashioned but impressive room bedecked with comfy chairs and sofas, a large blazing fire, a wall of books and huge glass windows overlooking what is now a black beach and invisible sea. All my lads stand facing. A smiling Jack appears from amongst them and points to a piano sat quietly in a corner minding its own business.

'Yours's I believe Jimmy.'

I head over and sit myself down. I lift up the lid. All the lads gather round. Nobody says a word. Other guests in the hotel I notice have also taken an interest. I start to play Chopin-Prelude 4 and swiftly lose myself in the music. I'm far away, lost in the clouds with my boys and then I'm back. I glimpse up from the piano and swear amid the living, Bert, Tom, Roger, Billy, Geoff, Eddie, David, Tommy and Mark are stood smiling watching me. I put my head back down then look again and they are gone. But I swear I saw them.... I saw them.

Later that evening I'm heading upstairs to my bedroom when I catch the drift of a conversation taking place on the landing in front of me. A man and a woman, 'Did you see that in the lounge earlier? It was so strange. All those young men with tears in their eyes listening to that older gentleman on the piano. Who was it? Do you know?'

'That was Manchester United my dear,' replied the man, 'Or what's left of them.'

Act Four
STATE OF GRACE

Wednesday 19th February 1958. Manchester United v Sheffield Wednesday. FA Cup Fifth Round. It's the day of the match and we've travelled back to Manchester and are staying at the Midland hotel. Its mid-afternoon and the tension is visibly rising for tonight's game. In my room I'm still wrestling with the team line up. Gregg, Foulkes, Greaves, Goodwin, Cope, Webster, Taylor, Dawson, Pearson and Brennan I've ten players after just informing young Shay Brennan he's in. The thinking being why worry the boy beforehand? Now he just has to concentrate on his performance. But god help me I have one position left to fill.

And it's Duncan's.

I have one in mind to help us through this bleak, dark tunnel. Not necessarily for the future but needs must. In last season's FA Cup final, Aston Villa's tough tackling-but talented wing half, twenty-eight-year-old Stan Crowther impressed and supremely irritated myself and Matt on the bench. His skill on the ball added to the way he cajoled the Villa players and got stuck into ours left a lasting impression. Not always fairly I may add but Crowther was determined to give everything to make sure the Villains won that cup.

I've phoned Aston Villa's manager Eric Houghton with an offer and he's going to put it to the player. Eric is a good lad and sympathetic to our cause.

'Sometimes it's better to do what's right Jimmy. You lads deserve help. I'll speak to Stan and sort it.'

  The latest from Munich-Whilst Matt continues to recover to the extent the Daily Express will tonight do a phone line commentary of the match to him, Duncan's

position remains frightfully precarious. Professor Maurer's voice on the phone failing to hide his concern that it appeared a terrifying and heart-breaking endgame was approaching.
'He's fighting Jimmy. Anybody else would be dead now but not your brave young fellow. Duncan developed severe haemorrhages that reduced the ability of his blood to clot. Immediately I arranged for police cars to race round to Munich blood donors. These were brought to the Rechts Der Isar and after several transfusions the bleeding was brought to a halt. But still Duncan remains dangerously ill. All my doctors have commented on his astonishing strong will to live. They cannot believe his fighting spirit and my nurse's queue to be by his bedside. Duncan is now conscious all the time but restless. He's confused but at times regains moments of clarity. I know the boy is scared despite the battle he rages. He shouts and screams and we try and calm him. I held his hand this morning and told him to try and stay quiet. To save his energy and not talk more than necessary…. Duncan looked at me and his word will live with me forever.'
'I understand chief.'
I could hear Professor Maurer's voice breaking….
'Anyway Jimmy, we are doing everything humanly possible to save your boy.
His Mother, Father and girlfriend Molly are constantly at his bedside. They leave only to sleep or to go and pray in our hospital chapel. I am not a man who believes in miracles for I've seen too much but I shall pray that one happens with Duncan. Goodbye my friend.'
Professor Maurer spoke of miracles. Do I believe in miracles?
You must be fucking joking...

There's a knock at my door. It's Jack.
'I've got some bloody good news Jimmy.' He's smiling wide, 'Jack old pal why are you grinning like a maniac?'
'I've just had Eric Houghton on the phone. He's on his way from the Midlands with Stan Crowther. He mentioned to Crowther that we were interested in him. He wasn't too keen to be honest Jimmy, didn't want to leave Villa, but Eric has got him to come to Old Trafford to watch the match later. And get this.
On the way up Eric had told him that he should help us out. Crowther moaned he hadn't brought any kit with him but guess what Eric said?'
'Don't worry; I've got your boots in my bag!'
He's bringing him straight here. You need to dazzle him with the old Murphy magic and then we have our eleven.'
'Blimey Jack, even if I can talk him round it's going to be tight. Plus, he's already played for Villa in the competition this season, so he'll be cup tied see.'
Jack smiles, 'Not necessarily.'
'Jack, you old dog what are you up to!?'
'I've let all the press boys know Stan is coming and the Football League has waived that particular ruling.'
'And have they?'
'Hardaker won't have any choice will he? For one day only the world is with us Jimmy. One day only.'

I'm down in the hotel foyer signing autographs for supporters when I get a tap on the shoulder. I turn around and its young Bobby Charlton, 'Alright Jimmy.'
He looks tired with eyes that have seen far too much for one so young, 'Hello Bobby son. Welcome home.'
'I know I'm not ready to play Jimmy but I want to be there for you and the boys tonight. Give me a little while

eh and I can help, I promise. I want to help so much. I want to get back on that pitch and put on a red shirt again.'

'Thanks son.' I put my arms around his shoulders, 'Tonight, you sit next to me Bobby and if you see me shaking, you grab my arm but don't let any bugger see! Agreed?'

Bobby smiles, my guess for the first time since before the crash. We shake hands, 'Agreed Jimmy. We're not going anywhere are we?'

'No chance lad. So long as there are stars in the night sky they're not getting rid of us. Now run along and go say hello to the other boys. They'll be over the moon to see you.'

I'm sat twiddling my fingers in a private hotel suite waiting for the arrival of Eric Houghton and Stan Crowther. Time is moving on. The boys have already set off for Old Trafford with Jack and I've a taxi on standby. The phone rings and I answer.

'Hello Jimmy Murphy.'

'Mr Murphy, this is hotel reception. We have Mr Olive on the line for you. Please hold.'

'Jimmy its Les, we have a problem.'

'Hello Les what's up?'

'It's the match programme. We need to go to print now or it'll be too late. Have you got the team line-up for me? Otherwise we're going to have to leave ours blank.'

'No, not yet. I'm still waiting on Crowther and then there's still no guarantee.'

'Very well, we'll go blank. Let the supporters fill it in themselves. We can always announce it over the tannoy beforehand. Good luck with Crowther Jimmy. Reel him in!'

'God bless Les. See you in a short while old pal.'
A knock at the door and it's the hotel Maître De with Eric and Crowther behind him.
The Maître de smiles, 'Jimmy your guests have arrived. I'll arrange for a pot of tea and some sandwiches to be brought in.' He leaves and I stand to shake both Eric and a surly looking and unsmiling Crowther's hands.
'Eric, Stan, thanks so much for coming, sit down lads please.'
I'm sat opposite, 'Stan I believe you'd like to help us out old pal?'
Crowther looks like he'd rather be anywhere else in the world, 'With time to think I'm not too sure Jimmy?'
'What's bothering you son?'
'Huge shoes Jimmy.'
'What do you mean?'
'Huge shoes. Duncan. Duncan Edwards. I'm going to have 60,000 supporters in my ear constantly comparing. They'll slaughter me. I can't match up to that boy. Nobody can. I wish you all the luck in the world Mr Murphy but I don't think I…'
'Listen Stan lad, you have to believe me. When you put on that red shirt those same supporters will cheer you to the bloody heavens. They'll appreciate you coming to us in our darkest hour and you'll be forever in their hearts. My other boys who'll be taking the pitch tonight. Some hardly out of school, they'll be wrestling with these same thoughts as we speak. How do you replace players like Byrne, Whelan, Pegg, Colman and Taylor? The answer is you can't. But what you can do is find men whom you believe may well not be blessed with the same talent but can match them in heart. That's what you showed last May at Wembley against United Stan. And that's why I

want you with us tonight. Raging against the dying of the light. Because with or without you son we are going to come through this darkest of nights. Even if I have to put on a red shirt myself to make up the numbers.'
A knock on the door and a waiter appears with the pot of tea and sandwiches.
'Even If I wanted to sign Mr Murphy. I've already played in the cup. I wouldn't be available for tonight.'
'Oh, you let me worry about that son.'
I pour tea for three and offer the sandwiches.
'So, what do you say Stan, time is short. I need an answer son? 'Crowther offers me his hand, 'You can count me in Jimmy.'
'Well thank goodness that's all sorted then,' laughs Eric. 'It's cost you the grand total of £32,000 and a cheese sandwich Jimmy!'
'I'm signing for you Jimmy,' says Crowther, 'I'm signing for you because I don't want you as an enemy for life!'
That makes me smile, 'You're wise as well as a bloody good footballer Stan. You'll do for me. Come on eat your sandwich and drink your tea, we've got a taxi to catch.'
  I stand. Now it's game on. I immediately ring Les. 'I've got our eleventh player. Ring Alan Hardaker at the Football League and tell him Stan Crowther is playing for Manchester United tonight. If he doesn't want the world to know what a complete and utter bastard he really is then he'll waive the rule of Crowther being cup-tied. Also, the press boys already have the story. And enjoy listening to him squirm Les. We're coming over now.'
'See you soon Jimmy. The scenes here are incredible old friend. We had to lock the gates at five-thirty. We've got

60,000 inside and easily the same amount locked out. The police are saying emotions are close to boiling over on the forecourt and ticket spivs are getting a right good kicking. It seems people are viewing their actions as dancing on our dead. Best get here soon Jimmy otherwise you won't get in the bloody ground! But prepare yourself, the atmosphere here is like nothing I've ever felt or witnessed. This isn't a football crowd gathering on these terraces tonight, it feels more like a congregation at a wake. Except they intend to wake the dead with their noise.'

I'm in the taxi with Eric Houghton and Stan Crowther and we're five minutes from the ground. Its approaching ten to seven, forty minutes from kick off and my stomach is starting to churn at what I'm going to say to the lads before they go out to play. With events so hectic I've not given it a thought but now: my god the reality is kicking in. I miss my friends so much. Tom and Bert. It's a lonely world without them. It's a different world. I've listened to people say that everybody lost something at the end of that Munich runway. Maybe so but we had the heart and soul of our football club ripped from us. It lay in the falling Munich snow, on puddles of blood and water. Amidst shattered wreckage and a silent ripped off fuselage that forever more will be the symbol of Manchester United and Munich. Munich.

……….. Once upon a time in Munich.

That we've garnered enough strength and indeed bodies to carry the torch onwards is being deemed in some quarters as a miracle. But not by me. Too much blood you see. Too much heartache has passed and I fear still to pass that the mere relevance of being able to put on a football match is hardly worthy of miraculous status.

Despite the millions of words written and spoken that mentions it the crass phrase 'Murphy's Miracle' makes me sick.
I was asked to keep the flag flying by Matt and this I've done. I've kept my promise and will continue to do so until my dying breath. Our football club founded in Newton Heath in 1878 and all but wiped out on a German runway eighty-years on has reached the lowest point in its history. Our future uncertain but spirit unyielding, it is now a question of tossing a coin and calling either salvation or disaster. If we lose tonight then even I may struggle to find the strength to go on. But a miracle? I think not.
Miracles are performed by those touched by god and me and thee? Well we are continuing to have problems…I'm nowhere yet ready to forgive this wretched massacre of all I've known and loved.

With the help of a police escort the taxi drops us close enough to avoid the frenzied crowds and race inside the ground. I noticed on entering our flag still at half-mast as a mark of respect for the victims and then it hit me.
This is no football match…It's a funeral without a burial service.
At ten past seven I enter the dressing room and the boys are already sat in their kit waiting. Crowther is stood next to me. All the faces stare across. For a moment I can't speak. I try but the words won't come out. I see a room full of red shirts but I don't see my boys.
'Lads,' Jack comes across and puts his arm around Crowther, 'I'm sure you all know Stan Crowther from Aston Villa. Stan is part of the family now. Make him feel at home.' He leads Stan over to his kit peg, 'Get

changed son. Jimmy will say a few words before we go out.'

Outside the roar of 'U.N.I.T.E.D' is blasting through the walls. I'm stood in the corner smoking. Jack joins me, 'You okay old pal?'

'I can't do it Jack. I can't speak to them.' He passes me a copy of the match programme. On its front cover our chairman Harold Hardman has penned some words.

'Although we mourn our dead and grieve for our wounded, we believe that great days are not done for us. The sympathy and encouragement of the football world and particularly of our supporters will justify and inspire us. The road back may be long and hard but with the memory of those who died at Munich, of their stirring achievements and wonderful sportsmanship ever with us. Manchester United will rise again.'

Then I looked inside and noticed the centre pages where against the Sheffield Wednesdays players was our eleven blank spaces. Jack points to them, 'You need to fill them in with your words for our boys tonight and those gone old pal. We've never needed you more.' My friend has tears in his eyes.

I nod and he smiles, 'Alright lads listen up,' shouts Jack to the players, 'The boss is going to say a few words.' With my cigarette still in hand I walk across. I look at Bill and Harry. My god a penny for their thoughts? Twenty-six-year-old Ian Greaves in at left-back for Roger Byrne and his usual deputy Geoff Bent. Both dead. Twenty-year-old Freddie Goodwin is playing right-half instead of Eddie Colman. Dead. Twenty-four-year-old former amateur footballer Ronnie Cope at centre-half for Mark Jones. Dead. Twenty-one-year-old Colin Webster on the right-wing for Johnny Berry. Seriously injured but

alive in the Munich hospital. At centre-forward our young battering ram Alex Dawson will lead the attack in place of Tommy Taylor. Dead. Seventeen-year-old Mark Pearson in for David Pegg. Dead.
Ernie Taylor for Liam 'Billy' Whelan. Dead. Stan Crowther in for the still gravely ill Duncan Edwards. And my biggest gamble-Shay Brennan. I can only hope this young local kid is as cool and laid back on the pitch tonight amid what will be a torrid atmosphere, as he is off it.
…Well Shay's and every eye is now upon me. I stamp out my cigarette and with hands in pockets pray the words will follow, I've only got a couple of minutes boys so I'll keep it simple. The ball is round to go around. You pass to your mate and he will pass to you. Everybody attacks, everybody defends. Now you play hard for yourselves…for the players who are dead and for the great name of this club you represent. Manchester United…' With tears falling down my face I can't carry on and have to step away. Jack takes over. He claps his hands, 'Right let's go lads!... Let's do this!'
I watch them leave until the dressing room is empty except for me and young Bobby Charlton. He comes across and is smiling. Bobby puts an arm around my shoulders, 'Come on let's go Jimmy. I noticed you never said play fair in your speech?'
'Not tonight Bobby lad, tonight we just win!'
  As we're heading up the tunnel a dreadful silence around the stadium is greeting the names of the Manchester United team over the loudspeaker. Broken only by sobbing or the screaming out loud of a dead player's name. In a voice shaking with emotion the tannoy announcer carries out his painful task. Then, to a

tumultuous roar, Captain Bill Foulkes and Harry Gregg appear followed by red shirted strangers in the Mancunian night. Old Trafford erupts with a monumental concoction of hysteria and excitement. The ground shakes! A tidal wave of emotion explodes, one that for thirteen days has remained dormant, just like the question.
Why? Just why the fucking hell why?
United are back but around me I witness scenes of utter heartbreak on people's faces. There's a cheer for every tear. Grown men weeping, only now when truly back amongst my adopted people can I feel their pain. It's still raw and is igniting passions beyond the heavens and burning the soul. Myself and Bobby take our seats. Supporters are trying to desperately shake hands but my mindset is only on the pitch. Beneath the glary haze of the floodlights I watch these eleven red shirts wave to the crowd before breaking to warm up. Deep inside me I have to admit a silent voice is asking them, 'Who are you?'
Around me people shout, 'We owe you everything Jimmy.'
'We love you Jimmy.'
'We wouldn't be here without you Jimmy.'
'God bless you Jimmy.'
Oh, please just leave me alone. Please…
To honour the dead, I notice many supporters have come dressed in black overcoats whilst adorning red/white scarves around their wrist or necks. The voices that scream out are almost primeval in their grief-stricken state.
I watch on as the referee Mr Bond, from London calls the two captains together. Bill and Wednesday's Albert

Quixall. The atmosphere that has engulfed the ground is unnerving and unnatural. A communal grief. Earlier in the season Sheffield Wednesday came to Old Trafford and gave us an almighty fright before going down in a close fought match 2-1. On paper all things considered our visitors from across the Pennines have been handed a great opportunity to earn a place in the FA cup Quarter-Finals. Unfortunately for Sheffield Wednesday as I look around they are up against not merely eleven players in red but a red army of 60,000 in no mood for nothing but a happy ending. At least to this night.

As I light up yet another cigarette the match begins and I feel Bobby stiffen up beside me. In a furious opening we are tearing into the Yorkshiremen.

The visitors are a fine side, tough but fair and in no way deserving the intolerable pressure being placed upon them as Mancunians let loose all the sadness, anger and despair of the recent two weeks upon their heads. A simple, cruel twist of fate has left them being the bad guys against those whom have simply refused to go without a fight gently into the murderous, Munich night. Sheffield Wednesday have walked into a cacophony of breaking hearts that is both deafening and unyielding and not willing to accept defeat. With Stan Crowther crashing into tackles and Ernie Taylor our new playmaker, constantly encouraging the youngsters around him we play as if lives are at stake, and in a cruel manner out of their skins. And into those whom have died. I look at my watch, fifteen minutes have passed almost unnoticed as Taylor with a fierce drive from twenty yards smashes a shot against the Wednesday post. The noise from the crowd greeting this near miss is simply unworldly. What does our club have to do to get a break, have we not

suffered enough? Still my lads press forward, on twenty-seven minutes we earn a corner. Deputising as a left-winger, Shay Brennan takes a corner that is fumbled by the keeper Ryalls on his goal line and we're in front!...
I punch the air and hug Bobby-Around me bedlam! A noise like a jet plane flying low over the ground as thousands weep tears of joy. Well done Shay son. Good lad, well done!

The second half wears on and still we lead. It's crystal clear to me and probably blatantly obvious to neutrals that the Sheffield players are not up to spoiling what is in all essence a cruel contest. For who would ever wish to cause upset at a wake? Throughout our football has been full of fire and passion and heart. They've done me and so much more importantly Manchester United proud by never stopping running. Ernie and Stan have been immense. Both have shown they are of huge character and we have chosen well. Two men thrown into this hellish Mancunian furnace of wrecked emotions and broken dreams. Where it's not just about the ball, the game and the result. It's about salvation. Whatever happens in this ground in the future, nothing I'm certain in generations to come and beyond then even, there'll never be such a night as this. And by god,
I hope with all my heart and soul there isn't….

Our football though forever thrilling with the boys trying to play to plan it's obvious we lack the quality of before. Our lack of understanding and class so clear at times, yet still they are defying all logic by playing so far above themselves. We are hammering away endlessly at the Sheffield Wednesday goal, shots are raining in but we need another, please god if you wish for me to reconsider our relationship then fucking do something!

There are twenty minutes remaining when Shay Brennan seizes onto a rebound from close-range to flash a shot past Ryalls. 2-0 and the world shakes on its Mancunian axis! I swear the chimneys that reach high into the black sky from Trafford Park over the grandstands are rocking also.

Five minutes remain and with Old Trafford watching on praying, screaming and hoping, Alex Dawson, a son of a Grimsby trawlerman, caps an unforgettable night of drama as he crashes a third low and hard into a besieged Ryall's net to confirm our place in the next round.

It's over…the full-time whistle. I rush down to the touchline. I'm being patted on the back all the way down.

'Fantastic Jimmy.'

'Bloody brilliant job Jimmy.'

For ninety minutes just the searing pain of Munich slightly easing only to surface instantly once more in the cold light of the last whistle. At the finish most of my youngsters are in tears with the overwhelming emotion of the evening taking a heavy toll.

Many are on their knees.

Once back in the dressing room, I call for quiet, 'After watching that performance I'm so proud of every single one of you. And I'm certain the boss and the boys over in Munich listening to that on the radio will be too. Not forgetting those we've lost, none will be prouder than those lads because that was a credit to their memory. That out there tonight was Manchester United and we, they and those supporters out there could not ask for anymore. It goes on boys. United are going on!'

I finish. Both Harry Gregg and Bill Foulkes are now sat together quietly in the corner. No doubt remembering dead friends. Their hearts and minds still languishing amid the snow and ice of that far away German runway. I think to head over but then change my mind. Best to leave alone. The lads have dealt with their demons in such an admirable way, but it is still so raw. There are no words from me now that could help what they're feeling. Young Bobby appears and shakes my hand, 'We had to win that Jimmy otherwise we'd all have died from a broken heart.' For a second Bobby's words make me dizzy. I compose myself. How true, how so very true… A Pathè news crew arrive unannounced armed with a bottle of bubbly to present to the players showing them enjoying a great victory. Though as they film there are few smiles to be seen, 'Go easy lads' I say to them, 'This isn't a celebration.' Nevertheless, my rag-tag team of crash survivors, youth players, reserves and new blood have combined to ensure that Harold Hardman's evocative words 'Manchester United will rise again' have been given real flesh and bone.

Most importantly we've proved that United are not willing to die anytime soon. Priceless breathing space has been earned tonight and the veiled dark curtains of despair that have lay drawn across this city are opened ever so slightly to reveal the merest chink of light. A state of grace you could say and now we shall see what the future holds.

It's Friday morning just two days on from the Sheffield Wednesday match. I'm in the office at Old Trafford and have just come off the phone to a distraught Professor Maurer. At this moment as the news breaks it will be difficult for those of Manchester United persuasion and countless more who loved the boy to breathe.

Duncan has gone.

He took his final breath shortly after midnight on the 21st February 1958. Though every soul we've lost at Munich is a spear through the heart, now, the loss of Dunc will be felt most profusely. More so because his injuries it was claimed would have felled lesser mortals. Not our Duncan though who fought on and on. To battle against all overwhelming odds to amaze and astonish the German doctors and nurses at the Rechts Der Isar hospital in Munich. They too whom have fought with equal grim determination to save him. Professor Maurer told me that when ultimately Duncan lost his fight for life, their tears fell equally as long and hard as those that will now be shed here. His Mother and Father and Molly despondent with grief.

In time as the years go by Duncan's legend will surely grow. That Duncan Edwards was actually seven-foot-tall, spat thunder and unleashed lightning bolts from both feet. But others, people like me who witnessed him play will tell you that was utter nonsense. We shall tell you the truth.

Duncan was better than that.

PROLOGUE:

ABIDE WITH ME: PART 11:

Matt walks into the Wembley dressing room. I'm behind him. All the players are sat in silence. I move to stand alongside, 'Alright lads the boss is going to say a few words now.' I step back. Matt looks around at the mostly unfamiliar faces. Harry smiles and nods towards him. So, does Bill and Dennis Viollet, now also back in the team. But the others? They stare at Matt like he's a stranger. Their eyes unsure going from myself to him.

'I can't do this Jimmy.'

Matt turns on his crutches and heads back past me to leave the room. Tears falling down his cheeks. Too raw and much too soon.
He's still on that runway.
I head out after him. We're near the top of the tunnel. He's wiping his eyes clear, 'I'm sorry Jimmy. I tried but could only see the boys we lost staring back.'
I notice the band are warming up and nearly ready for Abide with Me.
The words to this prayer so apt for myself and Matt here now. I grab his arm and gently guide him right to the edge of the tunnel so we have a bird's eye view.
'Come on Matt' I say, 'Let's listen to this, they're playing our song.'
And together we stand as the band starts to play.
Suddenly, somebody else comes to mind. Another old pal. I say to our lord, 'Give my friend here the strength to carry on and if you do?
Well then me and you are good again.'

ABIDE WITH ME

Abide with me; fast falls the even tide;
The darkness deepens; Lord, with me abide;
When other helpers fail and comforts flee,
Help of the helpless, oh, abide with me.

Swift to its close ebbs out life's little day;
Earth's joys grow dim, its glories pass away;
Change and decay in all around I see—
O Thou who changes not, abide with me.

I need Thy presence every passing hour;
What but Thy grace can foil the tempter's pow'r?
Who, like Thyself, my guide and stay can be?
Through cloud and sunshine, Lord, abide with me.

I fear no foe, with Thee at hand to bless;
Ills have no weight, and tears no bitterness;
Where is death's sting? Where, grave, thy victory?
I triumph still, if Thou abide with me.

Hold Thou Thy cross before my closing eyes;
Shine through the gloom and point me to the skies;
heav'n's morning breaks, and earth's vain shadows flee;
In life, in death, O Lord, abide with me.

THE END

C10
CHAMPIONS OF HONOUR

It was a heartbroken Real Madrid treasurer Don Raimondo Saporta who broke the news of the Munich air crash to Alfredo Di Stefano. On hearing Saporta telephoned the player at his home. A call which the player would later recall as amongst the 'Saddest moments of his life.' As news filtered through to Madrid, the extent of the disaster shocked Santiago Bernabéu. He spoke solemnly of this great tragedy and of his prayers for the dead and the survivors. None more than so than his great friend Matt Busby, who by God's grace had survived the crash but now hung on for dear life in a Munich hospital. Twice to be given the last rites...

Of the eleven Manchester United players who had lined up against the Madrileños in the two-legged semi-final, five died instantly; Roger Byrne, David Pegg, Eddie Colman, Tommy Taylor and Liam Whelan while Duncan Edwards fought on valiantly but lost his battle a few weeks later. Edwards' death touched Alfredo Di Stefano immensely and he told of the 'Magnificent impression' Duncan Edwards had made on him during the second-leg in Manchester. 'Such will to win and power in one so young. None deserved more the fullness of a great career.' What truly moved Di Stefano was being told how, in his last ailing days, Edwards had called out for his gold watch presented to him the previous season by Santiago Bernabéu following the semi-final in Madrid. It was a gift cherished by Edwards and after a swift investigation, a taxi was sent to the crash site, where astonishingly it still lay amongst the debris, and was returned to its rightful owner. Placed into his hand the watch for a short period appeared to have a revitalising

effect on the player, sadly such was the extent of Edward's internal injuries that he passed away in the early hours of Friday 21st February 1958. His solid gold watch nearby calling time on a footballing colossus respected and feared by the Madrileños.
'Los chicos' the Busby Babes were all but gone.

   In an act of wonderful generosity, the three times European champions offered to hand the grieving Mancunians the European cup for that season but whilst stricken in despair United politely refused, thanking in turn the Spaniards for their deep friendship. For this trophy had suddenly become so much more for all concerned with Manchester United and had to be one fought for and won. Too much blood had already been spilt, too many hearts had been broken to accept such an offer.
There was also much talk of Bernabéu loaning United the services of Di Stefano and Puskas for a season with the Madrid club paying half their exorbitant wages. Whilst it was claimed the player was willing, again the Old Trafford club baulked. Whether through pride or rumours that the petty pen pushers and insular attitudes of the Football League would refuse point blank the notion of a foreigner taking the place of a British player, it was hard to tell.
Perhaps more disturbing was the League's shabby at best decision to ban United from competing in the 1958-59 European cup competition, after being invited by UEFA as a grateful thank you for their "Service to Football." United gratefully accepted and found themselves drawn against Swiss champions Young Boys of Berne, only then to be informed that their participation had been

denied by the English hierarchy because they were not League champions. A spiteful payback by Football League chairman Alan Hardaker for Matt Busby going against his initial wishes to originally compete in the tournament.

But despite such ill feelings directed towards them on home soil, in Madrid at least hearts went out to the Mancunians in their darkest hour. In an act of extraordinary support, they came up with a special memorial pennant. It was conferred by Real Madrid to commemorate the destroyed English team and was entitled
"Champions of Honour."

 On it read the names of the dead players of which all considerable proceeds were sent to Old Trafford. A further show of Real's nobility of spirit came that same summer when they contacted Manchester United offering free holidays in Spain to Munich survivors with all expenses paid. Finally, and most importantly, a series of matches between the two clubs were swiftly arranged. Santiago Bernabéu not only agreeing to Matt Busby's plea for help but waived the normal £12,000 appearance fee charged by the Spaniards. A meeting took place in Madrid between Busby and Bernabéu where the United manager asked if they would consider accepting reduced fees, due to the cataclysmic effect the crash had placed upon his club. A generous Bernabéu insisted that the cash strapped United should, 'Pay us what you can afford.' With the Mancunians out of Europe and severely weakened, Busby realised how vital it was they retained the experience of playing against the world's best. Therefore, both teams agreed to treat the games as serious affairs. All would prove to be occasions with goals galore, the vast majority being scored by the team in white.

After a remarkable 1958-59 season during which United defied all odds to finish in runners-up position, the Mancunians had begun the 1959-60 campaign in more manic fashion, lying in sixth position at the time of Real's visit. The previous Saturday they had been taken apart 4-0 at Preston North End whom, inspired by veteran Tom Finney, were unlucky not to reach double figures. United were terrible as the wheels came off a half decent start to the campaign in gruesome style. Whilst dazzling going forward, defensively they were atrocious.

Busby was desperate for reinforcements before a bad run morphed into a relegation battle. Fine defenders such as Blackpool's Jimmy Armfield, and Rangers Eric Caldow were targeted without success. He also bid for Burnley creative Northern Irish midfielder Jimmy McIlroy but a move was turned down by chairman Bob Lord with a warning to the Mancunians not to return. Lord had little sympathy for United after Munich and hardly appreciated them attempting to take his best player from Turf Moor. It was the second time Busby had gone for McIlroy, the first time just before the crash. He would not go back again.

These were worrying times, at this stage of their recovery, a season where United veered from the sublime to the ridiculous on a weekly basis was driving supporters to despair. Following United had never been for the faint hearted, and that particular period they were capable of anything.

A thrilling goal-laden 6-3 win at Stamford Bridge over Chelsea watched by 66,000 evoked the best of memories pre-Munich. As did a 6-0 home crushing of Leeds. Then the dark side, a new phenomenon; a humiliating 5-1 drubbing at Old Trafford by Spurs and a feeble 3-0 surrender in the Manchester derby in which City outfought their neighbours was hard to stomach. As the inconsistency stretched into October there were many worried brows on the Old Trafford terraces.

The expectation that the Munich survivors; Bobby Charlton, Harry Gregg, Bill Foulkes, Albert Scanlon and Dennis Viollet would carry the team were huge and perhaps unfair but all had shown incredible bravery. None more than Charlton, on whose slim shoulders United fans placed most faith and the pressure was therefore the greatest. Charlton was regarded as one who spanned the pre-and post-Munich era; he was a living and breathing epitaph for the fallen who evoked the spirit of the Babes. With him around the future remained palatable.

It was hoped that Real Madrid's arrival in Manchester would provide a welcoming change from the weekly pitfalls of First Division football. A friendly match with nothing at stake. Just take a deep breath, relax and enjoy the football of a Madrid team whom would simply go through the motions.

However, under orders to perform at full throttle and on £50 a man win bonus, Real Madrid came to Manchester and cut loose in terrifying manner. United received a dose of cruel reality as they were handed a footballing lesson, the 6-1 scoreline saw United get off lightly and did little justice to the imperious Madrileños that night as Busby's patched up team were vastly outclassed.

Even more formidable than the pre-Munich team, the Spaniards lit up Old Trafford with an irresistible concoction of European and South American artistry and guile. None more than the irascible Magyar genius Ferenc Puskás. Rescued from footballing exile by Bernabéu, Puskás' god-sent ability and personable character added immensely to Madrid's already perfect storm. Wise as he was talented, the Magyar played the role of loyal Lieutenant to Di Stefano to perfection, he preferred to waltz gloriously in the shade of the all-consuming shadow of the Blond Arrow.

Also arriving in Madrid to perform alongside the holy trio of Di Stefano, Gento and Puskás was that other huge summer signing, the deceptively languid but utterly brilliant Brazilian playmaker Didi. He was joined by fellow countryman Canario and the wickedly gifted Uruguayan defender Jose Santamaria who was a marvellous footballer blessed not just in his ability to play and begin Madrid attacks, but also in the finest tradition of Uruguayan stoppers, willing when necessary to commit atrocities in defence.

With an emotional but deafening 63,000 crowd roaring them on, United started brightly and Bobby Charlton twice went close with thunderous strikes that Real goalkeeper Dominquez did well to save. Then, on seven minutes, as if annoyed that Charlton possessed the cheek to attempt such acts, the visitors opened the scoring. A delightful through pass by the dazzling Didi to Puskás caused gasps of awe from the terraces. The Hungarian maestro waited for Harry Gregg to commit himself then slipped the ball beyond the big Irishmen into the net. It was all done with the ease of genius.

It was soon 2-0 when on twenty-five minutes Francisco Gento set up Puskás who once more looked up and flashed a ridiculous, swerving drive past a flailing Gregg into the net. It was bewitching football. On the half hour it was 3-0: Real were relentless; with what appeared effortless skill Didi supplied a dagger of a pass into the path of an electric-heeled Alfredo Di Stefano who, without slowing, took the ball in stride before beating a besieged Harry Gregg with ease. Yet the best was still to come when moments before the interval Di Stefano delivered a moment of wizardry that bamboozled the United defence and made many in Old Trafford believe they were witnessing something quite unworldly. Standing by a goalpost, he produced an outrageous back heel after trapping the ball with his heel before turning and flicking it past a befuddled Gregg.

At 4-0, Madrid left the pitch to huge applause from a home crowd that watched through disbelieving eyes their beauty and majesty. The breathtaking images of those gleaming white figures under the Old Trafford floodlights re-ignited memories of heroes lost. None more than Di Stefano whose magical piece of artistry for Real's fourth goal earned him a moving reception as he vacated the stage from an adoring, if still silently grieving audience.

United came out for the second half determined to save face; Albert Scanlon went close before Bobby Charlton sliced apart the Real Madrid defence allowing winger Warren Bradley to run through from the halfway line and score from a tight angle. Maybe consolation only but for Bradley, loaned to Manchester United by famed amateurs Bishop Auckland as they strove to regain their feet after Munich, it was a special moment.

Warren Bradley's bravura effort served only to irritate the Spaniards and Real swiftly moved back into top gear. The ball was passed with a tenderness and technique but kept from United's grasp like a child clutching his favourite toy. On sixty-three minutes a grateful Puskás accepted Didi's delightful pass before crossing for the unmarked Pepillo to make it 5-1 from close range. Pepillo had signed that same summer from Sevilla and was yet another Madrileño superstar in the making. As for Didi, this night under the hazy glare of the Old Trafford floodlights was arguably his finest hour during a short and turbulent career in Madrid.

Twelve minutes from time and with United being dangled, toyed and prodded Francisco Gento suddenly got bored and exploded past a bedraggled United defence before almost breaking the back of the net with a ferocious finish past a desolate Harry Gregg. Beaten six times and at fault for none, Gregg was thoroughly fed up and cut a disconsolate figure.

Come full time and Real Madrid gathered in the centre-circle to take the acclaim of an adoring Mancunian public. Even the United players stayed behind to applaud the Madrileños off the pitch. It had quite simply proved a mis-match. Dennis Viollet spoke to the Manchester Evening News afterwards, 'It seems an odd thing to say after losing 6-1 but I have to say I enjoyed that! They were special.'

Munich had decimated Manchester United and a long time would pass before they could resemble a team good enough to give the European champions a real challenge. After the match Matt Busby was brutally honest in his summing up: 'They have walloped us 6-1 and in doing so confirmed what I already know, that we have a long, long way to go to close the gap.'

The newspaper headlines next day extolled Real Madrid's bravura showing:

THE DAILY HERALD: **GREATEST SHOW ON EARTH!**

NEWS CHRONICLE: **SHOOTING SENORS SMACK IN SIX!**

DAILY MIRROR: **REAL PERFECTION!**

 Two days later a touch of Di Stefano and Puskás must have rubbed off on Manchester United as 41,000 returned to Old Trafford to witness the Red Devils thrash Leicester City 4-1. Charlton's opener on five minutes was followed by Viollet (2) and another from Quixall. The grim realities of this post-Munich, though ever present, were for once temporarily put aside for ninety minutes as United on an Old Trafford pitch still sprinkled with Madrileño gold dust sent supporters home smiling. That itself a small miracle in such trying times.

  Wednesday 11th November 1959: Six weeks on from the 6-1 massacre at Old Trafford, a return match was staged in Madrid with Manchester United and Matt Busby given the red-carpet treatment by Santiago Bernabéu from the moment they landed till the moment of their departure. A pleasant stay was tinged with real sadness at memories of events only two and a half years before when the Babes arrived so full of life and captured the hearts of the Madrid public.
United went to Spain on the back of a 3-3 draw away to Fulham in which a late Bobby Charlton goal salvaged a draw. Lying in sixth place their league form remained patchy and infuriating. A bookies dream and a pundit's

nightmare. However, on their better days which could never be predicted, they remained a match for any team in England. A fact soon to be confirmed with events in the Bernabéu.

The affection and admiration for Manchester United was obvious amongst the Madrileño faithful as they handed the visitors a stirring welcome on entering the Bernabéu. As for the game, it turned out to be a remarkable match with United scaring the living daylights out of Real before finally going down in a 6-5 shootout! It was Boy's Own football.

An 80,000-crowd watched on in astonishment at the Estadio Bernabéu as the visitors raced into a shock two goal lead after only fifteen minutes. The first a penalty on twelve minutes after Bobby Charlton was cynically chopped down by Jose Santamaria, a man who clearly did not believe in friendlies. The goalkeeper Dominquez saved the initial shot from Albert Quixall, only to lie helpless as the United man got lucky and lashed home the rebound.

Quixall had been signed by Matt Busby to help rebuild his fallen empire in September 1958 from Sheffield Wednesday for a record fee of £45,000. The so called 'golden boy' twenty-five-year old cost £10,000 more than the previous highest transfer. His time up to that point had been disappointing at Old Trafford. Although rated highly Quixall struggled to live up to the huge sum spent on him. The fee for both sides was important though but for vastly different reasoning. Busby would later admit:

'I was determined to keep the name of Manchester United on people's lips. We always had to look as if we were doing something. Having been the greatest we could not settle for anything less. Quixall was part of that.'

As for Sheffield, their General manager Ernie Taylor was alleged to have said of the Quixall fee: 'The real price was £25,000. The other £20,000 was for Mark Jones and David Pegg.' Both Yorkshire schoolboys whom Wednesday had expected to have a career at Hillsborough and not Old Trafford, where fate's cruel hand clipped their wings far too early.

Sixty seconds later Albert Scanlon skipped clear of Marquitos and his long searching pass was picked up by Warren Bradley. Racing past the defender Pachin, Bradley let fly and his shot deflected off Santamaria and beat Dominguez to silence the stadium. The Madrid crowd were shocked and they soon let their heroes know about it.

However, at the opposite end they had no quarrel warmly applauding Harry Gregg, who after his nightmare experience at Real's hands in Manchester was busy banishing ghosts. Two sensational saves by the big Irishman as the Spaniards turned up the heat from Enrique Mateos and Alfredo Di Stefano brought the Bernabéu to its feet as Gregg staged a one man show of defiance. He was finally beaten on twenty-one minutes but only by a debatable penalty after a very soft handball was alleged against Bill Foulkes. Up stepped Di Stefano to thrash the ball past Gregg and halve the deficit. Immediately the crowd's spirits were raised and they shook life into a so far listless home side. Game on, but just when it was thought Madrid would switch into overdrive, United struck again. On the half hour the reds broke out en masse and a four man move between Freddie Goodwin, Albert Scanlon, Bobby Charlton and

Dennis Viollet saw the latter sweep the ball past Dominquez from five yards. It was football Madrileños style by the boys from Manchester! A feeling of bemusement filled the Bernabéu for, though classed only as a friendly, it was thought unthinkable for Real Madrid to be 3-1 down on home soil. The natives were restless. Gregg's heroics in the United goal hardly helped their mood as he threw himself around in order to keep out a barrage of shots. However, good fortune favoured the Spaniards once more when moments before the interval a clearly offside Mateos was allowed to run through and score. At 3-2 they had been handed a lifeline. It was cruel on the Mancunians whom knew they now faced a second half onslaught from the European champions.

Five minutes after the break normal service appeared to have been resumed as Real drew level. A brilliant through ball was latched onto by their latest wonder kid, nineteen-year old Seville born Manuel Bueno, who fired the equaliser past a diving Harry Gregg. A frustrated Gregg pounded the turf in frustration at being beaten. Bueno was a truly outstanding talent but due to such riches of talent at the Bernabéu his appearances were limited. Now the Madrileños turned up the gas. They pinned Manchester United back and hardly needed the helping hand of a clearly out of his depth French referee Monsieur Barberan who, on fifty-four minutes, produced another shocking decision by awarding a penalty for an innocuous challenge by Goodwin on Mateos. This proved the last straw for the visitors whom blazed in anger at the inept official. After having a quiet word with the United players, Alfredo Di Stefano appeared to gesture an apology to the crowd before purposely hammering his penalty over the bar.

There was class and then there was Di Stefano.
Two minutes later United had edged back in front when winger Albert Scanlon released Bobby Charlton to crash a powerful shot in off the post past Dominguez. Charlton had been wonderful throughout and appeared comfortable playing on such a stage. He was turning heads in Madrid and was the subject of overt flattery from Madrid officials which included an unexpected encounter at Madrid airport with Don Raimondo Saporta. The charismatic fixer embraced the startled United player before asking, 'So what do you think Bobby, would you like to come play in Madrid?'
Happily for Manchester United supporters, Bobby Charlton politely turned down the offer. He had no ambition to ply his trade elsewhere and no amount of Spanish gold would tempt Charlton abroad. Madrid had its attraction; the money, the sun, playing alongside Di Stefano and Puskás every week but it wasn't Old Trafford.
In the immediate aftermath of Munich, it was Charlton, still only twenty-years old and now without doubt the most talented of those still plying their trade at United who dragged them through the dark days. Though scarred from the loss of dear friends and forever to be haunted by his experiences in the crash, Charlton played like a man possessed in the red shirt.
The last half hour saw Real up their game significantly with Alfredo Di Stefano seemingly on a mission to make up for his deliberate penalty miss. The Blond Arrow proved unplayable, like a ghostly white wind he flitted across the pitch, impossible to mark and thrusting passes like swords through the United defence. Three times he shredded the thin red line and each was put away with

aplomb past Gregg by the sensational Bueno. It was a superb twenty-minute hat trick that left the visitors reeling, Harry Gregg speechless and the match surely safe for the home side.

Out came the white handkerchiefs in tribute; a rare moment in the sun for Bueno who acknowledged the crowds chanting his name. But still United came back, refusing to lie down they scored again in the dying embers of the contest when substitute, Alec Dawson, cut in from the touchline and hit a scorching drive past Dominguez making it 6-5.

A classic encounter finally ended and despite being light years away from the Madrileños in terms of class, Busby's men had shown a spirit that boded well for the future. Come full time both teams were cheered to the rafters as the Bernabéu showed their appreciation for a memorable spectacle.

That evening Santiago Bernabéu spoke at a money raising banquet organised by the Spaniards for the families of those killed at Munich. In a speech the Madrid President revealed once more of his huge respect for the United manager. He told the assembled guests that 'Matt Busby is not only the bravest, but the greatest man I have ever met in football.'

They were words spoken from the heart. They would meet again.

C11

THE 1963 FA Cup final: Manchester United v Leicester City

After finishing fourth to complete their best ever league season, Leicester started favourites to win the cup. If, not spectacular they were hard working and difficult to beat. The type of First Division team that Manchester United so often struggled against and yet even though fourteen positions separated the two sides, the mantle of underdogs did not sit well with United players and supporters. Matt Busby had selection problems, notably with Nobby Stiles who had suffered a hamstring pull in the recent Manchester derby. United's plight that day was such Stiles played on in considerable agony, thus aggravating the injury and all but ruling him out of Wembley. Into the side came Stiles' best friend and future brother-in-law Johnny Giles. In terms of natural talent, Giles was arguably the best player at Old Trafford, but a tetchy relationship with Busby meant this dark haired, tough but technically gifted little Irishman would soon seek footballing solace away from Manchester. He was later to haunt the United manager for ten years at Don Revie's up and coming Leeds.

In attempting to rebuild after Munich, Busby had never been afraid to spend big and his side that took to the field at Wembley back in 1963 cost in the region of £300,000. They were easily the most expensive team to reach an FA cup final. The quality of footballer available to Busby was the highest since the crash and if they clicked on the day capable of giving anyone a game.

Twenty minutes before kick-off drama occurred in the United dressing room when it was discovered Paddy

Crerand had disappeared. In his eagerness to witness the crowd singing along with the band, "Abide with me" the traditional cup final hymn, a curious Crerand had gone walkabout to stand in the tunnel. There he watched the pomp and ceremony unfold. On returning a frantic Busby quizzed his fellow Scotsman, before the bell rang and it was officially time to enter the pitch.

Led by Captain Noel Cantwell, Manchester United stepped back onto the Wembley turf for the first time since 1958. Football writers predicted widely that Leicester's strong defence would deliver for the trophy and send it to Filbert Street. With the highly rated twenty-six-year-old Gordon Banks in goal, and a defence marshalled superbly by their commanding Scottish centre-half and captain Frank Mclintock, they claimed Leicester were more than capable of handling the high-explosive concoction of Law, Herd and Charlton. Whilst at the other end of the pitch, United's much discussed Achilles heel, their own rearguard, was deemed likely to concede against a nun's eleven.

At first, all talk of a spectacle looked to have been muted as Leicester's tactics appeared to be to sit back and play on the break. Indeed, early on eight white shirts stood in their own penalty area as United's Maurice Setters took possession still inside his own half? When the Foxes did move forward the uncertainty in the Mancunian defence shown itself to be a curse that at any time could prove their undoing.

No more than goalkeeper David Gaskell. Three times in a mistake-littered opening fifteen minutes the error-prone Gaskell flapped to present Leicester players with clear cut opportunities, only for centre-forward Ken Keyworth and his fellow strikers to miss them. Having survived

United breathed heavy. Wembley was hard on both legs and minds. Bill Foulkes for one experiencing cup final nerves. He, along with Bobby Charlton, were the only crash survivors left in the starting eleven. The sheer emotion of an already draining occasion and the pressure to finally win silverware after Munich taking a heavy toll.

United hit back, Denis Law's menace and guile played in Albert Quixall with a superb pass. Quixall's inability to control allowed Banks to dive courageously at his feet and clear the danger. Never-the-less orchestrated by a probing Crerand, United built up an incessant passing rhythm, they dominated possession, their football neat and incisive. Bobby Charlton went soaring through and unleashed a typical rasping effort that Gordon Banks did well to save. Banks' ensuing kick out to Scottish inside-right Dave Gibson was robbed by fellow countryman Paddy Crerand. A typical act of swift thinking saw Crerand intercept, and spot Denis Law arriving in the penalty area. Law got the ball ten yards out and with his back to goal let the pass run behind him, turned and then in an eye blink lashed a low shot past Banks into the net. Manchester United led and their mass travelling support went mad. On the bench Busby was up celebrating but a season long torment meant any thought of victory remained folly, for he knew his team was capable of anything – good or bad.

Shortly before half time it should have been 2-0 when the scintillating Law sped like a red blur past Banks, shot goalwards and missed by an inch. It was all United, their play calm and progressive. Leicester were rocked but as the interval came they remained only a goal down and the game was anything but over.

The second-half saw a brief flurry from the Midlands club and a still shaky Gaskell dropped the ball at the feet of onrushing City midfielder Graham Cross, who inexplicably shot wide. Sadly, for their supporters whom tried in vain to rouse Leicester, they fell back into a first half mode of careless passing, and on fifty-seven minutes paid a heavy price. A long goal kick by Gaskell found the cunning Johnny Giles lurking wide-right. A touch of class followed as he beat his man before flighting a precision cross-field pass to an unmarked Bobby Charlton. Racing with deadly intent into the box Charlton let fly a shot straight at Gordon Banks. As Wembley held its breath the Leicester goalkeeper failed to hold and United striker David Herd swept the ball home.

Across the Wembley terraces a sea of red simply exploded in delight. A victorious, deafening chorus of "When the reds go marching in" erupted amongst them. With United so on top it felt already that the cup was won. As Paddy Crerand controlled the centre of the pitch with a calm but tough authority and Albert Quixall alongside having undoubtedly his finest match since arriving at Old Trafford, even Matt Busby appeared relatively content. He should have known better for from seemingly down and out Leicester struck back.

Ten minutes from time Keyworth's diving header beat Gaskell's flailing fingers to cut the deficit and reignite City hopes. Suddenly the Leicester faithful raised the volume and the 1963 FA Cup final was back on. Stunned but determined not to throw the cup away United roared back. Denis Law switched play to David Herd then sprinted forty yards forward into the penalty area for the expected return. When it came the Lawman smashed a brilliant arcing header past a desperate Banks, only for the ball to agonisingly hit the post and roll rather shamefully back into Bank's grateful hands. Ever the showman Law, in mock histrionics, collapsed to the floor.

On eighty-five minutes all doubts vanished when from another precise Johnny Giles cross, Denis Law jumped with Gordon Banks, who for the second time erred and dropped the ball at the feet of David Herd. Taking aim, a prowling Herd took advantage and flashed a skimming drive past two desperate Leicester defenders trying to block on the goal-line.

At 3-1 there was unbridled ecstasy amongst the red hordes. The cup was going to Manchester. Even when Captain Noel Cantwell threw it high, few worried he would not catch it on the way down. For on that sunlit Wembley afternoon it had been United's day. When interviewed after the match by the BBC's David Coleman, Busby claimed, 'Having so many big time players won us the cup.' Free from the lament of a trophy less period, there now existed a fervent hope of better days ahead. Mancunians revelled in glory. On returning home a city ignited in joy at being back amongst the land of the living. Hundreds of thousands lined the streets and pavements. Every sightseeing vantage was taken. People hung off lamp posts, on top of bus shelters. Others climbed rather warily onto high narrow window ledges. The bus carrying the victorious United team edged its way at snail's pace, showing off a trophy that was so much more than a simple prize. Munich still cut deep, those lost never to be forgotten but now life could go on.

On entering its final destination for a civic reception at the town hall, the bus went under a huge man-made red and white arch. A moment in time perhaps that signified when Manchester United had moved on from the end of that southern German runway. No longer did their supporters feel guilty at looking forward. As Matt Busby raised the cup high to the ecstatic crowds in Albert Square it was clear United were back.

C12

THE COMING OF GEORGIE BOY

Benfica v Manchester United: European Cup Quarter Final: Second Leg: 1965

On the morning of Wednesday 9th March, 1965, the city of Lisbon awoke to count down the hours before their beloved Benfica took on and destroyed the famous Manchester United. Portuguese confidence was sky high. As the United coach made its wary way to the stadium Benfica supporters held up five fingers to remind the visitors just how badly they were about to be beaten. Remnants of United's last visit to Lisbon when they were savaged by Benfica's great city rivals.

Always wise to any outcome Bela Guttman intended to use all possible advantages available. A ten-o clock kick-off wholly alien to the English champions would be delayed even further by the presentation to Eusebio of the European footballer of the year trophy in the centre-circle. It all adding to an atmosphere that verged into sheer, fanatical showmanship.

Wary of the attacking threat posed by United, Guttman, though confident, had reason to feel edgy. Benfica had not enjoyed a great season. Trailing heavily to Sporting Lisbon in the league meant success in Europe had become all consuming. There was intense pressure on him and his players to succeed and privately he forecast a troublesome evening. 3-2 down from the first leg at Old Trafford, it was essential they started well.

In the Manchester United dressing room beforehand tensions ran high. Nerves were fraught, players sat with their own thoughts as they listened to the crazy decibel of noise rising through the walls. Already the bell had rung to see them line up in the tunnel, only then having to return whilst Eusebio received his award. Nobody spoke and few moved, all except one. Paddy Crerand. The Scottish midfielder busied himself by playing around with a ball, only to cause ructions when he smashed a wall length mirror, shattering glass all over. Crerand felt the wrath of team mates whom already feared the worse and now had to contend with the seven years bad luck thrust upon them by their midfield lynchpin's bad aim.

Busby glared angrily towards Crerand but was too pre-occupied to comment. He called everyone together for a last team talk. Imploring them to, 'keep it tight in the early stages. Don't give anything away. As for George Best, well his thoughts must have been elsewhere...

Finally, both teams entered; firecrackers deafened and rockets ignited high above the stadium. A full moon disappeared behind a huge plume of red smoke. From the floodlight pylons the proud eagles of Benfica lit up in neon against a velvet black skyline. The Estadio da Luz paid homage to their heroes.

Named after the parish where the ground stands, Nossa Senhora da luz (Our lady of the night), many a silent prayer was said by the Portuguese to their holy mother, who it was claimed paid them a visit to Fatima only forty-eight years previously in the O Milagre Do Sol. (The Miracle of the Sun). Very shortly they were soon to witness another one of God's miracles, this one hailing from Belfast.

It took just six minutes for the Belfast Boy to work his magic – a foul on Bobby Charlton resulted in a free kick which Tony Dunne flighted into the Benfica box. Waiting to pounce was George Best who soared over two defenders to head past Costa Pereira and horrify the locals. Now two goals down on aggregate the home side roared forward, only to be caught again on twelve minutes by a quick kick out from Harry Gregg that found David Herd midway inside Benfica's half. Swift thinking by Herd saw him guide a header into the path of an onrushing George Best. As the Stadium of Light watched transfixed an accelerating Best took on and left for dead three Benfica players, before firing low past Pereira from a narrow angle. It was an outrageous goal from the Irishman; blistering pace, wonderful control and a devastating finish and it all but finished off Benfica. Across the huge terraces they watched grim-faced but fascinated by this slight red demon who slipped tackles with ease then teased and tormented their world class players. George Best appeared unplayable as at one stage five white shirts were left trailing in his slipstream, dazed and confused as if hit by a smoke bomb. Later on, recalling this memorable Lisbon evening, Paddy Crerand summed everything up by claiming, 'Besty just went daft!' With the game continuing almost in silence, Best looked to have completed a thrilling hat-trick only to be judged offside by famed Italian referee Concerto Lo Bello.

On fifteen minutes the visitors scored again! Charlton, Law and Herd all combined superbly to dissect the Benfica rearguard and set up winger John Connelly to lash a sensational third past a disbelieving Pereira. At 3-0 and 6-2 up overall, United were home and dry. For Benfica it was a collapse unparalleled in their history. A monumental thrashing, they were totally taken aback by the English champions attacking play and like a boxer they hung from the ropes reeling.

They had anticipated a tactical contest only to be caught

by surprise when their opponents had come out swinging. Bela Guttman bore a resigned look on the bench. No longer concentrating on how to pull back the tie, he instead wished only to avoid further humiliation. The myth of Benfica's invincibility at the Estadio Da Luz had been well and truly snuffed out. The old man knew well when a fight was up. This night belonged to the men from Manchester.

Half-time came and with the Portuguese players and fans in utter despair Paddy Crerand, who had been magnificent throughout declared to his jubilant team-mates in the dressing room, 'Anyone got another mirror?' Seven minutes after the interval Shay Brennan misjudged a lob and sent it soaring horribly over Harry Gregg into his own net. The sight of Eusebio rushing to retrieve the ball and restart proceedings momentarily galvanised the Portuguese crowd but as United led by Best, continued to carve open their defence at will, there remained little hope of a miracle. Guttman's men were a ghost of the team whom had terrorised Europe for the previous five years. With Eusebio under Nobby Stiles' lock and key Benfica played without any conviction or belief.

It came as no surprise when ten minutes from time United increased their lead further, Paddy Crerand scoring a much deserved fourth as he slid home after being put through by Law's deft side-footed touch. If George Best had been the catalyst and the fury then Crerand had been the instigator of this unforgettable Manchester United performance. It was already a well stated fact that when Crerand played well United performed and this was never truer than on that unforgettable evening in the parish of Nossa Senhora da luz.

In the dying moments Bobby Charlton capped a marvellous showing with a stunning run through the heart of a bedraggled Benfica rearguard before rounding Pereira and slotting home. The home supporters whom had waved five fingers at the United players beforehand had proved to be correct but they could never have dreamt it would have been in this manner. The final whistle signalled total mayhem on the pitch as hundreds converged from the stands to remonstrate with the Benfica players. Cushions rained down and fires started on the terraces. Some United players were jostled as they made for a quick exit down the tunnel. As for George Best, he found himself stranded in the centre-circle amid scenes of bedlam. Surrounded by Portuguese riot-police the Irishman was the focus of a hysterical mob whom were desperate just to be near him.

One crazed fan surged towards Best with a knife demanding a lock of his hair but was swiftly wrestled away. These were strange scenes unfolding in Lisbon. An adulation normally reserved for rock and roll stars was being heaped upon this United youngster's head. Matt Busby declared the performance, 'My finest hour.' As for Benfica, their season simply fell away. Guttman left that same summer for pastures new - the footballing gypsy off wondering once more.

The plaudits and acclaim for Best's individual performance had word smiths struggling to find phrases suitably apt. Geoffrey Green of the Times, in describing the Belfast boy's second goal penned a memorable line: "There was Best, gliding like a dark ghost past three men to break clear and slide the ball home. A beautiful goal." But the most famous would be by a local sports paper Bola that summed up the evening with its sensational headline: A BEATLE CALLED BEST SMASHES BENFICA!

A legend was born.

The following morning at Lisbon airport Best bought himself a huge sombrero and egged on by team mates put it on as they landed back in Manchester. Walking down the gangway a hundred cameras flashed and clicked and a smiling, Sombrero wearing Best entered the realms of 'Beatlemania.' Cue the next day's headlines with the photograph entitled EL BEATLE! The boy from Belfast in time would become the world's first instantly recognisable footballer. It was a monster that for a while would see him ride with angels, before he ultimately fell from a great height. But events in the Stadium of Light had been a rite of passage - George Best had arrived.

C13
BAD TIDINGS FROM BELGRADE
Manchester United v Partizan Belgrade: European Cup Semi Final: 1966

For Matt Busby it had been eight years since Munich, yet still the physical and mental pain remained to give him more sleepless nights than not. To be given the last rites once and survive must be a humbling experience, to have them delivered twice must make you doubt your mortality and treat every new day as a gift. But not Busby, for him it was the guilt, an obsession with conquering Europe and remaining dominant on the home front had, in his mind, resulted in carnage. Before the crash he was keen to push his boys on, afterwards it became a holy grail. Those lost had to have died for something, otherwise what was the point in going on? A deeply religious man, Busby had come close to losing faith in a god who at times appeared intent on breaking hearts. A path to salvation that came laden deep with traps and pitfalls had yet another in store for the Manchester United manager. A return to Belgrade....

Belgrade: Wednesday 13th April 1966: Hiding any fear or angst at returning to a city where his Babes played their final match, a buoyant Matt Busby declared publicly on the eve of the first-leg against Partizan, 'Manchester United have never played for a draw before and we will not start now.' True to his word Busby's team attacked from the off in Belgrade. With Partizan experiencing stage fright at being cast amongst such acclaimed company, United attempted to take swift advantage, and as eight years before hit early and hard. Though suffering injuries to George Best who played with his left knee heavily strapped, and Denis Law, both far from full fitness, they each missed more than presentable chances in the opening ten minutes.

First a wasteful Best shot wide when all of Yugoslav descent in the People's stadium had resigned themselves to going one down. None seemed more surprised than the wistful Irishman who it appeared was already limping. Then, as if determined to make amends Best left two Yugoslav defenders for dead, went around the goalkeeper before setting up Denis Law, who inexplicably lashed his shot against the crossbar from two yards out. The Partizan goalkeeper Milutin Soskic stood relieved and a little bemused that his goal had remained unscathed after the normally deadly Scotsman's uncharacteristic miss. Both misses combined to leave a feeling of dread among United supporters listening back home.

Seemingly in awe of their big-name opponents, the Yugoslavs had begun nervously and the passionate 55,000 capacity crowd had been reduced to a grumbling slumber. The visitors pinned back their hosts for long stages of the first half, but apart from a lone instance when a clearly unfit Law again struck the Yugoslav woodwork they failed to take advantage of almost overwhelming possession. At times United appeared complacent, such was their complete dominance. A European cup semi-final was not meant to be this easy. Though not playing well a Partizan team on an unusually attractive win bonus of a third of the gate were taking no prisoners. Hacking and slashing, they picked out their worst tormentor, the pulsating George Best, for particularly special attention. Already feeling the effects of a painful leg injury suffered in a recent FA cup tie at

Preston, and far too brave for his own good, the United forward at one stage actually stood on the ball to avoid the blood curdling swipes aimed towards him!

In truth, Best should not even have been out on the field but not wanting to let his manager and team mates down, when asked by Busby beforehand if he felt fit the young Irishman claimed he was fine. In reality his knee was close to collapse and Best had made a serious mistake - one that was soon set to cost him and United dear. Content with his team's performance up until this point Busby knew the pitfalls of a wonderful but unforgiving competition and remained wary. Opportunities at this heady level had to be taken when offered. On leaving the pitch at the interval United's reserve Noel Cantwell, who had watched proceedings from the visitor's bench, implied to Paddy Crerand that it was just a matter of time before they scored. This irked Crerand for he knew Partizan could not be as bad again in the second half. He was right. Two minutes after the break a revitalised home team took the lead. Looking sharper and quicker on the ball they caught United cold with a quick throw in, Partizan's raiding full-back Jusufi raced clear to place a high cross into the penalty area. Totally misjudging the ball, a despairing Harry Gregg allowed prolific Serbian born striker Mustafa Hasanagic, the idol of the Belgrade terraces to smash home a glorious header. Suddenly United were rocking.

Stunned by Hasanagic's goal, and taken aback by the technical brilliance and sheer fury of Partizan's football, a siege ensued. On the hour with Best and Law reduced to walking wounded, United cracked again. Partizan's finest players had risen to the occasion, the scheming box of tricks and lightning fast left-winger Milan Galic a constant thorn, whilst their classy sweeper Velibor Vasovic, now freed from defensive duties, moved up field and busied himself ripping apart the United defence with a series of sublime passes. After intense pressure with the home white shirts swarming all over their English opponents, it came as no surprise when a typically incisive ball from Vasovic wreaked havoc. Raiding midfielder Radoslav Becejac controlled instantly before firing past Gregg to send Belgrade delirious and the Mancunians into turmoil.

It was a devastating knock-out blow for Manchester United and clearly rattled them. Still, Partizan roared forward in search of a third killer goal. In fear of being overrun, Nobby Stiles and Paddy Crerand attempted to stem the tide of battle by crashing into tackles that erred towards street brawling. One instance involving the quick-tempered Stiles saw both full and empty beer bottles hurling down upon the Mancunian's head from the terraces. Belgrade was not a place to pick a fight. Crerand and Stiles swiftly decided it wiser to live and fight another day. The game descended into a series of nasty and niggling incidents that did not bode well for the return at Old Trafford. At the final whistle the Yugoslavs antagonised their opponents by celebrating like they had already won the European cup.

Outwardly Matt Busby accepted defeat with good grace. "I think we can still win in Manchester despite the two-goal loss. My players are sick with the chances we missed and at half time I would have given any odds on our victory. But congratulations to Partizan.'

Secretly Busby was reeling. The European cup he had sweated and given blood to win remained further away than ever. Memories of Belgrade first time around must have swept through Busby's head. Bobby Charlton's scintillating grass-cutting effort making it 2-0. The huge tension of the final moments as Harry Gregg refused to be beaten. The after-match party, the laughter and the songs. Enduring friendships, some doomed to last no longer than a day. ''We'll meet again.'' Roger Byrne and the boys. "Don't know where, don't know when. But I know well meet again…

There was more bad news for United as Best had badly aggravated the knee injury fifteen minutes from time and would require a cartilage operation, curtailing his season. Best's courage and youthful exuberance had backfired spectacularly. For in seven days' time when Manchester United attempted to pull back the 2-0 deficit, their most precious diamond would be sat amongst the crowd praying like the rest that the Red Devils could pull off a most unlikely comeback.

Manchester: Wednesday 20th April 1966. On a night tinged with high emotion and sheer unadulterated passion, Manchester United threw everything they had left at a resolute Partizan Belgrade defence. Roared on from the whistle by a deafening 62,000 crowd, they went for broke. However, George Best's replacement, John Anderson, proved inadequate at this exalted level and a Yugoslav team desperate to make it to Brussels by any means necessary simply swatted him aside.

Partizan coach Abdulah Gegic had shown great tactical acumen in plotting Partizan's route to the semis. So much so that Europe's elite clubs, including Real Madrid, had inquired about his services. But as the Mancunian skies turned black and the noise from the home crowd threatened to rip the roof off Old Trafford, Gegic's final team talk came solely down to 'Defend for your lives!'

This was an experienced, battle-hardened Partizan and the vast majority had played vital parts in Yugoslavia's impressive showings in recent European championships and World cups - reaching the final in one and the semi in the other. Old Trafford held no fears and they stood ready to go to war with Manchester United.

The first half saw United bombard the Partizan goal without creating anything resembling a decent opportunity. Every long ball and mishit pass came etched with hints of desperation. As the clock ticked down tempers on both sides frayed - a simmering undercurrent from the match in Belgrade that threatened at any time to erupt. Finally, it exploded when Nobby Stiles snapped after one to many attempts by Partizan defender Ljubomir Mihajlovic to dissect him at the midriff. With the Swiss referee Dienst's back turned Stiles took retribution and punched Mihajlovic to the floor. Suddenly chaos descended as players from both sides became involved in a free for all. In an unfortunate case of mistaken identity by his linesman, Dienst took wrong advice and sent off Paddy Crerand for allegedly flattening Mihajlovic. An irate Crerand tried desperately to argue a case without actually naming Stiles but it was to no avail. As if to confirm Dienst's highly dubious decision, Crerand became involved with Partizan winger Pirmajer, who was taunting the Glaswegian and telling him to get off the pitch. This was before Crerand clocked him with a left hook that would not have shamed Muhammad Ali! And so, with just twenty minutes remaining a tearful Crerand was finally led away, knowing that if United did pull off a late miracle, he would be barred from the final.

As for Nobby Stiles, his night took an even more frenetic twist when with just seventeen minutes remaining he finally grabbed a goal back. Running into the penalty Stiles shot past a fumbling Soskic from twelve yards out. Old Trafford went mad and Matt Busby came onto the touchline urging his team for a last great effort. The dream was still alive and just one more goal was needed to level the tie.

A fraught Partizan steadied themselves for a final onslaught. United came again, this time Bobby Charlton let fly a tremendous volley that hissed inches over Soskic's crossbar into the Stretford End. With time almost up few could hardly bare to watch. Busby stood and stared, as if in a trance, his dream in tatters once more. There was to be no miracle and at the final whistle Partizan celebrated a ferocious backs to the wall showing. They would go on to play Real Madrid in the European cup final. For Manchester United all was despair as for the third time running they had been eliminated at the semi-final stage.

In the dressing room no one spoke. A spluttered cough and the clack of boots being removed the only sound. One by one the players drifted off, finally only Paddy Crerand and his manager remained. The two men had grown close over the years, a distraught Busby opened up to his fellow countryman to tell him it was over. Crerand recalls, 'I was sitting in the dressing room and Matt was the only other person there. He was in a bad state and looked crushed. He kept mumbling about never winning the European cup. But I said 'you hold on here, because in two years we will win this thing'. I really believed it.' That same evening there was a banquet for both teams at the Midland hotel in the city. A still fuming Paddy

Crerand angrily confronted Partizan's Mihajlovic, who he accused of getting him sent off. The Yugoslav ended up locking himself in a toilet cubicle to escape the Scotsman wrath! Finally, the night ended and a miserable episode in the history of Manchester United came to a close. For Matt Busby a decision had to be made on whether he could summon the strength to go on and his mood hardly improved when the following Saturday saw United suffer further heartache by losing to Everton in the FA Cup semi-final.

However, an incident occurred two days later when he was travelling to Old Trafford for training that made Busby's mind up.

'I was fed up and everything else, but driving along I stopped at the crossing near the blind school. There I witnessed seven little children with sticks being led across the road. I just sat in the car and thought. Matt what problems have you got? You've got no problems compared to these poor kids. At that moment I thought one more go. Just one more go!'

A day of reckoning was drawing near.

STRICTLY BUSINESS

Manchester United v Real Madrid: European Cup Semi Final: 1968

It was a beautiful, gentle spring evening in Manchester when thirty-four-year-old Francisco Gento stepped out at the head of his team into the Old Trafford sun. The dazzling all white strip still made the heart race faster for Manchester's football romantics, despite the dose of 1960s pragmatism that Real had arrived with a five-man defensive plan intended to ensnare and strangulate United's attacking flair. It was the modern way. They, like United knew it was essential to avoid defeat. A draw in Manchester would all but finish off Busby's men and leave them indefensible in the torrid cauldron of Estadio Bernabéu. Then you would see the Real Madrid.

The Romantics with fond memories of Di Stefano, Puskás, Gento, Edwards, and Taylor would have to wait until the second-leg, for now the Madrileños came baring gifts; flowers and goodwill off the pitch - on it, it was strictly business. For this was the European cup. The absent heroes would have understood...

Real Madrid were in good health. Miguel Munoz's team arrived in Manchester as newly crowned Spanish champions after a 2-1 home victory the previous weekend over Las Palmas. Goals from Velásquez and Pirri ensured an astonishing seventh consecutive league title as the Madrileño's dominance on home soil continued unabated.

To counteract Manchester United's forwards Munoz had opted for a well-drilled, swift and ruthless when required defensive rearguard; Gonzalez, Zunzunegui, Sanchis,

Zoco and Luis. A white cloak, orchestrated, pushed, pulled and ordered into position by the magnificent sweeper Pirri. The full-back Manuel Sanchis was handed the unenviable task of man-marking George Best. The cunning Munoz had chosen well for this was an electric-heeled player, blessed with great concentration and tactical awareness. He was perfectly suited to his task. Though denied the skill, pace and deadly prowess of Amaro Amancio through suspension, Munoz remained supremely confident that with Velásquez, Grosso and the ageless Gento to counter-attack, they could return to Madrid with a favourable result. For after all was this not their tournament? The white knights of the Bernabéu were set once more to win back a trophy for a seventh time. But first Manchester United, a dear old friend, had to be dealt with.

Only the jarring pain of a cortisone injection and sheer courage allowed Matt Busby to name Denis Law in his line-up, but in all reality a serious knee injury had curtailed Law's genius to the point where he was a mere shadow of his true self. Busby knew a win was essential, he needed at least one goal to take to the Bernabéu. Anything less and United would require a miracle in Madrid to get through and Busby no longer believed in them.

A watching world-wide audience of 150 million and a huge 63,500 Old Trafford crowd held their breath as the two teams came out to do battle. At first glimpse the all-white strip still possessed the charisma to send a cold chill down the spine. However, any feelings of nostalgia and goodwill towards the Madrileños would be temporarily shelved for ninety minutes, as the home crowd concentrated on helping their team topple the Spaniards from their imperial perch.

The songs from the Stretford End both amused and deafened. Chants of 'Hand off Gibraltar' and 'Franco out, Busby in' resonated loud. A few hundred Madrid followers lay scattered loud and proud in the Cantilever stand, happy to make themselves seen and heard with an impressive array of banners and the traditional mass of white handkerchiefs.

United opened brightly when from a superb George Best cross John Aston powered in a header which was brilliantly turned away by the goalkeeper Betancourt. From the ensuing corner Denis Law set up Paddy Crerand to smash in an effort which crashed against the Madrid post - it was a storming start from the home team but one which soon ran out of steam. Madrid took control, their ball artistry delightful and dangerous. None more than captain Francisco Gento, no longer flying but still capable of wreaking chaos as he showed with a deft defence-splitting pass that sent his compadre Miguel Angel Perez clear on goal. With just Alex Stepney to beat the recently signed Argentine Perez took aim and shot past the goalkeeper to horrify Old Trafford, only for the infamous Russian referee Tofik Bakhramov, forever to be remembered as the linesman who controversially allowed England's third goal by Geoff Hurst in the 1966 World Cup final, to blow for offside. It was an act the Spanish took great exception to but it was also a disturbing reminder for Busby's team. A timely example of what awaited if they dared to switch off. Despite United's two early opportunities, Real retained a strict defensive discipline. There was no air of panic amongst the white shirts despite the wall of noise that emanated

from all four corners of the stadium. None were more supreme than Pirri, looking calm and assured. Sublime technique, he was the epitome of a true Madrileño, football's equivalent of a Hollywood superstar.
With Denis Law's injury reducing him to a forlorn straggler, the Old Trafford faithful looked elsewhere for inspiration to break the deadlock. On thirty-six minutes they got their wish when a sweeping United move ended with Aston jinking past Gonzalez on the left before squaring for George Best to fire a snapshot past Betancourt into the top corner. It was a stunning finish by Best, hit first time with his left foot showing wonderful technique and with an ease only great players possess. As the terraces erupted a black cat raced the length of the Old Trafford pitch – an omen perhaps? Comrade Bakhramov's whistle blew for half time and Manchester United had edged in front.
But a first half resembling a chess match had shown beyond doubt there was not a needle's thread between the two sides. The second half saw little change with United having the bulk of possession but few opportunities. Munoz's team were proving exceptional at snuffing out any dangers posed. George Best met his match that evening in the form of the limpet-like Manuel Sanchis, who tracked and second guessed the Irish genius's every move. It was a remarkable performance by the twenty-five-year-old Valencia born defender and one always remembered by Best who would recall 'Sanchis was amongst the hardest opponents I ever faced.'
With United's front four shackled and firmly under lock and key, Real Madrid looked to press forward. An equaliser looked certain when once more Perez went careering through, only for the deputising centre-half, the

versatile David Sadler in for the injured Bill Foulkes, to catch him at the last. Sadler was yet another unsung hero but one destined to play a huge part as this epic clash ran its full course over two legs. The game finished 1-0 with neither side particularly pleased or disappointed. The final whistle was greeted with muted applause from a knowledgeable Old Trafford crowd whom knew United now faced an awesome task in Madrid to make the final. Matt Busby hid any doubts regarding what was to come in the second-leg and remained bullish in post-match interviews, 'I think we will win through because I am convinced we are the better side.' However, many supporters feared the worst for Real had already shown in brief attacking spurts that they possessed enough flair to deeply trouble the Red Devil's defence.

In Madrid the war drums had already began to beat loud as they waited impatiently to end United's torment. For although they wished them well, Mancunian redemption, an almost absolution of sin would not be allowed to be earned on their turf. They like their forefathers before them stood ready once more to turn out the light on Manchester United. There would be warm embraces for their friends from Manchester. They would speak well of times past. Shed tears at those 'Champions of Honour' whom had been taken so cruelly. But once the last toast had been drunk and the Bernabéu crowds had gathered baying for blood, the Madrileños would have no choice but to obey –

it was nothing personal, this was strictly business.

   It was the best of times, the worst of times. For the Madrileños an age of unsurpassed glory, for Manchester United an age of unrelenting pain. In Madrid summers of light, in Manchester winters of despair. As Real Madrid swept everything before them United's Babes lost everything. Now they would clash again. The footballing gods so ironic, determined to milk the last bit of emotion out of a journey that had left Manchester United all but spent. A loss in Madrid would have meant more than simple elimination from the European cup. For the Mancunians would surely have thrown in the towel. They would have one last chance - there would be ghosts present in the Bernabéu. Red ghosts.

On Saturday 11th May 1968, a city was divided like never before. Come the final day of the domestic season both Manchester clubs were level at the top of the table but with City slightly ahead on goal difference. With United at home to Sunderland and the blues facing a tough away trip to Newcastle, it was generally regarded that come full time the reds of Manchester would be smiling having won another league championship. However, a shocking 2-1 loss at Old Trafford blew a hole in such wishful thinking and cast dark shadows over Manchester's red half, whilst causing untold joy on the blue side. United's defeat and City's dramatic 4-3 victory two hundred miles north meant the First Division title was on its way to Maine Road for the first time since 1937. Already two goals down to the visitors, a lone George Best strike hit early with venom from twenty-yards on the stroke of half-time proved insufficient.

This football mad metropolis would find itself for once resonating to chants of 'Champions' from those of a blue persuasion. A capacity Old Trafford crowd stood stunned. The pubs and bars of Manchester promised to be a painful place for United supporters that evening. Hiding his bitter disappointment, a gracious Matt Busby went straight to the Granada Television studios after the game to offer his congratulations to City manager and close friend Joe Mercer. Then, Busby disregarded events on the home front and all thoughts turned to four days' time and a date with destiny in Madrid. No matter how painful it was, they could ill afford to be scarred by losing out to City. Such disappointments had to be put away in a box and forgotten. For a much bigger prize lay at stake.

The Wednesday previously Matt Busby had flown over to Lisbon to watch the other European cup semi-final between Benfica and Juventus. Despite the home side winning 2-0 and almost certainly booking a place in the final, the Portuguese were, in Busby's opinion 'eminently beatable.' Though Eusebio remained a thunderous talent and showed few signs of waning, elsewhere in the Eagle's ranks the United manager sensed they no longer soared to past heights. Now a little slower and susceptible to pace, he felt if Real Madrid could be overcome then Benfica's wings on Wembley's wide-open spaces could well be clipped. He even admitted as much publicly, 'If only we can survive in Madrid then I feel that we have an excellent chance of winning the European cup.'

On the Mancunians arrival in the Spanish capital, Real President, seventy-two-year-old Santiago Bernabéu, welcomed them with a courtesy and charm typical of a man and the football club he proudly represented, 'I want Manchester United greeted and treated as the greatest football club in the world. And as our friends for many years nothing must go wrong. If we are beaten by United in the European cup on Wednesday then we shall have lost to a great team. We have met them on many occasions and it is about time their luck changed.' They were kind and generous words by Don Santiago, but come the time when battle was most intense, when stakes were raised and tackles flew high and fierce, it was highly unlikely Bernabéu would be so magnanimous. In a concerted effort to remain isolated from the prevailing madness consuming Madrid, the visitors stayed in a mountain retreat thirteen-miles outside the city. On the morning of the match the Catholics in the United team went to a local church. There, Nobby Stiles placed a 400 Peseta note into the collection box. Accompanying Stiles was Paddy Crerand who immediately blurted out, 'Bloody hell Nobby that's bribery!'

The Estadio Bernabéu was host to 125,000 fanatical supporters. Paying £20 for a return flight from Manchester, United also had unparalleled backing for a European away match, around 5000. But though loud the vastly outnumbered Mancunians would sound like a whisper in a thunderstorm compared to the noise set to erupt from an expectant home crowd.

Like gunshots fired across the massed terraces that towered up to the heavens thousands of firecrackers ignited and banged. The two teams represented first by pensive looking Captains Bobby Charlton and Francisco Gento came into view. The tension etched on both faces. Experienced Italian referee Antonio Sbardella led them to the centre-circle; there they broke and gave a quick dramatic wave to the crowds before posing for a final team photo. Real would kick off, their goal scoring superstar Amaro Amancio, back from suspension, appearing like a man rushing to make up for lost time. The Estadio burned like days of old, Madrid so expectant and demanding.

Yet any sentiment that may have resonated from their president's welcoming speech was disregarded as Real Madrid began with a determination to blow their Mancunians compadres into kingdom come. A Real line-up containing six of the Spanish national side pressed and probed. A Gonzales corner was headed against the bar by Amancio with Stepney well beaten and lashed clear by Tony Dunne. United employed their normal defence abroad with a five-man rearguard. Bill Foulkes was back from injury to line up alongside the versatile David Sadler with Nobby Stiles close by. This left Brian Kidd and George Best to forage for scraps up front. They swiftly became isolated as the Spaniards dominated playing in a manner so different from the white shirts seen in Manchester.

Back on home soil and with the arrogance of a bullfighter biding his time, it was surely a matter of when not if. Real were superb; Zoco and Grosso were highly impressive but it was the darting Amancio who truly stood out. Quick and aggressive, forever looking to run in behind United defenders. He and Nobby Stiles were involved in a ferocious tussle both on and off the ball. Stiles had been handed the task of shackling 'El Brujo' but the 'Witch' was proving hard to lock down as his Mancunian jailer attempted to stem Amancio's deadly threat. Stiles snapped and snarled at the Spaniard's heels, always just within the laws, just, but irritating him no end. Amancio raged and implored the referee to intervene. Theirs's would be a battle vital to the game's outcome, one set to become increasingly taut, if at times not downright scandalous.

On the half hour the Madrileños took a deserved lead when Amancio's precise free kick found an unmarked

Pirri, who soared above the United defence to head fiercely past Stepney from twelve yards. Matt Busby had warned his team in the dressing room only moments before they took the field, 'If Real do get an early goal to equalise on aggregate watch yourselves, because for a spell you will think they have gone mad!'

Well not only their footballers but an entire city went crazy, for now it was advantage Madrid - their patch, their crowd and for most of the first half, their ball. Real came again, a whirlwind, the confidence now flowing, their football freewheeling and incise, every loose ball picked up by a white shirt. Two minutes before half time a Bobby Charlton free kick was cleared and picked up by an exuberant Velásquez, who immediately attempted to feed Amancio on the right wing. However, it was defender Shay Brennan who moved swiftly to intercept, only to miskick horribly allowing Francisco Gento to sweep behind him with a clear run on goal. As one of their favourite's son took aim the Bernabéu held its breath. The years and the yards melted away as Gento sprinted into the penalty area and smashed a low drive past Stepney to put Madrid ahead on aggregate. The stadium went into meltdown, they had them. Manchester United were on the floor. As for Brennan, the boy who became a man during the unforgettable ninety minutes of that strange night against Sheffield Wednesday, 10 years before, he was disconsolate with his error. But this was no time for self-doubt as United re-started looking to survive until half time without conceding further.

Yet the fates once more teased the senses, delivering yet another twist. Straight from the restart a long, hopeful ball hoisted into the Real box from defender Tony Dunne found unexpected reward. To the home crowd's horror,

Ignacio Zoco, who had been arguably Real's best player until that moment inexplicably sliced an easy clearance spectacularly past Betancourt into the net. The tall, blond haired Zoco cut a despairing figure. Wholly disbelieving his sad misfortune. At 2-2 this semi-final was once more even and despite being hugely outplayed Manchester United remained in the European cup.

As Sbardella prepared to blow for the interval Real swarmed forward one last time. An astute left-wing cross from the ever-impressive defender Sanchis was met with astonishing technique and a magnificent drive past Stepney's smoking fingers by Amancio to send the home crowd into more raptures. The Bernabéu was a scene of utter chaos! An ecstatic Amancio took the salute of an adoring support. His had been daunting shoes to fill and yet as Madrid bowed in awe Amancio appeared destined to fit the bill of the legendary heroes of the past. It was a cacophony of joy, noise and relief not felt or heard since Enrique Mateos signed off a 3-1 victory over the Mancunians eleven years before.

Cornered and on the ropes, United's hopes waned just when they appeared to have regained a fortunate foothold back in the contest. One more blow and it was surely Adiós. As in 1957, to use Matt Busby's dramatic phrase, 'The world came tumbling down.' The European albatross that hung around Busby's neck weighed heavily once again. The nightmare looked set to go on.

The visitors' dressing room resembled a morgue. In an attempt to lift his best friend's broken spirits Bobby Charlton offered a kind word, only to be silenced by Shay Brennan, who angrily shot back there could be no excuses. He had erred badly and knew it. No words could ease his pain. The sorry sight of the United players with heads down and sick with disappointment as yet another European campaign (perhaps the final campaign) looked set to end in failure. So badly hurt was Nobby Stiles after a kick out from Amancio that he sat pouring whisky onto an open leg wound. The thought of not carrying on never entering Nobby's head. At the back of everybody's mind was Munich, always Munich. Always........

Busby had to literally scrape them off the floor. He spoke up, telling the players to forget the scoreline. Even at 3-1 down they remained just a goal behind. All was not lost. He recalls, 'I told them they were only 3-2 down on aggregate and to go out and play.' Paddy Crerand remembers listening on with incredulity, 'It could have been five or six in the first half and here was the boss telling us to go out and have a go at them! Well some of the lads were smiling by then. Here we were, having been totally outplayed and this man was telling us to go out and attack them!'

To receive such a mauling and remain in with a chance meant anything could yet happen. Real Madrid had played well, brilliantly even but the mindset could now change. It was a dangerous ploy to torture the bull when it still possessed life to lash out; United had been wounded but not finished off. Busby's last words as his team left the dressing room, 'Come on boys, remember we are Manchester United. Let's have a go at them.'

As the United players headed off back up the tunnel it was obvious by the demeanour of many of their opponents that they already considered the game won. It was a cockiness that riled those in red. Sensing a simmering fuse, the referee pulled aside Nobby Stiles and Amaro Amancio. Smashing his fists down, Sbardella intimated to the two that there were to be no more antics.

Both nodded in agreement then re-joined their teams with the official's warning already forgotten. So, began the second-half with Amancio wasting no time getting in his retaliation first. Knowing Stiles was all but playing on one leg, he went to finish him off. Only then to suffer the irate Mancunian's wrath when behind Sbardella's back, he was knocked out cold by a right hook. The punch caused howls of derision to sweep down from the terraces. Only to be met by a gentle shrug of the shoulders from the man christened with great irony 'Happy' by long suffering team-mates. It was a marker laid down by the United man that left his Spanish opponent felled and in great pain on the turf.

From that moment Amancio's influence waned and he disappeared as a threat. To further infuriate the masses, Stiles gently tapped the referee on the shoulder and pointed out the distraught Amancio, 'He's injured ref.' For his troubles the Mancunian was hit with a ripe tomato hurled from the crowd and a shoe that missed by an inch! Nobby Stiles would forever be known in these parts as the 'Assassin of Madrid.'

Real had begun to strut, their Olé football not appreciated by Manchester United Midfielders Stiles and Crerand whom ripped into challenges to upset the Spaniards' rhythm. The pace and momentum which had blown away the visitors in that blistering first half was no more. Suddenly it was United who posed the more potent threat, as a well-struck effort from Paddy Crerand flew narrowly over Betancourt's bar. Then, Charlton robbed Perez in midfield before moving forward to unleash a similar effort that the Madrid goalkeeper was happy to see fly inches wide. A nervous air engulfed the Bernabéu. All was not yet over. Brian Kidd raced to the goal-line and crossed dangerously, only for Betancourt to save at his near post. On the bench Busby and Jimmy Murphy urged United to keep going forward, for it was clear the sheer enormity of the occasion was affecting their opponents. United pushed on, all was rushed as the clock ticked down. For the Mancunians the hands of time raced wretchedly fast, while for the Spaniards it appeared to stop. Oh, for a Di Stefano, to tear a strip off those Madrileños who appeared more intent on blaming team-mates rather than ensuring their opponents did not dominate the ball.

The stadium was aghast, fraught with nervous exhaustion. For the first time the away supporters could be heard. With twenty minutes remaining Paddy Crerand urged Bobby Charlton further upfield as he raced to take a free kick. Crerand's lofted chip into the Real penalty area found George Best, who flicked on dangerously to the far post. Arriving late came David Sadler, unmarked from six yards he forced the ball into the goal and set off in celebration around the back of Madrid's goal to earn the fury of the seething locals. He cared little, for at 3-3 as the game entered its final stage all was set to win or lose. Told to abandon his defensive duties and play upfront by Busby, the twenty-two-year-old boy from Kent had to the abject horror of his Spanish hosts levelled the tie.

With the thought of losing everything at such a late stage simply overwhelming both teams became pensive in possession. All except one that is: thirteen minutes remained at the Bernabéu when Paddy Crerand's throw in found George Best wide on the right-hand touchline. Faced by Zoco and his arch-nemesis Sanchis, the United winger turned and twisted to leave both trailing in his

wake, before tearing into the Real penalty area. On reaching the goal-line Best glanced up to deliver a cut back, only then having to look again when he noticed who stood waiting for his pass. The same man who had staggered out of that inferno at the end of a Munich runway,
thirty-six-year-old Bill Foulkes had arrived in the penalty area as if urged by his long-lost pals…
Best's glorious pass was as close to perfection as possible but the unlikely figure of Foulkes finishing low past Betancourt with a precision side-foot effort that would have done credit to Denis Law, was out of this world. A despairing Betancourt pounded the turf as Madrid's hearts lay broken. Bill Foulkes, a no nonsense former pit miner from St. Helens, plucked by Busby to play for United, relates the grand tale as if it was yesterday.
'The atmosphere was so strange: they were not really playing and we were holding on to what we'd got. Then I shouted to Pat and could see the shock on his face because it was me. I kept running and Pat threw the ball to George. He went past one, then two and I kept moving up. I was only jogging but I can tell you I was the only red shirt in the box. George feinted to drive it to the near post then flipped a perfect pass for me. I just hit it in the opposite corner.'
Normally used to the sight of Foulkes ballooning the ball over the crossbar or screwing a shot haplessly wide, United players watched astonished as the granite man of their defence kept his cool and scored arguably the most important goal in the history of Manchester United Football Club. Paddy Crerand remembers thinking, 'What's that big idiot doing up there?' Bobby Charlton's first reaction was, 'Oh no not Bill!' Yet their worries

proved unfounded as Foulkes kept his nerve and finished off the Madrileños. Buried in red shirts Foulkes appeared determined to shrug off the compliments and return to his centre-half position as there remained sufficient time for it all still to go horribly awry.

But Real had gone in mind and spirit, their confidence and belief wiped away in the emotional slipstream of United's dramatic comeback. Yet still they found enough to go to the last. Seconds remained when Velásquez went flying down the United left and fired in a low shot that was deflected and safely cleared. By now few could watch, the tension unbearable. The visitors broke with Brian Kidd setting up George Best to shoot straight at Betancourt.

Again, Real swept forward only for Zoco's pass to be picked up by the referee who called proceedings to a halt on an unforgettable night of drama in Madrid. Across the field United players fell to the turf. Exhausted and filled with emotion. None more than Bobby Charlton as the memories of lost friends vividly returned amid the feelings of ecstasy evoked in the Spanish capital.

Onto the pitch streamed hundreds of jubilant United supporters to embrace their heroes. The Madrid police were too stunned and dazed to care. The United players embraced Matt Busby as they left the field. His smile was wide enough to light the Bernabéu as he waited for the team next to the tunnel. For Real Madrid it was a monumental loss and one it would take a generation to recover from. Thirty-one years would pass before Real won the European cup again. A sporting Miguel Munoz sought out the victorious United manager to shake his hand and wish Busby all the best for the forthcoming final against Benfica. Meanwhile, high in the Presidential box Don Santiago Bernabéu applauded the Mancunians' moment of triumph. Though sick with defeat, Bernabéu would later admit, 'If it had to be anyone, then I am glad it was them.'

The Manchester United dressing room whilst hectic and joyful was also awash with tears of relief and sadness. Matt Busby sat quietly. He was crying. Despite all attempts to console him Busby was heartbroken, 'I can't help it,' he sobbed, 'I just can't help it.' Busby was embraced by a similarly distraught Bobby Charlton and Bill Foulkes; three survivors together, now so close to a journey's end that at times had been too painful to bear. The next day on arriving back in Manchester, Busby was mobbed by the press within moments of disembarking and asked his thoughts on finally reaching the European cup final. A still emotional United manger, his feelings in turmoil but knowing he was expected to deliver a triumphal victory line, declared with a beaming smile, 'In the immortal words of the great Satchmo, (Louis Armstrong), it's a wonderful world!'

C15
THE BOYS OF 68
Manchester United v Benfica: The European Cup Final:1968

It was the morning of Wednesday 29th May 1968 and across Manchester special masses were being prepared. The countless Mancunian priests who received free season tickets from Matt Busby were having their markers called and would be expected to play an unworldly hand in United's attempts to overcome Benfica. Their task; to call on an ever-higher force to create a deflection, a gust of wind or in desperate needs maybe even a bolt of lightning to bring the cup home. Candles were lit, prayers whispered and rosary beads clasped tight. A ten-year journey in which they had staggered and stumbled, only to always get back on their feet, had finally neared Heaven's Gate. A footballing redemption set to deliver them from the living nightmare of Munich. In the name of the father and of the son and of the holy…Please, please let Manchester United beat the hell out of the Portuguese and win the European cup. Lord graciously hear us...

Two weeks following the second-leg in Madrid, United headed south by train to deepest Surrey. They stayed at Great Fosters, a historical country Manor hidden away in Egham where it was alleged Queen Elizabeth I was said to meet her secret lovers. The United players joked that it was lucky for her that George Best was not around at the time!

The team were heartened to receive news that a win bonus of £1000 per man would be paid to beat Benfica. Confidence was high; surely after coming so far, they would not blow it now? 'Their hearts are ready that is the most important thing,' Busby commented on the eve of the final. He appeared completely at ease and ready for whatever fate and Benfica had ready to throw at his football club. There was much talk that the real final for United had been the second-leg against Real but such idle chatter was quickly dismissed by Busby, for he knew Benfica were not just coming to Wembley as extras in the bigger picture of a glorious Manchester United victory. There was no script, no guarantee. They were in London to win. The Portuguese had never beaten United in European competition and the 5-1 thrashing in the Stadium of Light still cut deep.

What finer place to bury the demons of that infamous night for the Eagles two years previous when they suffered such humiliation in front of their own supporters, than to return the medicine at the grand old home of English football. In the intense build up to the final, legendary Benfica Captain Mario Coluna made it his personal mission to remind team mates of the indignation and criticism following the aftermath of that debacle. Revenge was in the air.

Though not the ferocious force of past campaigns Benfica remained a potent threat and utterly capable on their day of taking apart the very best. Among their ranks were some of the finest players in Europe: the class and finishing ability of the huge centre-forward Jose Torres, the fast and explosive Antonio Simões and Jose Augusto on the flanks and the guile and sheer presence of the inspirational Mario Coluna. Then, there was the player United fans feared more than any. Ready to be unleashed again upon Busby's team was the truly magnificent talent of the 'Black Panther' the kid born under the Mozambique stars was coming to get them. Given an inch Eusebio could destroy United on his own and the job of suppressing this phenomenon fell once more to twenty-eight-year-old Norbert Peter Stiles. Collyhurst's finest, he was an unlikely looking hitman yet upon his slim shoulders rested United's hopes.

Stiles had enjoyed considerable success against Eusebio both for United and England in the World Cup semi-final with his streetwise concoction of Mancunian nous and superb defensive awareness. By fair means and the odd foul, he kept the lid on the great Portuguese superstar. Stiles was not averse to bending the rules and occasionally breaking them completely. Yet despite the public perception of Stiles as being nothing more than a short sighted, toothless hatchet-man with limited talent, the specialist man-marking was a job requiring intelligence, tenacity, speed, tactical awareness and no little skill. It was testament to Stiles that both England manager Sir Alf Ramsey and Matt Busby viewed him as an integral part of their (successful) teams. Moreover, Nobby Stiles previous battles with Eusebio were memorable for the sporting manner in which both went about trying to outwit the other.

  During training Matt Busby and Jimmy Murphy would pull Stiles aside many times to drill into him the importance of not letting Eusebio get a shot off on his dynamite right foot. Keep him on his left, shackle and harass, cut off his supply. To quote Murphy, 'Don't let that bastard breathe!' Nobby Stiles had form for this particular task and Busby was supremely confident Eusebio would be snared. Nobby was no longer the broken hearted young apprentice who had cleaned out the playing skip when it returned from Munich with tears stinging his eyes. The Belgrade mud had still been fresh on the kit from those that perished and Stiles was given Eddie Colman's boots for a keep-sake – there was little doubt who would be in Nobby's mind when the final kicked off.

In the days leading up to Wembley, George Best was named English football writer's player of the year. He was the youngest ever recipient of the trophy. For Best, whose Northern Irish blood meant he was denied the opportunity to ply his remarkable talent at international level in the World Cup, the opportunity of playing in the European Cup final were there to be grasped. Feared hugely by Benfica after his masterful display in Lisbon, Best knew he would by targeted by Portuguese defenders intent on ensuring history was not repeated. But such was his self-belief and desperation to be recognised as a world star: to ensure adoration on the beaches of Rio and across the planet, the 29th May 1968 had to be the day when George Best proved he was good enough to stand alongside the likes of Pele and Eusebio.

Sadly, for another of the Old Trafford terrace idols, a much worse fate had conspired against him. After an endless onslaught of pain-killing injections, strappings and stitches, Denis Law's knee gave up and three days before the final he was admitted to St Joseph's Hospital in Whalley Range, Manchester for an operation. There the surgeon removed a one and a half piece of damaged cartilage and for the first time in three years Law was pain free. That season Denis contributed seven goals in twenty-three league appearances despite almost constant agony. He mustered a further two in three European matches. Though rushed back by Busby to play in the first-leg of the semi against Real, it was a gamble that failed and come the return leg Law was taken to Madrid for purely, psychological purposes. It was clear then that should United make the final, Law's chance of playing was minimal. Instead he would watch his adopted Mancunian's day of destiny in the relative comfort of a hospital bed, surrounded by close friends, sister-nuns and doctors, all wearing United rosettes. And with copious amounts of alcohol nearby should the need arise!

For one young man it was a birthday like no other. On the 29th May Brian Kidd would be nineteen-years old. Unlike other lads of his own age, Kidd would not be celebrating down the local pub with a few friends but in full view of 100,000 people singing 'Happy Birthday' to a boy living just a short bus ride from Old Trafford. Born into a family of reds – blues, his father was a City supporter whilst Brian's brother Jimmy was a United fanatic. Jimmy would be watching and praying on the terraces praying that 'Our Brian' would have the night of his young life and help United finally lift the coveted trophy. From Saint Patrick's Livesey Street to Wembley's field of dreams, Brian Kidd was set to enter Manchester United folklore.

And then there was two.

Bobby Charlton and Bill Foulkes - ten seasons on from surviving the catastrophe of Munich they stood ninety minutes away from finally honouring the lives and deaths of their lost pals. Never men to talk about such feelings instead they spoke through their actions in a red shirt. For Charlton and Foulkes, defeat to Benfica was simply not an option as they prepared to give everything they had left and more. Too much pain and sorrow had passed. The Portuguese would be respected, but they would also be beaten. The best of times, the worst of times. It was time to come full circle.

From Manchester they came by train, car and coach in their tens of thousands. An estimated 80,000 of the 100,000-capacity crowd were said to have travelled south. A religious pilgrimage with the motto, 'Thou shalt not fail.' Matt Busby's red and white army would ensure their team received rapturous support. London was daubed red, the sounds and colour of the expectant Mancunians filling every watering hole near Wembley stadium. The club had also invited the families of the Munich victims as special honoured guests. There to witness with their own eyes an appropriate end to what their boys had begun. Twenty-four parents, wives and team mates from the crash including Harry Gregg, Jackie Blanchflower, Johnny Berry and Albert Scanlon. No doubt Roger Byrne, Geoff Bent, Mark Jones, Eddie Colman, David Pegg, Liam Whelan, Tommy Taylor and Duncan Edwards would also be there, cheering louder than any if Benfica were overcome.

It was the end of a ten-year journey in which the club had stumbled so many times, but always kept going.

Onwards, driven, incessant, never daring to look back to the image of the stricken fuselage and the bodies of the fallen. The 1968 European cup final would not be played for glory, fame or prestige but solely for the memory of the Busby Babes and the only proper memorial to their passing.

The boys of 68 daren't let them down.

Manchester United: Stepney: Brennan: Dunne: Crerand: Foulkes: Stiles: Best: Kidd: Charlton: Sadler and Aston

Benfica: Henrique: Adolfo: Humberto: Jacinto: Cruz: Graca: Coluna: Augusto: Torres: Eusebio and Simões

Wembley stadium has witnessed so many magnificent dramas and there had been none more dramatic or tense

than the 1966 World Cup final. But as Manchester United and Benfica prepared to do battle in the 1968 European Cup final, this grand old sporting theatre threatened to self-implode with emotion and excitement. The teams came into view to be greeted by a raging sea of red and white flags and banners. The welcome that thundered out from the terraces produced a cacophony of noise; a symphony for the fallen. A deafening, throaty, lustful scream almost primeval in its longing for the night to go well. A defiant roar to tell the world we are still here.
Led by captains Bobby Charlton and Mario Coluna, the teams made their way onto the field. United resplendent in white tracksuit tops with an away change of all blue strip beneath, Benfica in white. The referee was the flamboyant, well-known Sicilian Concerto Lo Bello. Smiling for the watching world-wide audience, Lo Bello strode imperiously before the teams, basking in his moment of glory. An estimated 250 million people around the globe tuning in.
Suddenly, the crowd broke into a wonderful rendition of 'Happy Birthday' for Brian Kidd. It was a magical moment for the youngster, one he could happily take to the grave. Lo Bello called the captains together in the centre-circle where they exchanged handshakes and pendants. Charlton and Coluna shared a quiet word. Idolised by the Benfica supporters, the thirty-three-year-old Coluna, nicknamed O Monstro Sagrado (The Sacred Monster) was playing his fiftieth game in the European Cup. A great respect had developed over the years between he and Charlton, men whose paths had crossed many times for club and country.

Seconds before United kicked off Eusebio raced into the centre-circle to shake hands with Charlton. It was a gesture typical of Benfica's number ten. Then, as Wembley held its breath the game began. United opened brightly with left-winger John Aston taking on and beating Portuguese right full-back Adolfo Calisto. It was a taste of what was to follow from Aston who was to give the unfortunate Adolfo nightmares and an evening under the London stars he would never forget. George Best was targeted early by Benfica when left-back Fernando Cruz and centre-half Jacinto Santos combined to bring the Irishman to ground. Best reacted with a few choice words in Cruz's direction when he went to catch him with a sly raised elbow. Portuguese intentions were clear -they did not intend to take prisoners.

The first chance for United came from a Paddy Crerand free kick that David Sadler failed by inches to control from six yards, though this apart it was cat and mouse. Neither dared risk all for fear of being caught on the break. Nerves took hold, only the direct running of the flying John Aston carried any real attacking intent on either side, as he took on and beat Adolfo at every attempt. The cries of 'Johnny Aston' ringing out from the United supporters, it was acclaim that one rarely heard within Old Trafford where all too often Aston found himself the scapegoat when results went awry.

On ten minutes Nobby Stiles introduced himself once more to Eusebio with a double lunge. The first just below his waist, the second knee high. Lo Bello sprinted in with whistle in mouth warning Stiles no more. United's number six backed away with a comical look of remorse etched upon his face. From the resulting free kick the fuming Eusebio smashed the ball high over Alex

Stepney's crossbar, much to the delight of the massed ranks of United fans behind the goal who goaded the great one. Two minutes later George Best carelessly lost possession and the ball fell at the feet of a still outraged Eusebio. Stiles again flew in with a cynical tackle but was this time left sprawling as on went the Panther in full flow towards the United penalty area. As if to prove a point he unleashed a vicious swerving shot that crashed violently against Stepney's bar and rebounded to safety. Thirty-six goals in thirty-eight European cup games meant it not wise to mock such genius.

United hit back and should have taken the lead when Kidd's wonderfully timed through ball split Benfica's central defenders for David Sadler again to run onto and shoot, only to pull the ball horribly wide from just eight yards. The groans of disappointment from the terraces told their own story, for these were heaven-sent opportunities that United could ill afford to squander. Overall the first half was a dour, drab affair littered with mistakes and with defences well on top. Aston's personal duel with Adolfo was the exception, negativity ruled. The exquisite threat of George Best snuffed out by any number of Portuguese white shirts queuing to eagerly kick the Belfast Boy back across the Irish sea at every given opportunity.

Meanwhile, Nobby Stiles, with an impressive if grim enthusiasm and ruthless professionalism, had got on top of his charge and was winning his personal battle with the Panther hands down. The piercing shrills of Concerto Lo Bello's whistle for half- time brought proceedings to a temporary halt and rather surprisingly there were a few boos from a frustrated crowd. It had been a sparse contest lacking the attacking football anticipated. However, what it lacked in quality was made up for in drama. As a nervous applause accompanied both teams back down the Wembley tunnel, a knife could slice the tension-racked London air. Mancunian expectations were being re-assessed as the wildly optimistic had received a dose of reality. Benfica were not about to roll over.

Under orders from Matt Busby, United began after the interval at a much faster pace as crosses a-plenty flew with intent into Benfica's penalty area. Busby's pre-match belief that the Portuguese would struggle to cope with pace looked to be coming to fruition as Aston continued to flourish and Best was now beginning to have an impact from wide positions. Suddenly, the noise level lifted a notch and belief was restored among the red hordes.

Eight minutes into the second half it reached volcanic proportions when a menacing cross from David Sadler found a leaping Bobby Charlton, who with deadly intent directed a stunning header past goalkeeper Henrique into the far corner. Charlton raced away with arms raised to be mobbed by a sea of blue shirts. United led and Wembley ignited with joy! Off the bench came Matt Busby and Jimmy Murphy as celebrations ran wild across the stadium.

Looking to kill the game off Paddy Crerand stole possession straight from the re-start and played in George Best who ran through and flicked a sublime finish over a stranded Henrique only to be called offside by an eagle-eyed Lo Bello. Benfica were rocked, another for United would surely end the contest. Still the blue shirts came forward, the pressure relentless. On sixty minutes an electrifying Best again latched onto a terrible error by Cruz to race through with just Henrique to beat. Knowing it was game over if beaten the goalkeeper kept his calm and foiled the Irishman. Somehow Benfica were still alive as the 1968 European Cup final entered a dramatic final quarter. A renewed sense of urgency or was it panic, surged through the Portuguese ranks. This night too bore historical references for Benfica. A third European triumph in eight years but it was Crerand and now more than ever Bobby Charlton controlling the tempo of the match. Always one eye on the clock, just see it home, make no mistakes.

The Portuguese champions attacked, their passes aiming for the head of the giant Torres. His knockdowns waited for, anticipated then cleared by Bill Foulkes who had marshalled the United rearguard superbly. Benfica came again; eleven minutes remained when the heavens crashed on Manchester United. Jose Augusto's long cross was headed down with great precision by the 6'4 Torres, for the onrushing midfielder Jaime Graca to shoot low past Alex Stepney from eight yards and break Mancunian hearts. Wembley was shaken. The Portuguese contingent present let loose their emotions. Bobby Charlton remembers the sickening feeling in his stomach as the ball hit the net, 'It was my worst nightmare. I couldn't see him missing and he didn't.'

Written off from the start Benfica now looked favourites. Matt Busby watched on as if sat waiting for the inevitable. His team shattered as the Eagles soared. Sensing a truly remarkable winner, Benfica went all out to bury this myth perceived by the English that all Manchester United had to do was turn up and win the final. Eusebio probed, looking for gaps where previously none had existed in a now leaking United defence. He sprinted across the halfway-line leaving a weary Stiles in his wake, only for Tony Dunne to cover a relieved teammate but the Panther was loose, uncaged. Then, a rare foray forward from Mario Coluna, who belying his thirty-three years sprinted past Shay Brennan and crossed for Jose Torres to leap high, but luckily for Manchester United and Stepney head over the bar. Again, Eusebio threatened. Midway inside the United half and surrounded by four blue shirts, a swift thinking one-two with Torres saw him roar clear before running on and letting fly a tremendous drive straight into a grateful Alex Stepney's midriff. The United supporters once more held their breath, they could not take much more and implored their team to simply play the ball forward rather than just keeping hold.

Finally, the crowds' wish was granted as Paddy Crerand's long pass found Bobby Charlton on the edge of Benfica's penalty area. However, a fine challenge from Humberto robbed Charlton and Antonio Simões sprinted away towards the halfway line. Convinced fellow defender Bill Foulkes stood covering behind him, Eusebio's jailer Nobby Stiles moved to intercept the Benfica winger, only to realise with horror that Foulkes was out of position and the Panther had gone. From a wonderful pass by Simões, Eusebio just had to pick a spot from twelve yards past Alex Stepney and win a magnificent third European cup for Benfica - Wembley watched aghast as Eusebio fired goal wards.

Matt Busby shut his eyes. The search for redemption was surely set to continue.

Unbelievably he shot with his weaker left foot straight at Stepney who held on to the ball and earned the gratitude of every Manchester United supporter forever more. Ever the sportsman, Eusebio attempted to congratulate the goalkeeper on his courageous save but Stepney gave him short shrift, waving away the Portuguese striker.

'I smothered the shot and felt the ball go soft. It either burst when he hit it or when it hit me, either way it took away some of the sting. But the marks are still there and I've had Mitre written on my chest ever since!'

Still Benfica looked for a killer goal as they massed with deadly intent and encamped around the United penalty area. From the wings came the 'Eagles' as Augusto's cross was met superbly by Eusebio's header that flew within an angel's breath of winning the day for the Portuguese. With time almost up United broke out…. Georgie Best darted through Benfica's defence only to be run wide of goal before firing into a relieved Henrique's side-netting. Disappointment and anxiety etched with excitement engulfed Wembley stadium as Concerto Lo Bello blew for full time. It finished 1-1 and another thirty minutes on an unbelievably humid and sweltering Wembley evening awaited the two teams. All but out on their feet, Nobby Stiles later admitted, 'we were spent and another ten minutes they would have beaten us.' Busby and Murphy walked amongst their Players, urging and cajoling. Some of the United lads noticed also that the Portuguese appeared more worse for wear than them. It was a point reinforced by their manager, 'They're finished' he said. 'You're throwing the game away. Keep possession, get the ball to George and Johnny and start attacking.' Now in the final strait with the finishing line so close Busby would trust his footballing principles and three minutes into extra time Manchester United were back in front.

A long clearance from Alex Stepney was flicked on by Brian Kidd into the Benfica half. Just when Cruz looked in control of the ball it was taken off him by George Best, who raced twenty-five yards into the penalty area, dummied Jose Henrique and twisted left before rolling the ball home as a desperate Henrique dived in vain. Rehearsed on Belfast's cobbled streets then performed to a world-wide audience - now they knew his name! In a career that from this moment would start to diminish, Best's wonderful individual effort proved to be the defining image of arguably Manchester United's greatest ever player. What should have been a glorious beginning sadly turned into George Best's epitaph. But on 29th May 1968, as Wembley stadium exploded once more and a beaming Best fell into the arms of joyful team-mates, it felt like Georgie Boy would live forever.

Now United went for Benfica's throats. A revitalised Bobby Charlton fed the amazing John Aston who simply pushed the ball past the beleaguered Adolfo and ran the entire length of the Portuguese half before finally being brought to ground at the expense of a corner. The words unsung hero seemed to have been invented for the magnificent Aston.

Across ran Charlton to huge applause from the United supporters. His right foot delivery swung over toward a melee of bodies, reacting quickest Brian Kidd turned in a close-range header that was bravely blocked by a flailing Henrique, before the birthday boy forced home the rebound, arcing his effort over the prone goalkeeper and into the goal. From the heaving, dancing terraces a torrent of noise greeted Kidd's' goal. It was a joyful awe-inspiring crescendo. The red half of Manchester knew their team were almost there. As Wembley saluted the nineteen-year old Kidd, a brave but surely beaten Benfica looked dead on their feet. Charlton again, 'When that ball

went in I had to fight back the tears because I knew it was all over. Benfica had gone. We just had to guard against stupidity and we had finally won this thing.'
Straight from the re-start Aston careered once more over the half-way line before finding George Best wide on the right. Racing into the Portuguese penalty area Best's astute clip bounced off the Portuguese crossbar and away. United were rampant! Playing to Busby's instructions Paddy Crerand and Bobby Charlton kept the ball. Teasing and prompting the exhausted Benfica players, their hearts and legs equally shattered.
On ninety-nine minutes United roared forward again as Bobby Charlton with socks down around his ankles fed a raiding Brian Kidd to sprint down the touchline. Off soared the long-legged youngster before placing a perfect cross onto the right foot of a waiting Charlton, the boy on whose slim shoulders the hopes and dreams of every United supporter had rested since Munich. Charlton swept a majestic effort past Henrique into the top corner. Years later an emotional Charlton related, 'That was for Dunc and the boys. My pals.'
With such grace and artistry the European cup was won. First to congratulate Bobby Charlton was George Best who jumped into his arms. Both men were quickly joined by ecstatic team mates. Up came a laughing Crerand to embrace Charlton who gestured to his Scottish colleague, 'That's it. It's over.'
Lo Bello blew to end the first period of extra time and Manchester had simply blown away Benfica. Fifteen minutes of blistering attacking football had been dragged from who knows where when they appeared to have nothing left. The Wembley crowd were on their feet. A sense of wonder and disbelief filled the ranks.

Again, Matt Busby and Jimmy Murphy implored their players to keep the ball. Murphy stood over Bobby Charlton massaging his legs. The shy young kid from the north east who arrived at Old Trafford and was meted out for special attention by Murphy, who knew that here was a truly, exceptional footballer. Murphy had knocked off the rough edges and polished up the rest and Charlton's two superb goals on that long-gone Wembley evening epitomised everything the 'preacher' believed. A ripe apple that had borne wonderful fruition.
'We shall not be moved' sang the crowd.
'We shall not be moved.'
The final whistle: amid a hub of well-wishers a beaming Matt Busby strode onto the pitch. Trying desperately to fight away the tears and keep his composure Busby headed towards the centre circle to sportingly shake hands with the forlorn Benfica players. However, his path was cut short when a crying Bobby Charlton fell into his arms and the pair embraced. No words were necessary. The best of times.
Avoiding the mad huddle of cameras and flashlights exploding all around walked Jimmy Murphy. Never one for the spotlight, this proud Welshman stood content in the knowledge that it had really not all been for nothing. Munich would never go away but for one night the pain would ease, his boys could salute a job done well. A victory earned the Manchester United way. First you raise spirits, then you break hearts. Then you rise again and prevail. A wink to the stars and the fallen and Jimmy Murphy vacated the stage.
So, the time came for the presentation and the United players, Paddy Crerand foremost amongst them tried desperately to persuade Matt Busby to go and raise the

famous trophy high. Two years had passed since Crerand had talked his manager out of retirement in the dressing room after the bitter semi-final defeat to Partizan Belgrade, it felt like a lifetime. However, all efforts were in vain as Busby refused point-blank and instead insisted his captain Bobby Charlton be first up the Wembley steps to collect the Holy Grail.

On being handed the trophy a smiling Charlton lifted it into the air and Wembley stadium erupted! Looking drained and close to collapse he made his weary way back down. It was to be a strange night for Bobby Charlton whose thoughts even today never appear to be far away from those dear friends he had lost in the crash. To them went the glory and spoils of victory. A man who has dedicated almost his entire life to Manchester United, and for whom a piece of his heart will remain forever on a far off German runway.

C16
MATT AND JIMMY: FALLEN ANGELS: 1969
A Stage-Play

Against a backdrop of Old Trafford.
Facing audience:

Jimmy is sat smoking a roll up whilst gazing out over Old Trafford. When Matt approaches up the steps.

MATT
Jimmy.

Jimmy looks across to Matt, then back over the pitch, obviously not impressed.

MATT
Jimmy, I was going to tell you, but it's been crazy with the press boys. I just couldn't find the time earlier. I'm sorry.

Still Jimmy stares, totally ignoring Matt.

MATT
Oh, Jimmy, please talk to me?

Finally, Jimmy looks over at Matt.

JIMMY
Congratulations Matt, I hope you have a wonderful retirement. I really do. There, do you feel better now? If you could've been bothered to tell me you were going then me and Winnie would've bought you something. Some Cuban cigars, maybe a nice scarf or a hat. Red of course.

MATT
Come on old friend, I think we need to talk. It's been far too long and too much has remained unsaid. It's time to clear the air. I'm tired, I need to put things right with you. You're like a ghost around here.

(Matt sits down.)

JIMMY
A ghost? You've looked through me for ten years and now you want me to bare my soul. Is that it?

MATT
I just want to make things rights between us.

JIMMY
What, am I on your list of things to do before you walk off into the sunset with the crowd singing 'There's only

Matt Busby.' Do me a favour Matt. I think it best you just go.

MATT
I can't Jimmy. I just can't. I need to try and explain why I acted like I did.

JIMMY
No, you've left it far too late. But I genuinely wish you and Jean a long and happy retirement. I really do Matt.

MATT
Do you hate me? Do you? I couldn't blame you if you did.

JIMMY
Of course, I don't hate you, I don't understand you, but I don't hate you. How could I after everything we've been through man. What a stupid bloody question.

MATT
Well then give me this one chance to explain myself? Please Jimmy?

JIMMY

Give me one reason why I should listen to a word you have to say when after ten years you've done your damn best to act like I don't exist?

MATT
Fallen angels?

JIMMY
Ah, that's not fair Matt…That's not fair at all.

MATT
Please, old pal. I need to do this.

JIMMY
What, after all this time you finally want to open your heart? You want to tell me how everything changed after the crash. How you ever so surely over the years pushed me aside. And broke my bloody heart.

MATT
There was a reason. Selfish, aye, maybe but it was how I had to be. When I left the hospital at Munich my surgeon Doctor Maurer told me the pain in my body would in time ease, but I had to find a way or seek help for what was in my head. But I never did see. I felt the best way to face it was if I never mentioned it to anyone, it would all go away, but it never has. It never will. And yet you, you stepped up after the crash and saved the day…I don't

think I could have done what you did. The loss and the grief would've broken me. You were stronger Jimmy.

JIMMY
I'm not stronger and what are you on about, it did break me. It broke my bloody heart. But I had no choice, everyone was crying, numb with grief. I just had to grit my bloody teeth and make sure no one saw me cry. But cry I bloody did.

MATT
Aye, so many have told me what a grand job you did whilst I was lying in that Munich bed. Murphy's marvels keeping the red flag flying….

JIMMY
What is it with you? If I'm not mistaken you sound jealous?

MATT
Ah away with you Jimmy, that's ridiculous.

JIMMY
I never took you for a jealous man Matt. Hard and stubborn at times, yes, but jealous? I always thought you were bigger than that.

MATT
Jealous, me? What did I have to be jealous about?

JIMMY
You really don't know? Oh, come on, you can fool yourself man, but don't try and think you can fool me.

MATT
Explain yourself Jimmy.

JIMMY
You wouldn't want to hear it from my lips, believe me.

MATT
No, you're wrong, I really do. I need to know.

JIMMY
Okay then, if you insist I'll tell you. That at the time you believed people were saying I kept United going whilst you were lying in that Munich hospital.

MATT
Well you did and….

JIMMY

And that without me the board, your good friends would've closed the doors and called time on our club. And I can assure you they were close. Very damn close. But I talked them round see, I told them over my dead body would I allow that to happen. Over my dead body, I said.

MATT
What's your point?

JIMMY
My point? My point is that without me fighting, scrapping, pleading and bastard begging, there would've been no Manchester United, and you would've come home from Munich unemployed and looking for a job. It wouldn't have been Matt and Jimmy anymore, it would've been Jimmy and Matt and you could never handle that. What with your ego: losing the power of being Mr Manchester United would've been too much for you and so you turned on me like a…. like a….

MATT
You don't honestly believe that Jimmy? Please tell me you don't?

JIMMY
You tell me then, am I wrong?

MATT
That I could be such a jealous and vain man to see you denied any credit. Yes, you're wrong. That's not true at all. I'm better than that. At least, well at least I thought I was.

JIMMY
Well then tell me the truth, what was it, what happened back then? Why did you cut me out? Why did you break my heart?

MATT
(Tearful)
Jimmy please? Please tell me you don't believe that…Please…

JIMMY
No…I don't believe it. How could I? But something changed Matt. You changed and for the worse. The man who went to Belgrade was not the same one who returned. You pushed me away and just never stopped pushing. I became invisible to you. You treated me like a leper and I could never understand why. Damn it I still don't!

MATT
Do you know why? Can I tell you? The answer is quite simple and isn't one I'm proud of.

JIMMY
Aye well, bloody took you long enough man. Speak then. Go on….

MATT
It was because we, I, lost our boys Jimmy. We lost our boys They got on a plane and never came home and that's what changed. All our hopes and dreams died at the end of that damned runway.

JIMMY
Oh Matt….

MATT
And even after finally winning the European cup last May, did the pain ease? Aye, yes maybe for a night, but it returned. I saw it in the eyes of Duncan's mum who I met after the game. I looked at her and I could see Big Dunc Jimmy. I could see him…. And she said to me how much he loved me. How much he loved playing football and how much he loved Manchester United.

(The two go quiet. A tearful Matt light his pipe.)

JIMMY
There is not a day goes by when I don't think of Duncan. His last words to me in training before you all flew to

Belgrade. I got all the lads together see, I promised them if they got a good result, well, I would go easy on them in training when they got home. Duncan's voice boomed out, a huge grin on his voice, 'We won't let you down Jimmy'.... Ah Matt, this is going to hurt both of us.

MATT
We're no strangers to pain Jimmy.

JIMMY
We weren't strangers once. This strangeness between us is all your doing. So many years wasted when we could've helped each other. My family could never understand why you went like you did. Winnie said it was my imagination, but I knew, I saw it in your eyes. You couldn't face me. And I'd done nothing wrong.

MATT
I was a broken man when I came home. I couldn't think straight. I couldn't understand why I was alive and all our boys had died. I should've reached out to you Jimmy. I know that now, but at the time I was in a dark place. I couldn't see or think straight. I couldn't sleep, I just walked around in a daze.

JIMMY
Yet you were happy to let others close? But not me? You had your pals. Paddy McGrath, Johnny Foy, so why

crucify me? What the bloody hell had I done to deserve such treatment?

MATT
Because you knew what I was going through.

JIMMY
And what was that?

MATT
Oh, come on Jimmy, don't play games. I was grieving.

JIMMY
Grieving? Let me tell you something oh Mr Sir Matt Busby. Mr Father of our bloody Football team. Do you think you have the moral high ground on grief? Those days after the crash I cried till I had no tears left see, but I could never do it in public, because I was always drying somebody else's eyes. I couldn't let anyone see me break, because I was all they had. And it wasn't bloody fair Matt, it wasn't bastard fair what happened. Why us, why me, I'd whisper under my breath as I watched young boys, girls, just kids sobbing on the forecourt. Grown men stood there with eyes glazed, oh they could cry, but not me, not me, so please…. don't you try and tell me about pain? And then what happens, you come home and treat me like I've done something terrible to you man. Me….

MATT
If it makes you feel any better I did the same to the Almighty as well. I lost faith, so you were in good company Jim.

JIMMY
Aye well, me and him had words as well afterwards, More than a few. The fact he let you live meant we went back on speaking terms. For a while anyway.

(The two go quiet for a moment…. It's a bitterly cold December day and both men are wearing overcoats. Matt fastens his and puts his collar up. Jimmy's is open.)

MATT
Fasten your coat Jimmy, you'll catch your death of cold.

JIMMY
You've retired remember, you can't tell me what to do anymore….

MATT
(Smiling)
No, but I can tell Winnie when you're coughing and spluttering at home.

JIMMY
(Fastening his coat)
You fight dirty!

MATT
Aye well, I learned along the way.

JIMMY
When we played you were the artist Matt, the ball player, and me, well I wasn't called Tapper Murphy for nothing!

MATT
You'd have kicked your own ma you if she had tried to take the ball off you.

JIMMY
Ah she would never dare! …
(The two smile)

MATT
Do you remember when we met in Bari, 1943

JIMMY
How can I forget. Never been one for time keeping Matt, time just rolls on. But we were so young then. It was a world of killing and death. Dark, dark times but somehow it was all so normal. The Nazi bastards just had to be beaten.

MATT
Aye, Southern Italy. A beautiful country but drenched in so much blood. I watched you refereeing those soldiers like it was an FA Cup final. They saw it as a kickabout, but not you, not you Jimmy. I knew from that very moment if I was ever going to manage a football club after the war I wanted you alongside me. I remember when we spoke you had a football under your arm. You said to me, 'Do you see this Matt. Amongst the carnage, this, has kept me sane.'

JIMMY
Me and you were the lucky ones back then weren't we. Because we'd been professional footballers we were never really in the thick of it.

MATT
Aye, they made us pt. Instructors instead. We still saw terrible things though Jimmy. Man's inhumanity to his fellow man. What we are capable of when pushed.

JIMMY
Awful. In North Africa, I saw men fall to their knees and break down and cry just on seeing the ocean after returning from the front. Some started to swim and just carried on over the waves…. never came back…never came back.

MATT
The war at that time was far from over, but you told me one day it would be and pointed again to that ball and said, 'This will matter once more. Just a bag of wind in the great scheme of things, but there will come a day when the whistle will finally blow on this madness and life…. Life can begin again.'

JIMMY
I remember when I got your letter two years later asking if I would join you in Manchester. This bloody damp, cold, smog filled place and a club with neither a ground or a penny to their own. But it was our dream to conquer and it was a beautiful thing. And this city, it was reduced to rubble by Hitler's bombs, but it had something. It had guts Matt, it had heart and it had soul. They, like us just wanted to live again and enjoy their football and we were determined to make it happen.

MATT
And we did, me and you together, Matt and Jimmy. I could never dream in my worst nightmares that I'd live to witness such carnage as what had gone before, but I did. As if we hadn't suffered enough, me, you, Manchester, and yet our friend upstairs decided to bring on Munich

JIMMY
Maybe this is wrong to admit but for a time after the crash, there was a part of me that wished I had been on

that plane. To be with the boys when it happened. The chance I could've helped, maybe save lives?

MATT
You would've been sat next to me Jimmy. Where Bert Whalley was and he was killed outright. You could never have helped anyone from beyond the grave old son. No, the angels spared you for another task.

JIMMY
It wasn't the bloody angels, it was you Matt. You said I had to go manage Wales in Cardiff. It was my duty to do so and in saying that you saved my life.

MATT
No, it was a decision taken by angels Jimmy. Out of my hands. A decision taken by the angels. They spared you for a reason.

JIMMY
Aye, small mercies. So, they were to blame….

(The two go quiet. Jimmy smoking his roll ups, Matt his pipe.)

JIMMY cont.
So, explain to me. What happened when you came back then? I mean, let's be honest now, we were never like

brothers Matt, good pals yes, but all that ended. It was like a shutter coming down between us or a light being switched off. You just cut me out, why? I need to understand. What on earth caused you to do such a cruel thing.

MATT
Words can't express how sorry I am for what I did and how I acted towards you Jimmy, but you have to try and understand that I was nursing a broken heart myself. I still am, it's still broken and always will be. Every day I went to the ground and I saw ghosts, I heard their voices. Down every corridor at Old Trafford. When it went quiet I heard Eddie Colman's laugh, Duncan's broad black-country accent. I thought I was going mad. I honestly thought I was going crazy. As for you, well I knew you were suffering just as much inside, but there was just too much pain. It was killing me. I couldn't bear to reach out to you because that would've simply finished me off. A trouble shared they say, but my God, not this one. I needed to keep my feelings inside. And just seeing you every day…. and knowing like me, you were slowly dying to. I do regret what I did, I really do. But I simply wasn't strong enough to reach out.

JIMMY
You could've tried.

MATT
(Tearful)

I am so sorry Jimmy.

They go quiet once more.
JIMMY
It was the bloody oranges for me…I can still smell them now.

MATT
Oranges?

JIMMY
After the game against the Israelis, they presented me with a box of oranges that I carried home back to Manchester. But that is another story. Damned things. Then, from London Rd railway station, I jumped into a taxi that took me to Old Trafford still carrying those bloody oranges. I had no idea what had happened. Not a clue. I do remember it was mid-afternoon and there were dark angry skies and it was freezing cold and raining heavy. The rain splattering on the taxi window and as I looked, I also remember a man with a bowler hat who recognised me as we drove past…. And he was crying? So strange what stays in your mind after all these years Matt. Strange what stays in your mind…. On arriving I remember I gave the taxi driver an orange. He hadn't shut up all the way from the station to the ground but he was a good lad. I got out, I went inside, I was whistling, I was in a great mood. We'd just made the European cup semi-finals and I was on top of the world I was. So proud of you and the boys. And then I saw Alma and she was crying. She had tears rolling down her cheeks. She told

me there had been a crash, but didn't know who was alive or dead. That night, was like stepping into the pits of hell. There can never have been one so dark and so very long Matt.

MATT
I can only imagine Jimmy.

JIMMY
Oh, I don't think you can old son. I wouldn't want you too. Something clicked in me and I knew I had to get down to business. It felt like there was only me and Alma left, the phone was ringing off the hook. I got a call from the Express who confirmed the dead…. It was surreal. I went through Alma's list of family phone numbers. Ticking off as I rang. My heart breaking each time I dialed the numbers.
Roger Byrne. I spoke to his wife Joy. She sounded in shock and spoke almost in sniffling joking terms, but I could hear her heart breaking over the phone. 'I've only known him three February's Jimmy,' she said. 'The first he crashed our car into a lamp post. The second into Matt Busby's neighbour's garden and now the third he's gone and got himself killed in a damn plane crash.' She let slip also they were expecting a baby and Roger didn't know…. She was going to tell him on returning.

MATT
Oh Christ, Jimmy.

JIMMY
Tommy Taylor, Big Tommy and Barnsley's finest. I cried on the phone with both his mother and father, Viollet and Charlie. 'He loved you Jimmy' said Viollet. 'And he loved Manchester United.'
David Pegg's mother Jessie sobbed through tears and I sobbed too.
Liam 'Billy' Whelan. Billy, you know wanted to be a priest, but only the love of a ball saw him pull on our red shirt and not a cassock. I had no number, but I knew the name of the Dublin road: St Attracta, so I found out through the operator, a neighbour's phone number. I rang them and asked if they could possible go and put Liam's mother on the phone. She already suspected Matt, 'I knew Jimmy' she said. 'I could feel my Liam's spirit soar. He is with the angels.' I will never forget those words…. With the angels.

MATT
God bless young Billy. He was always so worried when he first came over that we would steal his real name and in the end, we did. He became Billy.

JIMMY
Mark Jones' pregnant wife June screaming down the line. Geoff Bent's wife Marion, she wept till there was no tears left to fall. 'What do we do now Jimmy' she cried. 'I already have one five-month-old baby child, Karen, and another on the way.'

Eddie Colman's dad Dickie said little but I could hear his heart breaking in Salford across the river. He left the house in just his pajamas and slippers and they found him hours later sat on a bench in Piccadilly, crying his eyes out. Eddie was their life. Their every breathing second. His grandfather Dickie Senior, whom all the players adored. Young Bobby Charlton and Wilf McGuiness in particular. They'd gather in Eddie's living room and the old man would enthrall them with tall and terrible and wonderful tales of his past escapades. There'd be singsongs and joy and laughter in Archie Street. That ended forever on Thursday 6th February 1958.

MATT
Eddie had a smile that could light up a city. That hip swerve of his could send a whole grandstand the wrong way. A cheeky chappie. A lovely boy.

JIMMY
My boys…. My golden, golden apples. Wiped out. Gone. And I hadn't even thought about Duncan. I never had time. He'd been confirmed as critical, but where there was life a grain of hope remained and in Big Dunc's case he was bigger than life itself. So, let anyone try to take him before he had conquered the world, I remembered thinking. But, in the end even he died and on hearing this none of us could breathe. A colossus and such a brave lad, The best. I don't know how, but, from somewhere God gave me the strength to make it through that darkest of nights. He was probably nursing a guilty conscience mind you…. I have never known pain and deep, deep sadness like it Matt. Never.

MATT
At first, I was spared the mental pain, because, well, they had given me the Last Rites twice hadn't they. I wasn't supposed to make it. You mentioned about wanting to be on the plane. Well, I was and I'm so, so glad you weren't and saw what I did. What I witnessed, the horror and the screams and the crying of our lads in the German snow. It tormented me to the point that when I was in the hospital bed I didn't care whether I lived or died. For I truly believed I had killed those boys, and I still do.

JIMMY
You can't seriously blame yourself for what happened Matt? It just isn't true.

MATT
(Tearful)
Do you blame me Jimmy? Do you blame me for what happened?

JIMMY
You're not God Matt. You never caused that plane to fall from the skies.

MATT
You haven't answered my question.

JIMMY
I think I have, you're talking nonsense.

MATT
So, the reason we lost our boys was because of the act of an evil god, and it was nothing to do with me pushing to get us home so we didn't forfeit the match against the Wolves the following Saturday?

JIMMY
You cannot torture yourself like this man. You're being far too hard on yourself.

MATT
Am I Jimmy. Am I really? Oh, I know what people said then and still do. Though never to my face. The families, players and supporters. Why did Busby let them get back on that plane for a third time? Why did he risk the lives of our boys? And why, most importantly, why was he allowed to live when they died?

JIMMY
Nobody ever said anything like that in earshot of me and I wouldn't have stood for it if they had. By god I would have sorted them out I would.

MATT

Much appreciated old pal.

JIMMY

I remember going over to Munich the day after the crash and first seeing you. You were unconscious in an oxygen tent. Like your Sandy, at first I didn't recognise you, I thought who is this stranger before my eyes? I sat down beside your bed and placed my hand on yours. You looked forty-nine going on eighty. Alright Matt, I said. I told you it wasn't time to go because we still had so much work to do. I reminded you'd once told me that together we would take United not just into the heavens, but beyond the stars.

That it just wasn't time to say goodbye because we had still to knock that bloody Real Madrid off their damn pedestal…. And I couldn't do it on my own, I told you. I needed you by my side. Matt and Jimmy together. Our red devils. It was my job to stoke the fires and light the flame in their bellies and you supply the gold dust. The magic. A bunch of bouncing Busby boys…And then, I suddenly felt a movement in your hand. Your eyes flickered open and you immediately recognised me. Yours was a tortured smile and you were clearly wracked with pain. You tried to speak, but it was nothing more than a strained whisper. I leant in close and could just about make out your words, 'Keep the flag flying till I get back Jimmy,' you said.

'Keep the flag flying.' Then, your eyes closed once more and you drifted off back into unconsciousness. But I had my orders see, and something told me that you, Matt Busby was going nowhere fast and it was down to me to hold the fort until you returned.….

MATT
The dreams Jimmy, they still come to haunt. There are times when I wake and I swear the sheets are wet with melting snow from that runway. I'm back there with the smell of burning petrol filling my nose and the dreadful sound of screams in my ears. I open my eyes and I see, I shut and I see. There is no escape. It is like being in a prison of my nightmares.

JIMMY
All these years you've waited to tell me this. All these years Matt. You should've told me then. I could've helped, you could've helped me and together we could've got better. Cos I've had the dreams as well. I'm back in the gym talking to the boy's coffins. I'm telling, no begging them to wake up. Praying it was all just a nightmare and when I wake they would all still be here. Fooling and clowning around, taking the mickey out of each other. But they never wake, the night is so dark and sad and each morning as my eyes open, my hearts breaks with it.

(Jimmy has a tear in his eye and Matt passes him a handkerchief.)

MATT
Here you go old son you have something in your eye.

(They both smile)

JIMMY
Thanks Matt.

(Again, they go quiet.)

JIMMY
So, it really is all over then? You're handing over the reins to Wilf. He's a good lad and bleeds red for this club he does. United through and through. Although I can't imagine this place without you. Like a church without a priest.

MATT
(Smiling)
Well I'm not really retiring as such Jimmy. I'm become general manager. Wilf will handle team affairs, I'll be looking after everything else. Let him concentrate solely on team matters. He's going to have enough to deal with.

JIMMY
Maybe I can help him? Give him a shoulder to lean on. Lend him an ear when he needs it. Wilf is full of enthusiasm, but tends sometimes to react if pushed. He's going from 'good old Wilf' to the boss. That's a big jump, especially with some of the characters knocking

around here. He will need a steadying hand. I could give him that.

MATT
Thanks, but it won't be necessary Jimmy.

JIMMY
Why not? Surely you know he's going to need help. If he's on his own there are players here who will chew him up and spit him out.

MATT
Well he won't need you because that's exactly what I'll be doing. Anyone stepping out of line, specifically our George, then Wilf tells me and I deal with it.

JIMMY
Hold on Matt, you're not stepping away at all are you? I should've known, you're incapable of living without this club. Wilf will be nothing more than your puppet. You'll still be pulling the strings.

MATT
No not all Jimmy, Wilf will be his own man.

JIMMY

Of course, he will, maybe I should ask him myself if he wants me around?

MATT
You're out Jim. I'm sorry. I really am.

JIMMY
(Smiling)
No, you're not. You don't want me around because I know you too well. I know what is going on here. You think you've pulled the wool over everyone's eyes, Wilf included, but you haven't mine Matt.

MATT
Are you questioning my integrity Jimmy?

JIMMY
(Smiling)
No, I would never do that. Just your reasoning.

MATT
What in choosing Wilf? Wilf is loyal.

JIMMY
Aye he is that, Wilf will do what he's told. If you want loyalty get yourself a dog Matt, not a football manager.

MATT
No, you don't understand Jimmy. United is more than a football club now, we're an institution that is worldwide. Wilf needs to be protected from that. He is going to need the guiding hand that I will provide. Not you.

JIMMY
And you swear to me now that you won't be interfering in picking the team?

MATT
Like I said, I will be a guiding hand.

JIMMY
Matt, listen to me please, you're not being fair. If Wilf is to succeed it will have to be on his own terms with his own people around him. He loves you, but you'll be like a huge shadow that in the end will blind him and the players will quickly realise he's just a front man and you're still the real boss.

MATT
I'm treating Wilf like a stooge you mean? Is that what you're saying?

JIMMY
Well, aren't you?

MATT
Ah, away with you Jimmy.

JIMMY
Matt, your presence will strangle him. Trust me it'll happen. You owe Wilf a chance to do this on his own. Let him stand or fall on his terms. Because, if, when it all goes wrong and you have to sack him, then he will hate you for it.

MATT
Your faith in Wilf is overwhelming Jimmy, I thought you two were close. Isn't Wilf one of your 'golden apples?'

JIMMY
Our golden apples you mean. And yes, we are close. I love Wilf, but I know him and this job with you not giving him room to breathe will destroy him. I beg you Matt, let me do it, you step away. You're still and will always be Manchester United in the eyes of our supporters and the entire world. Why not go now with trumpets blazing and the crowd singing your name. Or at least stay away from the football side of things. Let last May at Wembley be your epitaph.

MATT
(Smiling)

I maybe Mr Manchester United Jimmy, but back before Munich you're the ones our boys always loved.

JIMMY
That's not true they loved you too.

MATT
No, you're wrong they respected me, but they loved you Jimmy. Bobby Duncan, Eddie, Tommy, all of them. They were more your boys, your golden apples, not mine. You were with them every day in the mud and rain out on the training pitch. Screaming, cajoling, loving and teaching. Teaching the Manchester United way. I would watch you Jimmy, but I could never be you. Like you could never be me. Do what I did. You were hard, but did it with tough love. I was the one who ultimately made the decisions and broke hearts. That was my job. You, when the deed was done, you would place an arm around their shoulders and take them for a drink in the pub or a cry in the chapel...Good old Jimmy. We both had our roles old friend and I don't remember you complaining back then….

JIMMY
Complain about what? You sound bitter for no reason Matt. Why? I don't understand. They were your boys equally as much as they were mine.

MATT

But you didn't kill them Jimmy, I killed them. It was me.

JIMMY
Oh, now you're talking nonsense again see, you have bottled this up for years and it was never your fault man. An act of God killed our boys.

MATT
(Bitter Smile)
Oh yes, I forgot. It was an all in the hands of our one loving god whom we both worship who decided to rip us from the sky and splatter our blood all over that Munich runway. It was our one loving god who decided to give you the job of ringing the boy's families to tell them their fathers and sons were dead. Left dying in burning flames, a snowstorm from hell. It was our loving god that…

JIMMY
(Shouting)
Matt, for heaven's sake, that's enough! Stop this now!

MATT
Well then, be honest with me Jimmy, stop the bloody babysitting and speak your mind. Admit that I let our lads down. That it was all about playing the Wolves the following Saturday and getting home and not being docked points by that damned Football Association and Alan Hardaker.

JIMMY
That bastard….

MATT
It wasn't Hardaker that killed them Jimmy, I was the one pushing to get home. I risked everything on a larcenous throw of the dice that fell horribly wrong all for the sake of two damn points. We should've stayed over and come home the next day. I know that now and if I'm honest I think I knew that then. I put our boys at risk for the sake of two bloody points. Admit it Jimmy, go on you can say it, I won't blame you. The responsibility for their deaths lies with me.

(Jimmy starts to light another roll up as Matt stares at him.)

JIMMY
(Quietly whilst rolling his cigarette to his lips.)
I'm admitting nothing old friend because it just isn't true. You have demons in your soul and you're trying to convince yourself of a guilt that you don't deserve. It makes sense to me now what happened after Munich and I can see now why you tried to pretend I didn't exist. You were scared to death of me blaming you for what happened. Even though I would never have done so. And you know me well enough to know that god forbid I heard any bastard say such, I would've knocked their bloody head off their shoulders. Not caring who it was.

I almost throttled that damned Bob Lord at Burnley over some rubbish he sprouted about the crash. It took most of our boys to hold me back and if I had heard anyone talk wrong of you, a bastard tank regiment would not have prevented me sorting them out.

(The two men stare for a moment and then both start to smile.)

MATT
Aye, I can quite believe that…

JIMMY
Two bloody tank regiments!

MATT
For how I've treated you there can be no words. But I'm so, so sorry my friend. I can only hope and pray that somewhere in that huge Welsh heart of yours you find the strength to forgive me.

JIMMY
And Wilf?

MATT
It's not up for argument. Can we agree to disagree?

JIMMY
What you're doing is wrong and selfish.

MATT
I'm doing what I believe is right. This isn't Munich, it's not life or death. I'm doing this for the good of the club. As for how I've treated you, I deserve a penance.

JIMMY
Give over Matt, can you hear yourself? I'm a football man not a bloody priest. You just promise me you'll stop blaming yourself for what happened.

MATT
Wish I could Jimmy lad, but that will only end when I stop breathing.

JIMMY
You know something Matt, this game of ours that is supposed to be so simple. Just twenty-two men kicking a ball around. Be it in wind, rain, snow or fog and here in Manchester probably all at the same time. This game of ours as Bill Shankly often says is really about life. The passions involved. Love and like it or not, hate. The desire to win, the sheer pain of loss. The togetherness, friendships made and lost.

MATT
Aye, friendships made….and lost.

JIMMY
All for one and one for all and then, in the blink of an eye your career is over. This game of ours…. We were blessed to be allowed to come back into the game and do what we did. Watch what we witnessed. From the cradle….and sadly, for many of our boys to the grave. Death was never meant to cast its ghastly shadow over our beautiful game and our beautiful boys, but it did. Though we were truly blessed for a while Matt….
This game of ours.

MATT
Aye, this bloody game of ours. Can't live with it, can't live without it; and does it care? Oh, it will take you to the heights of ecstasy, but also to the depths of hell. Some game Jimmy….

JIMMY
It's a drug, no other word for it…it gets in your blood and you're hooked. There's no getting out.

MATT
(Smiling)
Exactly….

JIMMY
Then why the bloody hell did you retire man?

MATT
Let's not go there again Jimmy. We're never going to agree.

JIMMY
The mad old king that's you….

MATT
(Smiling)
Aye, maybe but I wasn't always like this, there's so many more responsibilities now Jimmy. It's not just what happens on the pitch anymore. United is changing. We have to look to the future off it. It's almost the seventies. A different world. Business matters off the field are equally important now.

JIMMY
Not changing for the better in my opinion.

MATT
Nothing stays the same old friend. We can't afford to sit still.

JIMMY

We have an ageing team that has to be sorted first and foremost. Otherwise we'll get left behind. That should be the priority, not building new stands or whatever else goes on in that bloody boardroom.

MATT
We still have Bobby, George and Denis. Willie has come in; young Kiddo is going to be a player. We're not weak.

JIMMY
We need new blood Matt, I can feel it around the place, and on the pitch things are not right….

MATT
(Smiling)
Let me sort it…. trust me. Will you?

JIMMY
No choice have I. You're not bloody going anywhere.

MATT
Good lad. We had a dream once didn't we? Remember the chat we had after watching Hungary beat England 6-3 at Wembley back in 1953, Ferenc Puskas and his wonderful magicians playing a brand of football we'd never seen. They appeared from behind the Iron Curtain like magicians and wizards to put a spell on all of us who loved and thought about the game.

JIMMY
Aye, how can I forget! A Welshman and a Scotsman watching them do that to England! It was bloody marvellous see. I remembered we shared a dram or two! What a team they were. Puskas, Hidegkuti, Czibor, Kocsis. Wonderful, wonderful team and their passing and movement. Those cherry red shirts caressing the ball with a wizardry, a magic that we'd never seen. Lightning fast. Like ghosts, red dervishes, ah I loved them Matt.

MATT
(Smiling)
Poor old Billy Wright!

JIMMY
(Smiling)
When Puskas dragged the ball back from Billy 's clutches and smashed it into the net that moment changed the game forever Matt.

MATT
(Smiling wide)
That's when we truly knew isn't it Jimmy. That we had to grow our own apples. Schoolboys: get the best, teach them that football is indeed a beautiful, but more importantly a simple game.

JIMMY
Pass the ball to your mate, make room, always help him out.

MATT
The ball is round for a reason. It is meant to go around. Make angles and when you get that chance, you aim low and you fire!

JIMMY
And you bloody well score!

MATT
(Smiling)
Aye, that was the idea!

JIMMY
Oh, I had them in tears at times, but it was always for their own good. The boys had to understand that not giving everything could never be tolerated at United. If I spotted one of them was just a little off I would be on him like a pack of wolves. But they learned and they learned fast…. But I loved them all I did. Every last one of them…. And I still miss those boys.

MATT
Oranges?

JIMMY
Excuse me?

MATT
(Smiling)
Oranges! You mentioned earlier?

JIMMY
(Wry Smile)
Those bloody oranges. The following day after the crash I went home to get changed before flying out to Munich. I passed those oranges to my Winnie and she put them under the stairs and we forgot all about them. Months after in the house there was a sticky aroma until we finally remembered they were still there! To this day the smell of an orange reminds me of those dark days. I can't even bare to look at one now, never mind eat one.

MATT
I still don't know how you did what you did after the crash Jimmy. How you coped. A miracle.

JIMMY
It was no miracle Matt. No angels. There was nothing miraculous going on, it was just darkness. A sea of grief that overwhelmed the city and somehow by sheer hard work, goodwill and a determination to keep the devil from our door we hung on. But those days after the crash

before the next match against Sheffield Wednesday were simply horrendous. Not just for me, but for all of us who were left.

MATT
Poor Harry Gregg and Bill Foulkes. Lads who were in the crash who played against Sheffield Wednesday. I simply cannot imagine what on earth was going through their heads.

JIMMY
I, we, United needed them, simple as that. They wanted to help and we were on our knees. We were like each other's shadows afterwards. I'm still not sure whether I was keeping an eye on them or them me.

MATT
I was told a story of you playing the piano in Blackpool at the Norbreck hotel where we always stayed.

JIMMY
(Smiling)
I had a little dabble.

MATT
It was Harry's and Bill's idea I believe?

JIMMY
It was. They came into the bar where I was drinking to tell me that all the lads were waiting in the hotel lounge to watch and listen to me on the piano. Their reasoning being none of the younger or new boys had ever heard me play. They knew only one Jimmy. The one obsessed like a madman around Old Trafford and the cliff. The one ranting and cajoling on the training pitch.

MATT
And Harry and Bill wanted to give them a glimpse of what had gone before?

JIMMY
(Smiling)
So, they did….

MATT
(Smiling)
Let them know that the band was playing on. Especially the piano man.

JIMMY
I've been playing the organ and later the piano since I was fourteen years old Matt, but I don't think I had ever been as nervous as at that moment. Harry called over. He said, 'Come on Jimmy, show the boys you're not all just growling and sandpaper voice. Show them the magic in that Welsh soul of yours!'

MATT
And so you played?

JIMMY
Aye, I played. I lifted up the lid and began to play Chopin-Prelude 4 and swiftly lost myself in the music. I was far away, lost in the clouds with my boys, and then I came back. I glimpsed up from the piano and I swear Matt, amid the living, they were smiling at me. All of them. I put my head back down, looked up again and they were gone. But I swear I saw them…. I saw them.

MATT
Grief does strange things to the mind Jimmy.

JIMMY
Later that evening I was heading upstairs to my bedroom when I caught the drift of a conversation taking place on the landing in front of me. A man and a woman. I heard it all. The woman saying, 'Did you see that in the lounge earlier? It was so strange' she said. 'All those young men with tears in their eyes listening to that older gentleman on the piano. Who was it?' She asked him? The man looked at her, 'That was Manchester United my dear' he said. …. And then added… 'Or what's left of them.' I just stood there listening.

(Again, the two go quiet.)

MATT
I know Arsenal came for you whilst in Blackpool.

JIMMY
Oh, they came for me, a spiv he was, sharp suit, I knew straight away. I recognise the sort. He first tried to pass himself as a travelling salesman but I didn't like what he was selling. He told me to jump off the sinking ship before I drowned with it. I told him exactly where he and his club could go.

MATT
(Smiling)
Aye, I heard!

JIMMY
(Smiling)
Sent him back south with his ears ringing and tie around his neck. Bloody cockneys.

MATT
Juventus, also, I believe came for you at the end of that season.

JIMMY

How the bloody hell did you know that? You spying on me Matt?!

MATT
(Winks at Jimmy)
Ten thousand pounds a year and you didn't go? That was a king's ransom. They asked Johnny Charles to pass it on I believe. John is a lovely lad. You must've been tempted?

JIMMY
How could I? Would you have gone?

MATT
No.

JIMMY
Well there you go. For the very same reasons you could never leave United is why I turned them down. That's why.

MATT
Unfinished business.

JIMMY
There was a debt to be honoured.

MATT
The European Cup.

JIMMY
For Manchester United.

MATT
Our boys.

JIMMY
Our golden apples.

MATT
Roger, Geoff, Billy, Mark, Eddie, Tommy, David and Duncan. May they all rest in peace.

JIMMY
Duncan. 'Big Dunc.' I know we're not supposed to have favourites Matt, but I dearly loved that boy. I remember managing Wales against England at Ninian Park. Before the game I was giving a last team talk. You know how I like to get carried away a little?

MATT
A little!?

JIMMY
Aye well, I was going through the England team one by one. Slaughtering them I was! When I finished Johnny Charles shouted out, 'What about Duncan boss? You forgot about Duncan Edwards?' Well I just smiled see and replied to John, 'Just stay away from him son. He'll murder you!'
(They both laugh.)

MATT
Di Stefano was the greatest player I ever saw, but our Duncan, would, if he had lived have been better. In time, he would have left them all in his wake. Alfredo, Puskas, Pele, Eusebio.
Duncan would have stood alone.

JIMMY
'What time do we kick off Jimmy?' He said to me when I visited him in the hospital. 'Get stuck in,' he smiled. The lad had so many wires coming out of him it was heart-breaking to see. I broke my heart crying when I left that room.

MATT
They never told me when he passed. Doctor Maurer believed I was not ready for such grim news. Finally, when I was stronger, the doctor broke down himself on telling me Duncan had gone. We both cried. Everybody cried in that place when he stopped fighting. Nurses, they

told me were in floods of tears. No one could believe that he survived so long with the damage inflicted on his body. The boy was superhuman.

JIMMY
No, he wasn't superhuman Matt…. He was just Duncan. (The two go quiet and just stare out over the stadium.)

MATT
Remember when we first seen this place after the war?

JIMMY
A bombed out wreck it was. Look at it now. A grand sight Matt. A perfect stage for our boys. There is a magic about this place. The smell of the grass, the grandstands. Even when it's empty it makes my blood chill.

MATT
If I shut my eyes Jimmy I can still see them down there. Duncan powering over the halfway line with players bouncing off him. He passes it wide to little Eddie Colman, who's snake hips leave a defender on his backside. By now the stadium is on fire. Eddie makes it to the by-line….

JIMMY

He crosses and Tommy Taylor rises like a salmon and thunders a header into the bottom corner past a diving keeper…. Old Trafford goes wild!

MATT
(Smiling)
A smiling Duncan looks over to the bench and gives us both a thumbs up.

JIMMY
'Piece of cake chief' he would say.

MATT
Another season and we would have beaten Real Madrid. I'm certain of it. Their president, Santiago Bernabeu, he knew we were coming for them. Santiago was a worried man. Did you know he offered me a pirate's treasure to become their manager in 57. He said to me, 'I will make it heaven and earth for you Matt.'

JIMMY
And what did you tell him?

MATT
I wrote Santiago a letter thanking him for his offer but told him my heaven and earth was in Manchester.

JIMMY
(Smiling)
He's a good man. Heart of gold. Nobody helped us more after Munich then Real Madrid.

MATT
Aye, and what was the first telegram we received in the dressing room last May after beating Benfica. It was off Santiago. 'Congratulations from your friends in Madrid.'

JIMMY
You can't buy class Matt.

MATT
No, you can't. And you can't buy what you have Jimmy.

JIMMY
What's that then?

MATT
You see the game with a poet's eye. even amid the mud and rain with players kicking lumps out of each other, you find a beauty that few others can spot. Aye, you would rant and rave and swear like a trooper, but it would be with so much passion and fire…. you could set the world ablaze. Those players, those boys would do anything for you. They would die for….
(Matt stops mid-sentence.)

JIMMY
(smiling)
It's okay…. Anything we did was done together Matt. You're right I do see the beauty and the magic in this game. I love a rainbow from a sudden storm on a sunny day. But one thing I'm not is naïve. I know what it takes to be successful in football. To be a manager. You need to be tough. To be able to deal with the crooks and the shysters.

Those who exist in this game of ours to just take and corrupt. You needed to be a real bastard at times to survive. To play the game not on the pitch, but off it. In board rooms with the rich and powerful, to be able to stand your corner and not just survive but win…Win! Most men can easily be turned, but you.

You were never turned. Oh, you were hard. Ruthless at times, yes, but you always maintained a common decency. A prince amongst many thieves and knaves and I don't say this lightly. You know me well enough to understand I would only tell you the truth….

MATT
I would expect nothing less off you old friend, but I was never no prince Jimmy. You think far too highly of me. I did my share of dancing with the devil, but there was no choice if I wanted to get United back to the top. There were things done and things not done of which I'm not proud of. After Munich, I could have tried harder to get the club to do more for the injured players. I should have pushed it and taken the player's side but I didn't.

Because right or wrong, Manchester United for me comes before all else. So, I am no saint.

JIMMY
There is no such thing as a saint on earth Matt. Saints belong in heaven not down here. You know I'm a god-fearing man like yourself. I go to church, I take communion, but I don't believe anybody is infallible. The Vatican can canonize a million priests and a thousand nuns, but for me, there is simply no such thing. 'Too err is human' don't they say? And 'to forgive is divine.' Your only crime my old friend is being human.

MATT
(Smiling)
You would have made a darn good priest Jimmy.

JIMMY
What, with my language!? Bugger that….

MATT
(Smiling)
Aye, the many priests who sit around our bench at Old Trafford will testify to that. I would watch them crossing themselves after listening to you.

JIMMY
(Smiling)

I always repent in confession. You know that. Besides that lot have given me enough Hail Mary's and Our Father's in payback. Been there half the bloody night sometimes!

MATT
I'm really glad we have been able to talk. I've been a fool, and there's nothing like an old fool. Especially a selfish one.

JIMMY
Why selfish?

MATT
I should have shared our pain.

JIMMY
I don't think it would've been any less old friend.
I remember when you first came home and you walked into the Wembley dressing room before the cup final against Bolton. I was behind you. All the players just sat in silence. I moved to stand alongside, I told them the boss was going to say a few words and then stepped back.

MATT
I looked around and hardly recognised anybody Jimmy. I remember big Harry Gregg, Bill Foulkes and Denis

Viollet smiling towards me, but the others? They stared at me like I was a stranger. Their eyes unsure, going from you to me. And I simply could not do it and left the room in tears. All was just too raw. Too soon. I was still on the runway because as I looked around at those in red shirts all I could see was the boys we lost staring back……

JIMMY
After we walked up the tunnel and I noticed the band was warming up and nearly ready for Abide With Me. I thought the words to that song were so apt for me and you. I grabbed your arm, do you remember?

MATT
Aye I do.

JIMMY
(Smiling)
Come on Matt, I said. Let's listen to this, they're playing our song! And together we stood as the band started to play. I thought that you and me could carry on like before, but sadly it wasn't to be…. Water under the canal bridge now though…. What's important is that we've cleared the air. At least on what happened after Munich. I thank you for that….

(Matt and Jimmy gaze around the empty stadium.)

MATT
It's getting colder…

JIMMY
Aye, there's definitely snow in the air.

MATT
We still want you around the place Jimmy. No one has an eye for a player like you. Your opinion will always count for something here.

JIMMY
That's very gracious of you Matt. I'll try my best not to get in the way.

MATT
A hint of sarcasm there Jimmy I think.

JIMMY
No, I honestly won't, but if anyone needs me I'll always be around. Until you say so of course. Can't have the past dictating the future can we Matt.

MATT
Nothing lasts forever Jimmy lad.

JIMMY
Aye don't we know that.

MATT
We lived through both paradise and hell, didn't we?

JIMMY
You speak as if everything is over Matt. We've just won the European cup for God's sake. That has to be the start of something, not the end and its down to you to install that in everyone here now. Otherwise we have foundations made from sand. Don't throw it all away.

MATT
This is United Jimmy, we're too big now. We'll always be at the top old friend.

JIMMY
It doesn't work like that Matt. We can't afford to rest on our laurels. For ten years we struggled on that path for bloody so-called redemption and when Bobby raised the trophy against Benfica it was for the boys lost. A fitting epitaph to our dead, yes, but not the end for the living. You have to ram that home to everyone here Matt. Otherwise we shall fall from the stars in a lot quicker time than it took us to reach them. Do you understand?

MATT

(Smiling)
I understand that you're worrying far too much Jimmy, and I get the passion, it's you, you'll never change, but the battle is over. It was won at Wembley last May. United will go on, but it won't be a journey laced with what's gone before. I'm pretty certain there will be triumphs and losses as we continue but no tragedies. Time to stoke out the fires my friend. Put your feet up a little and enjoy a well-earned rest. You've deserved it.

JIMMY
Do you remember the young man you met back in 1943 screaming at those soldiers because they weren't giving their all?

MATT
(Smiling)
How can I forget.

JIMMY
Well he's still bastard here! Inside me. Oh, I maybe older but don't you kid yourself, the fires will burn inside me for this club and game of ours till they put me in a coffin. I have lived and breathed United for twenty-three years. That is suddenly not going to change because you simply believe I should let the candle just burn out. It doesn't work like that and it shouldn't in you either, because if it is does then this club is doomed.

MATT
My fires still burn Jimmy.

JIMMY
Good, I'm glad to hear it.

MATT
I best be getting back soon. I've promised the press boys a private audience to keep them quiet.

JIMMY
Just promise me this one thing Matt, don't leave Wilf out to dry if it all goes wrong. I know him, he's going to give this job everything, but deep inside he's a worrier and will be desperate not to let you down.

MATT
I will have his back Jimmy.

JIMMY
Aye, you will need to have his front as well. Get him a couple of players in, dust the cobwebs down on the club's coffers and buy Malcom Macdonald and Colin Todd, they are just what we need. New blood and proper United players.

MATT

Let me speak to the board and we'll see.

JIMMY
Come on Matt, you're the board, you tell them to jump, they ask how high. Get them in, I promise you won't regret it.

MATT
(Smiling)
You think too highly of me Jimmy. It can be a spider's web in that boardroom. It's a different world and even I have to tread carefully. All about power, the scheming and politics involved, aye I can play but I'm by no means infallible. One day someone will come along and have me out to. I promise you.

JIMMY
I very much doubt that, I really do.

MATT
(Smiling)
Well we shall see. Look at us. Me and you. Out here in the freezing cold chatting about times gone past just like a couple of old pals.

JIMMY
(Smiling)
Matt and Jimmy.

MATT
(Smiling)
Jimmy and Matt.

(Jimmy reaches inside his jacket and produces a whisky hip flask. He shows it to Matt.)

JIMMY
For medicinal and special occasions. Would you care to share a wee dram?

MATT
(Smiling)
Be rude to say no Jimmy lad!

(Jimmy pours Matt's into a small cup and he keeps the hip flask.)

JIMMY
Let's have a toast Matt.

(Matt raises his cup.)

MATT
To our boys.

(Jimmy raises his flask and clinks Matt's cup.)

JIMMY
Fallen Angels.

(The two drink and then sit quietly staring around the stadium.)

It starts to snow…

                              The End

C17
WILF: NOVENA: Part One)

It's a bitterly cold April spring morning. Under a clear blue sky with a fake sun, thirty-one-year old Wilf McGuinness takes a deep breath and checks himself out in his car mirror. His hair neatly combed, he's clean shaven and looking and feeling dapper in suit and tie. This is the day.
If only his mates killed at Munich could have been here to witness it. Not a day goes by when Wilf doesn't miss them.
If only, if...

Thursday 6th February 1958. It is late afternoon in Manchester and twenty-one-year-old Manchester United footballer Wilf McGuinness, and close family friend Joe Witherington, a sales rep with the News Chronicle, are walking up Princess Street towards Piccadilly. Wilf has been to visit an orthopaedic specialist, a Mr Poston, whose diagnosis after examining his cartilage is that he faces at least two months out on the sidelines.
Wilf is filled with joy and despair; joy at United having advanced into the European Cup semi-finals stage for the second year in a row the day before, after a truly dramatic 3—3 draw away in Yugoslavia against a brilliant Red Star Belgrade team. And despair that his long-term injury will hinder his attempts to cement a place in United's first team.
'Never give up Wilf. Never stop fighting.'
That was Jimmy Murphy's set phrase with fist clenched whenever he passed Wilf in the physio's room at The Cliff. That's all very fine, he thinks, if just up against a mere mortal. Then Jimmy's words may hold more than a

candle with Wilf. But he's up against Duncan Edwards. The greatest player Wilf has ever seen. He's up against a colossus.

Wilf's and Joe's attention are struck by a paper boy ahead of them screaming loud, with a large crowd gathering around him. He's shouting out 'UNITED IN PLANE CRASH!' The two men rush over, a limping Wilf behind Joe, who reaches the paper boy first. He pays and grabs a newspaper off the stand.

'Does it say if anyone is hurt?' He's not unduly worried for Wilf has flown abroad with United on several occasions. Bumpy landings and air turbulence are common and he's convinced the story is simply being over-egged.

'A storm in a teacup Joe mate,' smiles a nervous Wilf. But after reading through the stop press reports, Joe isn't so sure.

'Come on' he says, grabbing Wilf's arm. 'We'll go to the Chronicle's office and see what they know.' Wilf sees something in Joe's eyes. He looks scared.

'No way Joe,' he adds. Trying to assure his friend, a United supporter also. 'They'll be okay.'

As soon as they arrive at the Chronicle it's clear something catastrophic is occurring. Everywhere people appear panic stricken. Loud voices shout down phones, one young secretary is crying as she struggles to cope with orders being barked at her by journalists suddenly finding themselves engulfed in a maelstrom of rumour and misinformation.

A Reuters news agency wire machine is spewing out streams of paper containing the latest facts and speculations of events on Southern German soil in Munich. Wilf looks on in shock.

'Give me a minute' says Joe, as he swiftly disappears amid the madness to try and find out information. He seeks out a journalist friend of his who hands him some copy. Wilf watches on as the two speak. The journalist looks across and nods towards him, his face ashen grey. Wilf raises a hand to acknowledge and smiles weakly.
'What the fucking hell is going on?'
Joe returns and motions for Wilf to follow him. 'We need to talk,' he sits Wilf down in a relatively quiet corner of the frenzied surroundings. 'I'm afraid it's bad Wilf. First reports say there have been numerous fatalities, although we have no names.' Joe shrugs his shoulders.
 'Nobody knows who is alive or dead.'
Wilf slumps back in his chair, not able to take in what he's being told. If not for his injury he would have been on the plane as cover for Duncan Edwards. The next few hours pass in feverish, haunting manner. Wilf listens out across the newsroom floor for the mere mention of a name, but there's nothing. He prays. Wilf prays like he has never done before that the lives of his mates will be saved. But slowly the death toll rises.
'Jesus Christ, this is a bloody nightmare,' screams a journalist who has just received more reports of deaths. Seven to nine, to twelve. But no names. It is torture. Finally, Wilf rings his father who tells him they too have heard nothing. Lawrence McGuinness tells his son to come home. Here is where he should be at a time like this. Wilf hangs up, he can't take much more. He's in a daze and asks Joe to drive him home to 51 Westleigh Street in Blackley, North Manchester.
The drive back up Rochdale Road is strange for the normal busy traffic has vanished. An entire city lies in morbid wait of forthcoming radio and television

announcements from Germany. Above sit black clouds and dark foreboding skies. There are no stars in the Northern heavens on this night. Mancunians brace themselves. They fear the worst. They fear the end of their world.

On reaching home Wilf collapses into the arms of his father, a veil of tears. It's too much for Joe to bear. He waves over to Lawrence and Wilf's mother, May, and heads back to the Chronicle office. Agonisingly, as the night goes on news begins to emerge and on the radio, some of the survivor's names are released: Bobby Charlton, Dennis Viollet, Albert Scanlon, Harry Gregg and Bill Foulkes. Duncan Edwards too, even though the BBC reporter states that he is 'Grievously injured.' And then he stops.

 No more names.

'What about the others! 'Exclaims Wilf. 'Eddie, Tommy, Roger and the rest. What about them?'

'Calm down son,' his father says softly. 'Nobody knows for sure. It'll be chaos over there.'

May puts her arm around him, 'Wilf there is a Novena (a Catholic devotion) at church tonight. We should go. I'll get our coats.' Lawrence looks at his devastated son. It feels like only two minutes ago he was making him the proudest father on earth by signing for Manchester United. He so wanted his boy not to experience what he witnessed during the war. Lawrence hoped Wilf would never live through such a day of loss as this.

Mount Carmel church is packed to the rafters. People are openly sobbing. Prayer, it appears, is the only option left to prevent the heavens falling down upon them. Wilf's entrance flanked by his mother and father causes a lot of head turning in the aisles. Men are wearing United rosettes or scarves.

'Hail Mary, full of grace the Lord is with thee. Blessed are the fruit....

Please let them live. Please, please... please.

1969: 'Please Please…'

Wilf snaps himself back to reality and dries his eyes. 'Not a day for tears Wilf lad,' he says to himself. 'Happiest day of your life this,' he switches on the car radio and Louis Armstrong's 'It's a Wonderful World' is playing. The boss's favourite song. Wilf smiles. The car is on the final stretch of Chester Road heading towards Old Trafford. He begins to sing along, ''I see friends holding hands, singing how do you do.''

He pulls up in the club forecourt and gets out the car. Wilf is now whistling 'It's a wonderful world' as he strides into the ground through a side entrance, marked up with a Staff Entrance sign above it.

'Fucking hell Wilf, are you in court today?' It's a grinning Paddy Crerand. Paddy is in collecting tickets for a forthcoming match. Wilf says nothing but gives Paddy the middle finger and saunters off. Hands in pockets and still whistling Wilf heads towards the boss's office. Could it soon be his office?

Sir Matt: I feel no sadness or pain in today's events, just a sheer sense of relief. I suddenly recall Sinatra's words. ''And now the end is near'' but myself, I face no such final curtain. This is still my club and will always be so until I pass my last dying breath. There will be no last goodbye. Of course, Wilf will enter centre stage today but I shall be watching his every move in the wings. He's the Chosen One.

Wilf is United, he's family and can be trusted. And so, the show will go on. But I will ensure in these uncertain times that if Wilf is in need of gentle persuasion then my door will always be open. He'll listen. For he's a good lad.

I've called the press conference for later today where we shall officially announce it. I hear Wilf whistling and can see his shadow outside the door. And so, this is it. I pretend to be writing and take a deep breath.

It has been a privilege and I did it my way.

I took the hits, more than any, most men could bear, and I'm still standing.

Regrets?

What do you think?

'Calm down Wilf son,' he says to himself. 'Calm down.' He comes to Sir Matt's office. He checks out his reflection one last time on a glass door panel. He straightens his collar and tie and hair one last time. He makes the sign of the cross and then knocks on the door.

'Come in' I shout. I look up from my pretence of writing and smile. 'You're looking smart Wilf, sit down.'

'Cheers boss.'

'Wilf, there's no easy way of putting this, so I'll come right out with it. Congratulations, son. You are the next manager of Manchester United.'

Wilf remains outwardly calm, the only sign of his acknowledging the unimaginable weight of the boss's words and how much they mean comes through a simple nod of the head. Inside his heart is racing - if you're listening in Eddie and Duncan and Roger and all the angels in heaven, have a drink on me lads.

'Now you won't be known as the manager straight away because I feel the title will only add extra pressure on your shoulders. You're going to have enough on your plate son. So, I've decided you'll be referred to as chief coach.'

Wilf nods sagely. I smile wide. 'The good news is Wilf, I'll still be around as a General Manager. I'll keep this office, you can have Jimmy's old one down the hall. He'll be sharing with Joe Armstrong. In matters of discipline, transfers and such, I'll keep an eye on those. Regarding wages... I look down at the sheet of paper in front of me. 'Yours will rise from £38 to £80. Over double Wilf lad. So, don't let me down.'

For one of the few times in his life Wilf McGuinness is speechless. No wise cracks, no jokes, just respect. He wants to cry with joy, he wants to hug the old man and open his heart on everything that has lain dormant since the late afternoon of Thursday 6th February 1958.

A cleansing of the soul - a Novena.

But now is certainly not the time, for the old man is in business like mood and certainly in no state of mind to witness his heir apparent suffer an emotional breakdown. For this is not how a Manchester United manager, sorry chief coach, behaves. These are heady times for Wilf and this is the best day of his life. All he can think about is that the great Matt Busby has chosen him to carry the torch onwards. 'I'll make you proud boss. I'll make you so very proud,' Wilf beams.

Official Manchester United club statement:
The board has given further consideration to the changes which will occur at the end of the season and has decided

to appoint a chief coach who will be responsible for team selection, coaching, training and tactics.

Mr Wilf McGuinness has been selected for this position and will take up his duties as from 1st June, and in these circumstances it is not necessary to advertise for applications as we first intended. Sir Matt Busby will be responsible for all other matters affecting the club and players, and will continue as club spokesman….

C18
'TWISTED BLOOD' GEORGIE

There was a time when the Busby Babes would travel to the 'Big Smoke' to London town with all the pomp and swagger of visiting Hollywood movie stars. Their arrival would be greeted with huge excitement. They were showbusiness - glamour and glitter. Nothing of their ilk had ever been witnessed. Londoners found it hard to believe. Footballing superstars from Manchester? Whatever happened to the cloth caps and the ferrets and the chimneys poking through dark satanic skies? These boys in their sharp suits, smiling with a wink and a handsome smile to the ladies, so full of fire and youth and talent beyond the heavens, who played with a devil on their shirts and in their play.

'It's grim up north' claimed the London papers. Well a dash of red sprinkled with gold dust and Matt Busby and Jimmy Murphy put paid to that.

And then Munich put paid to them. Was it all simply a mirage? The lights once more went out in the north and for Londoners the magic waned. The fairytale of those kids who had bloomed for a while under northern skies faded from memory. They reverted to type – Spurs became the glamour team, the birth right of all cockneys. But then came George…

Saturday 30th September 1964: Chelsea v Manchester United - Stamford Bridge. It was a performance that reduced his father to tears and left Matt Busby speechless. He knew more than any other that this slip of an eighteen-year-old kid was special. Busby knew something extraordinary existed within his thin balletic frame but what he never counted on or realised was the swagger. The courage and the sheer joy at putting on a show for the crowd.

In the capital at this time there was no better stage to introduce yourself than the glitzy surroundings of Stamford Bridge. A football club that acted like a magnet to the movie, music and theatre stars who resided in West London. An awed Chelsea crowd that came to watch Charlton, Law and Crerand take on their own exciting, vibrant team captained by a young Terry Venables, were left marvelling at the thin, red, scrawny like whippet, tearing apart their right full back, the highly regarded and experienced Ken Shellito.

It never appeared just enough to simply beat him, the kid seemed intent on turning the unfortunate Shellito into a gibbering shaking wreck. He would turn him one way then another, the ball would go through his legs, Shellito would move to turn, only to find George was already past him. It was cruel, yet beautiful to watch.

A sleight of foot, a conjuror's touch with the ball obeying his every command; it was if all present had fallen for this magical Irish waif whose smile could light up a city and in time would melt and break the hearts of millions of both sexes. George walked off at the end, head bowed and embarrassed as the entire stadium rose as one to hand him a standing ovation.

'Shellito must have twisted blood after that,' claimed Paddy Crerand in a post-match interview, as the word went out and the whole world gasped at the sight of 'Georgie Boy.'

Sir Matt Busby remember that day so well. He later joked, 'Whenever we went to Stamford Bridge, I thought I ought to phone the police and warn them a murder was about to be committed!'

C19

WHAT THE HELL: GEORGE

The Brown Bull, 1970: Fast asleep under a coat, amid broom handles, crates of ale, boxes of crisps and cigarettes is the great George Best. Too drunk to drive home or even to make it up the stairs to his own room given to him by the grateful landlord Billy Barr, the greatest talent in world football has been put to bed by the American landlord under a rain coat with a cushion wedged under his head.

It had been another crazy night at the Bull with the usual television and pop stars amongst the clientele, but as ever all eyes, both male and female were on George. It's all about George. Celebrities and every day punters came and went but come the end George was still going strong. Never stopping, his glass never empty. Eyes glazed, incapable of even talking. Finally, when he could drink no more and after many failed attempts to get him up the stairs, Billy made the decision to let him sleep off the booze in the back room.

The noise of early morning traffic and the rattle of freight trains making their way across the nearby rail bridge out of Manchester brings George back from his slumber. George opens his eyes, and for a second has no idea where he is. Then remembers, he checks his watch. There's an outside chance he could make training but decides against it. He couldn't handle another shouting session with Wilf, a lingering stare of disdain from Bobby and a lecture off the old man. He'll take the fine. It's only money. There's plenty in the bank. He checks in his pockets and pulls out a bundle of scribbled pieces of paper. Girl's phone numbers. He smiles and just wishes he could remember what they looked like.

George stands and yawns, he rubs his eyes and notices a small chink of light shining in through the dark, dank walls. He stands on an empty crate to look through and finds a gap in the brickwork, harbouring a view from a foot high up of the outside street. George peeps through, like a prisoner in a deep dungeon, staring forlornly at the outside world, as people go about their morning business. It fascinates him. He feels safe, for once it is he who is prying.

A bespectacled schoolboy no more than twelve years old is sat on the upper deck of a bus going past the Brown bull. It stops opposite at the traffic lights. He looks across and notices a man's eyes staring back up at him. He recognises the face. No, it can't be. The schoolboy takes off his glasses and rubs his eyes. He looks again. It is. It's George Best!

The lights change and the bus drives off with the boy continuing to stare. George has caught his eye. He smiles. The schoolboy grins back. Nobody will ever believe him.

Nobody.

George climbs back down. He spots a bottle of vodka on the shelf.

What the hell...

C20

Wilf: Let It Be: (Part Two)

The Cliff: Monday 28th December 1970: I'm sat at my desk. I look at the clock; it's time to see Wilf. My boy, my Wilf. There's a knock at the door.

In the corridor outside a track-suited Wilf McGuinness stands. He shuffles nervously. Pensive. He straightens his hair and is shocked to find a small strand has come off in his hand.

I call out, 'Come in.' Wilf enters. I smile, 'Sit down and take a chair son.'

'Cheers boss' replies Wilf. He sits but is clearly uneasy. I wonder if he senses what I'm about to say?

'Wilf lad, I've got some bad news. It is not working out. The board have decided to make a change.'

'What kind of change?'

I take a breath, 'It's over son. You're out. I… we can't risk relegation and the board feel unless changes are made it could happen.'

'Fuck off,' says Wilf. He's angry and shocked and now he lets fly.

'I can't believe you of all people have stabbed me in the back. You, who I've worshipped since I was a kid. I thought you were different but Jesus Christ. You're just like the rest.'

'Wilf, what am I supposed to do? I've been hearing stories; the players aren't happy.'

Wilf goes mad, 'They're not happy. Fuckin' ell, I'm not happy Boss. I'm glad they're not happy. They should be ashamed of themselves.'

This isn't going well.

'The Board have insisted son. My hands are tied. They're worried. I'm going to step back in until the end of the season and then we shall see.'

Wilf is trying to hold back the tears. I can see he's choking.

'And what about me?'

'Well I've had a chat with the board and they're willing to let you have your old job back with the reserves. Obviously, your wages will have to change to match the new position. But you'll still be one of the family Wilf.'

'One of the fuckin' family! You do this to me after everything I've given to the club and you expect me to simply tip my hat and go back to the stiffs?'

'I expect you to show some respect. And maybe a thank you?'

'Thanks for what? For shafting me? Well I can't accept this. There's no chance I'm going to step down and make it easy for you. Do you know something, it feels like all my life has been spent trying to please you? Well not this time, this is wrong. No way.'

'Wilf please, don't put me in this position. The decision has already been made. It's out of my hands.'

'Oh please, don't treat me as an idiot. Are you seriously trying to say that you don't agree with them? Anything you say to Edwards, him and the board just jump and ask how fuckin' high? Now just be honest with me. You can do that can't you? After all these years you can do the courtesy of telling me the truth.'

'What can I say except you're out Wilf.'

I can see the hurt in his eyes.

'I have to get this off my chest,' he says quietly. 'And may God forgive me. For twelve years it's been eating me up. When you were lying in that hospital bed in

Munich and I heard you had been given the last rites I spent whole nights praying you'd pull through. I lost so many pals, good friends that were like brothers. But you? I honestly thought if you didn't pull through then I really couldn't see any future. Any hope. And when Duncan went, may he rest in peace, I so nearly lost it. It was only the thought that you'd come back and make everything right that kept me going. I told myself in time life at Old Trafford would revert back to what it was like before the crash. 'Paradise' as Bobby calls it. But it never did.

'The place went stale, it lost its soul. Too many strangers, new faces who just didn't get what Manchester United truly means. It wasn't just Tommy and Eddie, Roger and Duncan and the rest that we lost on that fuckin' runway. Somewhere along the line we lost our spirit. United lost its spirit. Nothing has been the same since. Nothing. Oh yes we carried on, kept the red flag flying fuckin' high and we came back and won the damn thing. But it was never the same. Bobby knew, he just never talked about it. He still won't. But I see it in his eyes. He's still on the plane. Every day I see him still looking around for Duncan and the others. Force of will and a determination not to look back kept him from going mad with grief. And me. And Jimmy. And you? My god, we can only guess what kept you sane?'

Wilf is in tears. Forgive me but I can't help myself but feel anger towards him.

'Sane. You have no idea Wilf? Do you think there hasn't been an hour of every day since when I've not thought about the boys that I lost? It's not been easy for any of us who came through that hell but we have had to move on. Of course, things changed after the crash, we had our hearts ripped out. Something like that hardens men, lad.

It makes them what they are. What they become. Manchester United must come before everything and so despite everything - this is where we are today. I'm sorry son. I really am.'

Wilf sits back down. He wipes his eyes dry. He straightens his hair.

My heart is breaking.

Wilf is sweating, never before has he spoke to the boss like this and inexplicably, despite what has happened to him, he feels guilty. He takes a deep breath, 'Now, I am not going to beg. We don't do that where I'm from. My Mum and Dad would disapprove but I'll ask you one more time. Reconsider. Give me a few more games, I can do this. Get me a few players in and I can turn this season around. I swear I can do it. Christ, you haven't let me spend a bloody penny apart from Ian Ure and you bought him. Loosen the purse strings then at least I will have a fuckin' fighting chance!'

I stare straight at Wilf. I push a piece of paper over the desk towards him.

'I want you to sign this. Your letter of resignation. We'll tell the press that you came to us and for the good of Manchester United stated you wished to go back to your old job. That's the deal.'

Wilf looks at the sheet of paper. 'And if I don't sign it?'

'Well like you have said, things have changed.'

Wilf smiles and gently pushes the sheet of paper back towards me.

'They were good day's boss,' he says. 'They were the best of days.'

Wilf stands and walks out the door.

I pick up the resignation letter, screw it up and throw it in a waste paper basket. I lean back in the chair and shut my eyes.

Wilf is in a daze. He rushes past Jack Crompton in the corridor. Knocking him aside. He turns to apologise, 'I'm sorry Jack mate,' then he continues on in haste. Wilf can't get out of the training ground quick enough.

Jack takes one look at Wilf's face and he knows.

I appear, 'Bad news Jack, I've had to let Wilf go.'

Jack glowers at me, 'He was family boss.'

'I had no choice, we're on our way down. I have to step back in.'

Still Jack stares, 'Jack please.' I need him to understand. Indeed, everybody to understand. What I've done is for the good of this club. Of Manchester United. Surely Jack knows I'm hurting inside?

Finally, he shakes his head in disgust and turns to walk off.

Wilf gets in the car and is trying hard to keep his eyes dry. He switches on the radio and the Beatles 'Let it Be' is playing:

''When I find myself in times of trouble,

Mother Mary comforts me.

Speaking words of wisdom,

Wilf finds himself singing along and the tears start to flow……

C21
WHEN THE LIGHTS WENT OUT
Manchester United v Manchester City: 1974
In April 1974 Paul McCartney and Wings release Band On The Run. The Sting starring Paul Newman and Robert Redford wins the Oscar for best movie. Billy Joel is singing about a Piano man. The Watergate scandal rages on as Nixon attempts to lie and scheme his way out of a hole. The worlds' tallest building, The World Trade Centre opens in New York City, where it is claimed she will stand forever more. In Great Britain industrial strife is wreaking havoc and as a three-day week blacks out the nation into a candle lit existence, the lights are set to go out on Manchester United football club.

Saturday 13th March 1974: The Battle of Maine Road. With City and United struggling at the wrong end of the table, Welsh referee Clive Thomas would have had more use of a bell than a whistle as red and blue clash in one of the most bitter and vitriolic derbies of recent times. Both sides forget about the ball and decide to kick lumps out of each other.
On the terraces it is equally violent with scuffles constantly breaking out between supporters. United's infamous red bedecked hooligan following intent it appears, on tearing apart their rival's ground brick by brick. Back on the field no quarter is given or asked as tempers explode on the ball and off it. Private vendettas and petty feuds simmer dangerously and it all culminates in a remarkable Wild-West type brawl on the touchline involving City's Mike Doyle and United's Lou Macari launching into a full-scale boxing match!

The diminutive Macari refuses to back down and goes hell for leather with the infamously 'red hating' Doyle. After a short if brutal exchange of punches both men are dragged apart by linesmen, team mates and staff from the benches.

Thomas has no option and shows each the red card but they refuse to go. Instead Doyle and Macari stand their ground testing the referee's authority. After consulting a policeman Thomas blows his whistle and orders the teams off the field. In a shameful episode Manchester football is being dragged through the gutter. Maine Road is in uproar, what happens next. Will the match be abandoned?

Minutes later they reappear minus Doyle and Macari. By this time police lines are formed around all four corners of the ground. Whether this is to protect the players from the supporters or the other way round is uncertain. No surprise the game finishes 0-0 with points shared but not pride. Not on this day.

In a mad, crazy, last-gasp cavalry charge Tommy Docherty's United go all out in search of salvation and to stave off relegation. It gains instant results for just when the nails are being banged into the Old Trafford coffin, a sensational 3-1 win at Stamford Bridge against Chelsea offers hope where previously none existed.

Tommy's boys are magnificent. A stunning, long range rasping drive from Willie Morgan puts United in front and two second half goals from youngsters Sammy McIlroy and Gerry Daly seal a most unexpected if welcome victory. Docherty is delighted after this victory. He tells the waiting press, 'We have tried to play tight, to play defensively and it hasn't worked because it goes against our natural game. You may as well ask a cat to bark! So, from now on Manchester United will go forward. We will attack and damn the consequences!' What follows over the coming weeks defies belief as seemingly freed from unnatural defensive shackles, United rediscover their attacking instincts to score thirteen goals in a six-game spell and gain ten points out of a possible twelve. A thrilling 3-3 draw at Burnley is followed by three straight wins over Norwich, Newcastle and a 3-0 hammering of high flying Everton at Old Trafford. A tight, uncompromising point is hard earned against a fellow relegation struggler Southampton at The Dell and suddenly, redemption. A chink of light shines. If not a miracle then a huge slice of luck is required to stay up but so long as they keep winning it could happen. It really could.

On Wednesday 15th April 1974, Manchester United travel the short distance to Goodison Park to take on Everton, a side United have only recently beaten with some ease on home territory. They have to win and pray elsewhere at St Andrews Birmingham City, the chief rivals for survival, slip up at home to Queens Park Rangers.

As half time approaches United are the better team at Goodison and look more than capable of gaining two invaluable points. Then, news filters through from the Midlands that Birmingham have scored not once but twice in swift succession and suddenly United appear nervous.

A tense second half unfurls and as the visitors try manfully to regain their first half swagger, disaster strikes when Everton's Mick Lyons ignites the home crowd and sends the vast United following into despair. It finishes

1-0 and with Birmingham victorious the most frightful scenario now exists with just two games remaining. Norwich City are bottom with twenty-nine points whilst United are above them on thirty-two. Occupying the third relegation spot are Southampton with thirty-four. Just outside the drop zone are Birmingham City clear by one. United still have a lifeline, but it is slim. If Birmingham lose at home to Norwich and they win the last two remaining games then the Midlands club would fall and not the Mancunians.
It's too close to call.
United's next game? At home to Manchester City and a certain Lawman, now wearing blue set for a date with destiny.

Old Trafford: Saturday 27th April: Manchester awakes to a bright morning sun in late spring with snatches of early summer in tow. A city divided, one half praying for salvation, the other desperate to deny them. A Mancunian showdown of the like this fair city has never experienced. Families and friends ripped apart. Eyes opening with both dread and joyful expectation. For the blues, this isn't a question of loving thy neighbour but burying them. For the reds they can only pray a season of torment and mediocrity can suddenly transform itself into something resembling a miracle. Few hold out hope.
Denis Law arrives at Old Trafford and getting off the Manchester City coach he's mobbed by United supporters. 'Hope you're keeping well Denis?'
'Missing you Denis!'
'You're still the king Denis!'
'Make sure you don't score today Denis!'

He's busy signing every autograph book thrust in front of him when he feels a hand tugging on his arm.
'Come on Lawman, we have got a job to do'
It is Mike Doyle. Here on enemy territory he's receiving merciless stick, 'I hate this fucking place Denis. It gives me the creeps. Let's make sure we put this lot down today then no need to bother coming here next season.'
Denis smiles but inside he's churning. He's already spoken to the manager Tony Book about being left out who responded by giving him the armband! A red heart in a blue shirt.
'Make sure you go in the right dressing room Denis,' laughs Francis Lee, as they enter Old Trafford. Everywhere people appear to shake Denis's hand.
His is a fixed grin but it's a joker's smile. Denis is dreading this game like no other. So many memories, good friends: Paddy, George, Shay, Nobby. Jimmy. His initial anger after the harrowing exit towards the old man has vanished. Now, all Denis remembers are the good times. There is one he would dearly like to make suffer. Though in wreaking revenge on Tommy Docherty it would only in turn break the hearts of so many he cares about. But Denis knows his is an instinctive talent. He simply can't help himself. If a chance arises then may God and all the angels in heaven forgive him. Because he'll take it.

As kick off draws ever near Old Trafford resembles a nervous, fraught arena and no place for the faint or half hearted. 57,000 gather and erupt in a cauldron of noise as both teams come on to the pitch. The Stretford End explodes into a frenzied mass of red and white defiance. If this is to be the day they fall from the stars, they'll go down breathing fire and screaming out the two things their under-achieving team hasn't been able to take from them.

Pride and Passion.

The thunderous roar that greets the men in red is one of sheer mortal defiance. On this wooden fortress where boys become men, fuelled on Double Diamond and Watneys Party Seven, these red legions raised on glorious tales of yesteryear. Of Edwards, Taylor and Colman - those taken too soon and then Best, Law and Charlton.

Their songs sung with such gusto across the land. Loyal, fanatical, troublesome - 'downright hooligans' the authorities scream. All together now for one last carnival of sorts. Nobody ever promised them a happy ending. Six years of trouble and strife since winning the European Cup have put paid to that, but as the outside world waits to read the last rites on Manchester United Football Club, those who hold it dear are damned if today will be their last stand.

This isn't a disaster, nobody more than United supporters understand this. Dying is a disaster. Losing a team at the end of a runway is a disaster. Whatever happens today, whichever way the wind blows, United will rise again.

The teams appear from the tunnel, never has Old Trafford been so wracked with nerves. Grown men finding it hard to talk. The atmosphere is raw. This isn't about football it's life. Denis Law heads into the centre circle to shake hands with United Captain Willie Morgan and is given a standing ovation by all four corners of the stadium.

'Behave yourself today Denis,' smiles Willie.

Denis shakes his hand but says nothing. His emotions in turmoil, his heart racing.

The 90th Manchester derby is under way.

Manchester United's 36 consecutive seasons in the First Division is on the line. They twice go close in the first half. A Jim McCalliog effort is cleared off the line by Willie Donachie and Sammy McIlroy sends a header just wide of the post. United are trying everything but it is all effort and hustle.

Everything is rushed.

A first half littered with mistakes unfurls. City are sleepwalking, occasionally causing heart attacks on the Old Trafford terraces by meandering into United's half. Suddenly, a huge roar from the terraces as news filters through that Norwich have taken the lead at Birmingham! The noise level rises. Red voices scream towards the heavens. It is if a passing train is roaring past your face. There is hope, slim but a real sense the day may end well.

City come forward and Denis Tueart slides in Colin Bell to fire a shot from twenty-yards that screams past Alex Stepney's post.

The nerves return, City have woken up.

More news from Saint Andrews and it is enough to stop you breathing. Birmingham have scored twice in quick succession. Kenny Burns and Bob Hatton. The city fans roar with delight whilst the red hordes reel. The momentarily glimpse of salvation has gone.

It was asking too much. Like standing in front of a firing squad and praying they would miss.

Half time comes and goes, a strange sense of trepidation has settled over Old Trafford. Something is going to happen. Nobody knows what, but it's in the air.

A United corner, mayhem ensues and city defenders scramble the ball away after Gerry Daly looks certain to score. But no, it goes on and the clock ticks forever down. The home side are almost spent and the visitor's sense it's time to end their pain.

Tueart crashes a fine effort against the crossbar. City are now rampaging, Tueart again is foiled at the last with a magnificent stop by Stepney. United are on their knees. There are nine minutes left to play and the stage is set for the return of the king.

Midway inside the City half Mike Doyle tackles Willie Morgan. He passes to Summerbee who in turns send Colin Bell racing through the centre circle into acres of space. As the United defenders retreat Bell feeds Francis Lee, who is pushed wide in the penalty area. Hovering nearby is Denis Law. Lee's cross finds him and from eight yards Denis instinctively backheels it and the ball flies low past Stepney into the net.

The roar goes up from the City supporters.

The Lawman's face says it all.

'My God, what have I done?'

C22

ONE NIGHT IN MANCHESTER

Manchester United v Barcelona: European Cup Winner's Cup: Quarter Final: Second Leg: 1984

Wednesday 21st March, 1984: A 58,000 capacity crowd paying record profits of £200,000 gathered by the River Irwell praying for a miracle. Old Trafford under floodlights catching in their misty glare the ghosts of past great European nights. Georgie Best running amok past defenders, Denis Law's acrobatic overhead kicks and Bobby Charlton lashing in a thirty-yard screamer. Here in a stadium notably not of the grandeur of the Nou Comp but equally rich in passion and memories.

A Mancunian field of dreams. It was time for new heroes.

The Stretford End behind one goal a seething mass of red and white. Normally it would be from there that United's most vociferous support would roar but on the evening that Barca came to town the entire stadium was ablaze with a furore not witnessed for years

Wearing their change colours of yellow shirts with a Barca dash of red/blue stripe and blue shorts the Catalans prepared to fend off the coming Mancunian storm. So unfolded one of the darkest night in FC Barcelona's history. As expected United flew at Barca from the off. Their highly, precocious barnstorming, eighteen-year old Northern Irish international Norman Whiteside who missed the first leg through injury making his presence known early when he sent the bruising Alexanco crashing into an advertising board. Moments later a mistake by Javier Urruti whose attempts to come for a Ray Wilkins cross almost ended in disaster when stranded off his line, Whiteside lobbed him from twenty yards only for the ball to drop agonisingly onto the crossbar and over.

The Catalans were edgy, nervous as the noise generated from the Old Trafford terraces drove on the home side. Any attempts by the blessed Barca duo of Diego Maradona and Bernd Schuster to keep possession and bring calm to a frenzied atmosphere was immediately seized upon by the ferocious Bryan Robson and Remi Moses who snapped, wrestled and tore back the ball to begin yet another attack. It was pressure relentless and finally it bore fruit on twenty-two minutes, when from a corner flick on the dynamic Robson swept in the opening goal from close range.

As Old Trafford exploded Maradona stood alone in the centre-circle with hands on hips, a sombre figure staring back at the penalty area. His team now needed him more than ever because suddenly a realisation had dawned on all concerned with FC Barcelona that it was going to be an awful long night under Mancunian stars.

A first half dominated almost totally by United saw Maradona shine only sporadically. His few touches of class rare as mostly the Argentine was hounded, harassed, elbowed and mauled by the man-marking of Graeme Hogg, ably assisted by the small but fierce competitor, the black bushy-haired Moses never giving him room to breathe. Only once did he truly escape when a pass from Schuster freed Maradona and his instant snapshot across the goal was hit straight at United keeper Gary Bailey. This apart Diego was a ghost.

The Mancunian cavalry charges continued after the interval with Barca just not being allowed to settle and constantly pressed. Mirando Gerrardo was experiencing a hellish time at left back. On fifty-minutes Gerrardo again found himself in trouble when trying to move forward, instead surrounded by pouncing red shirts he passed inside to Moratalla, whom immediately played the ball back to an unsuspecting Schuster. The German's attempt to play his way out of trouble rebounded badly when the thundering hoofs of Whiteside caused panic in the Barca rearguard and a panicking Javier Urruti became forced to mishit a dreadful clearance.

  From that instance the Catalans comedy of errors only worsened as Remi Moses raced over to the touchline and picked up the loose ball before firing in a cross which was met first time by the sweet right foot of United midfielder Ray Wilkins. Disaster struck for the Barca keeper when he failed to hold the England man's fierce low shot and again waiting to pounce was Bryan Robson to score to take the roof off Old Trafford!
Urruti looked aghast, his error levelling the tie at 2-2 and the Catalans in serious danger of elimination. It was turning into a one man show, Not Diego Maradona or Bernd Schuster as might have been expected but the United and England Captain who was taking on and beating FC Barcelona on his own. With a seemingly now half-hearted Maradona all but anomonous Barca were on the ropes.
Five minutes later they were on the floor.
Again, it was United's talismans creating havoc as he delivered a wonderful left footed cross-field pass into the feet of on-rushing defender Arthur Albiston's path. At full pace Albiston tore down the left wing before finding the ever-dangerous Norman Whiteside at the far post, out-jumping three Barca defenders, Whiteside's header flew back across the face of the goal to be met by the right foot of United's centre-forward Frank Stapleton

who smashed it into the net from four yards. Barca were being destroyed by a rampant Manchester United. Not an hour played and their two-goal lead had gone.

The Catalans had thirty-five minutes to save their skins. Shortly before the third goal Maradona for once escaped the red shackles of Hogg and Moses, only to lose the ball and instead of trying to retrieve possession he simply stood and stared as the action moved away. Archetypal of a player no longer caring for the badge upon his shirt. The sacred Blaugrana. But come the restart with Barca now in desperate need of a goal Maradona at last appeared to shift into gear. But this was a night when even a consummate magician like Maradona found his conjuring powers struggling to produce rabbits from a hat. A red swarm descending upon him whenever the ball came.

There were moments, precious few when the Argentine caused gasps on the terraces with either a drag down or a hidden pass but nothing came to fruition. One chance came when he broke clear on the right to set up Schuster whose lifted effort missed Bailey's far post by inches. But it was never enough.

As the game entered its dying stages the noise from the Old Trafford terraces increased to even higher level of mayhem. It was a night not witnessed in Manchester for many a year and Barca were not being allowed to ruin it. One last time Maradona raised his game and flew into the United area, only to then dismally throw himself to the floor as he raced between defenders Mike Duxbury and Kevin Moran. A terrible dive and one which saw Mancunian wrath rain down upon him. A sad sight for those who came to view this much talked about footballer.

Finally, the drama ended and amidst wild emotional scenes the home supporters flooded the pitch and lifted high their Captain, who with his magnificent performance that night had entered into the annals of Manchester United legend. Robson found himself carried off in triumph. An epic occasion and one that even today United supporters still recall as amongst their finest hours. As for the yellow shirts of Barca they skulked off well beaten and home to a firestorm of criticism. It was one night in Manchester they would swiftly want to forget.

C23
THE SCOTSMAN COMETH: 1986
A Stage-play

Act One
BOJANGLES
Tuesday November, 4th 1986: Southampton v Manchester United: Third Round League Cup Replay: 4-1. After having just witnessed his 'magic circle' being ripped apart by a seventeen-year-old magician called Matthew Le Tessier, Bojangles was not in dancing mood. A horrific start to the season that saw United ravaged by injuries and poor form has left them lying second from bottom. The slaughter at the Dell placing increasing pressure on the manager. No funny quips or jovial remark from Bojangles on this night. Instead he twitches uneasily. Manchester is a long way off and the knives would surely be sharpening. Will they already be planning his execution?

Bojangles vents his spleen:
'Four-one to Southampton? Oh, Sir Robert is going to love this, more ammunition to fire the bullets, twist the knife and spread his poison. Whisper in the chairman's ear, 'He's not for us Martin, he isn't United, loves himself he does. Spends more time on the sunbed than the training pitch.'
Well what was your management career like Sir Robert? Did wonders at Preston North End didn't you? Worked out well didn't it?
I know what you're up to. I know what happened in Mexico at the world cup.
Promised the Scotsman my job, keys to the kingdom and

all that. You believe he's a better man, more United?
Never liked me has Sir Robert, he hates me in fact. How they forget. A poison chalice
Nobody wanted this job. Lawrie Mcmenemy, Bobby Robson and Ron Saunders. They all turned you down. Three wise men, but not me. I saved your neck Sir Robert, I said yes. I got you Robbo.1.5 Million of sheer gold. If it wasn't for me he'd have signed for Liverpool. Yes, Liverpool and you think you have problems with them now? Imagine that Sir Robert, imagine that. Robbo in a Liverpool shirt?
And now you want rid of me?
Well two FA Cups in five years isn't bad. Better than your managerial career Sir Robert. As for the league? So close then more injuries. Injuries, injuries, injuries….
Ten opening wins on the run we had last season, ten wins, we looked unbeatable. Norm, Jasper, Wee Red and Sparky. We played football from another planet. Ran riot The United way, my way. Like Sinatra sang,
"Much more than this I did it my way."
The title was wrapped up in a big red and white bow. Mancunian not Merseyside, eighteen years of ignominy, embarrassment and mockery.
Tear gas and Munich chants.
Very classy.
But we were finally back! Name on the trophy.
Then the Christmas period, time of good will to all men. Well not me because we fell like a tree. Injuries, injuries, injuries. Robbo went down and we came fourth in a two-horse race.
They came back.
"Liverpool, Liverpool, Liverpool."
But this year will be so different, get everyone fit

especially Robbo.

Then watch us go. Knock those smiles off the Scousers up the East Lancs. I just need luck that's all. I need a large slice of luck and no injuries. They have short memories in this city, such short, short memories. Forgotten already Wednesday 21st March, 1984. Barcelona at Old Trafford, 54,000 in the ground screaming their heads off.

My boys my United. Two goals down from the first leg at the Nou Comp. We didn't have a prayer claimed the wise and bloody know-alls. Well we did it. I did it, my United did it. Maradona and Schuster never got a touch. We blew them away 3-0. Three nil!

Robbo, Norm, Arnie, Remi and Frank. My boys.

The roof came off. Tears of joy, dancing in the aisles: we nailed them!

'A great night' the Mancs said. A Special night that brought back memories.

My United, my United, my United. Not yours Sir bloody Robert, not yours, mine. I just need luck that's all, a little more time.

………Get Robbo fit.

Well, what is it to be then Sir Robert? Are you going to twist the knife deep?

Official United statement:

It is with great sadness that Manchester United have been forced to terminate the contract of Mr Bojangles. The board of Directors would like to wish him all the best for the future and thank him for his efforts…Next

Act Two
THIS IS THE ONE
And so, Sir Robert was granted his wish for Mr Bojangles to be sacked. Good old Wilf, Frank who, the Doc, boring Dave and now Bojangles. All fell short.
None could ever hold a candle to the 'Old Man.' Pygmies following a giant. His was a shadow so overwhelming that it engulfed all who followed. Choked ambitions and drained confidence. Took away time, never enough time. A poisoned chalice for which there appeared no known cure. Then, suddenly word reached Old Trafford of a miracle-maker in the faraway north. Sir Robert sent forth his Mancunian emissaries, they travelled 350 miles to Scotland. To the 'Silver city' of Aberdeen.
Sir Robert keeps the old man informed:
'This is the one boss, Glasgow boy and Govan raised. Worked in the shipping yards, a toolmaker, family man, catholic wife with three sons. He supported Rangers as a lad, blue stock but nobody is perfect.
I can see it in his eyes, ice blue they are, pierce right through you. Hard as nails but a football man, one of us…United.
Coming for the right reasons also, bonuses apart he could have earned more by staying at Aberdeen. But there is a savage hunger to succeed, frightening.
A history maker.
I spoke to him in Mexico this summer when he was managing Scotland. Just a friendly chat. Told him to stay calm, we're coming. Be patient,
………United are coming.
His record in Scotland defies all logic, miraculous almost. He smashed the domination of the Old Firm with Aberdeen. Aberdeen!? It's extraordinary. Three titles,

four Scottish cups and a European cup winner's cup trophy beating Real Madrid. Did it the right way just like you boss. He presented the Real coach Alfredo di Stefano with a vintage bottle of whisky beforehand.

A class act, United style. A man of substance with an iron will.

A winner.

Great news that Martin has finally seen sense don't you think boss? Typically, Bojangles treated his sacking as a big joke by throwing a party.

'No regrets' he claimed. Never for us, never United.

Not like the Scotsman. He's coming and is going to give us back our club. Our dignity and pride. Win the league and then the European Cup.

Remember Wembley 1968, remember my two goals, they were for you and the lads that died. My pals, our United boss, our United.

The great days will return, I promise you. This is the one……

This is the one.'

Act Three
AN IMPOSSIBLE DREAM

On Thursday 6th November, 1986, the Scotsman sat down before the world's press at Old Trafford to be unveiled as the new manager of Manchester United. With the club lying second from bottom of the first division, surely when questioned about his first priority the manager's answer would be to talk about avoiding relegation and seek mid- table security. Not for the Scotsman as he boldly declared, 'We can still win the league.' Straight off new standards had been set, bars raised. A wind of change albeit only slight blew across

the Old Trafford pitch, over the stands and forecourt to settle softly on the River Irwell. Hardly raising a ripple. But the rising had begun.
The Scotsman admires his new kingdom from the centre-circle:
'Look at this place, a bloody cathedral. But what do they worship, mediocrity that's what. Aye well that ends of now. Nineteen years without the league title. I can smell the desperation all around, the frustration, hopelessness and it makes me sick. Reminds me of a dog that's been beaten so badly it flinches whenever anyone comes near. I'll have to act fast, shake things up.
Nineteen years defies belief, why has it been so long? So much betrayal, treachery and lies. When it comes to footballing politics they say Mancunians can make Machiavelli look like an amateur. Smile to your face then stab you in the back at the first opportunity……….
Well I come from Govan.
I met the players earlier today, great names but not impressed seeing them close up, 'Good to see you boys, I'm the Scotsman. Everybody starts with a clean slate, reputations mean nothing. Hopefully you feel guilty and are all hurting at seeing Bojangles get sacked, because if so then we have a chance. There will be no looking back, we go from here. You're playing for a great team and need to keep yourselves super-fit so you can look after your families. As for the drinking? It ends now. It's my way or no way.' Straight away I could smell the booze on their breaths.
I looked around at glum uninterested faces. Only Robbo stood out, the thirst for a new challenge still evident in his eyes. The others clearly weighing me up. How far can they push me? Let them try, aye,

just let them try.

As for the drinking? Wee red told me in Mexico of all day boozing sessions, 'Bojangles does nothing about it' he said, 'Too close to the players.'

Madness, madness. This has resembled for too long a social club, a haven for cheats, has-beens and boozers. The two Irishmen are the worst I'm told, Norman and the big Irish. Never off the treatment table but first away from the training ground into the Pubs and bars.

It's a shame because they are both bloody great players and could've been useful to me. But I could never trust those who put alcohol before their careers. I'll play it clever, consoling arm and all that. Give them another chance but I can't have it. I just can't have it.

They are already history here. Finished

Different situation with Robbo though, they tell me he drinks hard but trains harder. Have to get him fit.

Aye, get Robbo fit.

Liverpool. Liverpool, Christ they hate them here. But what a challenge.

It'll take time but we shall do it, get under their skin. Wear them down then take their crown. Refereeing conspiracies, United against the world, biased hacks. I can do it, I've done it before. I brought the Old Firm to their knees. They loathed us, us, little old Aberdeen! They despised me, good, because I never backed down. I hated it, the religious bigotry from both sides, the arrogance when we went to Glasgow and put them in their bloody place. 'Who did we think we were?' They sneered.

'Never heard of us' they mocked. Well they know us now.

Aberdeen, the silver city, my city.

Aye, they know us now.
As for Liverpool? They may have a smirk on their faces at the moment but nothing lasts forever, I guarantee that. Liverpool.
'Walk on'
they sing.
'With hope in your heart and you'll never walk alone.'
United supporters once sang it they tell me, but no more. It's sheer hatred now. Pure tribalism. So many seasons having their noses rubbed in it. All-out war when they clash. I can use that, knock them off their lofty fuckin' perch.
Bring that Liver bird crashing down. An impossible dream they tell me,
we shall see.

Act Four
AS TIME GOES BY
Whilst playing his trade for Aberdeen and Scotland, Wee red experienced at first hand the harsh realities of working under the Scotsman. Now, just when the nightmares had ceased he learns his former mentor is coming south to manage him at United. A once good relationship that soured dramatically when the player made the same journey three years previous was set to be rekindled. The cajoling and bullying, that sheer monstrous desire to succeed. Demanding everything and all from his players. All the time, every training session, every game. Wee red awaits with trepidation the Scotsman's imminent arrival in Manchester.
Wee red bemoans his luck at being followed south by the Scotsman:

'Of all the teams in all the world he walks into mine. Just my luck! I've already warned the lads that the beast from the north-east of Scotland is coming to make their lives a misery. Life under Bojangles will have felt like paradise compared to what awaits them. I shook everybody's hand in the dressing room. Told them I'm off. Half-joking maybe, but then again maybe not if the Scotsman carries a grudge. For when I left Aberdeen we hardly parted on the best of terms. I wonder if he's mellowed old 'furious?' That was our nickname for him back then. I hope so but seriously doubt it! More chance of him growing wings and playing a harp.

He's without doubt the most evil, cunning, tactically-astute, genius even, obsessed football man it's ever been my misfortune to come across.

The Scotsman detests losing, bans it even. We were not allowed to get beat!

Also, winning had to be achieved by playing in the correct manner. We played good football. A passing game. Be it at Pittordrie or the bear pits of Ibrox and Celtic Park, he insisted, nay demanded that his side attacked. Unbelievably, beneath that gruff, inhuman exterior their beats a footballing Romantic!

You either bought into his scheme of things or were hurled out of the club, usually by the throat! But the rewards for loyalty and giving all to the Scotsman's cause were immense in the manner of trophies, titles and becoming part of Aberdonian folklore.

And now, once more the man whose dark side could black out the sun is back in my life! We shall renew our acquaintance! Ducking from flying tea cups, being screamed at inches from my face. Flogged like a work horse in training.

But United need him, we need him because standards have slipped, players have lost focus. Under Bojangles, of course we cared, but did we care enough? Other things became equally important such as the drinking.

The boozing sessions have become legendary across Manchester. Days to night, then morning. Only once did I join the lads on their jaunts and then couldn't tie my shoelaces for three days after! Never again.

The Scotsman will come down on that like a hammer smashing a pint glass.

Also, he'll ensure our fitness levels improve so we can compete properly every week. Not like under Bojangles when only once every red moon we played to our true potential. On the day a match for anyone but so very few days. The beating of Liverpool but humiliated by Bournemouth in the FA cup. Bournemouth? We let Bojangles down there. He never deserved that performance. But that was us, the Magic Circle?

A Ferrari fuelled on alcohol.

Reverting back at a fools-whim into a team of individuals that flattered to deceive. It couldn't go on.

Given time I'm utterly convinced the Scotsman will be successful. That's if he doesn't spontaneously combust in a fit of rage on the touchline. Make no mistake this place will be turned on its head. It will get bloody, many casualties, careers and friendship will be tossed aside, there will be tears, anger and broken hearts a plenty, but he will get it back.

Under the Scotsman United will rise up and shake the world.

For he will not rest until this club has won the lot and then he'll insist we do it again! Believe me, I know

what's coming because I've seen it before. His way or no way. 'As time goes by?'
God help us!'

Act Five
THINGS CAN ONLY GET BETTER
On Saturday 8th November 1986, Manchester United played their first match under the guiding hand of the Scotsman. It was a disaster. A 2-0 defeat against Oxford at the Manor Ground acted as a dismal showcase for all that had turned rotten at Old Trafford. A side decimated by injuries, lack of fitness, heart and passion lay down and died a slow agonising death. Like condemned men sure of their fate by a seething executioner on the touchline they gave up. And this in the Scotsman's burning eyes was the ultimate sin. They awaited with dread the final whistle. For he would be waiting.
The Scotsman draws a line in the sand:
'Right sit down!
What the hell was that?
You call yourself professional footballers, Jesus Christ that was beyond embarrassing. Not one of you can honestly look me in the eye and say 'I gave all today.' The only thing I recognised out there associated with Manchester United was the red shirts on your back.
It was bloody shameful.
Looking around this room I see international players, seasoned pros, men who should care about their personal pride. But obviously you don't. Only cowards and cheats perform like that. You lot have just been turned over by a team with only a modicum of your talent. For that there's no excuse.

How do you sleep? Outfought, outclassed, outrun, fuckin' outrageous.

I will remember today's line up. Turner, Duxbury, Albiston, Hogg, Moran, Big Irish, Blackmore, Moses, Stapleton, Davenport, Peter the dribbler.

When this club is back where it belongs, you can hang your head in shame because that performance will act as a benchmark from where we will go on. For things can only get better.

That Bloody Maxwell after the final whistle.

'Thanks for the game,' he said to me. Thanks for the bloody game!?

We are Manchester United, where was your hearts? Have you left it in the Griffin or the Park? Maybe the Roebuck? Or the Four Seasons…Eh, big Irish?

I know what's been going on. Big time Charlies! Can't pass a pub never mind a ball on today's showing. I got advised to play you in midfield today. They told me you could handle it, 'He has a presence' they said. 'Mobile, brave, good pace and skilful, 'Big Irish won't let you down gaffer,' they said. Well they forgot to tell me that you can't run. No stamina. Substituted because you can't run anymore. Take a good long hard look in the mirror Irish because you're on a road to hell. Now, you lot listen and think hard. Sort yourselves out because what happened to Bojangles is never going to happen to me. Under him you got away with murder, well no more.'

Act Six
RAVE ON

In terms of all round ability few centre-halves ever came close to surpassing the big Irish. Brave and strong, technically brilliant, formidable in the air and blessed with blistering pace, this tall, graceful defender ranked amongst the best in Europe. On the field he exuded confidence, few forwards could ever outpace or outwit big Irish. He contained what team mate Kevin Moran called a 'Fifth gear.' A priceless gift that enabled him to shift unerringly into overdrive whenever required. Mr Bojangles christened him his 'black Pearl' upon which United's defence was built around. Sadly, like so much during Bojangles reign, a scratch beneath the surface unearths a totally different reality because off pitch big Irish's life was in permanent turmoil.

Big Irish looks in the mirror and sees the Scotsman staring back at him:

'I'll not look at him,

Just let him rant and rave.

Rave on Scotsman, rave on.

Because I'm not listening,

I'm not going to change.

……I can't change.

A black lad from Dublin raised for the first ten years of his life by monks and nuns who beat me, terrorised me. Every morning in that place I awoke from nightmares to a living one. And you sit there shouting and think you can scare me? You think I haven't heard worse, much worse, so much worse?

Vile, racist, diabolical.

Bullied by the best of the lord almighty's army here on earth.

I've heard it all before.

You don't even register Scotsman. I'm going to drink and drink till the pain goes away.

So, rave on Scotsman…….Rave on.

I want to drink,

I have to drink.
When I'm drunk I become normal. I can walk in a crowded room, look people in the eye and feel their equal. A black lad growing up in Dublin, beaten, mocked and ignored. You don't know the half of it Scotsman, you don't know….
Bojangles never spoke to me like this. He played fair, he was grand. I would go into training utterly wrecked. 'Big Irish is hammered again!'
Me stood there staggering with a daft grin on my face. Oblivious to all.
Bojangles would take me to one side, 'Sort yourself out for Saturday and we'll say no more about it. Keep it in house, amongst the family.
The Magic circle.
'We need you, we need you, we need you.' I was sheltered, safe from those who wanted to save me from harm. Deliver me from temptation.
I would get away with murder because come the match when it really mattered I was there for him. Never let him down. Count my man of the match awards Scotsman. You're a great one for statistics, you do the maths.
Let's do a deal, leave me alone and I'll perform. Either way I'll not look you in the eye.
So, rave on Scotsman, you're wasting time and breath. Rave on.'

Act Seven
ONE MAN BAND
Bojangles referred to him as 'Pure gold' the press naturally decided on superlatives and went with 'Captain Marvel.' To the supporters he was simply Robbo. Their driving force. A shining light in an age of United

mediocrity. A one-man band. Amongst the world's elite midfielders, inspirational, irreplaceable and unfortunately cursed by endless injuries. It was he in the tempestuous wake of the Scotsman's laying down of the law for his new regime who gathered together the players to steady nerves and more than anything, urge caution. For it made little sense tap-dancing in a minefield. Explosions were certain to occur so why pre-empt them?

Captain Robbo calls a meeting of his team mates in a local hostelry run by United legend, Paddy the landlord:
'Right lads, first of all has everybody got a drink?
Cheers Paddy and one for yourself.
Now, let's get cracking.
I know after Bojangles the new gaffer is a shock to the system, but I believe in the long run he's going to be good for us. Those of you who think he was a little over the top after the Oxford game had better get used to it because according to Wee red that was mild compared to when he really loses it.
You all know I'll stand your corner both on the pitch and off. I like a drink as much as anyone, if not more,
but this guy is not messing around.
Ask Wee red how he tore into his team live on the telly only moments after they won the Scottish cup? Claimed they hadn't played well enough.
'A bloody disgrace' he said.
How he knew where every player was on their days off. Spies all over the city and we know about that don't we? Even staked out their houses, made sure they behaved and if caught? If caught then god help them.
Another round please Paddy and a drink for yourself.

All I'm saying is that when you go out and have a beer, watch where you go, don't take liberties. And stay off the shorts!

Because believe me if you upset him he'll have you out of United.

No need to turn into monks just be sensible. Play hard, work harder. When he's in your face just think of the win bonuses. You're going to hate him but I guarantee you this, he's good.

Cheers Paddy, c'mon lads drink up and we'll have another.'.......

Act Eight
BETTER DAYS

Old Trafford had become like an old lady's home who in her day was a real beauty. A heart-stopping Belle of the ball. But as the years go by and she loses her looks, the house also starts to go downhill. Until on the day she dies it finally resembles a mothballed-dust-filled shell.

Creaking of old memories, happier times, better days. There's only one way to bring back former glories, that's go back to basics and clean the thing out from head to toe. With all the sensitivity of a hand grenade the Scotsman goes to work.

At 7-30am every morning the Scotsman arrives at the cliff and sets out his plan for future world domination. 'From now on they train twice a day, mornings and afternoons. Let them attempt to weave their way through the early morning traffic. Let them feel like they have a real job. Then I'll be waiting. Keep them busy, minds focused. Tactically, I've seen pub sides better prepared.

So many goals given away unnecessarily. All down to naivety or more likely players being lazy and just not doing their jobs.
I'll change that.
Players have treated this club like a movie set for their own personal glory and not a place of work. I'll change that.
Shoddy appearance breeds laziness, lacklustre. From now on clean shaven, short hair and club blazers to be worn on official business. No fuckin' hippies in my team.
Act United.
Think United.
Play United.
For too long we've been viewed as a music hall joke.
'Have you ever seen United win the league?' Chant the Scousers.
Believe me,
I'll change that.
There are better days to come.
As for the famed United youth system? A con, bloody mirage. A hall of mirrors arranged to hide years of neglect. I've inherited an ageing first team that appears more interested in getting drunk than playing football. Our scouts seem to have had the life sucked out of them. It's ridiculous. All we get is the scraps off City's plate who seem to have Manchester sewn up.
I can't have this,
I won't have this.
That lot are not even in our world, never mind class! Something has gone badly wrong. What the hell was Bojangles doing these past five years?
His so called 'Magic circle' 'once in never out' was an illusion. That's all he cared about and in doing so has let

everything else go stale. If you're winning leagues and cups every year then fine, such an attitude could be tolerated if not understood. But to concentrate all your thoughts on just the first team to the detriment of everything underneath, when you've won just two trophies in five years? That isn't arrogance it's bloody stupidity.

And now we're paying the price.

All those hours on that sunbed must have sizzled his brains. The whole place needs re-igniting. First thing I'm going to call a meeting, shake things up and demand to know why our conveyor of talent has ground to a halt.

My rules, no more best kids on the street or in the school. Even the city. I want the cream of the country. For Christ sake's Aberdeen has more scouts in Ireland than United have? That in itself is a scandal.

Everything is going to be restructured, new attitudes, new faces.

I'm bringing in Kiddo, United legend, local boy and a good lad. The son of a bus driver. Real United they tell me………Real United.

Eat, sleep, drink United. I'm reading every book that's been written about this club. Formed on a mud patch in Newton Heath. Old Trafford almost destroyed by a stray Luftwaffe incendiary bomb. Then came Munich. Eight players dead, United all but finished. Yet still they came back to win the European cup ten years on. If it was a movie no one would believe it.

Real United? What exactly does that mean? I'll speak to the Old man and pick his brains.

Act Nine
AN OLD MAN'S TEARS
The Old man sits in the office and lights up his pipe. It's a sparse room, only a telephone that never rings and a notepad adorn the table. He still makes the journey every day. On the Old Trafford forecourt people politely wave and offer to shake his hand. They still realise the Old man's importance and appreciate the sheer magnitude of what he achieved for their club. Even if those who now run United would rather he just went away. However, there was one on the inside who still valued the Old man's opinion.
The Scotsman seeks out the Old man for advice and to discover the real United:
'This place is sick son.
It needs drastic surgery, a new heart and that's you.
Nobody asks my opinion anymore. Sir Robert apart that is, but he's a good lad. Cares deeply about the club. This thing of ours. United.
Old Trafford is sprinkled with gold dust. You can't see it but it's there.
It's a great healer and it helped me.
After Munich I didn't want to know anyone or anything. My family, football, nothing. All I cared about had been taken away from me on that German runway. I should've perished son, my body was crushed, my spirit broken.
I was given the last rites, live or die I never cared.
Made ready to enter heaven whilst I was suffering hell here on earth.
But, somehow, I don't and will never know why, God spared me.
Then I became angry, outraged at this undeserved act of mercy.

Why me?
Eight players and so many good pals suffered such a cruel fate and yet I survived? In time I returned to Manchester but all my boys were long buried.
I missed the funerals, small mercies.
Dark clouds over the rainy city son. It rained tears.
Jimmy Murphy kept our flag flying. Only he could've done that. Kept United alive did Jimmy, fought tooth and nail when others were convinced our time had gone. So sad that we rarely speak now. That's the dark side of football. Sometimes friendships fall by the wayside because you're too stubborn to realise their importance. Only when it is too late does the sadness strike home at what you lost.
But you speak to him also, a wise man, a great man. We were like brothers once. You remind me of him son. Fire and passion, lives for the game….
This thing of ours.
Once back at Old Trafford when sat in my office, on quiet days I could still hear their voices echoing down corridors. Distant laughter, the rattle of football boots on concrete…. I still hear them now.
Big Duncan, Eddie Coleman, Tommy Taylor. My boys. They died in pursuit of a dream. My dream. Unfinished business son. The European cup.
That inspired me to ignore the pain and nightmares and concentrate on winning that trophy. And we did it ten years on, we did it!
Such relief son……end of a rainbow.
We had a party afterwards and invited all the families of those who died at Munich. I sang 'It's a wonderful world' with tears in my eyes. I thought of my lost boys, imagined their faces. It was a strange evening. Tinged

with the atmosphere of a boisterous Irish wake. I raised a toast, many toasts in their name and for that one night the sadness eased.
Though come the dawn as my head cleared it returned.
The real United son, it will show itself.
Strange and magical things happen here. We've always taken the tough path to success, but this only makes the journey more exciting. United never know when they are beaten. Constantly surprising, overcoming insurmountable odds.
Never give up son, fight your corner and always be bold. That's the real United
Look for players with hunger in their eyes, good temperament, but most importantly who can play. Get them raw, mould them, ferment your own apples. Clear out the bad ones. The city is blessed with boys who would give everything for this club. Find them. Bring them through together.
It will take time, years even but they will show themselves. And as they take flight the European cup will again come into our sights.
There's an inner strength in you son, you're the one.
My door is always open, now you bring it back!
This thing of ours............
The real United.'

Act Ten
PLOUGH LANE
A goalless draw away to Norwich and a narrow 1-0 win at home against Queens Park Rangers handed the Scotsman a satisfactory, if hardly spectacular response to his demands for more from his underachieving players. The next match would prove whether the heart for a

battle did exist at United or whether their reputation as having no bottle when it came to a scrap was justified. For Wimbledon away at their broken down-ramshackle ground was the ultimate test for any visiting team. A ghetto-blaster ripping through the changing rooms walls. Obscenities raging, threats and punch ups in the tunnel. War with a ball and the opening whistle signalling mayhem. Welcome to Plough Lane.

Harry the beast offers his players some gentle advice before taking on the world famous United:

'Turn that ghetto blaster down Fash,
I can't hear myself rant.
Right lads, we know who is here today. How they look down on us. Some of this lot earn more in a month then you do in a year Remember that when they get precious with you.
But today there is one ball, our patch!
Plough Lane!
A burial ground where the great and good crash and burn. Vinny, get after them from the off in midfield. Don't try and play, what's the fuckin' point? Just kick them, any of them. Get in their faces, don't let them settle into any passing rhythm. Word has it on good authority from Manchester that this lot would rather be on the lash than a football pitch.
Fash the bash have you sharpened your elbows big man? Good, because you should fill your boots out there today son. Reap carnage. They are a team of drunks with no heart. Players in name only. Make sure you see red out there boys. See red, give them hell.
I don't want to see that ball on the floor all game do you fuckin' understand? Keep it high and long. Unsettle them, torture the flash northern poofs.

Give them neck ache.

Turn it into a scrap because this lot couldn't fight their way out of a nunnery. So, forget the legends lads, the Old Trafford glamour. Georgie Boy, Lawman, Sir Robert and the fuckin' glory years. Those facing you in red today are not fit to clean their boots.

Now let's go nail the bastards!'

Wimbledon 1 Manchester United 0. During the ninety minutes at Plough Lane all of the Scotsman's worst fears are realised. Weak in defence, devoid in midfield of creativity and upfront toothless. But worst of all, gutless. The full extent of just how huge his task would be to turn this ailing giant of a football club into genuine title contenders hits home to the Scotsman with all the ferocity of a striking lightning bolt. There was going to be no quick fix and no miracle solution. Divine inspiration was still six years away and plying his trade as an ill-tempered teenager in Marseille. For now, it was crystal clear to him that this present lot had to go.

The Scotsman almost kicks the dressing room down and confronts those he feels have disgraced the United shirt:

'So be it,

this is how it's going to be.

Well thanks for that fiasco today. Thanks for nailing yourselves to the cross because you've saved me the trouble.

Did you hear our fans? They can see it, smell it. There's no hiding from them.

Well now the curtains have been well and truly pulled back and exposed you for the frauds you are. You were beaten by a team whose best player is a hod carrier by trade and a lump up front whose best asset is his elbows. But I wish they were here in this dressing room wearing

red shirts, because at least they have the fuckin' guts for a fight.
Today, I saw things unacceptable. Players pulling out of tackles, afraid to pass the ball. Bullied and intimidated like little schoolboys. Pathetic!
Can't defend, create or score goals.
Players out of breath, wheezing, on their knees because they are so unfit.
Jesus fuckin' Christ!
Get changed and get on the coach.
……… You make me sick.'
As the Scotsman let fly at his players, United winger Peter the dribbler stayed hidden in the bath:
'I don't need this. The man is a lunatic.
That's it, first opportunity I'm out of here.
If I show my face in there he'll rip me to pieces. Does he want footballers or deranged maniacs charging round the field kicking people?
I'm a winger, an England international. A brilliant one at that. I beat defenders with my skills. Put them on their backside with my flair and artistry.
I played for Manchester City, West Bromwich Albion, Leeds United and Coventry city. I won Double PFA player of the year when he was still managing a fishing town called Aberdeen.
Whereas I?
I played against Italy and tortured the infamous Azzurri hitman Claudio Gentile. Put the ball through his legs, made him appear a fool. Clemence, Neal, Cherry, Wilkins, Watson, Hughes, Coppell, Keegan, Latchford, Brooking and Peter the dribbler.
'A superstar is born' screamed the next day headlines.

I even had my own Peter the dribbler football in all the shops. It sold thousands. All the kids in Manchester had them. They loved me.
President of the Junior blues! Happy days.
And now this….
Did you hear him yelling at me in the second half!?
Acting like a nutter on the touchline, his veins bulging, he looked purple! I daren't even look, although I felt his eyes follow my every move.
Did you hear what he called me? It was outrageous!
Me! Peter the dribbler. Mancunian legend. Beats defenders for fun.
Those were not challenges on me, they were assaults. GBH!
If I hadn't jumped out of the way several times they would have chopped me in two. I never even got a decent half time cup of tea because we found out our hosts had put salt in the kettle. I ask you is this any to treat a legend like me?
Others will snap me up.
A queue of clubs as long as your arm will form for Peter the dribbler. Double PFA winner, Claudio Gentile tormentor. A dying breed, one of a kind I am.
I beat defenders for fun………'

Act Eleven
THE REAL UNITED
Two consecutive 3-3 draws home to Tottenham Hotspur and away against Aston Villa give the Scotsman a tantalising, if infuriating glimpse of all that's good, bad and downright ugly about his team. Inconsistency incorporated: Breath-taking going forward but suicidal in defence. The much-needed return of Robbo and Norm

after injury acted like a blood transfusion to United in attack. And, although their exasperating habit of self-exploding at the back continued unabated at least the Scotsman had something to grasp onto.

For the first time since arriving at Old Trafford, the Scotsman had seen the real United:

'It was against Villa that I sensed for the first time the sheer sense of occasion and excitement surrounding whenever United came to town. Before the game an expectancy that something special is set to occur. A full house, every viewpoint taken. The manic desperation to beat us, hate us, but so much want to be us.

A club that hasn't won the title for nineteen years, yet still possesses the pulling power of a visiting Hollywood movie star.

Like an Ali-Frazier super fight, Sinatra playing Caesars Palace or Red Rum racing clear in the Grand National, the sense of drama with United is overwhelming. Priceless.

It can't be touched, but exists.

The old man spoke about, 'This thing of ours.'

Inside Villa Park I understood exactly what he meant. I could almost touch it, the electricity in the air, the pulsating atmosphere that covets the stadium is all consuming. So much that you find it hard to breathe. Make no mistake Liverpool maybe champions but we're a scalp comparable if not one much more so. To compete and cope with this scale of hostility on a weekly level I need players of special character. Winners, men of substance and capable of rising to a challenge. There's going to be previously unseen levels of hatred and loathing, enemies to spare. For if there's jealousy now when we're winning nothing, what price the animosity against a successful United?

It'll be like old times when I declared war on the Old Firm then sat back to wait for the reaction. Typically, it was forthcoming, a Purple rage tinged with heady doses of Sectarian garbage. In short, they were so busy hating us they forgot how to beat us. It'll be fun once more firing the bullets, circling the wagons and staving off Scouse slings and arrows of supposed injustices. Then, whilst they seethe and grind their teeth we get on with collecting trophies.

I'm going to decimate the present squad.

Only a handful will survive the cull for their lack of physical and mental strength is embarrassing and can't be tolerated. When I next meet with Martin I'll tell him we need a new team. I've my list of names. An expensive list. All great players, potentially true United players.

No doubt he'll listen then shake his head. Martin has already pleaded poverty, 'Bojangles spent it all' he claimed. But there's money here, I can smell it.

Not surprisingly, he told me we would have to sell before buying.

History tells me this lot, if possible tend to do things on the cheap. Milk the United name and proud history for all its worth before giving out an extra penny. But given enough arm twisting, threats and ego soothing, I'm told by Sir Robert, Martin can always be talked round. We shall see.

Besides, our pot will already be half-filled with Bojangles' dead wood. The directors simply have to put their hands in tight Mancunian pockets and make up the rest. Glory days don't come cheap. Ask the last five managers before me? Given luck and patience, but most

importantly enough financial muscle, great things can be achieved here. I want a 'real United' one that will truly represent me and the supporters.
In time I'll make the Old man proud.
…. And Liverpool sick.'

Act Twelve
BOYS FROM THE BOOTROOM
From a small room deep in the heart of Anfield, three wise men plot and scheme to keep their club at the helm of English football. King Kenny, nice guy Roy and Ronnie the mouth keep alive the Shankly and Paisley traditions of the Boot room. Over a steaming hot brew they chat and dissect tactics, discuss players. Who needs a kind word or bringing down a peg. They talk of events elsewhere, who if anyone posed a threat to their superiority. Of knocking them off their Liver bird perch. They talk about the Scotsman.
Ronnie the mouth holds court in the famed Liverpool boot room and relates his feeling towards the Scotsman cometh:
'All these years dancing in our shade like a drunken uncle at a wedding. Staggering and stumbling, making a fool of themselves, whilst we, the glorious Liverpool football club waltz magnificent on the dance floor. All pomp, proud and strutting. It takes time to build a dynasty. Bob and Shanks started this thing of ours and now we carry the torch. Here in this very room, our sceptre throne.
We walk on.
Nothing or nobody is strong enough to take us on.
Their mistake was failing to replace the Old man with anyone of real substance. All were either too

inexperienced or outsiders not suited to their way of doing things. Strangers in the dark. Blind to what the Old man achieved for that place. Oblivious to how and simply too arrogant to learn.

Now, finally it appears they've got someone with a backbone and true sense of history.

The word is this Scotsman is ripping that place apart. Slicing egos and breathing fire. Our biggest nightmare has always been that someone comes along and awakes the sleeping Manc giant. For once it is stirred then God help us for a generation and one. But nothing is set in stone boys, they may believe their path to glory has begun, but walk on I say.

Let them come.

Will they ever learn in that grey, foreboding miserable city? Same old, same as.

He's going to deliver them from our evil. All mouth the Mancs, look at the history books and count their titles compared to ours. Count their European Cups. Shouldn't take too long.

Talk is cheap and so boys I will quote you from our anthem.

'Don't be afraid of the storm.'

Chances are the Scotsman will win a medal this season, the OBE.

Out before Easter!

We play them next and it is essential he's left in no doubt his cause is hopeless. That the sleeping giant is not merely slumbering but dead and beyond resuscitation. Let's kill this horror out on the pitch before it becomes real.

Show them a little hope is a dangerous thing. That blind faith in false prophets leads not to the Promise land, but disaster.
Bring on Boxing day.
For at Anfield we will show the Scotsman a real football club.

Act Thirteen
WELCOME TO ANFIELD
Boxing Day: Friday 26th December 1986. Liverpool 0 Manchester United 1. After being pummelled by a rampaging home side for almost the entire contest, United produced a smash and grab raid courtesy of Norm to snatch unexpected victory. It was a jubilant Scotsman that punched the air at full time before saluting the vast throngs of travelling Mancunians who delighted in taunting their unwelcoming hosts. Laced with a stench of hatred, driven by history and poisonous jealousy this is no ordinary rivalry. In many ways two cities so alike, not a needle thread could be darned between them. But in matters of football they remain a chasm apart. Chants of 'Who's that dying on the runway' and 'Munich 58' answered by 'Murderers' and 'Shankly 81.' Welcome to Anfield……It's a Northern thing.
The Scotsman reflects on a memorable victory over Liverpool at Anfield:
'What a game, what an atmosphere, what a place.
Aye, not much of that famous Scouse sense of humour on show here today. We bring out the worse in them. 40,000 screaming for our blood. Intimidating but scintillating. A white knuckle ride. War without weapons but a war nonetheless.

No surprise they took defeat bad. The boot room boys shook my hand, well touched it anyway. Ronnie the mouth couldn't resist a last dig, 'Although you won we were the better team,' he claimed.

As for King Kenny? Heavy lies the crown, comes to mind. Man of few words where I'm concerned and even less when beaten.

Norm's winning goal was a magnificent hit past Bruce the clown. Only the highest calibre of player can do that. Norm is one. He's a special talent, just twenty-one, but in so many ways already a seasoned veteran.

Signs, I saw real signs today. I asked them to show me something that the challenges I've set isn't beyond their capacities as just footballers but most importantly men. From the first minute we showed cool heads and huge hearts. Both were evident in abundance and now they have to continue with the same level of attitude and concentration. I demand this, nothing else will be sufficient here.

Turner, Sivabaek, Gibson, Norm, Moran, Duxbury, Robbo, Wee red, Stapleton, Davenport, Olsen. A true test of their character will come tomorrow after we've played Norwich at Old Trafford. Only then will I know if this team of mine has what it takes to sustain a proper title challenge.

Big Irish and Robbo were magnificent. Their courage and ability to play when under pressure sums up for me the real United. They gave all for the cause and others followed. For the first time that felt like my team today. Such a tragedy the same duo plus big Irish give me nightmares off the pitch with their boozing.

They must begin to understand and believe that the next match is the most important event in their lives. Not the drink. Never the drink.
I spoke to Robbo about this and told him straight that if he could find me one single asset that booze adds to an athlete's body then I would lay off him and his other red brethren who overly indulge.
He couldn't answer me.
None of them could when asked the same question.
The rest of their lives can be spent propping up a bar. What matters now is football, playing week in, living clean, enjoying a career that millions would happily give anything for. It's a crime not to take it ultra-serious.
Aye, its bloody maddening.
For when the full-time whistle has long gone and they are old men wanting to tell tall tales about their glorious youths. When grandkids are sat on their knee with scrapbooks and adoring eyes wanting to hear of the glory days.
When supporters are asking to see their medals, to hear about the great games, the wonderful goals. Thanking them and wanting to shake their hands.
When they were kings……
For this club creates legends like no other.
When that time comes nobody will care or have the slightest interest in how they got absolutely legless twice a week with team mates whom had little respect for themselves or others. Who knows if the players are listening or even care what I say? All I know is that this time tomorrow, today's result will either have been a real turning point in our season or yet another false red dawn. I'm not holding my breath.'

Twenty-four hours later: Manchester United 0 Norwich 1.
… And Robbo pulls a hamstring.

Act Fourteen
DERBY DAY

Whilst the Scotsman breathed fire in his attempts to revitalise United fortunes across Manchester, their local rivals City were deeply entrenched in yet another struggle against relegation. The glory days of the late sixties, early seventies are long gone. The times when they went toe to toe with United for every major honour a distant dream. Now, it was all about survival. So far the eighties had proved eventful only in terms of heartache and disappointment. Therefore, the possibility of beating United at Old Trafford when the two clubs were drawn together in the FA cup Third Round was viewed as a god sent opportunity for short term redemption. Relegation and financial ruin may well have been hurtling into sight on the near horizon but if the long-suffering blues could just beat the rags?

Beat the rags, beat the rags, beat the rags. …..

The, legendary ex right-winger 'Buzzer' was regarded as one of City's best ever players and on the eve of 'Derby day' he puts up a spirited defence of his beloved club:

'Another relegation battle dawns and we're in dire straits again. A curse, a rag gypsy curse cast upon us, forever tormenting us. 'Twisted and bitter' we're called by that lot. Infatuated, riddled with a sky-blue envy.

Although, what we have to be jealous about I don't know because how many leagues have they won in the last nineteen years?

And who was the last Manchester team to win the First Division?
Saturday 11th May 1968. The rags got beat 2-1 at home to Sunderland, whilst we and yours truly win 4-3 at Newcastle to clinch the title. I got the first, a smashing shot into the top corner from six yards. Typically, the television cameras and trophy were at Old Trafford. But we were the champions, English champions. City from Maine Road.
Our coach Big Mal declared, 'City would be the first team to play on Mars!' That's how superior we were to everybody else. For once we were the headline makers, top dogs in Manchester.
Then what happens?
Two weeks later the rags somehow fluke a European cup against an over the hill Benfica. Always in their shade outsiders say, well not me, not City.
We've hurt them,
done them many times. Broke their rag hearts.
I scored the goal that clinched a league cup semi-final in 69 at Old Trafford.
I started the move from which the Lawman scored to send them down in 74.
Great times, a wonderful day. The Lawman cried, so did I.
Tears of laughter.
We shall go there and give everything. Suckling, Gidman, Wilson, Clements, McCarthy, Redmond, White, McNab, Varadi, Grealish, Simpson.
A Manchester Derby day always starts with a knot in the stomach and ends in either joy or despair. Forget our league position, this is the cup and our year for Wembley. We shall start by making the rags cry in their

own backyard. Seven thousand blues will show them how true Mancunians support their team.

A magnificent club like City deserve success, not perpetual torture. One day a blue moon will shine above our fair city.

……One day.

Saturday 10TH January 1987. United 1-0 City.

C24
WELCOME TO MANCHESTER
…Saturday 26th December 1992…
Alex Ferguson knew he had something special with Eric Cantona early on at the Cliff training ground when sat in the office, his assistant a smiling Brian Kidd rushed in.
'You're not going to believe this? Its Eric.'
Immediately Ferguson thinks that his new boy has head butted a tea lady or even worse. He leans back in his chair waiting for bad tidings, 'What's up Kiddo?'
'Just look out your window boss?'
Ferguson turns around to see a lone figure on the training pitch with a host of balls firing them at the goal.
 'It's Eric. He didn't want to come in, asked if I could let him have another twenty minutes.'
   A smiling Ferguson shakes his head in disbelief, 'Get some of the apprentices out there. I don't want him on his own.'
'Will do and don't worry about him being a loner. This fella is good as gold. He knows the score. Eric was born for this club.'
 Kidd leaves the office whilst Ferguson appears mesmerised as Cantona continually firing the balls into an empty net from different angles. A smile comes on the United manager's face, 'Good lad' he says quietly.

   With Eric Cantona adding that touch of guile, it allows players like Ryan Giggs, Lee Sharpe, Andrei Kanchelskis and Mark Hughes to run into positions, certain to expect an exquisite flick, or perfect pass from the beguiling Frenchman. The results are instant and United are now in fourth place, only two points behind the unexpected leaders. An unfancied Norwich City.

Cantona has so far scored one goal, a late equaliser at Chelsea as he slalomed away from defenders and smashed a low shot into the net.

Whilst not spectacular Ferguson is pleased with his new signing. Early signs are that Cantona is forging a partnership with Mark Hughes and his trio of exciting young wingers. A huge test is this Boxing Day match away at Hillsborough, Sheffield Wednesday, and after an hour, United are being slaughtered.

Its 3-0 to an on-fire Wednesday and on the United bench a glum looking Ferguson fears utter humiliation in the Steel city.

Step forward Eric Cantona.
Suddenly, rather than fold the away team's number seven drops a little deeper to start attacks rather than finish them. Freeing Brian McClair upfield and finding United's wingers with killer passes behind the Wednesday full-backs.
Five minutes after the home side's seemingly third killer goal, McClair breaks from Cantona's pass and makes it 3-1. Suddenly, the jumping mass of red and white at that same end in the Leppings lane sense hope.

It goes on-pressure unyielding, red shirts swarming forward with Cantona, mesmeric, picking holes and a sleight of foot that has Wednesday defenders swaying and rocking like trees in a fierce wind. Chances are being created by the handful and missed-Ferguson loses patience with a misfiring Giggs and replaces him with a Ukrainian bolt of light called Kanchelskis.

Now with him on the right and the electric dancing feet of Sharpe on the left, the charge of the red brigade continues. Unable to clear their lines a terrible mix up between the Wednesday defenders allows McClair in to grab a second with ten minutes remaining. Again, the supporters from across the Pennines go wild. There's still hope of a most unlikely point. The United management of Ferguson and Kidd are off the bench. They too sense something special.

Cantona is probing and causing nightmares amongst his opponents.

A voice in the Sheffield crowd behind the home team's bench picks out a worried looking manager, Trevor Francis, 'Fuckin' ell Trevor. I can't believe you had that French bastard on trial and let him go?'

A nutmeg, drop of a shoulder and he's away again. Cantona is putting on a show that is both delightful and at the same time dismantling the Wednesday defence. 'He's like a fuckin' can opener,' says Ferguson to Kidd on the touchline.

He is that boss' replies his grinning assistant. 'And he's ours.'

With time almost up another astonishing scramble in the home penalty area, and as the ball bobbles loose, it's Cantona who forces it over the line. 3-3 and immediately he's swallowed up by the United supporters who swarm onto the pitch. Mobbed by a blazing swarm of ecstatic Mancunians who have a new hero. A new song…A new day.

In the away dressing room after the match an exhausted but joyful Cantona is shepherded away from thankful team mates by his manager. 'Well done Eric,' smiles Ferguson. 'And welcome to Manchester United!'

C25
A SENSE OF WONDER
…Saturday 9th January 1993…

As the referee Mr Peck, from Kendall, blows to end the match Old Trafford erupts. All certain that on this cold, dark Mancunian, January afternoon, they have witnessed something quite extraordinary. Not just a performance laced with wonderful flair and three points that have seen them go top above Norwich, but for a moment of pure genius on fifty-two minutes.

It came not surprisingly from the conjuring right foot of their number seven. The tall striding Frenchman with a pass of such sweet touch and beauty it caused gasps from a crowd normally reserved for the Ballet and not a simple football match.

United were already one up through a first half Eric Cantona header. Their talisman ably abetted by a supreme blistering supporting cast in Giggs and Sharpe on the wings. And later Kanchelskis.

With Hughes and McClair in equally explosive form and wreaking havoc, it was nothing more than waves of red shirts running riot against a shell-shocked Spurs team, whom from the first minute to last haven't known what's hit them. Even the full-backs Paul Parker and Denis Irwin were hurtling over the halfway line at every opportunity to join in the carnage. Certain that every run would be found by Cantona's inner radar. His ability to pick out a pass sometimes verging on the supernatural, with balls not so much passed, but guided by mystical powers.

Ferguson watched on from his seat with a look of satisfaction, but like everyone else in the stadium a sense of wonder also. And no more than seven minutes after half time when Cantona played a one-two with the darting Irwin, that didn't so much dissect the Spurs defence, but put a spell on them.

A delicate, unerring chip shot, collected by the Irishman to run onto and fire gloriously past the diving goalkeeper Erik Thorvstedt.

Old Trafford went wild! Enraptured and even after the cheering had died down for the goal, a special whispering hush settled across the stands. One that signalled something truly special had just occurred.

In an eyeblink of magic Cantona opened every United supporter's wide.

Just what the hell had they got on their hands?...

C26
NEVER AGAIN
…Saturday 20th March 1993…

The vast majority of the 37,000 here at Maine Road are on their feet and delirious after winger Ricky Holden's cross has just been headed powerfully by centre forward Niall Quinn, past a diving Peter Schmeichel, to give city the lead in this, as ever a bitterly fought Manchester Derby.

Fifty-seven minutes have passed in which United have missed a host of glorious chances. Wayward finishing from Ryan Giggs and surprisingly Eric Cantona has left Alex Ferguson spitting fury on the visitor's bench.

Cantona was unlucky with one effort, a downward header that was tipped superbly round the post by city goalkeeper Tony Coton.

However, there could be no excuse for another later in the half when the Frenchman, too casual by half, could only stroke a weak shot straight at Coton,

And now Manchester United have paid the price for such sloppy finishing.

'That's been fuckin' coming,' declares Ferguson through gritted teeth to Brian Kidd. Around them City supporters letting him know in no uncertain terms their feeling regarding the neighbours from across the city.

'Take that Fergie!

'You're gonna fuck it up again!'

Words striking home with the United manager. United have recently met fellow title rival Aston Villa at Old Trafford and fought out a highly entertaining and keenly contested 1-1 draw. A match that shown there was little between the two sides and the fight for the title could go right to the death. Coming into the Derby they are level at the top of the table, but Ferguson after last season's collapse, house of cards style, knows he can't let his player start to believe it's happening again.

With Maine Road resonating loud to the sound of City anthems, the home team now have something to hold on to. A victory today and there will be parties in the streets and alley of surrounding Moss Side and all points Mancunian blue.

Marshalled superbly on the field by their still influential and highly effective player-manager, the grey-haired Peter Reid, who along with the lung-busting young local boy Gary Flickroft, alongside him are more than holding their own in the middle of the park against Paul Ince and Brian McClair.

But United are still creating opportunities as the so far misfiring Giggs at full pace, dribbles his way through a crowd of blue shirts, only then to shoot wildly wide. Not even forcing Coton to make a save.

Ferguson shakes his head in disbelief. 'What the hell is wrong with him today?'

United are coming again, though nowhere near their fluent best they remain capable of ripping City apart when the mood arises.

A sprinting Lee Sharpe from the left-wing crosses wonderfully for Cantona to soar majestically and dip a powerfully header past the grasping fingers of Coton.1-1! Ferguson and Kidd are off the bench punching the air and the thousands of United supporters behind that goal in the Platt Lane and those scattered around the stadium celebrate.

The ecstatic Frenchman races over to Sharpe to thank him and they are swiftly joined by the rest of their teammates.

The game finishes level and local pride is shared.

On his way to the United dressing room Ferguson remains calm. He knows it's important after last season run in, where maybe him losing his temper with them one too many times had a negative effect.

'Well done boys' he shouts on entering. 'You were the better team by a fuckin' mile. Last season we stopped creating chances, this year that's not happening. You're making them by the hat full.

Just one thing, I want you all to do me a favour?'

. All eyes turn towards him.

He points over to Ryan Giggs, 'If you do make a chance don't pass to him over there!'

Any disappointment over the result melts away as the room lapses into guffaws of laughter. Ferguson sits himself down next to Giggs.

'Ryan son, if I even want anyone to assassinate me I'll pick you!'

Giggs smiles and with an arm around the supremely talented if still erratic, young Welsh winger's shoulders Ferguson knows his point has been made. Unusually subtle for the man from Govan but he like all at United has learnt from last year.

'Never again' appears to be the mindset amongst both players and staff.

'Never fucking again.'

The race for the title goes on…

C27
RED RAIN

…Monday 5th April 1993…

The sleepy Suffolk outback of Norwich, a city hardly noted for its ferocious pace of life has just come face to face with a footballing equivalent of blitzkrieg. In just a nine-minute spell an Eric Cantona inspired Manchester United blew away fellow title challenger Norwich City at Carrow Road with a brand of football, rarely witnessed on these shores.

On leaving the ground Norwich supporters are obviously devastated at the result, but many remain a little bewitched at some of the football played by their opponents from the far away north.

One in particular of older vintage is still purring when being interviewed by a local radio station, 'It was like Puskas and his bloody Magyars coming at us in that first half! Anyone who plays football like that deserves to win the league. Good luck to them.'

It was a game in which if United had lost they would have been four points behind the leaders, Alex Ferguson's predecessor, Ron Atkinson's Aston Villa. Norwich, also, are still up there battling away. But this result could do equally as much damage mentally as points wise such was the difference in class between the two sides.

In a calculated ploy perpetuated by Alex Ferguson the Mancunians retreated and lured a skilful entertaining Canaries team forward.

Then, when the ball was won back they hit on the break with such remarkable, blinding pace, deft touch and sheer power that the 20,582 crowd were left as breathless as their hapless Norwich defenders.

At times it resembled tortoises in pursuit of rabbits…

Their yellow shirts chasing the wind when up against the lightning swift Kanchelskis and Giggs. A masterclass in counter attacking football that began on thirteen minutes. Lee Sharpe's twist, turn and incisive pass to a lurking Cantona in the centre circle. In a blur from all around him, red shirts burst forward and the Frenchman delivered a delightful through ball to a rampaging Giggs. With an offside trap not so much broken, but exploded by three United players, the young Welsh winger jinked past goalkeeper Bryan Gunn and slotted home. Mike Walkers high fliers were stung. Nervous and unsure in possession, for one loose pass or bad touch and they were being torn apart in an instance.

But knowing this is a game Norwich could ill afford to lose Walker kept urging his side on from the touchline. Only for six minutes later the klaxon horns to blow loud again as Manchester United poured forward like a red rain over Carrow Road.

Pallister, with a measured pass from his own penalty box to Sharpe, then Ince wide to McClair, followed by the Scotsman's magnificent first-time ball to a jet paced Andrei Kanchelskis, who streaked away down the right-hand touchline, into the box, around Gunn before firing low in to the net.

Before Norwich players and fans could catch their breath, they were hit again direct from the re-start. Paul Ince breaking over the halfway line leaving a trail of flailing yellow shirts in his wake. Ince went on to face off a totally isolated Gunn, before passing wide for Eric Cantona to strike regally side-footed into the top of the goal. 3-0-and a match already won with an hour left to play.

A home team left staggering like survivors walking away from a plane crash. Brutal, breathtaking and over.

Norwich's are punch drunk, their title surge in tatters. They will never come back from this. In boxing terms, it would be deemed a clear knockout.

As for Alex Ferguson's Manchester United?

They are closing in on a historic title and few can see them failing now...

C28
UNITED SOUTH

…Wednesday 21ˢᵗ April 1993…

With the title now so close they can taste it fifteen thousand Manchester United supporters have turned up at Selhurst Park for the game against Crystal Palace to roar their team over the line. News filters through by radio that Villa are already behind at Ewood Park. A cheer goes up, then another. It's 2-0 already! Suddenly, amongst the United supporters the noise level switches from nervous excitement to near euphoria as the realisation hits that they are almost there! Win their final two games at home to Blackburn and away back here at Selhurst versus Wimbledon, Manchester United will be champions.

Nothing, not fate, injuries nor fixture congestions. Or no amount of screaming diatribe from Leeds Liverpool or City can halt that fact.
But there still remains a job to be done against Crystal Palace and with the Seagulls involved in a desperate relegation scramble it promises to be anything but a walkover. The game begins and not surprisingly with so much at stake it's a cagey affair. United playing in their third strip of yellow/green shirts can't settle, the passing misplaced and there's little fluency in their play.

Another roar goes up from the Manchester United supporters as more news emerges that Blackburn are now three up against a Villa team whom appear to be in meltdown. The passion and furore that's now erupting from the away masses lifts high into the South London evening.

Back on the pitch only Eric Cantona is rising above the hundred miles an hour kick, rush, boot-see what happens football from both sides. His touch sublime, and composure on the ball when others around him are treating it like a hand grenade, a sight to behold.

Ironic on an evening when calm heads amongst the Mancunians are in short supply, it's the supposedly tempestuous, 'uncontrollable' Frenchman with a legendary short fuse the length of a matchstick, who's an oasis in a storm when all around are losing it. None more than the usually unflappable Peter Schmeichel, here on the half hour. His quick throw out to an unsuspecting Ryan Giggs sees the Welsh youngster immediately robbed by Palace's Eric Young. A pass inside to Gareth Southgate, whose slick through ball is latched onto by the speeding home centre-forward Chris Armstrong. Taking it in his stride, Armstrong lashes in a shot that clips the foot of Schmeichel's post. A close call and not surprisingly the Big Dane turns to roar abuse at Giggs. His stare back saying more than any amount of words could ever achieve.

Halt time arrives and Alex Ferguson rises swiftly from the visitor bench with a look of relief. He turns to Brian Kidd, 'Thank fuck that's over. Let's get them in Kiddo.' Once inside, 'Alright listen up' shouts Ferguson as the United dressing room goes deathly quiet. 'The good news is Villa are being hammered at Blackburn. There's no way back for them. We're almost there lads. All you have to do now is calm down and remember you're so much better than this lot it's not fuckin' real. Keep possession; pass it to your mate. Be patient and the goals will come. You're Manchester United players and that comes with standards. One is you treat the ball like it belongs to you. You don't fuckin' give it away cheaply. Okay?'

There are nods and acknowledgement from amongst the players.

Ferguson smiles, 'Good, now one more thing. When you go back out there, look around on the terraces. For you'll see more United supporters here tonight than Palace have. You lot are honoured. You're paid to wear that badge on your shirt. This lot wear it in their hearts. For many the club is their life. Their bread and fuckin' water. Families go without food to pay for season tickets. Jobs are lost, divorces happen, so don't you dare break their fuckin' hearts and blow this thing now….

Don't you dare.'

United have reappeared second half a team reborn, the football now crisp and incisive. Cantona at their very heart, probing and setting the tempo as yellow/green shirts now at last responding to his sleight of touch, deft flicks and short but devastating passes. Some so sharp and unexpected they cut faster than a paper clip. On sixty-five minutes Cantona attacks down the left and his wonderfully delivered cross finds the right foot of Mark Hughes. Steadying himself Hughes lets fly a thunderous volley that flies like a cannonball past the Palace goalkeeper Nigel Martin and into the top corner! A magnificent hit and Hughes' 100th league goal for Manchester United.

One that's greeted by United supporters with scenes of sheer utter joy. Aston Villa have been beaten. If the score remains so victory over Blackburn five days from now at Old Trafford will secure the first title in twenty-six years. The songs are loud, proud and victorious, but still many don't dare to dream.

Ten minutes from the end with United now looking to see the game out, Schmeichel fails to hold a weak effort from Palace defender Chris Coleman. The ball bobbles clear, only to fall at the feet of Chris Armstrong. As all in Selhurst Park hold their breath, Armstrong shoots but screws his effort horribly wide. Roars of relief from the United supporters, despair amidst the Palace.

The game rages on, a minute remains from what's been a battle royal. Cantona has the ball at his feet, the noise from the crowds deafening. There are tears on the faces of United supporters. So close. So fucking close.

This is Manchester south…

Spotting a run from Paul Ince, Cantona finds him with astute ease and the cockney lad with a Manc heart runs on and fires low past Martin to signal unbelievable riotous scenes on the United terraces! Only a collapse of biblical proportions can stop them now. A journey that began in black and white Manchester is set to be realised in modern times with a party the likes this city has never witnessed.

Ferguson is on the touchline hugging Kidd. He punches the air for he knows. Almost there. If Villa don't beat a struggling Oldham Athletic at home on Sunday, the title is already Old Trafford bound. But that really is asking too much. Surely?

C29
WHEN THE SEAGULL FLEW
ERIC CANTONA:
Book:

Introduction:

THE UNVEILING

…Friday 23rd November 2012…

No surprise in Manchester the rain has made an appearance, but neither storms nor dark clouds can dampen this occasion at Old Trafford. Mancunians paying tribute to arguably the greatest football manager of all time. It's a day when the drum roll and the red flags should have flown high just for one man. Sir Alex Ferguson.
But appearing through the crowds that stand waiting for the unveiling of Ferguson's statue on the forecourt strides a heavily bearded man with scraggly overgrown hair. Wearing a long black jacket with a dark open shirt and blue jeans. His walk is unmistakable, more of a strut. Forty-six-year old Eric Cantona is back in town.
An invitation from Ferguson to attend one Cantona didn't even have to think about. Two men who once upon a time in Manchester conspired to end twenty-six years without a league title for United. Around Cantona grown men appear like children, women swoon, even the great, the good and the famous watch with admiring eyes as the Frenchman without even trying or desiring steals the limelight from the supposed star of the day. A smiling Ferguson stands from his seat to greet him, 'Eric how are

you son? Thanks for coming.' Around them mobile phones and television cameras record for posterity the return of the king coming face to face with his one-time manager.

But in truth so much more.

'It is my pleasure and my honour. Nobody deserves this more than you.'

'Aye well' smiles Ferguson, 'I wouldn't be stood here waiting for them to unveil this if it wasn't for you Eric.'

'No, you wouldn't' replies Cantona.

Both men start to laugh.

'Hopefully I'll see you later,' says Ferguson, 'We'll have a good chat. Just me and you and a good bottle of red.'

Cantona smiles, 'That will be wonderful. Enjoy this moment, you so deserve it. I was called the king but they were wrong. You wore the crown. As one of your heroes Mr Sinatra always claimed. You took the hits and did it your way. You were the magic man. Not me.'

He walks away with every eye upon him. Leaving an emotional Ferguson fighting hard to hold back tears. His wife Cathy pulls his arm, 'Are you okay Alex?'

'Aye, I just have something in my eye, that's all.'

She smiles knowingly, 'Of course you have dear.'

Later that evening Cantona stands alone on the Old Trafford forecourt staring up at the Sir Alex Ferguson statue. There's not a soul around. The distant sounds of traffic and a busy city enjoying the delights of a Mancunian Friday night drifts through a darkened sky. Lit only by a plethora of stars and a half moon.

For Cantona, so many memories exist in this place. The name lit up in neon. *Manchester United.* Seven years that saw him emblazoned for many reasons into the rich tapestry of United's history. Cantona appears lost in thought when suddenly a voice shakes him back to reality,

'You have nae got any eggs have you son?'

He turns around and Ferguson is stood grinning wide. Cantona smiles, 'I just wanted to see this on my own before I fly home in the morning. It's a beautiful thing.'

'Aye' laughs Ferguson, 'I'm a handsome bastard don't you think?'

'So, how long before you are in your carpet slippers driving Cathy mad and tinkering on the piano?'

'Not until I've put our new noisy neighbours Manchester city back in their box. Of all places for the Arabs to land it had to be in Ardwick? Or that is' he says smiling, 'Until I keel over on the touchline.'

Cantona nods in agreement, 'Somehow I thought you would say that.'

'Do you ever miss it Eric?'

'Every single day. I miss the friendship and togetherness of the dressing room. The walking out of the tunnel onto the pitch and the crowd singing my name. The battles against our rivals.'

He looks across at Ferguson, 'I miss you.'

'They still sing your song,' smiles Ferguson, 'Every bloody week. *Oh, ah Cantona*. Home and away. You were always a hero here but that night at the Palace turned you into a legend.'

'All the great games and the trophies we won together. I hope you don't mind me saying boss. But that remains my favourite moment.'

Ferguson smiles, 'Aye, well. Looking back I can see a lighter side of it now. On the night I could have bloody swung for you son!'

Cantona laughs, 'I remember when you wouldn't meet my eyes coming off the field. At that moment I knew I was in big trouble and had let you down badly. It never helped my mood when I looked up and Simmons started mouthing off. Next thing I knew I was in mid-air.'
He stops walking, 'I never really thanked you for what you did for me back then.'
'We were good for each other,' replies Ferguson.
'But standing by me after Selhurst Park with the court case. Coming to Paris. The way you stood up for me. They were the actions of a father, not a manager. You will always be in my heart for that.'
'Well you paid me back in fine manner. Aye, it was a hell of a time Eric. A hell of a time'
'It was the very best of times,' replies Cantona, whilst pulling the collar up on his coat. Ferguson notices this and smiles wide, 'Some things never change.'

THIS IS ANFIELD

…Sunday 26th April 1992…

Earlier this same day Leeds have won at Sheffield United meaning to retain any chance of winning the league title and ending a twenty-five-year drought, Alex Ferguson's Manchester United have had to win at Anfield.
It's been a horrific collapse by United to let Leeds back in and ironically in a stadium and city where they wish the Mancunians nothing but bad tiding the last rites have been handed out.
Laced with a stench of hatred, driven by history and poisonous jealousy this is no ordinary rivalry. In many ways two cities so alike, not a needle thread could be

darned between them. But in matters of football they remain a chasm apart. Chants of 'Munich 58' answered by 'murderers' and 'Shankly 81.' Welcome to Anfield. It's provincial, it's nasty, it's sick.
It's a northern thing.

Playing with all the desperation of a man being chased by a tiger knowing he just has to keep running or else, United have produced a brave last stand. A performance brimming with guts and no lack of skill though on a day when lady luck not so much turns her back but spits in your face, they have gone down 2-0 in a Scouse bearpit, that's now joyfully revelling in their bitter disappointment.

Before the match began deep in the legendary Anfield Boot room, a war council took place. Three men themselves once at the helm of English football but not anymore. Former midfielder and now manager Graeme Souness and his back-room staff, Liverpool stalwarts Ronnie Moran and Roy Evans. They discussed the importance of beating United and keeping the Old Trafford genie in the bottle.
A scathing Ronnie Moran held court, 'All these fuckin' years dancing in our shade like a drunken uncle at a wedding. Staggering and stumbling making a fool of themselves, whilst we the glorious Liverpool football club waltzed magnificent on the dance floor.'
He looks towards Souness, 'It takes time to build a dynasty Graeme lad. Shanks and Bobby started this thing of ours, Kenny for a while and now you carry the torch. Here in this very room, our sceptre throne. We walk on.

United's mistake was failing to replace Matt Busby with anyone of real substance. McGuinness, O'Farrell, Docherty, Sexton and Atkinson…
All were either too inexperienced or outsiders not suited to their way of doing things. Strangers in the fuckin' dark. Blind to what Busby achieved for that place. Oblivious to how and simply too arrogant to learn. With these in charge we were always safe for they were never going to win the league.
This Manc holy grail that luckily for everyone at Liverpool football club is for them a crown of thorns. But sadly, finally, it appears they've got someone with a backbone and true sense of history. Alex Ferguson.
I'll be honest boys, my biggest fuckin' nightmare has always been that someone comes along and awakes the sleeping United giant. For once it's stirred with their financial muscle worldwide? Then God help us for a generation and one.'

Moran smiles wide and claps his hand together, 'But nothing is set in stone. They may believe their path to glory has begun but walk on I say. Let them come. Will they ever learn in that grey, foreboding miserable city? Same old, same as. Ferguson, they claimed this season was going to deliver them from our evil. All mouth the Mancs, look at the history books and count their titles compared to ours. Count their European Cups. Shouldn't take too long. So, talk is cheap and so boys I will quote you from our anthem, 'Don't be afraid of the storm.' We've got to stop them today and put a marker down. That this sleeping giant down the East Lancs road is not merely slumbering but dead and beyond resuscitation. Let's kill this horror out on the pitch today before it becomes real. Show them a little hope is a dangerous thing. That blind faith in false prophets leads not to the Promised land, but disaster.'

So, it's proved as a Liverpool team pumped up and a crowd equally so danced on the grave of Manchester United's title challenge. Ensuring the wait would now extend to twenty-six. A veteran commentator for BBC Radio Merseyside stated, 'In all my years covering this club. All the trophies won. Never have I seen this stadium so fired up.' It has indeed been a cauldron of hate. At times hysterical. Here of all places United were never going to be allowed the grace of keeping a fading dream alive. Despite three times striking the woodwork through Paul Ince, Brian McClair and Andrei Kanchelskis.

From the eleventh minute onwards it appeared already written in stone, a game too far. Ian Rush, so deadly against any other team in Europe not just England, finally broke a gypsy curse of never scoring against Manchester United. At that moment Mancunian hearts must have broke for if there was still any lingering hope that ended it.

All wrapped up nicely for the Merseysiders in the dying moments when a Liverpool breakaway initially saw a Ray Houghton shot strike the bar, only to fall clear for winger Mark Walters who fired home the rebound to send three quarters of Anfield delirious with joy.

At the final whistle as Alex Ferguson shepherded his devastated players off the pitch, a smiling Ronnie Moran sidled up to him, 'Heavy lies the crown Alex. Always in our shadow.'

'We'll fuckin' see about that,' snarled Ferguson.

On leaving the ground to board the coach home to Manchester, two lads not wearing colours approach Ryan Giggs and Lee Sharpe for autographs. Both hand over paper and pens to sign which they duly do. Only then for the United players to be forced to watch on as they are ripped up in their faces and thrown on the floor.
'Fuck off you Manc scum,' delivered in a thick scouse accident as they walk off laughing. Ferguson notices and heads over, 'Ryan, Lee, you remember what's just happened here. This is what being a Manchester United player is all about. The jealousy and hatred at places like this is all they have left to hold onto. So, take a deep breath, close your eyes and remember their fuckin' faces. Because I promise you one day I'll knock these bastards not just off their perch, but smash it into a thousand pieces.
Now get on the coach.'
It was seven months before Cantona…

GAME OF THORNS

'Always be the first to hit.' Albert Cantona

…Wednesday 25th January 1995…

A damp and dark winter's evening. Manchester United are at Selhurst Park, South London and home to a struggling Crystal Palace side. United have to win in order to go top of the league above present leaders Blackburn Rovers. A new rival for the Old Trafford giant.
Lancashire old school. Old money. £600 million worth. Sixty-four-year old Jack Walker. His fortune made in

steel. An owner and lifelong fan. A rags to riches tale but real class in football terms comes not with one season's worth of determined mercenaries, more a generation upon generation of history. The type your grandchildren become bored of you retelling. But the Rovers are here now in the present and in Manchester United's face. The Mancunians find themselves dealing with an opening line few players can turn down, 'We'll double whatever they offer you lad.'
Welcome to Blackburn...
Jack Walker is determined that whatever it costs the title will be bought and delivered to Ewood Park.
A fanatical ABU, (Anyone but United.) His multi-million-pound team managed by Kenny Dalglish, and spearheaded by record signing Alan Shearer, are leading the table in the early weeks of 1995. The race for Alex Ferguson's reigning champions to catch them and secure a third successive title is on.
The previous Sunday a glorious Eric Cantona header against Blackburn at Old Trafford, pushed United even closer. Now, here at Selhurst with the game tight, scrappy and scoreless at half time the second period is under way.
Their talisman is having a frustrating evening.
In terms of class it's a mismatch, so Palace's central half Richard Shaw is resorting to what he knows best.
Tugging, scrapping and hacking away at United's much vaunted number seven in order to gain a reaction.
To rattle Cantona's legendary gallic short fuse and tempestuous nature. He's whispering into his ear, 'C'mon Eric, have a go. Fuckin' try it.'
But so far the Frenchman is yet to bite.

Many times Cantona has pleaded with the referee Alan Wilkie for protection, but is simply ignored. Ferguson himself has launched into the autocratic, diminutive, bald headed, moustachioed Wilkie in the tunnel at half time, 'Just do your fuckin' job and look after my player!'
For he knows more than any other the spark to ignite the fire is never out. Just always simmering.
In the changing room Ferguson urges Cantona to remain calm, 'Don't get involved with him. That's exactly what he wants Eric. He can't play, his game is tackling, so pass the ball around him. Kill him with your fuckin' skill.'
But as the match restarts Shaw continues his game of thorns. Each pointed to wind up Cantona and at 8.57, on forty-eight minutes, 18,447 watch on as he explodes. Annoyed and irritated beyond all manner by Shaw's niggling, Cantona finally hits back. From a long goal-kick by United keeper Peter Schmeichel, both players challenge just inside the Palace half. The Frenchman in what is nothing more than a petulant act lashes out at the defender by kicking him in the knee. Shaw collapses dramatically in a heap and cue unadulterated mayhem. Immediately, Wilkie is surrounded by the red/blue of Crystal Palace and black United shirts. It's occurred only six yards away from the linesman Eddie Walsh. The crowd are screaming behind him, 'You saw it, tell him linesman!'
'Send the fucker off.'
'Show the French bastard a red card!'
The roar grows louder, 'Off, off, off, off'…
Walsh comes on the pitch and nods to Wilkie who goes to his pocket and with indecent haste shows Cantona the red card. The noise greeting this from the terraces, United

away following apart, erupts like a bomb going off. It's party time in South London.

Ferguson watches on, his face not giving clues to the anger brewing inside. With every genius undoubtedly comes a curse and Cantona's is happening right here before his very eyes. He turns to United's kit man, Stretford born sixty-four-year-old Norman Davies. One of the great characters at United, Davies has been with the club since 1973 and is loved by all, 'Norman, get him down the fuckin' tunnel before there's a riot.'

'Okay gaffer' replies Davies, as he stands up.

A natural storyteller, Davies always loves to relate the tale of how unlucky he was to be the only National Serviceman wounded in Germany after the war. Davies was shot in a border skirmish with the Russians in an incident hushed up to avoid a diplomatic row and possibly World War three! He would soon have another even more outrageous tale to tell.

On the pitch Cantona starts to walk off, stopping only to give Wilkie a last look of disgust. Then, he turns down his collar. A sure sign that the battle is over for tonight and soon for the considerable future. Shaw has made a miraculous recovery. Back on his feet, job done.

This is the game, a game of thorns and it has pricked the life out of Eric Cantona until his blood has run red hot... He attempts to make eye contact with Ferguson whilst walking past, but the United manager is in no mood for consoling. He instead is busy staring the referee out. Bad tiding in his eyes, for there's still a game to be won.

It's now ten again eleven. A ferocious contest that was proving difficult has suddenly become irrevocably harder.

They have overcome bigger hurdles, but as he looks around Selhurst Park and the baying home crowd, Ferguson realises his team are really up against it. United are a long way from Manchester.

Walking along the touchline, the abuse rains down in torrents onto Eric Cantona's head. Davies has yet to catch up with him. Amongst the mob one in particular catches Cantona's eye as he races down the steps towards the advertising hoards. This is twenty-year old Matthew Simmons. Cropped hair, pasty skin and wearing an ill-fitting black leather jacket, a shirt, tie and jeans.

Simmons is screaming vitriol only five yards away at Cantona. With veins almost popping out of his face, contorted by hatred,

'Fuck you, you French Motherfucker! Fuck you!'…

Already spitting bad blood Eric Cantona's legendary thin fuse was simmering, sizzling and now ignites. His father, Albert, always told him since he was a child, 'Hit first Eric. Hit first!'…

Like lightning striking a power line Cantona explodes by launching himself over the hordes with a karate kick into Simmons stomach then follows up with a flurry of punches that has him backing off with a look of startled fear, horror and finally, sheer terror etched upon his face. Norman Davies, with the help of a steward grabs him back. The crowd stand mortified as the Frenchman, his eyes still ablaze and seemingly ready to go and finish off Simmons who stands with both hands up as if to suggest, 'What did I do?'

Stewards surround Cantona as Ferguson's assistant Brian Kidd helps Davies to pull Cantona clear, 'Come on Eric' says Kidd. In his broad north Mancunian accent, 'Let's get you the fuck out of here lad.'

A sense of hysteria and madness has drifted down upon Selhurst Park. Thinking their teammate has been attacked the United players led by Paul Ince charge across. A melee occurs with stewards, supporters, footballers and policemen in a stand-off. The fiery Ince stands before the crowds, 'Come on we'll fuckin' take you all on!' The boy from East London who has suffered equally the venomous wrath of outraged West Ham fans for posing in a United shirt before actually signing is another like Cantona, never one to back away from a fight.

Finally, tempers are doused as a level of sanity prevails and Wilkie and his assistants haul the United players back onto the pitch. Meanwhile, a striding Cantona is being led down the touchline by Davies and a clearly scared looking steward called Jim Page, 'I don't fuckin' get paid enough for this,' mutters Page, as the taunts and the insults fly.

Also, the huge figure of Peter Schmeichel has an arm around Cantona who walks tall with chest out and head high. Appearing totally oblivious to the screaming mob on the terraces chanting for his head. A plastic cup of tea is thrown and splashes on the four men and Schmeichel reacts with fury, 'Pack it in you bastards!'

Finally, they reach the relative safety of the tunnel area. Schmeichel turns to Davies, 'Get him into the changing room and lock the fuckin' door Norman.'

Davies nods and the keeper heads back onto the pitch. His reappearance is greeted by an even bigger barrage of abuse from the South Londoners. However, wound up and not in the mood to take any more Schmeichel bawls back, 'You're a fuckin' disgrace All of you!' Astutely delivered in the big Dane's distinctive Manc-Danish accent.

Once inside the changing room a still seething Cantona decides he isn't finished and heads to go back. Davies notices and jumps in front of the door, locks it and puts the key in his pocket, 'Norman, move out the way.'
Davies shakes his head, 'No chance Eric.'
Cantona stands with arm folded, staring.
'Now listen,' declares Davies, 'If you want to go back out on the pitch then you'll have to go through me and then break the door down. I'm not gonna let you get yourself in any more trouble son. So, calm down and how about a nice cup of tea? Just me and you?'
Suddenly the fires wane in the Frenchman. Like everyone else at Old Trafford he thinks the world of this kitman. Cantona nods and smiles.
'Good lad,' says a relieved Davies, 'I'll put two sugars in for you as well, seeing as the boss isn't around.'
Outside the roars of the crowd echoes loud through the walls. For the fifth time in his Manchester United career Cantona has been sent off. A self-destruct button he knows not how to switch off. There's guilt at letting his teammates and manager down, but when it comes to what happened with the foul-mouthed supporter? Cantona feels he got off lightly. But what of United? There's nothing more dangerous than a Ferguson side feeling ill wronged and on fifty-six minutes, centre half David May pounces at the far post from a Lee Sharpe left wing cross to send their supporters packed into a full half of Palace's Arthur Wait stand, wild with delight!
'Ten men. We've only got ten men!' Roars out from the travelling Mancunian hordes. Their numbers swelled by 'Cockney reds.' Derided by all but whose loyalty to United unyielding and beyond the cause of duty over the years.

The Stone Roses Ian Brown summed it up most succinctly and eloquently, 'It's not where you're from. It's where you're at.' On the touchline Ferguson turns to Brian Kidd, 'Now let's keep this fuckin' tight and get out of here and go home.'

'I wonder how Norman is getting on with Eric?' Ferguson doesn't answer, his eyes glazing over with quiet fury. Kidd knows best not to push the subject. Cantona remains sitting with head in his hands whilst desperately trying to follow proceedings on the pitch through the crowd noise. He knows United are one up but then a huge roar with ten minutes left can mean only one thing.1-1. As Selhurst Park erupts, Ferguson fumes. The chance of making even more inroads into Blackburn's lead looks to have gone. United's new record signing Andy Cole, a controversial £6 Million buy from Newcastle has misfired all evening. Its early days but the manager's mood is not softened when Cole goes clean through only to miskick and shoot horribly wide. Cries of mocking and derision from the home terraces. Sombre disbelief amongst the United support. What the hell have they bought? All of them, like Ferguson, still unaware of just what has occurred in front of their very eyes this evening. A night at the Palace few of them would ever forget. Alan Wilkie blows his whistle and the game is over. The Crystal Palace fans roar in salute of a vital point gained in their relegation struggle.

Ferguson shakes hands with fellow manager forty-nine-year-old Alan Smith. A man himself still coming to terms with all that's just unfolded. A Palace substitute whispers into his ear, 'Fergie hasn't seen it boss. He hasn't got a fuckin' clue.'

'Well I am not gonna be the one to tell him,' replies Smith.

In the United dressing room the returning players are met by the sight of Eric Cantona still sat in his football kit. All are quiet and reflective, but mostly in shock. Nobody speaks to him, except one. Roy Keane makes his way over towards Cantona. He saw everything from his position on the field, 'Fair do's Eric' smiles Keane, 'I would have done the same thing.'
Ferguson enters. His face flushed red with anger after handing out Wilkes another mouthful. Finally escorted out of the referee's room by a policeman, he was dragged away and into the dressing room by Kidd. Ferguson walks over to Cantona. Although at this time still unsure of what's occurred he's outraged the player allowed himself to get sent off, 'What did I say to you at half time? You've just cost us two fuckin' point Eric. That was stupid. Bloody stupid!' Cantona keeps quiet. There are few people in this world he will accept such criticism from. His father, mother, wife and the only other, undoubtedly this seething Glaswegian stood before him. Emotions are running high. A still fuming, Ferguson thinks best to put a little distance between himself and the Frenchman and heads off to the other side of the room. The atmosphere remains tense. No one is risking opening their mouth and incurring the boss's wrath. A breathless United lawyer Maurice Watkins enters the changing room and heads over to Ferguson, 'We need to work out something to say for the press Alex. I've been talking to the police. They have officers still out on the terraces taking statements from the public. This thing is already out of control.'

Ferguson shakes his head, 'Maurice, we've had a fuckin' player sent off. That's hardly ground breaking, not even for us. I'm not interested. They can go to hell. That's my statement.' That said he leaves the room.

Watkins appears bemused. The proverbial penny has not dropped with him that Ferguson is so far unaware of fully what's occurred. Outside the manager storms past a waiting press pack, 'And you lot can fuck off as well,' his parting words to them. 'I suppose that counts as a no comment lads,' says the man from The Sun.

'Well even Fergie can't stay quiet too long on this one,' replies the man from The Mail.

'I wouldn't fuckin' bet on it,' adds the man from The Mirror.

On that point they all sadly nod in agreement.

Police superintendent Terry Collins appears from the referee's room and calls across to the United manager, 'Mr Ferguson, may I have a word please? Just so you know sir, we shall be launching a full investigation into what has gone on tonight. It was a very serious situation and could well have ended in a major public disturbance.'

Ferguson stares non-plussed at Collins. Half convinced this man is making a mountain out of a molehill, 'Aye, you do that,' he replies. 'Speak to Maurice Watkins our lawyer. He handles these kind of things.'

That said he walks away leaving the policeman standing open-mouthed. Collins shrugs his shoulders, 'Bloody northerners.'

Whilst the United squad are in mid-air flying home to Manchester, the BBC's Sportsnight shows the incident in full and Gary Lineker tells a watching audience of millions, that Cantona has lost 'Le Marbles.'

On the plane few speak. Notoriously for his foul moods when events have gone against them, Ferguson appears even more angry than normal. Content to just stare out through the window. Deep in thought. A second sense is telling him trouble is brewing. There's a genuine feeling amongst his staff that the gaffer has been told, but just doesn't want to discuss it yet.

Little do they know.

Further back Eric Cantona still hasn't spoken. Unlike his manager he's in no doubt whatsoever of the storm that lies ahead. A moment of madness appears certain to have curtailed his Manchester United career. Cantona is convinced when day breaks over the 'Rainy city' his now spiritual home, the wolves will pounce and he will be ripped to piece by the press and media.

The plane lands shortly after midnight and Ferguson arrives home in the early hours of Thursday. He's surprised to find his wife Cathy and oldest son Jason still up waiting for him, 'Do you want to see it? 'Asks Jason. Thinking he's just talking about the match Ferguson dismisses the notion, 'I'll catch it in the morning Jason, I'm shattered son.' That said he goes upstairs into the bedroom and shuts the door.

Cathy stares at Jason. Unable to believe her husband doesn't want to watch an incident that's set to rock their world, 'Do you know something Mum,' says Jason.

'I think Dad's finally mellowing.'

Cathy looks up towards the bedroom, 'Aye Jason,' she replies. Utterly convinced he's wrong in his thinking, 'And I'm the next Queen of England.'

Later that morning around 5am Ferguson awakes from a short restless slumber. His mind racing, he decides to go and watch the video of the match. Quietly, so not to wake

Cathy, making his way downstairs. He slips in the tape, settles down on the sofa and watches with disbelieving eyes. Ferguson's immediate thoughts are that Cantona is finished. Such will be the outcry and this being United he's convinced the witch-hunt will prove too much to contend with. Cantona will be lucky to escape with a public flogging, 'What were you thinking Eric?' He says quietly to himself, 'What the bloody hell were you thinking son?'

Meanwhile, in Worsley, Salford, the man in question hasn't slept. Cantona's heavily pregnant wife Isabelle, is far from happy with him, 'Wonderful timing Eric' she declared in dramatic fashion as he walked through the door, 'I am six months pregnant and now we have to deal with this.' That said Isabelle goes back upstairs leaving her husband feeling even worse. If such a thing was possible.
Now, as the clocks strikes 6 am, Cantona sits and waits alone downstairs knowing that just outside his front door all hell is set to erupt and engulf them.

THE SEAGULL HAS LANDED

…Wednesday 25th November 1992…

It's a drizzly, miserable, grey Mancunian afternoon. Fifty-two-year-old Manchester United manager Alex Ferguson is in his chairman Martin Edward's office deliberating over buying a striker. United's goals have dried up dramatically. Just a measly seventeen in sixteen games, they now lie in a lowly eighth position, and are in serious danger of being out of the title race before actually ever being in it. A broken leg suffered by summer signing Dion Dublin from Cambridge and Mark Hughes and Brian McClair misfiring, means they have to move fast.

'What about David Hirst at Sheffield Wednesday?'

'Wednesday won't budge,' replies Edwards. 'We've bid up to £3.5 million, but Trevor Francis is annoyed. He's claiming we unsettled Hirst by leaking it to the newspapers. Ferguson shakes his head, 'And Saint Trevor, he never does such a thing?' Jesus Christ!'

'Who else is there Alex?'

'Nobody who really stands out. There was Alan Shearer who would have suited us down to the ground, but Kenny Dalglish has a blank cheque off Uncle Jack.

I understand even we can't compete with Jack Walker's money. What about Beardsley at Everton? He ticks our boxes.'

Edward's phone starts to ring and he picks it up, 'Oh hello Bill what can I do for you?' On the line is Leeds United's financial director Bill Fotherby, 'Martin, this is a long shot but our manager Howard Wilkinson would like to know if there's any chance Denis Irwin could be available for transfer? For a decent fee of course.'

Edwards puts his hand over the earpiece to muffle it. He smiles over to Ferguson and says quietly, 'It's Bill Fotherby from Leeds. They want to know if you would consider selling them Denis Irwin?'

One look at Ferguson's face gives Edwards his answer. He goes back on the line to Fotherby, 'I'm afraid not Bill, I've got Alex here with me now.'

Suddenly an idea comes into the United manager's head. He swiftly scribbles down a player's name and passes it

to Edwards, 'Before you go off the line Bill. What's the possibility of us having Eric Cantona off you?'
The line goes quiet and Edwards looks across to Ferguson. After a moment Fotherby comes back on, 'Well I know Cantona and Howard don't see eye to eye. He's a strange one is Eric. Let me have a word and I'll ring you back.' The phone goes down.
'What did he say?'
A shocked Edwards smiles wide, 'He's ringing back, but I think you could be on to something. Where on earth did Cantona's name come from?'
'Something Bruce and Pallister were talking about last month after we played Leeds at Old Trafford. Both of them couldn't stop eulogising about him. His skill and strength. It takes a lot to get those two big lumps excited because they just take everything in their stride. But Cantona?
That's why it's always stayed in my mind.'
The phone starts to ring again and Edwards answers. Once more it's Fotherby, 'Martin, Bill. I've just spoken to Howard. He wants to know when can we meet and where?' Edwards gives his manager the thumbs up and the grin on Ferguson's face could light up Piccadilly, 'They want to meet,' says a whispering Edwards.
'Tell them the Midland hotel in Manchester at twelve o'clock tomorrow.' Edwards does so and puts the phone down, 'My god Alex, you really do move in mysterious ways. But I'm sure you've heard the Cantona stories. The word is he's a special talent but a nightmare.'
'Aye' replies Ferguson, 'So is not being able to score fuckin' goals Martin. Don't worry about it, I can handle Cantona.'

The next day at 11.45 am, two men are walking up the steps of the Midland hotel. Both are smartly suited, handsome and undoubtedly French! Twenty-six-year old Eric Cantona, and his agent, thirty-seven-year-old Jean Jacques Bertrand. They are met in reception by United Club Lawyer Maurice Watkins who shakes hands with both, 'Welcome to Manchester gentlemen. If you will follow me please.' Watkins leads Cantona and Bertrand into a lift and then a luxurious third floor suite. Stood inside waiting are a smiling Alex Ferguson and Martin Edwards. Again, the two parties shake hands.
Ferguson puts an arm around Eric, 'How about me and you go and have a chat over there?' He points to two chairs and a table with a pot of tea and tray of biscuits upon it. He and Cantona settle down whilst Edwards and Bertrand sit elsewhere to hammer out a deal.
'I really hope this happens, have you managed to agree terms with Leeds?'
'Aye,' replies Ferguson, 'We've got you for 1.2 Million. If you ask me that's the steal of the century. Martin should wear a balaclava.' Both men laugh.
'Then I assure you dealing with Jean will not be a problem for Mr Edwards. Your club, Manchester United? It comes sprinkled with gold dust. The stadium is like a magical place where dreams can come true. Such a rich and wonderful but also tragic history.'
'We intend to make our own history. A new chapter Eric. And with you in the team, I feel we can win the league and then go for the European Cup. But I want to do it by playing football that takes people's breath away.'
Cantona smiles, 'I believe we are kindred spirits Mr Ferguson.' The Scotsman looks deep in the Frenchman eyes and what he sees warms his heart. A ferocious will

to win. This is a player that makes the difference. Who unlocks defences with moments of beguiling skill. Ferguson knows the signing of Cantona could be his last throw of the dice. Losing the title to Leeds last season after seemingly home and dry, only to collapse at the final hurdle through injuries and fixture congestion means time could well be running out for him. Ferguson has won trophies aplenty, but Manchester United and its supporters demand the league. Twenty-six years and counting…

He has to ask the question, 'The word is you can be a problem Eric. Is that true?'

'Inside I have a blazing passion to win Mr Ferguson. But I ask only one thing. That people respect me. If so, then trust me I will set fire to the Manchester rain and make dreams come true. I promise.'

Ferguson smiles wide, 'That's good enough for me son.'

When news breaks of this tumultuous transfer between these two old northern rivals and whose fans quite literally detest each other, the feeling is one of complete shock on both sides. It's like a nuclear bomb exploding over the Pennines and the fallout in Yorkshires verges on poisonous. Amongst the fanatical Leeds United supporters, Eric Cantona, has already achieved cult status in their league winning season the previous year. It was viewed by all as a proper love affair. Cantona's cryptic comments on the city's town hall balcony during their trophy winning homecoming, 'I don't why I love you, but I do' entered Leeds folklore.

Now, as a new reality hits home and Cantona is witnessed on television screens adorning the shirt of their most hated enemy. These same words are viewed in a different light. What many took for love was really complete indifference. He was simply passing through. For Eric Cantona's heart, it appeared was always that of a Red Devil.

On the Friday morning at Old Trafford a jubilant Alex Ferguson with the newly signed Frenchman alongside him in a club tracksuit begins the press conference by announcing, 'Mon Plaisir presenter Eric Cantona!'
As the questions fly at Cantona about why he left Leeds, in his former kingdom the Elland Road switchboard is close to meltdown with supporters demanding refunds on their season tickets. 'He could have gone anywhere,' they scream.
'Anywhere but those Manc bastards!'
Whilst back across the Pennines the laughter and joy from Manchester United supporters at seeing their rival apoplectic with rage is comic gold. Later on that morning in an empty stadium Ferguson and Cantona are stood in the Old Trafford centre-circle. The new man appears in awe as he gazes around, 'This is a field of dreams' says Cantona, 'Here it feels like anything is possible.'
Ferguson is enjoying his new boy lapping up the new surroundings, 'I wonder if you're good enough to play here Eric?' Cantona looks full circle around the stadium. The ghosts of the Busby Babes. Of Best, Law and Charlton echoing in the wind. He then stares across at his new manager and smiles, 'And I wonder if Manchester is good enough for me?' Grinning wide, Ferguson puts an arm around Cantona's shoulders, 'You'll do for me son, let's go and get a cup of tea.'

RED FLAG FLYING

…Thursday 26th January 1995…

Arriving early next morning at the Cliff training ground Ferguson finds already the place besieged by press and television. He drives straight through ignoring the barrage of cameras and microphones surrounding him. Desperate for a soundbite. Once ensconced in his office the first telephone call is off the Manchester Evening News' long standing United reporter, David Meek. One of the few journalists trusted by Ferguson, 'Off the record David, it doesn't look good. Eric may well have gone too far this time.'

It continues all morning. United chairman Martin Edwards enters the office carrying two paper cups of tea, He hands one over to Ferguson, Edwards smiles, 'What's it to be then Alex? A public hanging or should we just shoot Eric on the pitch before the next home game? I've had everyone but the Pope on to me already asking what we are going to do with him.'

'I think he's going to have to go Martin. I can't see any other way. Have you heard anything from the FA yet?'

'I spoke to Graham Kelly about ten minutes ago and gave him assurances Eric will be harshly dealt with. They can't act before their own disciplinary inquiry which means we've got fourteen days to come up with something.

Hoisted by their own petty petard there. They are initially charging him with misconduct and bringing the game into disrepute. It appears all their Christmas' and birthdays have come at once with this.'

'Aye, they are going to be rubbing their hands together at Lancaster Gate,' replies Ferguson, 'It will be open season on us.'

'What on earth possessed him Alex?'

Ferguson shakes his head, 'We've had nearly three years of Cantona and should treasure every moment, but it's like playing bloody keepie-uppie with a hand grenade. You can only keep it in the air for so long and then sooner or later it explodes and takes everything and everyone with it. He's a wonderful talent and a good lad, but this? I just don't know.'

Meanwhile, only a few miles away in Worsley, Eric Cantona opens his front door and is greeted by a sea of madness. Photographers, cameramen and reporters suddenly surge forward towards him. Cantona is surrounded but continues to walk towards his M registered Honda. Hardly the car of kings, but good enough for Eric.

Wearing jeans and a strange garish coloured jacket, he appears in no mood for journalists. Looking weary, heavy eyed and pissed off, Cantona bends down and steps in his car ignoring every microphone and recording device thrust towards his face.

'Eric, why did you do it?'

'Eric was you trying to kill him?'

'Eric, Eric, are you a Bruce Lee fan?'...

He starts the car and drives off. Cantona's face is a mask of indifference to all around him for already the Frenchman's mind is on an upcoming meeting with Alex Ferguson where his Manchester United fate could well be decided. This wasn't how he wanted his time at Old Trafford to end, but if so then Manchester will have proved just another port in a stormy sea for Cantona. It appears controversy stalks him like a red devil on his shoulder forever whispering troublesome tidings in his ear.

Eric Cantona knocks on and enters Ferguson's office. He looks up from his desk, 'Sit down son.'
Cantona does so.
'Did you sleep?'
The Frenchman shakes his head
Ferguson smiles slightly, 'Me neither. Eric, what the bloody hell happened? You hear the same crap every time we play, why now? How did you let that foul-mouthed idiot get under your skin?'
'I suppose it was just one too many times. I saw the look of hatred on his face. I heard his words and something snapped in me. I cannot help who I am boss.'
'And who's that Eric?'
He shrugs his shoulders, 'Me?'
Ferguson stares at him and shakes his head, 'We'll just have to see where the land lies over the next couple of days with this. But until then you speak to no one. You say nothing, do nothing, you disappear. Now they'll be after you. So far as the tabloids and the other bloodsuckers are concerned, beyond these walls you're now public enemy number one. Don't give them any more bullets Eric.
I promise you this thing is on the fuckin' brink. Do you understand?'
Cantona nods, 'I understand.'
'Good lad, now get out of here.'
He stands to leave but on reaching the door Cantona turns around, 'Boss, I know what I did last night was unacceptable to most. But if someone said of your

mother what he said about mine, then I think you would want to knock his fucking head off to.'
His piece said Cantona leaves the room.
Ferguson stands staring at the shut door, 'Aye you're probably right son,' he sighs, 'And a little more'…

Red slings and arrows covet en masse the television, newspaper and radio world. Outside on the Old Trafford forecourt former players are lined up for the price of a fistful of twenty-pound notes to mouth outrage.
Some honest and giving truthful opinions. Others simply playing to a media and public audience who have rushed with an unhealthy glee to crucify this alleged, crazy, mad Frenchman from over the channel.
He is just so un-English.
Alex Stepney: 'George Best was provoked all the time, but over the years he handled it well. Cantona would have been out in Sir Matt Busby's day. He's a disgrace to this club.'
Bill Foulkes: 'Going into the crowd like that is behaving like a hooligan. That's nothing to do with sport. He lost control of himself and that's very sad to see. But Eric is French and they are different to us.'
Shay Brennan: 'Sir Matt would never have stood for anything like that.'
Tommy Docherty: 'Cantona should be sacked by the club. But I'm not so sure he will be. Why? Because the club these days is all about money. You go into Manchester and see the shirts with his name on being worn by all the kids around this city. Double standards.'
Others outside the United 'family' were equally succinct and even more to the point. A certain Brian Clough claimed, 'They should cut his bloody balls off!'

But there was one other flying the 'La Marseillaise' flag for Cantona. Fighting a lone battle and telling every media outlet with a link to the outside world that United's talisman was more victim than criminal. Fifty-six-year old Paddy Crerand. Light grey-suited, grim faced and ready to start a war with the 82nd Airborne if they disagreed with his opinion was carrying the fight on the forecourt.

Fiery, ferocious, opinionated, hopelessly red-eyed and splendidly letting fly. Sky TV are currently feeling his wrath after inquiring of Crerand, 'Do you believe Cantona should be thrown out of Manchester United?'

'What a bloody stupid question. Let me tell you something. The abuse Eric had to take last night and every time United go away from home is scandalous. How would you feel if somebody walked up to you now son and started slagging off your mother? You answer me that?'...

Suddenly the Sky cameraman gets the nod to stop filming.

The reporter smiles, 'Cheers Paddy, thanks for your time.'

'No problem' replies Crerand, 'I only hope you fuckin' show that in full, but I very much doubt it.'

'Out of my hands' says the reporter, 'Not the agenda I'm afraid. You're a one-man band today Paddy. I'm sorry to tell you, but I think your man has pissed on his French fries for the last time.'

'We'll see about that,' smiles Crerand. He looks around, 'Now if you horrible Murdoch bastards will excuse me, I recognise the journalist from The Sun. I want a fuckin' word with him.' Off goes Crerand towards the Sun hack, 'Hey, don't you run off. I want to talk to you.'

'Oh no, here he is,' sighs the journalist. 'Crerand would keep the red flag fuckin' flying high in an earthquake. Hiya Paddy,' he sighs, as Crerand stands facing. 'To what do I owe the pleasure?' A red faced Crerand is fuming, 'Pleasure!? I'll give you fuckin' pleasure. What gives you the right to.' It goes on….

…Thursday evening…Edge Hill Hotel: Alderley Edge Cheshire...

For three hours, in the lush interiors of a private suite, Manager Alex Ferguson, Chairman Martin Edwards, club lawyer Maurice Watkins and United PLC Chairman Roland Smith, have discussed the pros and cons of keeping Eric Cantona on the payroll or getting rid.

Smith is adamant he has to stay, 'On the back of last night's fiasco our share price is dropping dramatically gentlemen. We fell £2.4 million to 77.2. Now let me tell you that's somewhat drastic in not even twenty-four hours. The Market isn't stupid. It understands the importance of losing our finest asset. I'm just saying this is something we have to keep in mind on deciding whether we keep Cantona on or let him go.'

Edwards nods in agreement, 'In the real world Eric is a licence for our marketing people. He's gold dust. It's his shirts the supporters crave around the world. Giggs, Keane, Kanchelskis, Ince? Even if you add them together they come nowhere near those of Cantona's. But then we have to measure all this against the club's name and how we must be seen to do the right thing. The whole world is watching. I was speaking to the FA this afternoon and they are already onto FIFA and trying to persuade them to give Eric a worldwide ban.'

Ferguson shakes his head on hearing this, 'Jesus Christ, why don't they just cut his fuckin' head off and be done with.'

'Why don't we,' replies Edwards. Thinking out loud, 'Why don't we suspend Cantona until the end of the season? Fine him two weeks wages. I mean that's £20,000 with win bonuses. In doing this we're showing that we believe the greater good of the game is above the needs and wanting of Eric Cantona. And, more importantly, Manchester United.'

'It could work' replies Watkins. 'We keep the moral high ground and maybe in doing this we blunt the FA's blade and stop them going too far over the top with their punishment.'

'It's worth a try' adds Ferguson. 'Mind you that lot would love nothing more than putting Eric in a cannon and firing him through the channel tunnel with a one-way ticket.'

'Now you've had a little time to think,' asks Edwards. 'What are your feelings on this Alex?'

…Ferguson appears reflectful as all eyes fall upon him. 'You all know I'm a football man. Through right and wrong my decisions are made for the good of this club. I understand the business side of United. The share price, the way we've gone. I don't like it as I've told you all many times.' The other three smile ruefully.

'I think it restricts our chances of doing better in Europe and competing against Walker and Dalglish and the rest of their mercenaries. But I deal with it.

Now, when I first saw what Eric did my initial thoughts were he had to go. No way could we besmirch the name of this club by letting him put on a United shirt ever again. But then I spoke to the boy this morning and I looked in his eyes? Eric is convinced he did the right thing.

Oh of course in the real world we tell the lads constantly to ignore what's hurled at you. Just kill them with your skills. And most of the time they listen to me. Keane, Ince, Hughes, Bruce, Schmeichel and Cantona. These aren't just footballers. They are tough young men who would run through a glass door for me and United, if I asked them to do so. This piece of work slagged off Eric's mother and ultimately that's what all this comes down to. For where he comes from in Marseille you can get your throat cut for less. It's the right thing to do standing by Eric and let's also be realistic. Both in marketing terms, but infinitely more important on the pitch, it's for the best if we keep him. Let me tell you something, I've got some very special boys coming through that are like nothing you've seen for a generation at this club.

Better judges than me are saying this is the finest crop of youngsters since the Busby Babes. And every single one of them worships the ground that Cantona walks on.

His skills, the strut. The collar up, his arrogance and belief. Most importantly the way he holds himself as a Manchester United player.

Remember these names gentlemen. Beckham, Scholes, Butt, and the Neville brothers. In time you're going to love them because they'll continue to fill the trophy cabinet and in your world Roland, Keep the money rolling in. So, Eric stays no matter what they throw our way.

Cantona remains a red.

Agreed?'

They all nod.

'Well we best batten down the hatches everybody,' smiles Edwards. 'For the proverbial shit is about to hit the fan.'
'Aye well' replies Ferguson, 'I wouldn't worry too much about that Martin, because according to the rest of the fuckin' world that's already happened. So, let's just get on with it.'

…Friday 27th January…12pm…

Maurice Watkins is stood on the Old Trafford forecourt in front of a watching world press and media. They stand primed. Like a lynch mob waiting for the body to fall from the trapdoor on the gallows and cheer justice. All are expecting Watkins to announce United will jettison their troublesome Frenchman. But as he goes on it soon becomes clear this isn't happening.
A feeling of disappointment is clearly visible amongst many of the Red top journalists. Watkins wraps up, 'In reaching our decision which the player fully accepts, Manchester United has had regard to its responsibilities, both to the club and to the game as a whole.'
Cue, cry havoc, the moans and groans of a disgruntled mob and let loose the journalistic dogs of war.
Immediately they can smell the scent.
Cantona is a hunted man.

MAGIC BEANS

…Sunday 6th December 1992…

In the second period wearing a number twelve jersey as substitute for an injured Ryan Giggs, Eric Cantona steps over the touchline onto the field of dreams and the white-hot atmosphere of a frantic and emotional 117th Manchester Derby. Old Trafford erupts as Cantona immediately receives possession and his first touch is a sublime cross for Mark Hughes who goes almighty close. United are already one up courtesy of a superb first half strike from Paul Ince. But City are fighting hard. Their player manager Peter Reid also enters the fray and immediately heads over to fellow Scouser and midfielder player Steve McMahon, 'Go and fuckin' sort Cantona out Steve. Give him a few welcome to Manchester tackles. Ruffle his feathers.' McMahon smiles wide and winks back at Reid, 'Leave it to me!'

Three times McMahon attempts to push Cantona's red danger button. Pushing, shoving and finally flattening him with a reckless, hacking swipe, 'Here we go' says Brian Kidd, to his manager, who's face is contorted with rage at City's blatant attempt to wind his new player up. As the entire ground holds it breath waiting for the eruption instead the Frenchman simply ignores the smirking McMahon's helping hand and gets back onto his feet. One glance of utter contempt towards the player in blue sufficient to show his thoughts on the matter.

On seventy-three minutes Mark Hughes with typical aplomb chests the ball down from fully twenty-five yards, and crashes a fierce drive past the City keeper Tony Coton to make the score 2-0 and surely game over? As the home crowd roar in delight, local pride once more secured, only for City to go down the other end and hit right back. Winger Ricky Holden crosses and a mix up between Peter Schmeichel and Steve Bruce is pounced upon by Niall Quinn. 2-1 and the men from Maine Road have a lifeline.

City rally and a late scare for United when Schmeichel more than makes up for his earlier mistake to pull off a courageous double save from Andy Hill and David White. Old Trafford sighs in relief. Finally, the referee blows to signal full time and Manchester is most definitely red.

On leaving the field Eric Cantona accepts the acclaim of his new supporters by applauding all corners of the stadium and none cheer louder than the Stretford End. A standing ovation.

As opening nights go it won't be one Mancunians will remember enough of to tell their grandchildren about. But one that in years to come people will always ask, 'Where you there when the King first stepped foot on Old Trafford's hallowed turf?' Cantona has performed a decent enough cameo. Nothing special, no gold dust as of yet, but the signs are there that roots are being planted. The magic beans are in the ground…And so it begins.

THE PRIDE OF THORNTON HEATH (Part one)

…Friday 27th January 1995…

Twenty-year old South Londoner Matthew Simmons, a double-glazing fitter and former ball boy and £300 a year Crystal Palace season ticket holder. Eric Cantona's arch nemesis has sold his soul and story to The Sun newspaper for just a couple of grand. With the promise of a lot more to follow. A likely tale… They currently have him holed up away from prying eyes in a hotel near Gatwick Airport.

Simmons is a worried man. Already he's attempted to ring Manchester United football club and speak to Alex

Ferguson to try and diffuse this powder keg of a situation. However, the woman on the switchboard simply refused to believe him and hung up. But this is no innocent supporter whose one moment of rash behaviour on a crumbling Selhurst terrace has rocked the footballing world. For Simmons has a past. An alleged history of neo-Nazi sympathies and a conviction for attempted robbery with violence.

He has attended British National Party and National Front rallies and in 1992 was convicted of attempted violent robbery when he attacked an attendant in a Croydon petrol station. He assaulted Sri Lankan-born Lewis Rajanayagam with a three-foot spanner striking him in the shoulder rather than the head only because the sales assistant took evasive action and ducked.

Simmons was seventeen when he attempted to cripple Rajanayagam. At his subsequent trial for threatening language and behaviour he attacked the prosecution counsel after being found guilty, leaping over a bench and executing a flying kick of his own. He was sentenced to seven days in jail but only served twenty-four hours. So, to say this young man has form is not to overstate the case. Which makes his somewhat watered-down version from Wednesday night rather hard to believe?

'All I did was rush down from my seat in the 11th row and say to the player, 'Off you go Cantona. It's an early bath for you.' He goes on to tell The Sun, 'I might have sworn at him, I'm not sure. But whatever I said it never gave him any excuse to do what he did. Cantona was the lunatic, not me. I was just in the wrong place at the wrong time.'

Meanwhile, in Croydon, South London. The scene of this most heinous crime that has shocked the great and the good and the hypocritical. In a special incident room at Addington police station, seven officers are devoting their full-time attention to the task of interviewing witnesses to the incident, whose names and addresses were taken on the night. An inspector walks in and they all stand. He smiles, 'Just so you are all clear on this matter. I want good news and even better witnesses. I want blood. So, put in the overtime and let's nail him. It's not on, fuckin' Mancs coming up here. Sticking their noses in the air. Thinking they can do as they please. Well not on my watch. If Cantona had pulled the same trick at Chelsea or god forbid Millwall, they would be dragging him out of the crowd piece by piece. It's a bloody liberty.

So, do your jobs and make sure we get what's needed. Does everybody understand? I want this French bastard locked up.'

The officers nod. His piece said the Inspector leaves, 'Fuckin' hell' exclaims one of the young uniformed policemen, 'I never knew the old man supported Palace.' 'He doesn't' replies another, 'He's a Liverpool fan.'

…Saturday 28th January 1995…

Old Trafford: Manchester United v Wrexham: FA Cup Fourth Round. Cantona's day. An occasion so many thought would resemble a wake. A remembrance service for their missing King instead has turned into an astonishingly vibrant and deafening display of defiance. Gone but not forgotten Eric Cantona's face adorns countless flags, shirts and banners.

From 43,222, 'Oh Ah Cantona' rings out like a war cry and not a wish you were here. This is a city and a football

club determined to let a watching world know that their love affair with Cantona burns bright as ever. Indeed, since his now infamous karate kick into Matthew Simmons' stomach, the Frenchman's fame has gone beyond legendary status. The enduring image of him leaping over the advertising hordes is already iconic.
A symbol, one that appeals to a red army, huge in size, loyalty unquestioning but sick and weary of 'Munich 58' chants and glory hunter tags. 'No more' and 'fuck you' is what Cantona's actions scream out to them.
A club's hardcore support despised by all those who don't have it in their hearts were with him in spirit as Cantona took flight into infamy. Manchester United 5 Wrexham 2.
They never had a chance on this day…
On Cantona's day.

A DAMNED UNITED

…Monday 8th February 1993…

Two days before Manchester United play the champions Leeds at Elland Road, death threats are sent to Eric Cantona's home, terrifying his wife Isabelle. That same afternoon at Crystal Palace's Selhurst Park, Leeds' supporters gleefully chant, 'Happy birthday dear Munichs.' To call this a hate fest directed at the Mancunians and Cantona specifically is pretty much an understatement of this or any year.
The arrival of a Manchester United coach at Elland Road is always cause for a burning torches and pitch fork brigade. Armed to the teeth with their 'scum' and 'Munich' songs and screaming bile at their Lancastrian

foes from across the Pennines. Maybe it's a hangover from the War of the Roses? A generic deficiency passed on through the generations?

Although more likely a throwback to the Don Revie era, when despite being undoubtedly the best team in England for nigh on six years, they never received a modicum of the publicity that was shown to a struggling Old Trafford club at the time by the press.

It was always deemed that Billy Bremner, Peter Lorimer and Johnny Giles were great players, but no Best, Law or Charlton. A fine club that won constantly but lacked class. And then there were the rumours.

The brown envelopes that Revie was allegedly fond of. A rotten twelfth man.

The stench of corruption.

A tale confirmed by Sunderland's manager Bob Stokoe, at the time whose reaction to Revie, when offered one was to tell him to 'Fuck off.'

In later years their own goalkeeper David Harvey admitted publicly as much that it went on. Harvey now ostracised in Leeds and by his former team mates. This stigma that has remained throughout the decades and a notion their supporters detest. A damned United.

Even last year's title triumph is still viewed by many in the media as the Mancunians racked by injuries and fixture congestion, blowing up at the last hurdle, rather than Leeds deservedly winning it. It's a pot over boiling with grievances and one set to explode in spectacular manner.

All this easily sufficient to create a lynch mob mentality when Manchester United came to town. But added to the betrayal in their eyes of Cantona's switch to the dark side. A fucking red devil without horns, but a devil nonetheless. Well, all bets are off.

Cantona's appearance at the coach door ready to step off signals a barrage of abuse and sickening taunts that goes not just beyond the pale, but all human decency. Fist clenching, eyes glazed, spouting utter filth about him and his family. 'Leeds, Leeds.'

Funny how far the crown slips in just a short space of time. From king to Judas. Nothing makes a heart turn quicker than lost love in somebody else's arms.

Especially when it's to the one true bastard you hate most in this world. Welcome back to a forsaken hole for any of Mancunian persuasion, Eric Cantona.

Once inside the stadium and heading to the sanctity of the away dressing room a couple of the United players try and cheers Cantona up, for he's clearly shaken by his overtly hostile reception. And indeed hurt. A Frenchman still relatively new to this country could never begin to understand the animosity between these two northern giants. The depths of sheer hatred. Ryan Giggs smiles wide, 'Thanks for that mate, it's usually me they save the bullshit for!'

'Why you?'.

'Not sure really. I do tend to take the piss a bit against this lot when I get the chance. I don't think they've much sense of humour around here.' Steve Bruce comes up alongside them. He's laughing, 'Might be best if you stayed away from taking corners or throw in's tonight Eric. If this lot drag you in the crowd, we'll have to call the SAS to get you back!' Even the pensive Frenchman can't help but raise a smile at this.

The reception on the pitch for Eric Cantona shocks even his usual laid-back team mates. None more than Giggs who stares incredulous at the hundreds of faces spewing pure bile towards Cantona behind the goal where they are warming up, 'Fuck me' says Giggs, almost to himself, as behind the net there's a sea of grown men doing the aeroplane gesture in reference to Munich.

Paul Ince sidles up next to Cantona. Who despite outwardly appearing unconcerned at the level of abuse aimed towards him is silently reeling. Ince puts an arm around his shoulders, 'Fuck em Eric, we're with you mate.' The United team continue warming up until Alex Ferguson appears in the tunnel and seeing for himself what's occurring motions for them to come in. All start to make their way off the pitch.

Except one.

Eric Cantona slowly makes his way towards the goal where his accusers sit. He takes a ball, juggles it for a moment and then unleashes a frightful volley into the top corner causing many behind it to duck. His point made, Cantona, head high, shoulders back and chest forward now leaves the field. The jeers grow even louder as he disappears from sight, but amongst many Leeds supporters there are now smiles also.

'The sheer nerve of the bastard.'

Leeds United 0 Manchester United 0.

GREETINGS FROM GUADELOUPE

…Thursday 2nd February 1995…

Eric Cantona's home is now the scene of a media and press stake out. The main road littered with tripods aplenty. Aerial and satellite dishes. Photographers forever primed with their cameras to catch the merest glimpse of life through the Cantona's closed door and curtains.

Hangers on and sightseers. Some merely curious, but many also of the red army desperate for news of 'Le God.' It's a circus, not one with lions or clowns and acrobats, but instead consisting of only one act. He's the biggest show and hottest ticket in town and Cantona is starting to feel like he can't breathe.

And then there's his heavily pregnant wife and eight-year old son Raphael to worry about. This can't go on-they need to get away. He rings Alex Ferguson, who is in no doubt of Cantona's next move, 'You have to disappear for a few weeks. Far away. Somewhere these bastards can't touch you. Concentrate on Isabelle and your son. Let me and the club handle it here. Do you understand?'

'Yes, thank you boss.'

'Have you anywhere in mind?'

'The Caribbean. They will never find me there.'

Cantona hears Ferguson laugh on the line, 'Jesus Christ, Eric! You don't mess around. Good for you son. When you come home hopefully matters will have settled down. We'll get the court case out of the way and then life should return a little back to normal.

Cantona smiles on hearing this, 'What is normal at this club boss?'

'Exactly' says Ferguson, 'But what's important, whatever happens. If by any chance they track you down. Don't, I repeat don't do anything stupid. You walk away Eric. Turn the other cheek.'

…Friday 10th February 1995…

Caribbean Guadeloupe Islands…

Just after 9am, experienced ITV news correspondent, forty three-year old Terry Lloyd enters the exclusive Club Med complex in the Guadeloupe islands. This is no fly-by-night, entertainment, long-lens journo; Lloyd is amongst the top men in his field. In 1988, he broke the news to a horrified world that Saddam Hussein had used chemical weapons in Halabja killing 5,000 Kurds. In 1995, he covered the Oklahoma bombings and in 1999, became the first foreign journalist to enter war torn Kosovo.

Lloyd immediately spots Eric Cantona enjoying a game of archery with Isabelle and Raphael. He walks across to him. Cantona stands with the bow in hand. Isabelle pulls Raphael towards her. They've been discovered and it's clear to see are horrified. A smiling Lloyd introduces himself and then puts out his hand which Cantona reluctantly accepts, 'It's great to meet you Eric. Would it be possible to do a five-minute interview? That's all, and then we'll leave you and your family in peace.'

'No' replies Cantona, 'I am on holiday.'

As no's go it's pretty emphatic, but Lloyd, whom for this is nothing more than a few days in the Caribbean sun is determined not to take this 'no' as any defining answer. He looks around, 'It's really lovely here. Is this where you're staying Eric?'

Suddenly, two security men appear and Cantona motions them over. They stand either side of Lloyd.

Cantona walks within inches of his face, 'Go away and leave me and my family alone.'

'Look' exclaims Lloyd, 'Be reasonable Eric. There are several of the red tops searching the Caribbean looking for you that are throwing money around like confetti. In a few days or so your cover will be blown mate, and all

Fleet Street and his dog will be on your doorstep playing with their buckets and spades and in your face.
But I promise you, one interview and then I'm gone and my mouth stays shut. So, what do you say? Five minutes for ITV news. Do we have a deal?'
Cantona smiles and then shakes his head, 'You people? What rock is it you crawl from?' The Frenchman nods to one of the security guards and they escort Lloyd away. He shouts back without turning, 'You're making a big mistake Eric. You really do need to play ball with us. You play fair with me and I'll be straight with you.'
Cantona goes back across to Isabelle and Raphael.
'Shall we pack?' Asks Isabelle.
He picks up Raphael and kisses him on the forehead, 'No. We're staying here. Besides, there's nowhere to run.'
They all watch as Lloyd and the two security men disappear from sight.
'Now come let's finish our game,' smiles Cantona.
'If I become good at this it will be handy when the journalists arrive.' Isabelle starts to laugh, 'First you think you are Bruce Lee and now Robin Hood? I want my Eric back.' He kisses her gently on the lips and pats her stomach, 'What do you think, boy or girl?'
I hope it's a girl so she can tell her stubborn father what to do. If it's a son then three of you? What chance do I have?'
They both smile as Cantona fires his arrow and hits a bullseye.

…Saturday 11TH February 1995...

Around 10am, the next morning Terry Lloyd and his film crew are on a public beach next to the Club Med resort. Suddenly, one of the crew points towards the other side of the sands, 'I don't fuckin' believe it! Looks like our lucky day.' They all stare over and on the far end of a jetty stretching out onto the crystal blue Caribbean waters are Cantona and Isabelle. Lloyd smiles, 'Come on lads. I want you to set up the camera about forty feet away from them and leave the rest to me.'
They head off.
Isabelle, wearing a loose fitting dark sun dress spots them first, 'Oh my god, Eric, look!' She points to an advancing LIoyd and the camera crew behind him. Already filming. 'Stay here,' says Cantona to his wife.
He jumps down off the jetty and walks towards Lloyd. 'Mr Cantona' says Lloyd, 'When do you intent to return to England?' Cantona stops within inches of his face and LIoyd starts to repeat the question, 'I'll ask again, when do you intend to...'
Before he can finish Cantona has him in a headlock and whispers into LIoyd's ear, 'Come with me. I want to talk to you.' LIoyd tries to continue the conversation whilst restrained, 'Come on Eric, no need for violence.'
Cantona lets him loose, but keeps an arm on his shoulders whilst guiding Lloyd off the beach. All the time watched by a startled camera crew and a worried Isabelle.
'Thank god I hid his bow and arrow' she says quietly to herself. On reaching the complex Cantona shouts over the manager who is stood with a security guard. They come across. The camera crew has also arrived on the scene,

'I want the film you took of my pregnant wife,' demands Cantona. 'No way,' says Lloyd, now free of the Frenchman's grip. 'That's a public beach. We've done nothing wrong and it's our property.'

'You couldn't spell wrong,' says Cantona. Quietly, but with menace. Two more security guards arrive and the manager orders them to confiscate the film. LIoyd attempts to intervene, only to be stopped in his tracks as Cantona launches himself once more Kung Fu style to bring him down. Sent crashing to the floor, Lloyd is slowly helped up by his film crew, 'You're going to fucking regret that!' He shouts angrily towards Cantona, who simply glares at the three ITV men with utter disdain.

'Go now, before I get mad again.'

'Come on Terry, fuck this. The guy is nuts,' exclaims one of the cameraman. LIoyd points to the film now in the hands of one of the security men, 'That belongs to ITV! You haven't heard the fucking last of this. I'm getting in touch with the British embassy.'

'Mr Lloyd,' says the manager, very calmly and smiling. 'You can contact her Majesty the queen herself. But we are dealing with a king here. Now good day to you.'

A sore LIoyd and his camera crew head off with him still grumbling loud.

Cantona turns to the manager, 'Thank you for your help.' He smiles, 'No problem Mr Cantona. I myself am a Manchester United supporter. I promise you won't be bothered against whilst your family are in my care. Isabelle has joined them and links her husband. She too adds her thanks and the two head back towards the beach. Together walking hand in hand along the sea edge. Half a world away from Manchester and the madness and

hysteria that is engulfing it in the aftermath of Selhurst Park. Utterly unaware that just around the corner their lives are set to take an even more turn for the surreal…
When new breaks in England of events in the Caribbean a huge amount of public opinion goes in Eric Cantona's favour. Being chased across the planet and the thought of a film camera crew trying to film him and his heavily pregnant wife whilst simply trying to relax on a quiet beach harvests much sympathy for Cantona's angry reaction.
None more than Alex Ferguson, who behind the scenes rages at this news and publicly goes so far as to state, 'To film without permission a man's six-month-old pregnant wife in her swimsuit sitting on a beach is deplorable. Any husband worth his salt would react. This ITV interviewer got off lightly.' The tide is turning, but Eric Cantona still has to face the long arm of the law and the wrath of the British Justice system. On returning to England he's officially charged with Common Assault in relation to the Selhurst Park incident.
Few would ever believe what happens next.

EMPIRES RISE AND FALL

...Saturday 6th March 1993…

It's thirty minutes to kick off in the Manchester United dressing room at Anfield and Alex Ferguson has just called for quiet amongst his players. All eyes fall upon him.
'Alright listen up. Ten months ago we came here with half a hope and a fuckin' prayer of winning the league. They beat us 2-0 and rubbed our noses in it. Not just the

fans, but their staff and players. Remember their faces, the laughing coming from their dressing room?
Aye, well today we're back and I've got a good memory.
Now you all know what I think of this place?
You can smell the vomit.
What they think of us? It's not a problem, they hate us, fair do's, we hate them back. Their history is like ours, steeped in glory. But I came here today and l looked in their eyes and they're worried. Liverpool are scared of us because we are coming and they know deep down it's over.
To them Manchester United are like a huge wave that's going to wipe out their history and make this place irrelevant.
Now think back to last year.
'Have you ever seen United win the league?'
'Always look on the bright side of fuckin' life?'
In our faces they sang and they laughed.
Ferguson points across to Ryan Giggs and Lee Sharpe, 'Do you two remember what happened outside the ground with the autographs?'
They both nod.
'Well when the bile starts up again today, you run that little faster, tackle that much harder, and if you get a chance make sure you don't miss. Because if we win today those same faces who ripped the autographs up in your faces will go to bed tonight crying in their fuckin' shellsuits.'
Ferguson turns his gaze back to the others, 'As for the Munich 58 chants? For this lot it's as natural to sing as breathing. And this is where you are today. Liverpool. Feel the love. A mutual fuckin' disrespect.
This is Anfield? Do me a fuckin' favour.

Now I expect you to not just win today, but to leave them and their supporters with a calling card that says I hope you enjoyed the ride because your time in the sun has gone. The days of looking down the road and laughing, saying where are your league titles? Twenty-six years? I'll say again.
Twenty-six fuckin' years? That's enough, no more, I want this league and this lot, in this hole of a ground, in this city that spits on the name of Manchester United are not going to stand in my way. And, more importantly are not going to stand in yours.
Empires rise and fall. And we, United are set to knock this fuckin' Liver bird off her perch for good. So, any questions?'
Total silence.
'Thought not,' smiles Ferguson
'The future is your boys. Time to put this lot in a cell and throw away the fuckin' key.'
Final score. Liverpool 1 Manchester United 2.

STITCH UP

…Friday 24th February 1995…

Set in the hidden beauty of a leafy part of Hertfordshire, The Sopwell House Hotel is playing host to what is now a world-wide media event. Here the Football Association will hand out their punishment to lump onto the back of Manchester United's already lengthy ban for Eric Cantona.
A black Limousine enters the grounds.
Along a winding, slim road it continues up to the main front doors of the hotel. Inside are Eric Cantona, Alex

Ferguson and a newly assigned personal bodyguard for the player, forty-two-year old Ned Kelly. A huge man, craggy features with equally sized long moustache and a face that tells of a battle and a scar or two. Kelly no doubt has many a tale to tell of past deeds. His job now to keep the press and media wolves at harm's length from Cantona. Or maybe just the other way round.

Ferguson is convinced the FA's desire to hammer his player and put extra nails in the coffin has been scuppered by United's swift action to ban Cantona until the end of the season, 'They wouldn't fuckin' dare add any more on,' he says to himself. Whilst staring out the window of the Limousine at the dozens of film crews and journalists from across the globe lying in wait on the hotel's grassy mounds.

'They wouldn't dare.'

Ferguson turns around and addresses Cantona, 'Always remember you are a Manchester United player and will remain so. Rise above it, say nothing and I promise we'll do right by you. Okay?'

Cantona nods.

Ferguson turns to Kelly, 'Keep this lot out of Eric's face.'

'Will do boss' he replies. Kelly smiles, that in itself a little unnerving, 'Don't worry, he's in good hands now.' Amidst a crescendo of loud voices shouting questions and being totally ignored, they step out. Dressed in attire suitable for a funeral. A sombre black suit, grey tie and white shirt, Cantona stares straight on. Oblivious to all and any. Kelly is swiftly earning his money, one look and a hand across the chest is enough to form a clear path. As Cameras flash and roll they head inside.

From an upstairs window in the conference room the FA Chief Executive Graham Kelly watches their arrival. His features solemn, for he knows in just a short time a certain Scotsman could well be hanging him out this same ledge and even contemplating letting go.
Behind enjoying a ridiculously expensive bottle of Bushmills whisky between them before proceedings begin are the other invisible esteemed members of the FA panel. Geoffrey Thompson. A Justice of Peace from the amateur county game in Sheffield. Ian Stott, Chairman of Oldham Athletic and Gordon Mckeag. A former Chairman of Newcastle United and now President of the Football League.
'Come sit back down and finish your drink Graham,' says Thompson. Instead he stays standing and Stott walks over and hands him a glass, 'Get this down you son. One feels you are going to bloody need it'
'Whatever they come up with we're going to throw the book at this lunatic,' adds Mckeag. 'Bloody French.'
'I'll drink to that,' smiles Stott.
'About time we put United in their place.'
He raises his glass, 'Agreed?'
They all nod and do similar. Except Kelly, who's in no mood for such joviality. For at this moment he feels more in need of a suit of armour.

The United entourage enter the Committee room and sit opposite Kelly, Stott, Thompson and Mckeag. There are muttered greetings on both sides and tepid handshakes. Watkins begins proceedings, 'Gentlemen, I would like us to start by letting Eric read a set statement. They all glare at Cantona as Watkins passes him a sheet of paper.

He looks up towards the panel with a wry smile on his face. Sat next and watching him closely is Ferguson. He's seen this look before. The manager's inner thoughts are written across his worried features and could easily be shown in a cartoon display bubble containing the words,
'Behave Eric.'
To the shock of the four men facing him Cantona begins speaking in perfect English, 'I would like to apologise to the chairman of this commission. I would like to apologise to Manchester United. Maurice Watkins and Alex Ferguson. I would like to apologise to my team mates. I want to apologise to the FA.'
At this point he switches back to French, 'And I would like to apologise to the prostitute I shared my bed with last night.'
On hearing this Watkin's face goes ashen-grey and he appears to be suffering a heart attack on the spot.
The FA Committee all smile knowingly. Unlike Watkins none speak French and clearly think these words are nothing more than a Gallic apology from the heart. Ferguson himself, no great linguist appears also to not have understood the gist of his player's comments. Although one look at Watkins and he knows Cantona has thrown in some kind of verbal grenade.
'Thank you Eric,' says Kelly.
'De rien.' ('Your welcome') Replies a straight faced Cantona.
By now Watkins has recovered and suddenly believes that if Cantona can get away with this then maybe god is a Frenchman? 'Tell me Mr Cantona?' Asks Thompson.

'Are you a Kung Fu expert?' The Frenchman looks at Watkins, then Ferguson before finally returning a quizzical glance to Thompson.
'Pardon?'...
Three hours later an exhausted United trio leaves the committee room to let the panel come to a verdict on what punishment will be handed out. Ferguson is whistling and appears a happy man as they are led into a nearby suite. There they settle down in armchairs as tea and biscuits are served.
'Well that seemed to go well Maurice?'
We have good reason to be confident Alex,' he replies. Watkins has decided not to mention Cantona's prostitute remark to him on the grounds why rock a ship that has possibly just missed an iceberg by inches?
He glares over at the Frenchman who just smiles and winks back. Cantona has little respect for these people who dare to put him on trial. For what? Hitting some thug who dared to tarnish his mother's name. Besides, he took one look at his accusers and believed none would have understood him anyway?
'But remember Alex,' continues Watkins. 'We've been here with these people before. They have one rule for Manchester United and another for the rest. So, best just wait and see'
'No chance Maurice,' smiles Ferguson. 'Not this time. I believe we're looking at a heavy fine for our boy here. Nothing more'...
'Let's hops so' adds Watkins. Still fearing the proverbial book will be thrown at United and Cantona.
The long history of bad blood between Manchester United and the Football Association means when it comes to second guessing all bets were off. Two hour

later a message is delivered to the United suite that a decision has finally been reached and their presence is required back in the Committee room.

'About bloody time,' says Ferguson, 'I thought those buggers had fallen asleep in there.'

Before going in Watkins taps Ferguson on the shoulder. He turns around, 'All I'm saying Alex is don't be surprised if they hammer us. Normal rules don't apply to Manchester United, you know that.'

Ferguson smiles, 'Don't worry Maurice. I'm the calmest man in the world. Now come on.'

Watkins, Cantona and Ferguson are back sitting down. Facing them the four members of the panel are wearing their most serious expressions. Graham Kelly begins, 'Gentlemen, thank you for your patience. We've come to an agreement after a lengthy discussion and it's as follows.'

He looks down to read, 'The Football Association are doubling Eric's' ban to six months, extending it worldwide and we are also adding an extra £10,000 fine of our own. I'm sure you'll believe me when I tell you this hasn't been an easy decision to reach.'

'Oh, I bet it fuckin' wasn't,' snaps an angry Ferguson. Watkins winces, for he knows what's coming.

'You've stitched us right up.'

'Now wait here Alex,' replies Ian Stott.

'It's Mr fuckin' Ferguson to you!'

Ferguson stands. He goes to walk towards the door and then turns back, 'What is it with you people? Ever since the fifties you've had a beef with this club. Matt took us into Europe against your supposed better judgement and since then any chance to twist the knife deep you do it.

You even took Bobby off United for a nothing international when they were fighting for their lives after the Munich crash for Christ's sake? What kind of organisation does something like that? Where others have hearts, you have rules and fuckin' requirements. What is this hatred? Is it a Masonic thing? Handed down in generations. Get United, different fuckin' rules apply.'

'Be care Alex, you're on dangerous ground,' interrupts a shocked Thompson.

'Fuckin dangerous ground?' Replies Ferguson.

'I've not even started. Your problem is you sit in fancy hotels behind these long wooden pine tables. You drink expensive whisky and pretend you matter. Let me tell you something. Manchester United matters, Liverpool matters. Arsenal matters. You lot? If you're lucky and behave we let you shake the player's hands on Cup Final day. You are Mini's to our Ferraris. It's like comparing Frank Sinatra to Chas and fuckin' Dave.

Small men with big egos and huge titles, but you live empty lives.

Your jealousy eats you up and so you lash out.

How can you justify doubling Eric's ban? It's criminal to do such a thing.'

Watkins stands and gently tugs on Ferguson's arm, 'Alex for God sake. Enough!'

Ferguson stares at Watkins, then Cantona, who has watched the manager fight his corner like no one he's ever seen. He decides at this moment whatever it takes and no matter how long he'll repay such loyalty.

Ferguson smiles, his face now reddened in anger, 'Go ahead do your worst. Nothing you lot can throw at us will take away the fact you need Manchester United more than we need you. You would all do well to remember that.'

That said Ferguson motions for Cantona and Watkins and together the three men stand to go.

'I really must protest Maurice,' says Kelly, as Watkins is almost out the door and last to leave.

'Who the bloody hell does Ferguson think he is?' Adds Mckeag. Thompson and Stott are too stunned to speak. Watkins comes back in and shuts the door behind him.

'Alex is a little angry. He'll calm down.'

'He was bloody outrageous!' screams Stott.

'Hear' pipes up Thompson. 'He hasn't heard the last of this.'

'Gentlemen' replies Watkins. 'Tempers and emotions are running a little high at the moment. Let's give it half an hour before we tell the waiting world what you've come up with here today. As for Alex? If I was you I'd take my advice. Stay out of his way for the next twenty years or so.'

Watkins smiles, 'Maybe thirty.'

Before a frantic army of media types with cameras flashing and blinding the two sides entered the huge hotel lounge to sit alongside each other whilst the FA's decision is announced. Alex Ferguson's face is like thunder, but he's calmed down enough to attend and keep his thoughts to himself. For now.

Later he would admit publicly, 'I don't think any player in the history of the game will get the sentence Eric got unless he kills the FA President's Bert Millichip's dog.' Like a hitman contemplating future hits a quick glance along the line at Kelly, Stott, Thompson and Mckeag is sufficient to show a watching world the man from Govan isn't happy and in unforgiving mood.

The hatchet not so much buried as out of sight and ready to be sharpened for another day.

As for Cantona, he remains cool, calm and collected on the outside. Neither speaking nor it appears even bothered by the circus that surrounds his every move. But inside, he like his manager is raging. For it's now a question of what does he do for six months without a ball at his feet? For the game is the air he breathes and this ban will surely suck the life out of him.

As silence is called for a hush goes around the room and Graham Kelly reads out a prepared statement.

'The members of the FA commission are satisfied that the actions of Eric Cantona following his sending off at Crystal Palace in the Manchester United match on January 25 brought the game into disrepute. Eric Cantona has therefore been in breach of FA rules. After taking into consideration the previous misconduct of Eric Cantona, the provocation he suffered, the prompt action taken by Manchester United, Eric Cantona's expression of regret to the commission, the apologies he conveyed to those affected and the assurances he gave to his future conduct, the members of the commission decided that Eric Cantona should be suspended forthwith from all football activities up to and including 30th September 1995, and in addition fined £10,000.'

On finishing the above statement, Kelly utters the immortal line that is heaven on earth to journalists, 'Any questions?'

This is the signal to see the room explode into a cascade of noise and frenzied excitement. Three hundred voices

shouting at once, but the one everybody wants answers from remains tight lipped.
His eyes defiant and giving nothing away. For Eric Cantona this is far from over, as next on his agenda is a return to the scene of the alleged crime.
South London, Croydon Magistrates court and a date with destiny...

A SENSE OF WONDER

...Saturday 9th January 1993...

As the referee Mr Peck from Kendall blows to end the match, Old Trafford erupts. Manchester United 4 Tottenham Hotspur 1. All certain that on this cold and dark late January afternoon they have witnessed something quite extraordinary. Not just a performance laced with wonderful flair and three points that have seen them go top of the table above Norwich City, but for a moment of pure genius on fifty-two minutes.
It came not surprisingly from the conjuring right foot of their number seven. The tall striding Frenchman with a pass of such sweet touch and beauty it caused the type of gasps from the crowd normally reserved for the Ballet and not a simple football match.
United were already one up through a first half Eric Cantona header. Their talisman ably abetted by a supreme, blistering supporting cast in Giggs and Sharpe on the wings. And later Kanchelskis.
With Hughes and McClair in equally explosive form and wreaking havoc, it was nothing more than waves of red shirts running riot against a shell-shocked Spurs team,

whom from the first minute to last today, haven't known what's hit them.

Even the full-backs Paul Parker and Denis Irwin were hurtling over the halfway line at every opportunity to join in the carnage. Certain that every run would be found by Cantona's inner radar. His ability to pick out a pass sometimes verging on the supernatural, with balls not so much passed, but guided by mystical powers.

Ferguson watched on from his seat with a look of satisfaction and like everyone else in the stadium, a sense of wonder also. And no more than seven minutes after half time when Cantona played a one-two with the darting Irwin, that didn't so much dissect the Spurs defence, but put a spell on them.

A delicate, unerring chip shot collected by the Irishman to run onto and fire gloriously past the diving goalkeeper Erik Thorvstedt.

Old Trafford went wild! Enraptured, and even after the cheering had died down for the goal, a special whispering hush settled across the stands. One that signalled something truly special had just occurred.

In an eyeblink of magic Cantona opened every United supporter's wide.

Just what the hell had they got on their hands?...

OH WHAT A CIRCUS

...Thursday 24th March 1995...

It's a clear Spring South London morning with a light touch of summer on the way. Ned Kelly is escorting Eric Cantona through a haranguing mob of hundreds of reporters and photographers outside Croydon

Magistrates. His only advice to Cantona, whom he has swiftly grown close to, 'Stay close Eric and leave the rest to me son.'

Earlier that same morning a senior police office had knocked on Cantona's hotel room and asked him about travelling to the courts, 'If you want Eric, to avoid the press we can sneak you in through the rear entrance in a police van?'

Cantona stared at him like he was mad, 'That would be the act of a common criminal. I am proud of what I did and I will walk through the front door.'

'Suit yourself' replies the officer, 'But it's going to be bloody crazy son. Having you here today is like having Take That and the Spice Girls combined.'

Cantona smiles, 'I will walk.'

The office sighs and shakes his hand, 'Well good luck to you then.' He walks off muttering glumly to himself, 'The lunatic must think they are going to part like the red sea to let him through. The man is clearly mad.'

In an astonishing display of just how much world-wide publicity the Selhurst Park incident has generated over twenty television crews are mounted in and around the courts. All vying for a decent view to catch a glimpse on film of this remarkable man, whose one moment of madness has enraptured, enthralled and outraged an entire planet. One journalist has even hired a hydraulic lift to give him the best possible chance of seeing Cantona's entrance into the courts. The atmosphere outside is tense and scuffles break out amongst the various media organisations. These same whose senior producers and editors claim that Eric Cantona should be hung from the highest gallows are rolling around in public, kicking and throwing punches. All in order to earn the right to be near him.

The word ironic doesn't do it justice.

Dressed to kill, wearing a pale blue jacket, black jeans and a grey Tee-shirt with a small replica of the Statue of Liberty pinned upon it, the effect of Cantona's appearance on the Paparazzi is that of a visiting A list Hollywood movie star. Dozens of snappers retreat before him, walking backwards. Flashlights go off. This feels more like the opening of a movie premier than a Common Assault charge to be heard in Court number one at Croydon Magistrates.

Eric Cantona has the world media spinning on its axis with the same ease his sleight of foot makes a premier league defender appear in the midst of a fit.

In an electric atmosphere and to a breathless packed court containing those both pro and against Cantona, plus a significant number of news journalists from both home and abroad. The local prosecutor Mr Jeffrey McCann with a dramatic sweep of his hand begins proceedings. Sensing a moment in the limelight never to be repeated, McCann is describing in the minutest detail, the dramatic events at 8-57, on the evening of Wednesday 25th January 1995.

Listening intently are the chairperson of the bench, fifty-three-year old Mrs Jean Pearch. A retired music teacher. And two local Croydon men, Brian Chapman and Chris Funnell. Mrs Pearch has been chosen specifically because she has no interest in football. The mother of four children now holds in her hands the liberty of the idol of millions. And equally one loathed by the same number. Not your everyday Friday morning here at Croydon Magistrates.

McCann continues, 'Cantona fell back, got onto his feet and went to strike Matthew Simmons with his fists, it appeared to all, two or three times. Having no choice Simmons naturally defended himself by punching back.' McCann points dramatically to the Frenchman who sits watching and listening to proceeding next to his esteemed barrister. A member of the Queens Council and hugely respected man in his field, Fifty-seven-year old David Poole.

'Eric Cantona, this man you see here with us today ladies and gentleman was restrained by officials and led off the pitch. It was only through good policing and stewarding that prevented this dreadful episode from escalating into a truly major public disorder.'

This goes on and on. Witnesses are called, thanked and dismissed. One who describes himself as neutral is called by McCann to describe Cantona's violent reaction. But not all goes to plan for the prosecution, 'He went mad, but this guy did scream out to him along the lines of, 'You fuckin' cheating French cunt. Fuck off back to France, you motherfucker. French bastard, wanker! So, I'm not really surprised he was a little wound up.'

At this point the Magistrate clerk Mr John Manning feels best to step in. Manning looks across to Eric Cantona, 'Mr Cantona, can you follow what the witness is saying?' Cantona smiles, 'Yes' he replies.

Much to the court's amusement which suddenly breaks into laughter. The tense atmosphere suddenly changed by this retelling of Simmon's manic rant. Now it's time for the defence to step up as Poole addresses the chair.

'I have a statement from my client which I would like to read out?'

'Go ahead' says Mrs Pearch. Like everyone present she can't wait to hear Cantona's version of events.

Poole begins reading the Frenchman's account:

'Shortly after half time I was dismissed from the field for an offence against an opponent. I was angry and frustrated with myself at my dismissal, but did not protest to the referee. In my opinion his decision was correct although I had been repeatedly and painfully fouled in the course of the match.

As I was leaving the field and making my way towards the player's tunnel I was deeply disappointed with myself for what had happened. I then became aware of a man to my right near the front of the spectators' terraces, one of a number who seemed to be shouting and gesticulating at me.

At first I could not hear what he was saying, but it was soon very clear that he was goading and taunting me because of the sending off.

His face appeared to be contorted and he was making an obscene gesture. He was shouting in abusive, insulting and racist or nationalistic terms.

I was obviously hurt and insulted and with the addition of this to my existing frustration, I reacted in a way I now deeply regret. By jumping up and kicking out towards the man's chest. I am very aware that I should not have done this and I am not seeking to justify it'…

Poole turns back to the Chair, 'This man you see before you is not who you read about in the newspapers or see on television. He's a family man. Sometimes a volatile and tempestuous footballer. But as we have already heard the provocation by Simmons was severe. It was aimed at my client's nationality and the sexual integrity of his mother. Now I ask all here. Would you have acted differently?

Maybe, but I'm sure there are many present who would have, as Mr Cantona did, and now regrets, lose your temper for moment and hit back.

Matthew Simmons is one of that regrettable minority who puts xenophobia before any love of soccer and expresses this by abusing footballers who are black and from overseas. We are all fully aware of Simmons background. This is a twenty-year old young man who already has a history of racist violence.

Whereas Mr Cantona has spoken out many times in public against racism.

A man of positively good character, acting out of character in a moment of extreme distress.

His charity work and I have letters of support for him here in my hand.'

Poole displays these to all.

'They speak in glowing terms of Mr Cantona's good nature and handsome generosity of spirit. There's also the fact that my client has already been punished enough, for what was nothing more than a rash of temper against a violent, racist hooligan.

His cost for this momentarily loss of control has been high.

£10,800, two weeks wages. The FA suspension until September 30. Unrivalled in its severity in the modern day. Plus, their further fine of another £10,000. And so because of this I ask the court for a conditional discharge for my client, and to see his good name not tarnished anymore.'

Mrs Pearch calls for a recess whilst they consider the evidence.

An hour goes by; Poole is sat next to Cantona in a waiting room, 'We'll be okay Eric' says Poole, 'I'm sure of it. This is an open and shut case.'

A bell rings to signal the time has come to return to court. 'Right then, here we go' smiles Poole. 'Let's get this over with and go home.'

The two men stand and head off.

An air of expectation and nervous tension has again engulfed court number one. With everyone in their places Mrs Pearch reads out the verdict:

It's just turned 11-47 am and Eric Cantona's world is set to take yet another leap into the absurd.

'I would like to begin by saying there will be absolutely no compensation for Mr Matthew Simmons.'

Immediately a smile comes on Poole's face. This is looking good. Mrs Pearch continues, 'We have in making our decision taken into account, Mr Cantona's plea of guilty, his apologies and previously good character.'

Suddenly, Poole goes ashen faced…He smells trouble.

'We do feel, however, that you are a high-profile public figure with undoubted gifts and you are looked up to by many young people. For this reason the only sentence that is appropriate is two weeks' imprisonment forthwith. This will take place at High Down. A category B prison.'

If somebody had let off a grenade in court number one the impact could not have been greater. There are loud gasps from the public gallery.

Cantona initially appears shocked, but then a half smile crosses his face. As if the verdict was ever going to be anything else? Poole is deep in discussion with Mrs

Pearch for bail, but she shakes her head, 'I'm sorry' she says. 'Immediate bail is refused.'
He walks back over to Cantona and shakes his head, 'I'm going to find another Judge to lodge an appeal and another application for bail. You may have to spend a few hours in a cell, but that's all. Will you be okay?'
'I'm Cantona' he smiles. 'Of course. It will be a new experience.'
'Good man. I'll sort this mess out and I promise we'll be back in Manchester for this evening.'
Poole disappears out of the court room. Inside he's a worried man knowing that possibly his very reputation rests on getting Cantona out of this place today.
'Oh, what a circus. Fucking amateurs,' mumbles Poole, under his breath. 'That was nothing more than a lynch court.'

With a young policeman by his side Eric Cantona is led off to the court cells. When out of sight and just the two of them walking down steps to the holding area, the policeman says quietly to Cantona, 'Just sit tight okay, it's a fuckin' scandal this. You'll be out of here in a couple of hours. I'm a cockney red. You're the king for me.'
The Frenchman turns and smiles at him. British justice may stink, but it never ceases to surprise him where United fans show up, 'Thank you' he says.
'No thank you sir' replies the policeman. 'I've got your back while you're here Eric. Don't you worry about that.'
They reach the cell and Cantona enters and sits on a bench. The policeman shuts the door and goes to stand

outside. He smiles, 'I'm not fuckin' locking it, no chance.'

Here Cantona stays whilst a seething Poole negotiates his freedom. Cantona is surprised but happy when his lawyer and good friend Jean-Jacques Bertrand appears and is allowed to stay in the cell with him.

'Well my friend' says Bertrand. 'Even for you this is a first.' The two men are close and Cantona smiles. He points to Bertrand's briefcase, 'Do you have a saw and some dynamite in there? Maybe we could stage a break out and escape back to France!'

Both laugh. Much to the bemusement of the police officer who's standing on guard outside the cell. Cantona points to him and says in English, 'That man out there is my friend.'

Bertrand nods in agreement and the young policeman is now wearing a grin that would light up London town...

Across the city at Buckingham Palace, Alex Ferguson, resplendent in kilt and beaming ear to ear with his family around him is posing for cameras after just being awarded a CBE off the queen in the New Year's Honours list.

Suddenly, he hears a journalist's voice shout loud from amid the sea of photographers from the crowd, 'Alex, what do you make of Cantona going to jail?'

Suddenly Ferguson's smile disappears. He appears stunned, like a man recovering from just having his wallet snatched. Cathy whispers into is ear, 'There's nothing you can do about it for now.'

Knowing as ever his good lady is right Ferguson smiles once more, whilst inside his stomach is churning. He ignores all other reporters' questions over Cantona.

Finally, after three hours Poole secures Cantona's release. The appeal is granted in court by Judge Ian Davies and the Frenchman is released on a bail of £500. Davies is equally shocked as Poole's by the initial Cantona verdict,
'Bloody ridiculous' he admits to Poole.
'Get him out of London and we'll set the appeal for eight days from now. Give time for sensible heads and a bloody good dose of reality to prevail. Talk about lunatics taking over the asylum? What Pearch has done is not even legally binding. You can't say you're locking someone up just because they are damn famous.'
Poole goes down to the cell and Cantona and Bertrand stand on seeing him. He smiles wide, 'Come on Eric we're going home.' On leaving Cantona shakes hands with the policeman, 'Thank you for being a good person.' The policeman appears close to tears, 'My pleasure Eric.' Cantona, Bertrand and Poole head off leaving him alone. The policeman wipes his eyes, 'Fuck me, I never expected this today.'

Just after 3pm, Eric Cantona with Ned Kelly on one side and a lady Police Constable on the other emerges from Croydon magistrates into the London sunshine. His appearance once more the signal for unadulterated chaos! There are cheers and boos in equal numbers from both Manchester United and Crystal Palace supporters who are gathered amid the army of journalists and cameramen. Chants of 'scum' and 'going down' are drowned out by loud, incessant chants of 'Oh ah Cantona!'

He stops to sign autographs for two young girls, no more than ten years old. Both wearing United shirts with his name on the back. One starts to cry tears of happiness and Cantona leans down and whispers to her, 'Everything is going to be alright. We are going to win.'

He stands back up and through the awaiting media scrum Kelly and the constable guide Cantona expertly through. His face as ever a mask of utter indifference to the camera flashes and shouted question erupting all around him.

Only one legal hurdle now remains left to overcome and for Eric Cantona, derided, mocked and at times treated with less respect than a sewer rat, his moment in the sun will soon dawn.

But worryingly for United and their supporters all this mayhem is being closely monitored in Italy. Inter President Massimo Moratti craves the genius of Eric Cantona like no other to lead his charge against almighty city rivals and all conquering AC Milan. Moratti is a man for whose fortune made in the petrodollar, means money is to him like others have water flowing from a tap. What Moratti wants he gets. And he desires above all else, Cantona.

AN EASTER MIRACLE

…Saturday 10th April 1993…

'We didn't start playing until the 90th minute.'
Alex Ferguson

Manchester United are at home and with just over an hour gone against Sheffield Wednesday, Old Trafford resembles a collective nervous wreck. It's a stifling hot day and United's play is littered with errors. There are many groans from an expectant crowd whom after recent blistering performances have gathered expecting a goal fest, but it isn't happening

The title race is now a straight shoot-out between United and Aston Villa. The Birmingham club have the edge in that if they win all their remaining games then the title is theirs. It's essential the Red Devil's don't drop points today, but as the sun's shadow dances across a huge swathe of the pitch hopes are dimming amongst supporters that a breakthrough will be forthcoming. Their clever ball players such as Eric Cantona and Ryan Giggs are experiencing a kind of day every magician must dread. When the rabbits simply refuse to emerge from the hat. Two sublime first half touches from Cantona that almost put his team mates through, but that apart,

nothing more.

As for the visitors, Trevor Francis's Sheffield Wednesday. They appear content to just sit and wait for an opportunity that will truly ruin the home side's day. With ex United player Viv Anderson and the gangling but effective Carlton Palmer defending heroically, all paths to goal appear to be blocked off.

A concerned Ferguson turns to his substitute and now elder statesman Bryan Robson. Eternally cursed by injuries, Robson still plays an integral part in matters of the United dressing room. And when fit and deemed necessarily he remains an important player for Ferguson. Respected beyond words by the manager for his playing ability, courage and leadership. He along with Brian Kidd a close confidante.

'Get yourself warmed up Robbo, you're going on soon if this doesn't change.'

'Okay gaffer' he replies and sets off running down the touchline.

Robson's appearance causing one of the loudest cheers of the day from amongst the home supporters. Suddenly, the referee Mr Peck pulls up injured and the game is halted. Struggling badly Peck motions he can't carry on and the whistle is handed to the substitute referee/linesman Mr John Hilditch.

We've had a seven minutes stoppage. Hilditch restarts and the game continues. The clock is already showing 4-30pm when Sheffield Wednesday winger Chris Waddle races into the United penalty area. He stands, drops a shoulder and goes to beat Paul Ince who sends him crashing to the ground. A small pocket of South Yorkshire roars loud and Mr Hilditch points to the penalty spot. No argument, a blatant foul by the United midfielder and up steps a boyhood supporter. A Manc John Sheridan, a lad from Stretford to possibly hammer a final nail into his home town club's title challenge. Twenty-six years could well become twenty-seven and the search for the Holy Grail will go on. Sheridan appears cool, calm and collected. His two brothers are the opposite, both watching on from an angst-ridden Stretford End. 'Please miss our kid,' one of them pleads quietly.

'Please.'

Many can't and simply refuse to watch. There's a strange silence around the stadium. The only voices heard are prayers and insults. Steve Bruce sidles up to Sheridan as he prepares to take the kick, 'You're a red aren't you

John?' He says smiling. Sheridan stares hard at him, 'Not today mate.'
Up he comes to stroke the ball past Peter Schmeichel with astute ease and a delighted Sheridan rolls away punching the air. Old Trafford watches on aghast.
Ferguson puts an arm around Bryan Robson's shoulders, 'Get on and fuckin' sort it out son.'
Robson smiles and nods. Theirs's still a battle or two in the old warrior yet. On he comes to replace Paul Parker and the game restarts. Suddenly, the noise level rises as the realisation hits Old Trafford that an entire season rests on this final twenty-minutes. Immediately, Robson is flying into Wednesday players for tackles like a man whose life quite simply depended on it. With Robbo alongside him Ince now finds a new lease of life and finally, after what feels like an eternity, Manchester United appear to be waking up.
Led by Robson, United huff and puff, but there's no magic forthcoming today. Its scuffles, blocked crosses and wayward passes. Still they are roared on by an equally desperate crowd who now know their team needs nothing short of an Easter miracle to rescue even a point. But still Wednesday are unyielding with Anderson and Palmer frustrating all efforts to get through. A chink of light as the stadium holds it breath when Cantona links with Hughes for the Welshman to batter his way through and hit a fine low effort. Only for it to be tipped around the post by the goalkeeper Chris Woods.
Heads back in hands.
Maybe its fate, destiny's child decrees some things are just not meant to be. You're allowed the odd cup competition and agony of coming second. We'll tease you with the dream, then like water dripping through

your hands, take it away and nail you to the fucking floor.
For never will you be handed the ultimate accolade of champions.
That belongs to London, Leeds Liverpool and Birmingham….
There are four minutes left to play and Manchester United have won a corner.
Ryan Giggs races across to take it. The boy from Salford, a United supporter, stolen from the grasps of City as a thirteen-year-old by Ferguson's legendary powers of persuasion. The man himself watches on. His eyes totally on Bryan Robson who's placed himself on the edge of the penalty area. In comes the Giggs' corner and as Robson starts his run, Steve Bruce meets it from twelve yards and produces a guided header high past Woods into the top corner. Old Trafford erupts in sheer unadulterated relief!
The Captain is mobbed by his grateful team mates and disappears under a sea of red. But still Ferguson's glance has never left Robson who followed in Bruce's effort and ended up himself in the back of the net. Taking two Sheffield Wednesday defenders with him.
'That man is incredible,' he says quietly as Brian McClair rushes to reclaim the ball. As they return to their defensive positions Pallister hugs Bruce once more within an inch of his life, 'You fuckin' star Brucie!'
The pressure for a late winner is now utterly relentless. Ince spreads a long raking pass wide to Ryan Giggs on the left wing and his cross almost causes an own goal by an exhausted Viv Anderson, who stabs it inches wide of the post for yet another United corner.
The baying crowd are on their feet.

The time has just turned five o'clock and still we go on. Giggs sprints to take it, this time from the left. It's cleared but falls back at the feet of the dancing Welshman. Looking up Giggs tries again, only for the ball to overrun and head over towards the far-right hand touchline.

There waiting is the unlikely, attacking figure of Gary Pallister. His cross is deflected back over the penalty area and lands heaven-sent into the path of an on-rushing Steve Bruce, who thunders another unstoppable header past Woods to send Old Trafford spinning wildly out of control!

No one is spared the madness and delirium sweeping over the stadium with even Alex Ferguson and Brian Kidd going momentarily crazy and becoming honorary members of the Stretford End. Ferguson charges down from the stand dancing a manic Scottish victory jig! His face gone to heaven and back. Whilst Kidd runs even further past the manager onto the pitch and slides to his knees. Arms raised. Eyes to the sky.

Sheer joy etched on so many faces, for this day, this hour and this moment. When fate, destiny and lady luck suddenly took a look around this famous old ground and changed sides.

Manchester United and Aston Villa remain within a hair's breadth of each other in the title race, but suddenly there's something in the air.

The final whistle 'finally' blows…

Am angry and disbelieving Trevor Francis mutters to himself, 'Fuckin'ell it's Sunday.' United have scored the winner seven minutes into injury time.

They now lead Villa by a point at the top of the table and it appears for the first time in a generation the footballing

gods are smiling upon them. Steve Bruce finds himself again being buried under a thankful flurry of red shirts. The popular skipper surely now set to be granted the freedom of three quarters of Manchester. And arguably more. He breaks free of his friendly mugging and for a moment stands alone.
Now Bruce can't stop himself as tears start to fall.
He wipes his eyes clear.
A smiling Cantona comes across and puts an arm around the genial Geordie's shoulders. The Frenchman takes in the astonishing scenes of revelry erupting around them.
'What kind of clubs is this Steve?' He asks.
A still emotional Bruce smiles through newly falling tears to answer, 'Eric mate this is Manchester United.'

SEAGULLS AND TRAWLERS

…Wednesday 31st March 1995…

At Croydon Crown court the circus is back in town! Dressed more discreetly this time around in a grey cashmere jacket, black waistcoat, white shirt and dark trousers, there still remained a part of Eric Cantona that couldn't resist turning his nose up to the establishment, whatever the consequences, by wearing light brown cowboy boots!
As ever, a media scrum reigns outside the courts as Ned Kelly with a fearful look of, 'Don't you dare fuckin' touch' in his eyes negotiates Cantona through a barrage of reporters and cameramen.
It doesn't take long for justice to put itself right.
After retiring for just thirty minutes Judge Ian Davies returns and in front of a hushed packed courtroom, he

throws out the previous ruling and instead sentences Cantona to 120 hours of community service.
His final summing up, 'Whatever the defendant's status he is entitled to be dealt with for the gravity of his offence and not to make an example of a public figure.' Davies' words are greeted with huge cheers from a public gallery that has been heavily infiltrated by United supporters. One more fanatical than most Mancunian Pete Boyle immediately races out of the hearing. Boyle charges throughout the main doors and announces to the hundreds of gathered media, 'The King is free!'
A smiling and relieved Cantona embraces his QC David Poole as applause rings out. He stands and raises an arm in acknowledgement to his supporters. One, thirty-nine-year old Gillian Priest comes over and hugs him. Gillian then kisses Poole hand, 'Thank you so much' she says with tears falling down her cheeks.
Maurice Watkins also appears and shakes Cantona's hands, 'I have something I wish to say to the world Maurice.' A shocked Watkins never expected this and is a little wary. He wouldn't put it past Cantona to now deliver an hour long expose of the British Judicial system by quoting the great French poets. And also re-start the hundred-year war between France and England as an afterthought. Watkins stares quizzically at Cantona, 'What exactly are you up to Eric?'
He simply smiles, 'You will see.'

Croydon Court hotel: At a hastily arranged press conference the world media have gathered to witness a now free Eric Cantona. Word has spread that he's finally going to speak and amid a blinding array of flashing lights and incessant clicking of cameras, Cantona enters with Maurice Watkins and Jean-Jacques Bertrand alongside him. They sit and face a hugely expectant audience. Suddenly, there's a hush as Watkins prepares to speak, 'Eric is just going to say a few words and won't be taking questions afterwards.'

All eyes fall on the Frenchman as the room goes deathly silent. Cantona begins,

'When the seagulls'...He stops to sip from a glass of water in front of him before continuing, 'Follow the trawler, it is because they think sardines…will be thrown into the sea…Thank you very much.'

That said, Cantona rises and leaves his tormentors open mouthed as he steps out the room. Watkins and Bertrand can't help but smile whilst across the floor there is much bewilderment, laughter and utter shock! Twenty words in fourteen seconds have stopped the clock as the world declares in unison, 'What just happened?'

In one act Cantona has set his own agenda and moved the story on to leave the Selhurst Park saga behind him and thrown the media a few more scraps to feed on in the process. Only this time no one got karate kicked or punched. Journalists and reporters are left fuming and feeling short changed because Cantona has refused to yield before them and indeed has had the last word.

'Seagulls and fuckin' trawlers!?' Exclaims the man from the Sun. 'Le Nutter!'

'What was all that about Maurice?' Asks the Man from the Mirror. 'Watkins smiles, 'Isn't it obvious?'

The man from the Mirror blushes.

'Where's Cantona gone now Maurice?' Inquires the man from the Mail.

'He's gone for a lie down,' replies Watkins, with a glint in his eye. 'Been a rather stressful day. Besides Eric

doesn't want to stay and talk to you lot. He's had enough and I don't blame him really.'
Eric Cantona would never for the remainder of his time at Manchester United speak to the British press again. For them, the seagull has truly flown.
But this story is far from over…

JUST LIKE HEAVEN

…Sunday 2nd May 1993…

It begins the day before. Just after 5-45pm at Mottram Hall golf course in Cheshire. The club bar is packed with members watching the dying embers of Aston Villa versus Oldham Athletic on Sky sports. The air is tense for the Latics are leading 1-0 with just seconds left to play. If this score remains the same then not only will Oldham have saved themselves from relegation.
But Manchester United will be crowed champions for the first time in twenty-six years.
Amongst those watching most intently is a fanatical United supporter and season ticket holder, Forty-six-year old Michael Lavender. Being too nervous to sit and watch the entire game Lavender has been out hitting a few balls on the course. He's only just returned because he thought the agony and the match would be over.
But still it goes on.
'How long to go George?' He asks the bartender, whilst ordering a beer.
'Anytime now Mike, They're in injury time.'
The barman hands Lavender his pint just as the referee blows and the entire room goes crazy with delight!

Drinks fly off tables and corks from Champagne bottles pop and fizz in the air.

'Where's Fergie?' Somebody shouts.

I'm sure he's around,' screams another.

Alex Ferguson is a member and arrived at the golf course hours before with his oldest son Mark. Utterly convinced that Villa would beat Oldham to keep the title race going into the final week of the season, Ferguson decided to simply not watch it and enjoy another of the great loves of his life. Golf.

A tearful Lavender is finding it all hard to take in.

'Twenty-six years. Twenty-six fuckin' years' is all he can say. The barman George Davies notice this and makes his way around the bar. He's also a red and whispers into Lavender's ear, 'Ferguson will be around the sixteenth or seventeenth green. Why don't you go and tell him he's won the league?' Lavender nods and smiles, 'Thanks George.'

'Champions Mike!' Exclaims George, 'Bloody champions!' The two men embrace.

Lavender heads off to his car. He drives up the path around the course until finally he sees two figures on the seventeenth. Lavender drives closer and his heart skips a beat. He heads over.

Alex Ferguson looks at his watch and son Mark starts to laugh, 'Forget it Dad, we'll know soon enough. Besides, if it was good news then somebody would have come out of the club to let us know.' Suddenly Lavender's car screeches to a halt nearby behind them. The startled Ferguson's turn around and sees him racing over. Red faced and out of breath, but smiling wide. He stops facing just a couple of yards away, 'Excuse me Mr

Ferguson,' says Lavender, 'I'm sorry to interrupt your game, but you, we are the champions. Oldham have won at Villa!'
Not certain at first whether this man is taking the mickey Ferguson stares hard at Lavender. But then he notices the tears in his eyes, 'You're absolutely sure about this son?' Asks Ferguson,
'Oh yes boss' grins Lavender, 'I've never been more sure about anything in my bloody life!'
Suddenly, Mark hugs his dad and Lavender thinks it best to just leave them alone. He heads back to the car. His moment in Manchester United legend forever immortalised as the man who broke the news to the man!
A grinning Ferguson takes off his cap and wipes his brow, 'Bloody hell!'
An emotional Mark tugs his arm, 'So, what happens now?'
'We win it again next year son.'
Mark starts to laugh, 'No, I'm talking about should we head for the eighteenth or go and celebrate?'
'Best go and tell your Mother first eh?'
They laugh and with Ferguson's arm around his son's shoulders they walk off back to the club house.

...*Monday 3rd May 1993*...

It was only fair that when dawn broke over the River Irwell on this day of dreams that the man in the sky should decree there should be sunshine.
That all beers should be drunk cold, that all songs should be sung loud.
That all tears shed should be tears of joy. That all things worn should be red.

And that all those we love should be hugged within an inch of their lives. Mother, fathers, brothers, sisters, wives and lovers. Those no longer with us put a scarlet ribbon on their gravestone so they can party too.
For it's been an eternity. Twenty-six long and lean years. But now there's a new word in Manchester. Not London, Leeds, Liverpool or Birmingham.
But Manchester. The home of the Industrial Revolution. LS Lowry, Alan Turing, Marks and Spencer. The city of the Busby Babes. Of Best, Law and Charlton...
And now of Cantona!

It's Monday 3rd May 1993, and a chant not sung for many a sun or moon can finally be shouted from the rooftops. Champions!
Across the city From Moston to Wythenshawe. From Sale to Shaw. Ardwick, Ancoats, Collyhurst and Newton Heath. All points north. On the council estates of Harpurhey and Blackley they are dancing in the streets. Toasting with strongbow and whisky chasers and half decent wine in Collyhurst.
The streets of Salford, that 'Dirty old town' signposted United red has simply gone mad! Stretford, Urmston and Flixton are out on the roads. Stick a traffic cone down, pull out the tables, crack open a beer and drink and drink to 'Eric the King. The leader of our football team!'
From the hostelries of Altrincham to the wine bars of Hale, Bowdon and Alderley Edge they raise their glasses in the air. The red, white and black flags across Manchester are not just flying high, they are covering the sky. The party has begun!

Amidst the chaotic revelry that has engulfed Manchester on this beautiful May Bank Holiday Monday, there still exists the small matter of a football match to be played at Old Trafford. Manchester United against Blackburn Rovers this evening in what is now nothing more than the supporting act of the champion's crowning.

A party twenty-six years in waiting and those with an invitation blessed.

Touts can name any price and many are doing so. If Jesus Christ was to return himself performing juggling, turning water to wine and curing lepers a ticket would be easier to come across.

From early morning the roads and streets around Old Trafford are crammed with excited supporters. Counting down the seconds to that glorious moment later on tonight when the trophy is presented in the stadium.

The hawkers arrive and set up shop. Finally, able to shift their chancer's arms, job lots of Tee shirts and baseball caps. Collateral damage from last season desperate climax to the league. These and those newly printed in the last twelve hours. Plus, scarves, flags, banners and cups.

All with one word inscribed.

As for those responsible on ending the curse and causing an entire city to jump in a barrel of beer, the players partied equally long and hard at Steve Bruce's house. What began as a small get together with close friends and neighbours swiftly grew into a full-scale celebration as team mates naturally migrated to their Captain's home. Soon, all were present and any thoughts of the next day's game disappeared. The unyielding pressure forever present in the closing months of the campaign giving way to one almighty blow out!

Last order didn't apply at the Bruce's.

Stood in the kitchen with Bryan Robson enjoying a quiet beer, the Captain looked through into the living room to see Giggs, Ince, Parker and many others at various points of no return. He smiled wide, 'God helps us against Blackburn Robbo. We're going to get bloody hammered 10-0 tomorrow!'

Nearing kick off next evening, hangovers have settled sufficiently for Alex Ferguson to name a full-strength team. In the dressing room he's gathered all his players and staff together. Ferguson stands in their midst as the crowd noise, their songs and chants echoes loud through the walls.

But as he begins you can hear a pin drop, 'I want you all to look around this room because without each and every one here we could not have won this league. Now you've all done absolutely marvellous. Aye, I'm bloody proud of every single one of you.'

He focuses his stare on the players. Many of them heavy eyed and still dog rough. Desperate not to catch the manager's eye. He smiles, 'Now, I'm not even going to ask what you lot got up to last night. I don't want to know.'

That said Ferguson's glance turns towards Steve Bruce, who puts his head down, but can't fail to hide a slight smile.

'But let me tell you I don't want this lot turning up here tonight and ruining it for everybody. Dalglish will have his players wound up and ready for a scrap, so if you're not up for it they'll turn us over. Now your fitness is good. Despite the rumours I've been hearing today and looking at the state of some of you.'

A few spluttered cough and embarrassed smiles as most players continue staring shamefaced at the floor.
'Whoever doesn't perform in the first half is coming off for Robbo in the second, so make sure you're on your game. And finally, this is one of the few occasions where you can just go out and enjoy it. So, express yourself. Soak it all up…But win!'
Laughter breaks out around the room. It's clear that despite winning the league defeat for this man can simply never be tolerated.

There have been many special nights under the Old Trafford floodlights. Wonderful atmospheres, spine chilling occasions, but as the cry goes out across the terraces, 'Bring on the champions' few have ever come near to matching or beating what is occurring here on this warm Mancunian summer's evening of Monday 3rd May 1993. Amongst the crowd, the flags, banners and scarves waving there are as many tears as smiles. Thoughts of those no longer present who didn't live to see this moment. Twenty-six years is an awful lot of funerals. United season tickets exist in families like DNA. The faces may change, even names, but the passion like Manchester United never dies.
The players led by Steve Bruce appear and are met with a wall of noise from the fortunate 40,447. They head into the centre-circle to wave and accept the acclaim of a rapturous red army. As Queens 'We are the champions' blasts out the home team break for a brief kick about. The anthems continue with a tribute to their latest hero and legend already in making.
'Oh Ah Cantona' begins and swiftly resonates from all parts of the stadium. Drunk on alcohol and euphoria an

ecstatic red choir are as one hailing their new king from across the channel. Cantona remains calm and cool. The trademark shirt collar up and ready for battle. His features etched in concentration for it's time to go to work.

As Alex Ferguson warned his team beforehand, Blackburn have turned up in a mood, not so much party spoiling, but more on the lines of putting a hand grenade in the punch bowl. United have started slowly with passes going astray all over the field. None in red appears capable of trapping a ball never mind create an opportunity. Even Cantona is affected, his first touch normally so sure, temporarily deserting him. Whereas Rovers are fast, hard tackling and seemingly intent on turning this Mancunian fiesta into a damp squib. On eight minutes midfielder Jason Wilcox plays a pass out wide for his full back Nicky Marker to cross low and Scottish international forward Kevin Gallagher lashes a sensation near-post effort past a stunned Schmeichel into the top corner.

On the ball hitting the net the roar of 'champions' starts up loud once more from the Old Trafford terraces to rouse their team. More importantly Ferguson heads down to the touchline, his face reddened with anger. A look that says more than a thousand threats and a message succinct and clear, 'Step it up or else.'

It's like the switching on of a light as United click in and start to resemble their true selves. The passing swift, incisive and slick with one man at its red heart. Cantona's radar is up and running. The runs of Hughes, Giggs and Sharpe are now being found by the Frenchman with the astute ease of a young child devouring an ice cream.

On twenty-one minutes Paul Ince is fouled and Ryan Giggs steps up from nearly thirty-yards, to flash a left footed free kick into the top right-hand corner past a stunned Bobby Mimms in the Blackburn net. Old Trafford explodes in delight at this wonderful goal by the prodigious Giggs.
Truly a moment worthy of a coronation.
Ferguson himself beams wide at this piece of supreme skill from the youngster who already has the footballing world drooling at his dancing feet. A boy wonder starting to remind many older supporters of a past United legend. A kid from Belfast whose lightning pace off the mark, bewildering dribbling and balletic grace and movement over the grass saw him illuminate not just countless grey Mancunian afternoons. But also cause hearts to burst, break and soar, both near and afar.
The word on Ryan Giggs is that even George Best rates him. Higher praise is hard to find.
Half time arrives and Ferguson as promised introduces Bryan Robson. The second period is one-way traffic as Manchester United now playing with a freedom of expression that comes only from knowing you're the best are producing some exquisite football. Not surprisingly Cantona is at the fore. Teasing and tormenting two Blackburn defenders in the penalty area before skipping past both and delivering an inch perfect pass for Robson to smash a ferocious fifteen-yard volley straight at Mimms, that nearly cuts him in two.

It's now a siege as on sixty-one minutes Cantona again is causing havoc. Looking for an opening, he produces a delicious slide pass that takes out three Rover's shirts for Paul Ince to race onto and fire low past Mimms from eight yards. A small cameo of the champion's season. Wonderfully vivid, a swiftness of mind and feet then rapier fast and ultimately deadly.

The class of 93.

In the dying seconds Cantona again beats two defenders on the edge of the penalty area and sets up Mark Hughes, only for him to be brought crashing to the ground. A free kick and there's just one Manchester United outfield player yet to score this season. As Old Trafford holds it breath, the big defender Gary Pallister is called for and wearing a huge smile he lumbers up field and casually lashes a right foot shot into the net that Mimms never sees. A perfect ending to what has been a sensational performance. Once the hangovers had shifted!

But now the moment all those with United in their heart have been waiting for…

On a star lit Mancunian evening in front of an emotionally charged and electrifying packed Old Trafford, Steve Bruce and Bryan Robson prepare together to lift high the Premiership trophy and officially signify the twenty-six-year drought is over. Hysteria, great joy and an overwhelming sense of relief fills the air. An albatross around the neck of all at Manchester United disguised as a Liver bird can finally be cast off.

Sat watching events unfold nearby where Bruce and Robson stand and wait is an elderly gentleman. Eight decades and three years old. He's forever and rightly immortalised in the legendary Spinners tribute song about the players lost at Munich. The Flowers of Manchester as 'The Father of this football team.' The old man in his thirties came to the club with a burnt-out ground, dying and on its knees after World War two.

Along with his assistant Jimmy Murphy they together built it into what United is today.

A worldwide phenomenon.

From the snow, blood-drenched runway of Munich to European cup glory ten years on. Then he retired and the walls to the kingdom crumbled. Manchester United fell from grace...Until now.

A smiling Sir Matt Busby watches on with tears in his eyes, but fiercely proud as amidst a thousand flashlights, blinding and illuminating this dark and memorable Mancunian night, Bruce and Robson lift together the measure of red dreams. Old Trafford erupts and United are back!

Each player follows and is handed the trophy to enormous cheers from a delirious and grateful crowd. But none more than the one ninth in line. When the name of Eric Cantona is mentioned over the tannoy the roars from the stands echo far away in northern skies. Andrei Kanchelskis passes to Cantona and as he lifts it above his head Old Trafford again self-ignites with noise and furore.

Watching on a smiling Alex Ferguson has the look of a proud father. His audacious gamble on Cantona now proving to be the work of a genius. The Frenchman's signing undoubtedly the catalyst that has brought about one of the greatest nights in the history of Manchester United.

THE KIDS ARE ALRIGHT

...Thursday 18th April 1995...

Eric Cantona begins the first of his 120 hours Community service at the Cliff. Manchester United's training ground. Not surprisingly the seagulls are out in force following the trawler with their long lens cameras. Scaling walls and watching on ladders. Journalist trying to sneak past or bribe security personnel to let them through. But none are biting, 'Stick your money up your fuckin' arse,' is heard muttered more than once.

'Just let Eric get on with it.'

It's been Cantona's own idea to coach local children from the Manchester area. There will be two-hour sessions twice a day for a month.

Some seven hundred boys and girls have been chosen. Taking this ultra-seriously Cantona has devised his own training schedule for the youngsters. He's determined to make a mark and in his own way start to pay back the loyalty this city has shown him after the events of Selhurst Park. The first amongst these arrive in a mini bus. A dozen 9-12-year olds from Ellesmere Park Juniors FC. All wearing United shirts and most with the Frenchman's name emblazoned on their back.

The excitement amongst them on the thought of meeting Cantona is giddy, verging towards meltdown! Few have slept. They are led into the Cliff gym where the coaching can take place away from prying media eyes.

A lone man stands with hands on hips in a United tracksuit waiting to greeting them. One of the boys shouts out, 'Look! It's Eric!'

He smiles toward them as in a mad charge they rush over and surround him. All jumping up and down and singing hardly surprisingly, 'Oh ah Cantona!'

Showing great patience and gentle humour Cantona sets about his task. He shows one youngster the best way to

finish. After the boy has shot wide and appears disconsolate, Cantona leans down and looking him in the eyes declares, 'Always concentrate on one corner of the goal my young friend.'
He points, 'Aim for that.'
Cantona stands up and throws him back the ball.
'Now' he says smiling, 'Let's try again.'
This time around the youngster smashes the ball low and accurate into the far corner of the goal. He turns and jumps into Cantona's arms.
The kids are alright…

THE PRIDE OF THORNTON HEATH (part two)

…Friday 3rd May 1995…

Back at Croydon Magistrates it's time for Crystal Palace supporter Matthew Simmons, Eric Cantona's 'alleged' victim to have his case heard in court. He stands fuming in front of three magistrates after just being found guilty on two charges of using threatening words and behaviour back on that infamous night under the Selhurst Park floodlights.
The court Prosecutor Jeffrey McCann (now acting against Simmons) is in the midst of wrapping up, 'On top of these charges I would also like to apply to the court for an exclusion order preventing Mr Simmons entering all football grounds'…
Then, in a moment of complete madness Simmons snaps and leaps to his feet. He jumps over a bench and karate kicks Mr McCann in the chest. Two policemen immediately race to grab hold of him.

Screaming abuse, a ranting Simmons is finally pulled away from the shocked prosecutor, 'I'm fuckin' innocent. I swear on the Bible it was that fuckin' French bastard'… Simmons is taken out of the courtroom in handcuffs and locked up to calm down. One of the policemen who rushed to McCann's aid is the same who looked after Eric Cantona, whilst he was held in the cell that Simmons now sits. Still raging with anger, he looks up towards the same officer who's smiling.

'What are you so fuckin' happy about?' Snarled Simmons, through the bars towards him.

'Just thinking about a good friend of mine,' replies the policeman.

Later that day Chairman of the Bench Mrs Mary Richards jails Simmons for seven days for contempt of court.

'Your violent outburst today was an obvious and serious contempt of court. We feel a term of custody is appropriate. You'll serve seven days and also be fined £500 and a further £200 costs in relation to your earlier charges. On top of this we are granting an excluding order requested by the prosecution that will see you banned from all football grounds for a period of twelve months.'

Lawyer Mr Adam Davis, saddled with the unfortunate task of defending Simmons, stands to speak, 'My client would like to deeply apologise to the court and to the members of the public and especially to Mr McCann for his regrettable actions here today. Mr Simmons has been under immense pressure and has suffered death threats since the Selhurst Park incident.

He has also been hospitalised twice as a result of severe panic attacks. In mitigation for the two offences of using threatening words and behaviour. I am sure you will bear in mind what happened to the other party in this matter. That Mr Simmons would not have found himself in the position he is in today, but for Mr Cantona's violent over the top reaction? In all I hope you will agree that these are thoroughly unique circumstances.'

Mr McCann now stands from his seat, `I am content to accept his apology and have no intention of pressing charges. But if Simmons thuggish behaviour has proved anything today, it's that Eric Cantona, whilst I don't approve thoroughly of his actions. I can now understand them.

Simmons glares at McCann with a look of utter loathing. McCann catches this and stares back, 'The feeling I can assure you is mutual young man.'

BATTLE IN THE EAST END

…Sunday 14th May 1995…

It's the final line in what has been a dramatic season's tale. Schmeichel, Neville, Bruce, Pallister, Irwin, Butt, Keane, Ince, Sharpe, Cole and McClair.

The tension unbearable and the stakes never higher as the fight for the title has come down to the last game. As it stands Blackburn Rovers will be crowned champions if circumstances don't change.

Manchester United are in the East End at Upton Park. A viper's nest where they are welcomed with all the warmth of an Israeli tank on the streets of Gaza's West Bank. At half time it's 1-0 to West Ham and the visitors have been outplayed by a Hammer's team free of relegation fears and enjoying torturing their northern

visitors. Raising their game to a level not witnessed in the home of jellied eels and the Queen Vic all season.
Older West Ham fans remember 1967, when United fans turned up in their tens of thousands to witness a title triumph and turn the streets around Upton Park into a Mancunian fiesta. Boot boys. Smashed bottles, bricks and coins. A battleground, one compared by those present to Hitler's Luftwaffe attempts to raze the area to the ground during the Blitz.
This time with the mood of defiance and expectation rising from Upton Park terraces, it was clear their team wouldn't be allowed not to give everything and more to prevent Manchester United players once more doing a victory dance on their hallowed turf.
And so far Harry Rednapp's men haven't let them down. Meanwhile, at Anfield where Blackburn Rovers were expected by many to be all but handed the trophy by Liverpool, Dalglish's men lead by a single Alan Shearer goal. Jack Walker's dream is close to fruition, but it's been no easy ride for the cash rich, great old Lancashire club.
Mancunian fears of a Liverpool surrender have not occurred with the Merseysiders giving a great account of themselves and not lying down. Made all the more surprising because of former Liverpool idol Kenny Dalglish's emotional return as Rover's manager. Many koppites are adorning Blackburn scarves. Such is their hatred of United and vice versa. For it's a poisonous rivalry that transcends so much more than just football. But one that has not today affected matters on the pitch.

In the United dressing room Ferguson fumes. His team appears to have given up and for him that's simply unacceptable. He stands in the middle of the floor, gathering thoughts. The players daren't meet his eyes, for they can sense what's coming.

'Right listen up, where's my fuckin' team gone? Because that wasn't Manchester United I've just watched out there. All the hard work you've put in this season is going down the drain. Is this how you want it all to end? A fuckin' surrender in the East End against a side who aren't fit to tie your boot laces? You don't even have to perform at your best to beat this lot.

For these stopping Manchester United winning the title is the biggest medal they will ever have to pin on their fuckin' chests.

Whereas you?

You're born winners. Otherwise you wouldn't be sat here today with a red devil on your shirt. All I ask is you go back out there and justify the trust that me, the board and the millions of United supporters put in you.

On days like this it's not about the money or the glamour. This is all about pride. Now we can't do anything about what's going on at Anfield. Blackburn could score another four in the second half and win 5-0, but I couldn't care less. If it's not to be our day, then so be it. But I want us going down giving everything. Spitting blood, screaming into the fuckin' wind as the title slips away. Let them carry us off on our shields.

But don't you dare go down without a fight…

Don't you fuckin' dare!

All I want from you, my team. My Manchester United is a second half performance that our lot who've travelled to watch you today can say in years to come. Oh, we may not have won the league, but do you know what. I was

there at Upton Park for that second half when United came out and took my fuckin' breath away. Okay?'
By now all eyes are locked on Ferguson.
He claps his hands together, 'So, come on! Wake up and let's show the world how real champions go about their jobs. Not the kick and rush of Blackburn Rovers, but with the passion, skill and flair our history demands. Let's go out and do it the Manchester United way!'
The second begins and its swiftly obvious Alex Ferguson's half time words are having an instant effect on his team. Suddenly the ball is being passed superbly around amongst the away team and West Ham players are chasing shadows. A Roy Keane cross is met superbly by the head of Lee Sharpe and his flying header is tipped spectacularly around the post by home keeper Ludo Miklosko. United have woken up.
Midfielder Paul Ince, back in a place where he's hated like no other is once more driving forward. On fifty-seven minutes Andy Cole wins a free kick which is hoisted into the West Ham penalty area by Gary Neville. Brian McClair leaps high and powers a glancing header past Miklosko and suddenly its game and title back on! Ferguson and Brian Kidd are off the bench punching the air.
They are coming again.
A Denis Irwin corner is cleared, only to be acrobatically put back in to the box by Ince with an overhead kick. From six yards out McClair swoops and meets it on the volley to flash the ball high over the bar. It's nerve-wracking, dramatic stuff!
Behind the goal United fans are once more starting to believe. But they also desperately need help from

elsewhere. And from a sworn enemy whom in normal circumstance wouldn't hand them an umbrella in a storm. Once more the dynamic Ince, to a cascade of boos runs straight at the heart of the West Ham defence and is brought crashing to the ground.

From twenty-five yards Irwin steps up and blasts a swerving free kick inches wide…It's a siege, nothing less.

Suddenly, as United earn another corner a huge unexpected roar erupts from amongst their supporters. News comes through on the radio that Liverpool's John Barnes has equalised against Blackburn!

Ferguson looks quizzically towards a steward who confirms this. A large smile comes on his face. Kidd's also, 'Now it's interesting Kiddo' says Ferguson. As he ruffles his assistant's hair, 'Let's see what Uncle Jack's lot are made of.'

Word reaches the United players that the race for a third successive title is back on. One more goal and their hold on the trophy will remain tight. The West Ham fans are worried. Their forever blowing bubbles long drifted away as the East End terraces have suddenly lost their bark and bite. For the real Manchester United have now turned up and the Hammers are hanging on by the most slender of threads.

Lee Sharpe's corner is cleared, only for him to pick up the loose ball. Again, Sharpe crosses and a flashing header from Mark Hughes is foiled by a magnificent leap from Miklosko, who turns it around the post.

An astonishing save!

Keane is replaced by the precociously talented flame-haired Paul Scholes. Undoubtedly a future United superstar. The Langley born Scholes takes up a position high in the field. Looking to drop a last grenade in the short time that remains. Meanwhile, going hell for leather Ferguson has gone just two at the back. Three minutes to play, nerves are shredded, the atmosphere torrid, emotional and utterly gripping.

Scholes chests the ball down on the edge of the penalty area. His sublime pass cuts open the home defence to leave Andy Cole with just Miklosko to beat. On the United bench hearts skip a beat as Cole hits it instantly but only straight at the keeper. Surely that's the chance and its now gone begging?

An extraordinary opportunity for Cole to cement his place in United folklore, but he's fluffed his lines badly. And he knows it.

Ferguson shouts at the referee to grab his attention. He taps his watch. The message clear, 'You better add some fuckin' time on!'

The ball is bouncing around the West Ham box like pinball. United have forced the home side so far back they are now defending on their own six-yard line. A scramble ensues once more. The balls again fall loose to Andy Cole with just the keeper to beat. A chance of redemption, heaven sent, but he haplessly side-foots it weakly into Miklosko's chest…

The ghost of Cantona haunting the Old Trafford club. As a devastated Cole shakes his head the ball is again hurtling around the West Ham box. Hughes' shot is blocked, as is Ince's. Claret and blue shirts are throwing themselves in front of everything. It's like the Alamo without the Mexicans.

Once more the ball is cleared and picked up by Scholes. He looks to ping in a cross, only for a West Ham boot to hammer it towards the halfway line. There stands Peter

Schmeichel. He kicks the ball back and a relieved Miklosko grasps and so gratefully holds it in his arms. The cheers from the East End are delirious and borne of relief. We are two minutes into three of added stoppage time. United are still going strong, Gary Neville's long throw causes mayhem in the penalty area before being hacked clear. And then a thunderous roar from the home fans,

It's over.

The final whistle signalling the end of Manchester United's reign as champions of England. But it's been a truly heroic second half effort. The last stand Ferguson demanded has been beyond even his wildest hopes.

The players go across to their supporters who warmly applaud their magnificent efforts. Chances have been made aplenty by United and horribly squandered. None more than Andy Cole who when his team really needed him has fell well short of the standard required.

Kidd goes across to Ferguson, 'Brace yourself Gaffer. You're not going to believe this but Liverpool are winning!'

'Not our year Kiddo,' smiles Ferguson, 'Just wasn't meant to be'…

Later that Sunday evening, at a now deserted Upton Park, a lone banner lies on the floor in the stand which was filled with Manchester United supporters only a short time ago. It's a French tricolor with a picture of a certain Frenchman absent this day. Never was his presence missed more.

Six days later at Wembley stadium, a weary looking Manchester United are beaten 1-0 by Everton in the FA Cup Final. A season that promised so much has evaporated to dust. The events of Wednesday 25th January ultimately overwhelming and returning to haunt them. The suspension of Eric Cantona, whom Alex Ferguson often referred to as their 'Can Opener' has dealt them a critical blow. At the final hurdle when trophies are handed out and a touch of Gallic gold dust is required to unlock the tightest and most grim defences.

A mesmeric flick or sleight of foot to dazzle and then destroy has been sadly lacking. The last week proving beyond all doubts how vital Eric Cantona was, and still is to Manchester United.

And that whatever happens they must ensure he remains at Old Trafford.

But faraway in northern Italy. In Milan, the self-styled city of culture and sophistication. Plans are already underfoot to lure the Frenchman away and into the blue/black of the Nerazzurri. FC Internazionale Milano and Massimo Moratti are watching…And waiting.

WELCOME TO PARIS

…Saturday 25th July 1995…

A new season is dawning and in order to up Eric Cantona's match fitness and ensure he still feels part of the team, Alex Ferguson has organised a low key, behind closed doors friendly against Rochdale.

All has gone well and Cantona has shown his manager enough to suggest that when the ban finally runs out on 30th September, he'll be ready to go again.

On leaving the pitch at the Cliff, Ferguson pulls him to one side, 'How are you feeling Eric?'

'I feel great. Like I can breathe again.'

Ferguson smiles, 'I need you firing and to hit the ground running when the times comes son. These boys, Scholes, Butt, Beckham, the Neville's, they worship the ground you walk on. All will be first team players this year. I want you to lead them. This summer we've lost Ince, Hughes and it's looking like Kanchelskis is going also. That's a big hit for any club. Even one like ours.'
Cantona nods. He appears in deep thought and for a moment says nothing. Then he turns and looks Ferguson straight in the eyes, 'I will be ready.'
Ferguson grins wide and puts an arm around his shoulders, 'Good lad.'
The two walk off…

…Thursday 30th July 1995…

Spokesman Mike Parry stands before a host of journalists on the steps of Lancaster Gate. FA headquarters. He prepares to read the most extraordinary, petty and vindictive statement. Word has reached Lancaster Gate of the friendly game between Manchester United and Rochdale at the Cliff. But, more significantly of Eric Cantona's involvement. Immediately contact is made with various newspapers, radio, television and satellites outlets. The message clear and succinct:
'It's in relation to a certain Frenchman so make sure you send somebody, because you don't want to miss out on this!' The hunt is on again
Parry begins, 'We've been made aware of the fact that Eric Cantona has taken part in a football match and have written to Manchester United asking for their observations. And to inquire under what sort of conditions this match was played. The ban imposed on

Cantona said that he should be suspended from all football activities until the beginning of October, so we assume United have a plausible explanation. We'd just like to know what it is and to clear the matter up.'

If Parry is expecting a tidal wave of excitement from his gathered audience, it appears he's going to be massively disappointed.

'Is that the big news you promised us Mike?' Asks the man from The Sun. 'A bloody practice match watched by one man and his dog and you want to crucify him for it?' The Sky camera crew and reporter are already packing to go. The reporter pissed off, 'If that's the best you've got Mike, you've wasted our time.'

A heavily sweating Parry can't believe the bad reaction to his statement. Clearly someone in the hallways of power behind him has underestimated the amount of support there now exists for Cantona in the media.

'But he could have broken the FA rules? Surely you can see the huge significance of this statement chaps?'

'Not really' replies the man from The Mail.

'Get a life Parry' shouts the man from The Mirror.

'This is a bloody joke. That particular trawler has already sailed.'

But for Eric Cantona this is the last straw. He's driving with Jean Jacques Bertrand alongside him when this is announced on the radio. Cantona stops and pulls his car up to the side of the road. He explodes in anger!

'These fucking people are never going to leave me alone until I walk away. I was wrong with what I said at the press conference. They are more like leeches than seagulls. Very well, they want rid of me, well I want rid of them. They can have their way.'

Cantona is close to tears. He turns to Bertrand, 'Contact United. Tell them I am sorry but I wish for a transfer. I feel it will be best for both them and me if I wasn't around anymore. If these people will be so vindictive as to stop me kicking a ball around in a game like that. Then they are never going to change. Every time I look at someone wrong they are going to come after me. So, what is the point of staying in England?'

'Are you sure about this Eric? 'Asks Bertrand.

'Because if you are I can ring Moratti at Inter and by next weekend you and your family could be living in Milan. But it's your call. Manchester and Ferguson in particular have been good to you'

'No,' replies Cantona. 'A clean cut is best for all. In time somebody else will come along and the United fans will sing their name and forget about me.'

Bertrand doesn't look so convinced. But it's his job to do as a client asks. Even if it's one of your best friends and you feel he may be acting more on impulse than on reason. But, then again. This is Cantona.

'Very well then if that's what you want I'll ring Martin Edwards and we will fax an official transfer request. Through whether they accept it is something else.'

Cantona is clearly tormented on letting down his manager. He knows of the trust that Ferguson was set to place in him for the forthcoming season. Of how he's rescued his career. Stood by when others would prefer to see him burnt at the stake. But his family must come first. Isabelle has given birth to their second child. A baby girl Josephine. The thoughts of losing the friendship of such a great man will forever haunt him, but blood must always come first. Although it will break not only Cantona's heart but millions of reds also,

Milan is calling.

The next few days sees in print, radio and on screen a massive display of support for Eric Cantona. Public revulsion for the FA's small minded and indeed what appears bullying rebounds in spectacular manner.
So much that they are forced to release another statement. Only this time, retreating faster than a man with a water pistol trying to take on a tank.
Again, spokesman Mike Parry stands on the steps of Lancaster Gate before an invited audience. His features glum. Knowing he's not so much fire-fighting, but rolling around naked in the ashes.
'What is it this time Mike? 'Asks the man from the Express. 'Has Cantona farted in public?'
A clearly embarrassed Parry glares at him, 'Okay then,' he sighs, 'Shall we get this over with.' Parry starts to read off a small sheet of paper:
'The Football Association have received a response from Manchester United in regard to our inquiry about Eric Cantona. We are entirely satisfied with their explanation and have conveyed this to the club. So far as we are concerned the matter is now closed.'
'Has Alex Ferguson been in touch with the FA Mike?' Asks the man from the Daily Star.
'You could say that.'
'And what exactly did he say?'
Parry smiles, 'I couldn't possibly comment'…

Alex Ferguson is staying at the Savoy in London for a book promotion when he first hears rumours through a journalist of Eric Cantona's transfer request. His initial thoughts are to dismiss it. But for peace of mind

Ferguson decides to ring Martin Edwards from his hotel room phone. What he's told shocks him rigid.

'He's going Alex. Eric's mind is made up. This fuss over the Rochdale game has tipped him over the edge. I'm afraid we've lost him. Besides matters are moving fast. I've already had Inter on putting in a bid for £4.5 million.'

'Turn it down Martin,' replies Ferguson. 'Let me speak to him.'

'Well if there's anybody can make him stay it's you. Good luck.' Edwards hangs up and Ferguson immediately rings Jean Jacques Bertrand.

He answers.

'Where is he Jean?'

'Alex you're wasting your time. Eric has already left the country. He is in Paris. The deal with Inter is done. All they need now is his signature.'

'Believe me without my blessing Jean, Eric is going nowhere. He's got three years left on his contract and I will make him sit on the bench for that time rather than sell him.'

'You don't believe that Alex,' replies Bertrand. 'How can you honestly believe me too?'

Bertrand is right. Ferguson is bluffing. He thinks too much of Cantona to ever do such a thing, 'Jean please. After what we've been through together. I deserve at least the chance to put my case. And if Eric still wishes to leave once we've spoken? Fair enough. He can go with my blessing.' Unbeknown to Ferguson, Cantona is with Bertrand and has been listening in. He nods across.

'Very well' says Bertrand to Ferguson, 'When can you come over?'

'I'm on my way now' says the Scotsman, 'I'll ring when I reach Paris.' That said Ferguson puts down the phone. Bertrand looks across at Cantona and smiles, 'He's coming. Rather you than me my friend!'

Cantona shakes his head, 'Can you arrange everything? At least I owe the boss a decent meal and a few bottles of fine red before he returns home to Manchester empty handed and disappointed.'

'Of course,' replies a grinning Bertrand. 'But don't be sure he'll be going back to England on his own. He is a remarkable man and very persuasive is this boss of yours.'

'He won't change my mind Jean,' he replies.

'When Cantona's mind is made up that is it.'

Still Bertrand is grinning at him, 'Of course Eric. I keep forgetting you are Le God'

Cantona smiles, 'I know what you are thinking. There is a Scottish hurricane heading our way.'

'Oh no, not our way' replies Bertrand, 'He is coming for you my friend!'

…Wednesday 9th August…

On arriving at Paris's Charles De Gaulle airport, Alex Ferguson makes the telephone call to Bertrand.

He answers, 'Hi Alex. Listen carefully. I've booked you into the Georges V hotel near the Champ-Elysee. Get a taxi straight there and wait for a telephone call. We have to be really careful because the Paparazzi have got word that Eric is in Paris.'

Ferguson does as Bertrand asks. He books himself in and waits patiently in the hotel bedroom to be contacted. At 8pm the phone starts to ring.

It's Bertrand.
He laughs, 'Please excuse all the James Bond antics. In five minutes a porter will knock on your door. Please follow him and he will bring you to me.'
'Don't worry' smiles Ferguson, 'I'm just enjoying my Martini as we speak. Shaken not stirred.'
There's a knock at the door and Ferguson goes to answer. Stood there is a hotel porter. A small bald-headed man with a friendly face, 'Mr Ferguson, my name is Louie. I am a friend of Jean Jacques Bertrand. Can you come with me please?' The two men make their way through a host of long, winding corridors and down a back staircase that leads into the kitchens. There, startled chefs in their big white hats and smartly attired uniformed waiters watch on in astonishment as the manager of the famous Manchester United and their very own Louie walk past. Ferguson smiles a greeting and they return it.
Finally, they reach a fire door exit which Louie opens. It leads into an alleyway. There waiting for them is a man on a Harley Davidson motorbike wearing a helmet and carrying another in his arms.
He takes it off and it's Bertrand smiling wide.
'Good evening Mr Bond!' Bertrand passes Ferguson the spare helmet. The Scotsman shakes hands with Louis, 'Thank you.'
'No problem Mr Ferguson. One day I shall tell my grandchildren about this day!'
Ferguson puts on the helmet and climbs on the pillion behind Bertrand, 'Hold on tight Alex,' he says, before the bike roars up and they swiftly disappear into the Parisian backstreets. For fifteen minutes with Ferguson clinging on for dear life Bertrand rides like a madman. Finally, they arrive at their destination. A small family restaurant

hidden away from the tourists in a quiet backstreet called L'Ami.

Ferguson steps off the motor bike and removes his helmet. His face windswept, reddened and shaken by the journey. Bertrand takes off his also. He's still smiling wide, 'Come, Eric is waiting for you inside. The men walk across to the restaurant.

'The owner is also a good friend of ours,' says Bertrand. 'He has agreed to close the place to the public tonight, so you can both have it to yourselves. Just Eric, the owner and chef. And a wonderful wine cellar Alex.'

Bertrand stops walking and faces Ferguson, 'I know you two are close and that he thinks of you as a second father. But I really do fear his mind is made up. Just promise me one thing. If you don't succeed. Please just shake his hand and tell him you understand. For I know him better than most people. It will break Eric's heart if he believes you no longer value his friendship.'

Ferguson nods.

'Thank you Alex,' says Bertrand, 'Now let us go say hello to Monsieur Cantona!'

Inside it's empty except for one man sat at a table. A smiling Cantona stands on seeing Ferguson and Bertrand. They walk across to him and Cantona kisses each of them on both cheeks. He points to a chair, 'Please sit down boss.' Ferguson does so. He pours himself a large glass of red wine already on the table and one for Cantona too.

'Okay then' says Bertrand, 'I know you two have a lot to talk over. I will leave you alone. Alex, when you have finished please ring me and I shall come and pick you up.'

'Oh no you bloody won't,' replies Ferguson. 'I'll get a taxi! The man is a lunatic Eric. He thinks he's Evil bloody Knievel!'
They all laugh.
A smiling Bertrand winks at them and heads out the door whilst Cantona sits back down facing Ferguson.
'Are you hungry boss? I can go and tell the manager to bring some food. The lemon sole here is delicious.'
'Anything but Italian for me,' replies Ferguson.
Cantona tries hard to not smile. He takes a sip of wine then looks at his manager, 'It is wonderful to see you boss. Always, but nothing you can say will change my mind. They will never leave me alone in England, so I am going to Milan. It is for the best.'
'You're going to be my Captain, Eric.'
'Boss please, I'…
'No, listen to me,' says Ferguson. 'This isn't you. The Cantona I know would run head first into a storm rather than away from it. If you leave United now everything we've done together will lose a bit of its magic. Oh, it will be in the record books, but there's still so much more to do son. Our journey is only halfway. These boys I have waiting to come through. They are talented beyond their years. Beckham, Scholes, but they need a steady hand. I can shout and bawl from the touchline and put an arm around them in the dressing room. But I need a leader out there on the pitch. Someone who they respect and will listen to in the heat of battle at Anfield or Highbury.
Someone who they love Eric. Someone like you.'
Ferguson smiles, 'I need a Napoleon to organise my troops.' He starts to laugh, 'Did you know young Scholes still has a huge poster of you on his bedroom wall? That

little fella is going to be a legend at this club. He has a temper to match his red hair. Aye, a nasty little so and so, but I swear the boy possesses a touch and eye for a pass that takes your breath away. He could be your sorcerer's apprentice. And with you, Scholes and the others. Beckham, Butt, Giggs, the Neville's. We are going to dominate for years to come.
'But only with you by their side to lead. What do you say?'
Cantona finishes a glass of wine. He refills his and then Ferguson's. 'Before you came here tonight I told myself whatever this man says or does to try and convince me to stay at Manchester United, it will not be enough. That no matter how bad I feel, I will stay strong and not change my mind. Which is why I must thank you from the bottom of my heart for coming, but still refuse. I have become a hate figure in your country and I can never promise you that what erupted in me at Selhurst Park will not happen at Anfield or Goodison. Or Leeds.
I am who God made me boss. Once the whistle blows again they will be howling like jackals and my every move will be watched like no other. I will try to control the demons, but they will always be there. And it only takes one moment of weakness and everything will be over. I am sorry that your journey has been wasted. But the answer must remain. No.'
Cantona feels terrible, but when he looks at Ferguson he's smiling wide, 'Let's try some of that Lemon sole!' The night goes on and the conversation almost inevitably returns to football and a subject close to the hearts of both men. The great teams and players.
Ferguson is in his element, 'The Real Madrid of the fifties and early sixties are the finest team I've ever seen

Eric. I was there at Hampden Park when they beat Eintracht Frankfurt 7-3. Di Stefano, Gento and Puskas. Absolute magicians. Then there was Del Sol and Canario. Those boys could catch pigeons. All wonderful names, magnificent players, but even such talent needed a leader. A conductor for the orchestra whose baton would wave and the magic would begin. And that man was Alfredo Di Stefano. The Blond Arrow.'

Ferguson grins wide as Cantona re-fills their drinks.

He continues on, 'They said Alfredo was an arrogant so and so. A pompous sod. Nobody could tell him what to do. A Generalissimo they called him in the dressing room apparently. Another Franco! But Alfredo didn't care. For he knew his worth to the team. He ran and scored more goals than anybody else. And so, he demanded respect. Not just on the pitch, but off it. By his own fans and others. And with that came six European cups and a grand place at the top table in the history of the game.'

Cantona listens on in awe as his manager speaks.

I want you to be my Di Stefano Eric,' smiles Ferguson, 'I want you to be my conductor.'

'You never give up do you boss?'

'Look,' says Ferguson, 'I understand the worries about the reaction that awaits when you start playing again. I'm not going to bullshit you Eric, there are times when you are going to get dog's abuse. They are going to be screaming vile rubbish. Hostile, revolting chants calling you and yours. I get it too. We all do. 'Anyone but United?' You've heard the phrase. Success breeds jealousy in England and they can't handle it. It'll get worse because we're going to get better. And if you stay they are going to scream even louder because you son. Whether you like it or not have a gift to set fire to the

Manchester rain. You admitted that yourself and that ultimately is what United are all about.'

Cantona stares at Ferguson. For a moment saying nothing and then he smiles wide, 'Okay, I will stay. But I can only promise that I will try with everything in my heart to make this work. If it doesn't, for whatever reason. We part as friends. A deal?'

A grinning Ferguson raises his glass and they toast.

'A deal'…

RETURN OF THE KING

…Sunday 1st October 1995…

At Old Trafford the moment Manchester United fans across the world have dreamed about for 248 days finally arrives and of all teams to face?

Those with a Liver bird on their chest.

Liverpool have travelled the short distance along the East Lancs Road to Manchester and Old Trafford. The Scousers are coming and like a jilted ex arriving at an old girlfriend's wedding day with bad tidings, they are determined to ruin the homecoming party.

Along Sir Matt Busby way, the vendors, hawkers and fanzine sellers gather trying to shift all things Cantona. Flags, banners, Tee-shirts, scarves and magazines. All adorned with the name and face of their returning hero. Sky television cameras are on the forecourt filming supporters showing off Cantona's name emblazoned on the back of their shirts.

Due to extension work being done on a new stand the capacity has been cut to 34,000, but there are thousands more content to just mill around until kick off, then head away to watch the match on television in nearby pubs. Inside the stadium hundreds of journalists from across the world are already entrenched in the press box, whilst 108 television camera crews are set up in place around the pitch.

As the grandstands rapidly fill up the stadium tannoy blasts out the 'Magnificent Seven' movie theme. Drowning out any verbal sparring between the United and Liverpool supporters. Mocking chants, brutal sick and derisory. Shankly and Busby songs. Blinded by tear gas. Munich and Hillsborough. Burning bonfires. Manc scum, Scouse bastards. A rivalry infected with no rules or lines in the sand. A raging light that will never go out. Manchester-Liverpool. Welcome to the north.

In the United dressing room Eric Cantona sits quietly next to Peter Schmeichel. The big Dane senses his friend just needs a little privacy at this time, so he lets him be. Around them there's an air of nervous intensity. Excitement and anticipation dipped in fear.

The final words of their manager Alex Ferguson's team speech from just a short while ago still ringing loud in the players ears, 'Don't you dare fuckin' lose to this lot!' There's also laughter, joking and plenty of mickey-taking. Gorton born youngster Nicky Butt is mercilessly pillaring the seriously, strait laced football, United-obsessed Neville brothers Gary and Philip. Aided and abetted in this by Ryan Giggs.

Centre halves Steve Bruce and Gary Pallister nicknamed 'Dolly and Daydream' by Ferguson are sat together watching the television, as yet another Cantona image flashes up, 'Bloody hell Eric,' shouts out a smiling

Bruce. 'You're on telly more than Coronation Street mate!'

Cantona laughs, they all do. Delighted to have their talisman back.

Roy Keane comes and sits down beside him, 'If any of those Scouse bastards start trying to wind you up today Eric, leave them to me okay? You walk away.'

Cantona nods his thanks as a smiling Keane stands and goes to get changed. Brian Kidd is alongside Andy Cole. He puts an arm around the nervous looking centre-forward. Still he thinks to prove himself to his United peers and supporters. 'If you get a chance today Coley, don't think just hit it okay? The boss thinks you're good enough, I think you're a fuckin' star, but you. You've got to believe you belong in the red shirt. Alright lad?'

Cole smiles and nods as Kidd ruffles his hair, 'Good man.'

. The bell sounds for the players to line up in the tunnel. 'Right come on boys,' bellows Bruce clapping his hands together. 'Let's go and murder this lot!'

As Cantona stands and puts up his collar the others are already making their way out of the changing room. The kitman Norman Davies comes across, 'Eric can I have a quick word? I just want you to know that your kit has never come out of the skip. I've never thought, well Eric's banned so I'll leave the shirt in the laundry. I've carried it all over with me. It's really good to have you back big fella. And as far as I'm concerned you were always with us.' Cantona embraces the tearful Davies. In the tunnel Ferguson makes his way down the line of United players where Cantona is standing last.

'How do you feel Eric?'

He smiles wide, 'Like I've come home.'

A pulsating Old Trafford holds its breath as a sea of French tricolors fly in their thousands across the terraces. A stadium drenched blue, white and red close to a collective meltdown. United supporters have been patient and loyal, but are desperate now to witness with their own eyes the return of the king.
To an ever increasing, deafening crescendo of noise both teams head up through the tunnel. It's almost time. Steve Bruce, Peter Schmeichel, Phil Neville, Gary Neville, Ryan Giggs, Gary, Pallister, Lee Sharpe, Nicky Butt, Andy Cole, Roy Keane and following behind the boy from Marseille. An adopted Mancunian and king not just for the day but for as long as the red flag flies. With eyes focused Cantona walks ever faster. He's business-like now, adjusting the collar for it's time to go back to work as once more he enters into sunlight and Old Trafford goes mad!
Sixty-seven seconds into the match and Eric Cantona is rampaging down Liverpool's left-hand side. Roared on by the crowd Cantona crosses into the box. The ball isn't cleared, falls loose and is finally latched upon by Nicky Butt who fires in a shot past goalkeeper David James. 1-0 to United and Cantona's name resonates loud around the stadium. It's like he's never been away!...

EPILOGUE

…Saturday 11th May 1996…

Wembley Stadium: FA Cup Final: Six minutes remain of what has been a brutally tight match between these worst of enemies, Manchester United and Liverpool. United are going for a league and cup double after hunting down

Kevin Keegan's Newcastle since Christmas and ultimately 'loving it' when the Geordies collapsed. Now, as extra time looms and even penalties come to mind the champions have a corner.

David Beckham swings it in only for the ball to be headed clear and fall on the edge of the penalty area. As it drops a certain Frenchman adjusts his body and with wonderful technique despatches a volley that flies past Liverpool goalkeeper David James into the back of the net.

Cue hysteria amidst the Manchester United fans behind that goal!

In one moment of genius Eric Cantona has surely proved the difference and secured yet another league and cup double. United's second in three years. A song etched with a strong Mancunian accent resonates loud over the grand old terraces of Wembley stadium. One that will be passed from grandfather to father to son and on and on...

'Oh, Ah Cantona!'

THE END

C30
DANCING WITH TEARS IN RED EYES
(Barcelona 1999)
The time was way past midnight when the last light was dimmed in the Nou Camp. High above the skies over Barcelona glittered with stars. Across the city there were riotous celebrations. The unmistakable tones of Mancunian accents rang out in tribute to the memory of the man known as the Father of their football club. For 26th May was the birthday of Sir Matt Busby and in his honour thousands of bleary eyed, drunken, ecstatic United fans sung boisterous renditions of 'Happy Birthday' to Sir Matt. Many were convinced that it was divine intervention on his part which finally brought the Germans to their knees.

'With Manchester United it is never over until the fat lady has had a heart attack.'
 Hugh McIlvanney

Wednesday 26th May 1999, a data forever etched in Manchester United folklore. Manchester airport was decked out in red white and black. Thousands prepared to make the pilgrimage to Barcelona. The charter flights hurtled off the runway in the direction of Spain. Already countless reds were descending upon Catalonia from across the continent and indeed the world. They came drawn as if by an invisible cord to the Nou Comp: all with one wish only-to see their team crowned European champions. Thirty-one years was a long time to wait for a club such as theirs. Bobby Charlton gave a rallying call. He declared that, 'It is time we put something on the table again.' Hopes and expectations were high.

However, there were many also that feared the worse. A double was already claimed. Surely it was asking too much for the Gods of football to grant them yet more glory? Bayern Munich were not coming down to Barcelona to lie down and die. They themselves were on course for a historic treble. Ottmar Hitzfeld had a good record against Alex Ferguson. It was he who had masterminded Borussia Dortmund's semi-final triumph against United two years previously. Hitzfeld felt his tactics were good enough to thwart the Mancunian's attacking instincts.

He placed huge faith in his defensive players. Andy Cole and Dwight Yorke would be shackled by Thomas Linke and the Ghanaian international Samuel Kuffour. Whilst his wing-backs Markus Babbel and Michael Tarnat would be expected to tame the threat of Ryan Giggs and David Beckham. Tidying up behind these four would be the unmistakable features of the legendary Lothar Matthaus.

During his exceptional career thirty-eight-year-old Matthaus had won every honour in the game. Everything that is except the European Champions cup. Barcelona would undoubtedly be his last chance to put this right. Matthaus was not about to let such an opportunity pass. The man every English football supporter loved to hate, but secretly admired, prepared to bring back home to Munich a fourth European cup. And nothing and no one was going to stand in his way. Little did Lothar Matthaus realise what lay in store for him and his team.

The night before the final Alex Ferguson took United's last training session wearing a replica shirt of the 1968 European cup winning team. It was a poignant act on Ferguson's part and showed his knowledge of just what this competition meant to Manchester United and their supporters. This was a club steeped in the history and tradition of this magnificent trophy. A trophy they had in the past spilt blood in their efforts to win. The loss of the 'Babes' on that infamous Munich runway in Southern Germany still cut deep into the emotions of all connected with the club. The final would also fall on the 90th birthday of Sir Matt Busby. Ferguson, more than any other was viewed as a worthy successor to Busby.

His inclination to give youth its fling bore more than a passing resemblance to Sir Matt's way of doing things. For Edwards, Colman, Pegg, Whelan and Charlton, read Beckham, Giggs, Butt, Scholes and Neville. Busby's 'Babes' never got the chance to win the European cup. Fate decreed it was not to be. Come kick off in the Nou Camp, Alex Ferguson would ensure that his Manchester United were playing for more than a simple trophy. They would be playing for their history. As birthday presents go it would suit Sir Matt Busby and his boys quite nicely if they were to succeed. Make no mistake,
they would be watching.

The loss of Roy Keane and Paul Scholes to suspension forced Ferguson into desperate measures. Beckham came in from the wing to cover his Irish Captain's absence, whilst Giggs would switch wings and Jespar Blomqvist would play on the left. He was convinced his team possessed sufficient firepower to counteract losing two such influential players. Although a huge gamble it was one in which Ferguson felt justified. Besides, if the match was not going according to plan he could always call on the talents of Teddy Sheringham and a Norwegian goal scoring machine called Ole Gunnar Solskjaer to come off the bench. For the man born at 667 Govan Road, immortality beckoned. Fifty-seven years previous on 31st December 1941, the city of Glasgow had given birth to Alex Ferguson. Now, in the early Catalan evening, the Nou Camp, daubed three-quarters blood red with the legions of United followers prepared to give birth to his legend.

The pre-match entertainment laid on by Barcelona was quite surreal. A worryingly overweight Montserrat Caballe was ferried onto the pitch by a golf buggy to perform a rather disturbing duet with the deceased Freddie Mercury. Freddie appeared from the stars courtesy of a gigantic video screen. Together they belted out their classic hit 'Barcelona.' Deep below in the bowels of the stadium the teams nervously prepared. For the managers this was the worst time. Their job was almost complete. Now it was down to the players.

Ferguson gathered his clan around him. He called for their attention, 'There is not a team in the world that can beat you,' he said, 'And that is why you must not be afraid. I am proud of you, and honoured about what you have already given me and the club. The only thing I regret is that I can't send you all out onto the pitch. Because without exception you all deserve it.' With that he wished them all the best of luck. His job done, he

could do no more. Now it was down to the eleven men in red. Or maybe twelve. Or maybe just thirteen.
Ottmar Hitzfeld too gave his final instructions. His players were briefed and everyone knew what was expected of them. Hitzfeld had already been quoted in the German media saying this would be their year. The absence of Keane and Scholes was a monumental bonus for Bayern Munich. Their powerful midfield of Jens Jeremies and the immensely talented if temperamental Stefan Effenberg more than fancied their chances against Beckham and Butt. Ferguson's surprised inclusion of Jespar Blomqvist had momentarily taken Hitzfeld aback, but he recovered swiftly to realise it mattered little. The plan would not change. Babbel would take the elusive Swedish winger and victory would be theirs.

Led by their goalkeeping Captains Peter Schmeichel and Oliver Kahn, the two sides came onto the pitch. The sheer size of Manchester United's support swiftly became apparent. Apart from one section behind a goal the whole of the Nou Comp's vast towering terraces was bathed red white and black. Flags and banners lay draped over every orifice of this wonderful footballing cathedral. The reception for Ferguson's team was overwhelming. Manchester had travelled en masse to Barcelona! Outside the ground there were a further 5000 supporters who were forced to follow proceeding s from the crowd noise and half sighted video screen. Manchester United dare not let such raw passion and undiluted love go unrewarded. They dare not.

All shook hands before battle commenced. Effenburg glanced around at the stadium as if to say, 'Where are our supporters?' Finally, the Champions league theme finished and the players broke ranks to warm up. Schmeichel and Kahn shook hands in the centre-circle. The noise was rising. The atmosphere close to melting point. The highly respected Italian referee Pierluigi Collina wished both his linemen a good game and with the Nou Camp verging on a collective heart attack he steadied himself.

For obvious reasons the city of Munich has and always will be synonymous with Manchester United football club. The coming events of the night of 26th May 1999, were to make the city of Barcelona equally so. United kicked off.......

C31
PRICELESS:
Manchester United v Chelsea: Champion's League final: Moscow: 2008: (John Terry's penalty)

  Even amongst the billionaire Oligarchs of modern-day Russian monarchy, one-time Siberian orphan Roman Abramovich stood alone. It seemed astonishing that a man who can buy the world is forced like 76,000 others in the Luzhniki stadium to simply watch and pray.
In the midst of a Moscow downpour, almost Mancunian in its ferocity a tumultuous occasion reached a heart-stopping climax. A goal apiece, fighting tooth and nail for every inch in what was an enthralling contest Manchester United and Chelsea fought each other to a standstill.
Not a needle thread could be darned between them and after two hours they were only wrenched apart by the hideous facade of penalties. Russian roulette, at first no one missed. Until ultimately an unexpected loss of nerve from United's Cristiano Ronaldo gifted a heaven-sent match-point to Chelsea Captain John Terry.
Handed a golden opportunity to win the Champion's League Terry strode purposefully from the centre-circle, adjusting his armband for all to witness, exuding self-confidence. The many critics of Abramovich's Chelsea claimed they were nothing but a footballing Frankenstein: soul-less, man-made, effective maybe but totally lacking any substance.
But winning the European Cup changes minds, opens doors and creates legends. Upon John Terry's' shoulders lay the immense weight of history. All the grand luxurious yachts, jumbo jets, fine art, limousines and

beautiful women. For Ramon Abramovich victory that night on home soil would have dwarfed all.
Priceless.
Up stepped Terry only to slip sending his effort crashing against Van der Sars' left hand post. Sir Alex Ferguson's team remained alive whilst Terry appeared distraught, his defining moment gone forever. The tears fell. Anderson came forward for United and an amazing night in Moscow went on….

C32

THE GINGER PRINCE
(Paul Scholes goal against Barcelona: 2008)

Old Trafford Manchester United v Barcelona: Champions League Semi Final Second Leg: Sir Alex Ferguson is hardly a man noted for sentimental nature so when he vehemently declares to the world's media that if Manchester United qualify for the Champion's League Final, 'Paul Scholes definitely plays,' journalists and supporters are shocked. Able to see a pass others can only dream of, sublime technique with a deadly eye for goal from near and far. Arguably the finest English player in a generation, but a streetwise temper that when roused in the heat of battle has at times proved his undoing. No more so than Turin back in 1999, when against Juventus a second booking cost Scholes a place in Manchester United's epic Champion's League Final victory in Barcelona. Ironically, it is the Catalans who now stand between United's 'Ginger Prince' and a place at Europe's top table. After a drab 0-0 in the Nou Comp, battle resumes at a raging Old Trafford with a full house demanding United show their true colours. But it is Barca who excel early, none more than the genius of Lionel Messi who leads the home side a mesmerising, merry dance in the opening exchanges. Messi explodes upon Manchester causing heart attacks amongst the locals and its with great relief on fourteen minutes that United finally awake from the magical little Argentine's spell to break out. Cristiano Ronaldo careers into a flurry of Barca shirts but is tackled by full-back Zambrotta, who in turn gives away the ball to an advancing Paul Scholes. Twenty-five yards out and with time to pick his spot Scholes rifles a ferocious drive into the top left-hand corner. Old Trafford erupts! Ferguson's dream of a second Champion's League trophy looms large and for possibly one last time in the shadow of Moscow's Red Square, Scholes will stand beside him.

C33

FLARES OF MANCHESTER: 2010

Here on Wednesday 19th January 2010, Manchester United have travelled across town to play neighbours Manchester City in the Carling cup semi-final first leg. In its short history Eastlands has never experienced such as this. It is a moment meant to signify the beginning of a new era. The coming of an empire that had its roots firmly ensconced in east Manchester, but funded by endless amounts of black Arabian gold. Oil.

A blue moon rising.

A launching pad for a club so tired of simply just existing in the depressing shade of United's seemingly endless trophy parades.

Antagonised beyond all reason by the mischievous banner that lies draped over the Stretford End declaring…. '34 years'….and counting. But now things are changing. The Sheikh's promise of providing world class footballers paid pirate treasures to adorn the blue jersey is proving no idle boast for they are coming by the fistful.

As kick off dawns the lights at Eastlands dim and blue moons are beamed onto the pitch and across the stadium. Finally, Manchester is blue and United at long last left blinded in the shadows. Suddenly, from behind one goal amongst the 6000 United supporters, red flares are ignited to illuminate the away end. With three quarters of Eastlands roaring out 'Blue Moon' and the defiant chants of 'United' deafening, never has Manchester felt such passion and fervour.

To United supporters the flares signify an act of defiance. Though wracked by the Glazer debt which shows no sign of releasing its odious grip over their beloved club they

are not prepared to go gently into the night. For Manchester United's own birthplace of Newton Heath lies only three miles away,
for lest we forget this is their city too!

C34
MURDER ON THE DANCE FLOOR
(Real Madrid v Manchester United: European Cup: Second Round: 2013)

On Wednesday evening at the Estadio Bernabeu, Manchester United and Real Madrid clash for the fifth time in European cup competition. Only once have United prevailed, when back in 1968 a late and rare Bill Foulkes goal secured a 3-3 draw and a meeting with Benfica in the European Cup final. The three other occasions have seen Real prove over the two-legs to be by far the best team. Their line-ups dominated by names that have lit up world football over the decades. All-time greats.

Alfredo Di Stefano, Paco Gento, Ferenc Puskas, Zinidane Zidane, Roberto Carlos, Raul, Luis Figo and now another stands between the Mancunians and a place in the quarter-finals. One who appears destined to stand alongside such legends. The kid from Madeira with the dancing feet. Once of Old Trafford and idol of the Stretford end. Then, eighty million pounds later of Real Madrid.

Cristiano Ronaldo.

Sir Alex Ferguson pre-match thinking will surely evolve around attempting to keep Ronaldo on a short leash. But how? Attempting to rein in this Portuguese firecracker means United could well employ a man marker. Rafael maybe? As Sir Matt Busby did in 1957 by surprising all and telling Eddie Colman to follow the explosive Di Stefano wherever he roamed, the same may apply with the young Brazilian come Wednesday. Hardly a task to relish but one if concentrated and on form the rapid and skilful Rafael could well take to with a relish.

As United fans have discovered over the years picking Ferguson's teams is akin to picking the correct lottery numbers. Who knows what is being planned in the Man from Govan's mind? Many dread United going to Madrid and attempting to simply defend, for they don't possess midfielders of sufficient defensive calibre to protect a defence that at times this season has leaked goals at a fearful rate. Much would rather prefer they adopt the same tactics that has seen them overcome Chelsea and Manchester City this season.

An archetypal Manchester United 4-4-2 with Wayne Rooney just off Robin Van Persie, two wingers and Tom Cleverley and Michael Carrick holding centre midfield. Lure teams in then hit them wide. But this is not Stamford Bridge or the Etihad. The Bernabeu bares comparison with the Maracana, with the Nou Comp. With Old Trafford. This is a theatre of footballing dreams. Of Madrileno dreams. White ghosts. And if not handled with the respect such a grand stage deserves contains the capacity to destroy you.

Stricken by inner fighting, bickering, dressing room revolts and a La Liga campaign verging on the disastrous, Jose Mourinho's last chance of glory this season depends on grabbing a glorious tenth European cup for Real Madrid. Mourinho and Madrid have clearly grown weary of each other. A love affair brief, for a time ecstatic now stands on the verge of meltdown. The debacle with Iker Casillas and Sergio Ramos whom appear to have declared civil war on their coach means it is now a certainty Mourinho will be plying his illustrious trade elsewhere next season.

However, nothing would delight the 'Special One' more than come May on a warm Wembley evening. (Maybe against Barcelona) it is his team. Real Madrid dancing around the pitch holding high that gleaming, glistening trophy. Then, as the cameras close in, he takes off his winner's medal, takes a bow and leaves the stage in style. To where? We wait and ponder. My guess, Paris Saint Germain for a season. Then, Manchester, the red side. As for Wednesday, my heart says a draw, 1-1. My head says United could well suffer the wrath of a young man equally a part of their own rich heritage as Best, Law, Charlton and Cantona.

C35

ONE NIGHT ONLY: Cristiano Ronaldo: 2013

For years Manchester United supporters have sung, ''Put him on a plane, bring him back from Spain, Viva Ronaldo.'' Well, the Portuguese genius is back!

On Tuesday 5th March 2013, Cristiano Ronaldo will step out once more on his old stomping ground at Old Trafford, only this time adorning the legendary shirt of a Madrileno. He treads in special footsteps. Di Stefano, Gento, Puskas, Raul, Zidane. Now, twenty-eight-years old and at the peak of his powers Ronaldo prepares to sprinkle his own particularly brand of gold dust and claim a rightful place amid such illustrious company.

A truly magnificent header to earn Real a draw on home soil and a muted celebration as a show of respect to his old employers and their supporters means his place amid United's all-time greats was duefully reinforced. Now, to have his portrait alongside past Madrilenos in Madrid's hall of fame and what more grand and fitting place to stake that claim than Manchester United's theatre of dreams? Once home but now at least for one night only, enemy territory.

At 1-1, the tie remains finely balanced. Jose Mourinho exuded huge confidence in his immediate post-match interview at the Bernabeu. The 'Special One' taking time out to admonish United for not playing into his hands by committing to all-out attack and instead preferring to play a clever and intelligent defensive game.

Mourinho was seemingly convinced Real will score the necessary goals and finish off the job in Manchester. Sir Alex Ferguson however urged caution. Too wise despite the away goal to even contemplate United had gained an edge, Ferguson agreed with his friend and counterpart that once battle re-commences at Old Trafford, events in Madrid will count for nothing.

The scenes at the final whistle of a tearful Ronaldo embracing Sir Alex Ferguson and later visiting his former teammates in their dressing room again gave hope to United supporters that one day the possibility, albeit highly unlikely of the prodigal son once more in red becoming real. But could such a pipe dream really happen? Ronaldo has made certain utterances regarding his state of mind at the Bernabeu recently. But these appear to be more a reluctance for the world and Barcelona in particularly to recognise that in his mind Ronaldo deserves equal billing alongside whom many consider the greatest footballer of all time.

The magical adopted Catalan from Argentina, the remarkable Messi.

Up until eighteen months ago Ronaldo appeared to be disappearing in the afterburners of Messi's genius. When aided by the bewildering, conjuring duo of Xavi and Iniesta he blew away teams and defences with all the ease of an X MEN character. But now whilst Messi's form has hardly wilted Ronaldo has come roaring back to stand alongside and even overtake his greatest rival for footballing sainthood in goals and in winning back La Liga with Real Madrid from Barca. More than ever the battle between the two rages on for whom is the finest talent on the planet. Most go for Messi, a notion that rankles Ronaldo more than someone stealing his hair gel. However, if Ronaldo explodes upon Manchester United on Tuesday week and sends them tumbling out of the Champions league. And with Barca facing a huge task of hauling back a two-goal deficit suffered against AC

Milan; the crown could well be up for grabs. The stage is set for Ronaldo, a hero's welcome guaranteed, but once that first whistle blows and the crowd roars, friendships both past and present matter none.

Whether one day United fans wish to see him once more in a red shirt does ever comes to fruition? Dubious in the extreme. Such a transfer and the extortionate sums involved would cause a collective panic attack amid the Glazer family and unless they do sell to said interested Arab parties e.g.: Qatar. Then there surely will be no second coming. Sadly, it appears Ronaldo will be heading home for one night only.

But it promises to be a hell of a night!

C36
THERE IS A LIGHT THAT NEVER GOES OUT
Manchester United v Real Madrid: European Cup: Second Leg: 2013

On Tuesday afternoon in Manchester the sight of United and Real Madrid supporters singing together the Morrissey song and Mancunian classic, 'There is a light that never goes out' only gives ruse to the theory that the special relationship that has existed between these clubs since the Munich air crash continues even to this day. That the two-legged tie was ultimately decided by a hugely controversial refereeing decision appeared overall to have little effect on the mutual respect shown by both clubs in this long running saga and tale of two cities. As ever both games were grand occasions. Epic clashes laced with huge drama, great skill and controversy. Jose Mourinho's wonderfully evocative turn of phrase on the eve of the second leg, 'The world will stop to watch this match,' never-truer as events unfolded, then exploded on a memorable Tuesday evening under the glare of the Old Trafford floodlights.

What began in the Estadio Bernabeu with Streford born Danny Welbeck giving United a surprise lead after coming under intense pressure from a Ronaldo inspired Madrid, ended with who else was it ever going to be? The magnificent Ronaldo scoring the goal that sent Sir Alex Ferguson's team tumbling out of Europe. The boy from Madeira again refusing to celebrate as previous with his ferocious headed goal in the Bernabeu. Ronaldo showing neither the desire, nor heart to twist the knife any further into the place he once called home and to those he still views as extended family.

As for Jose Mourinho, the 'Special One' carried himself with real class and rare humility throughout. Both he and Ferguson disappointing the media frenzy that waited with manic anticipation an eruption of words at some time between arguably the two greatest managers alive today. That Jose's respect for Sir Alex and undoubtedly a hardly hidden desire to covet the great man's seat when he finally retires to his horses and roses pruning (as if), maybe caused some to mention an agenda, the fact remains Mourinho did himself and his reputation huge credit.

'The best team lost, that is football.' Were you watching Bobby Charlton?

Sir Alex Ferguson's indignation and sheer fury at the dismissal of Nani meant he daren't risk putting himself before a press conference that could have served as nothing more than a launching pad for the man from Govan's slings and arrows into everyone from the besieged Turkish referee Cuneyt Cakir, to the first journalist who erred to mention the name of a certain Scouse born United player who never made the starting line-up. Instead, out came Mr safe hands and Ferguson's second-in-command Mike Phelan to fend off barbed questions armed with nothing more than banal sound bites and tired clichés. In the end the world that had stopped to watch gave up and left Phelan to it.

As for Wayne Rooney, Ferguson's issuing of his word at Friday morning's press conference at Carrington, that he will still be a United player next season surely ends all speculation of him moving elsewhere? But word or no word, Sir Alex is wise and canny enough to know that it may not be his decision. The cow in the other field may well rear its' ugly head once more. Player's super egos

and greedy agents these days sadly outweigh honourable aged old traits like promises and handshakes.
Hopefully Rooney settles down and helps United win what is now a much desired and needed Premiership and FA Cup double. For this season has in a way not really begun. The possibility of winning back the title from City and taking them on at Wembley in the cup means Wayne Rooney will have sufficient opportunity to end this campaign as once more a red shirted hero.
But for those United fans that dreamed of more European glory at Wembley in May, well those dreams have cruelly been ended. The opportunity to finally rid themselves of what occurred there against Barca in the 2011 Champions League final is now not to be. Finished off by a club whom many years previous after the horrors of Munich gave a helping hand when others simply turned their backs.
If it had to be anyone, so be it, I am glad it was them. As United and Real fans danced, drunk and sang together on Tuesday afternoon in a place the Spaniards once did so much to help, it appears this Tale of Two Cities goes on. And, indeed,
there truly is a light that never goes out.

C37
THE MAN WHO CAN'T BE MOVED
Sir Alex Ferguson: (The Miracle man) 2012

For a man who steadfastly refuses the advances of Father Time, Sir Alex Ferguson appears set for yet another all-out assault on football's leading prizes. Last season's collapse in the champions league and final day heartache in the premier league means the fire in Ferguson's belly must be raging and any as Wayne Rooney has already experienced who slip from expected standards will be ruthlessly dealt with. When needed the man from Govan can be all things to all men. Politician, poet, street fighter, bully and most importantly a managerial genius.

However, considering the structure and make up of this present Manchester United squad, if Ferguson wins back the title or even more remarkably grabs a third champion's league winner's medal, then it will not just be a case of commissioning a statue in the Old Trafford forecourt. They should name the stadium after him.

No arguments that the purchases of Robin Van Persie and Shinji Kagawa will infinitely bolster the United line-up. Moderate and good teams will come to Old Trafford and leave decimated. However, in the matches that fire the soul. The likes of Manchester City, Chelsea, Real Madrid and Barcelona, will United's much questioned midfield have the necessary guile and physical prowess to cope against the world's best?

De Gea, Rafael, Evra, Carrick, Vidic, Ferdinand, Cleverly, kagawa, Rooney, Van Persie and Valencia appears to be Fergusons preferred line-up when United are set to face a major rival. A side that is never going to bully opponents into submission more likely beat them by playing neat, intricate and incisive football. Something Ferguson's teams have always achieved but with the added punch of steel running through its core. Arguably, Vidic apart and the human grenade masquerading as Wayne Rooney when his head isn't right, United now lack that particular weapon in their armoury.

It will need a vast improvement of luck with injuries and United's own duo of Benjamin Buttons, Ryan Giggs and Paul Scholes to contribute hugely from the substitute bench for Ferguson's dream of a league and European double coming to fruition. This, allied with the firepower of Hernandez, Nani (cards marked for the January sales) and Welbeck means such a mouth-watering achievement is not beyond the realm of fantasy.

Hugely difficult and requiring the odd miracle maybe but for the Man who can't be moved, miracles are a large part of his forte. We shall see….

Post note: Sir Alex won the title back but dreams of European glory ended at the hands of Real Madrid and Ronaldo.

C38
FERGIE'S WAY
Sir Alex Ferguson's Retirement: 2013

Late Sunday afternoon as Sir Alex Ferguson makes that final walk from the tunnel alongside the touchline to his seat, the tears around Old Trafford will be enough to flood the red sea. So, it ends, 1986-2013. A footballing dynasty unsurpassed. Trophies plundered at such a rate Manchester United's trophy room glistened so bright it could be viewed from the moon. Teams filled with players that captivated and enthralled, exhilarated and at times when the red mist fell they exploded and appalled. Cantona, Keane, Hughes, Giggs, Scholes, Van Nistelrooy, Beckham, Rooney and Ronaldo. Men not just for all seasons but whose great deeds saw them enter the annals of United legend.

Footballing empires brought to heel, one especially dragged kicking and screaming to its knees. Liverpool. The Anfield cub reduced to taking twice a season pot-shots at their enemy from twenty-eight miles up the East Lancs road. This against a side they once swatted like flies as the Liver Bird soared high. Before as he so famously quoted, Sir Alex knocked it off its 'f-----g perch! Such has been the animosity and vitriol between these two giant bastions of English football Ferguson's retirement is for many Liverpool supporters being viewed as the end of a long-term jail sentence. Similar to Andy Dufrense in the classic movie the Shawshank Redemption. When Dufrense finally escapes his prison horror and becomes a free man.

There have been other challengers. Mighty enemies armed with great wealth. With Russian gold and Arab oil. Blackburn, Arsenal, Chelsea and now one so close to home you can hear them breathing. Manchester City. All have rose and temporarily toppled Ferguson's kingdom. Only then to feel the wrath of a man who reacts to losing battles, leagues and cups like a bad-tempered lion with a toothache.

On foreign shores in the champions league Sir Alex's greed and lust for success was never fully realised. Maybe his greatest regret was not winning one, maybe two, even three more. The two that were claimed came in remarkable circumstances. Barca 1999 and Moscow 2008 both heart-stopping victories that sucked the energy and drained the heart and soul out of every Manchester United supporter on the planet.

'Who put the ball in the German net, Ole Gunnar Solskjaer' and 'Viva John Terry' destined to be United terrace classics for generations to come.

For this man who came into my life twenty-seven years ago and along with my little boy being born has given me some of the best days and night of my life. There can be no word to describe how he will be missed. But this is not a eulogy. There is no funeral march, no pipers and minute silence. Instead it is simply to raise a glass to the future! Sir Alex is walking off into the sunset. Whether it be annoying the neighbours by tinkering on his piano. Reading his vast wealth of books or back to the sport of kings. A little advice, The Rock of Gibraltar is not worth the hassle. This Politician, this poet, this street fighter and what has been most importantly for United supporters, this true managerial genius.

The curtain is closing and one last bow remains. Oh, I am sure there have been regrets along the way, but really too few to mention. You don't reach the top of the mountain without encountering storms and making enemies. The records will show that Sir Alex took the blows and come the end did it his way. For that we are truly grateful.

C39

SILVER BULLET
David Moyes: 2014

For David Moyes, though he will never admit publicly drawing the European champions Bayern Munich in the quarter finals is equivalent to standing in front of a firing squad and praying they will all miss.

As Manchester United's disastrous premiership campaign dipped beyond pitiful and verged towards scandalous in last week's 3-0 debacle against Liverpool at Old Trafford,

Moyes faced hostility towards a United manager not seen since Dave Sexton had a shoe thrown at him by an irate woman from the Old Trafford stands back in 1978.

However, these days the slings and arrows and high heels are delivered through the different channels of social media.

Red supporters letting fly a torrent of abuse through fan forums, twitter and Facebook. The times early in the season when Moyes could rely on a significant amount of support online vanished in ninety-minutes of half-hearted nonsense and a betrayal in a performance of the red devil crests on the players' shirts.

Then came Wednesday and the Greeks baring gifts in the shape of Olimpiakos. And suddenly the red flag was flying high once more. A night of high drama, nerves, emotion and ultimately what this club is all about.

A throwback to Fergie time.

The old master on his feet in the dear seats roaring for the United defenders to not sit back. Old habits refusing to die as Sir Alex Ferguson's mask of just a watching (nothing to do with me anymore) punter finally revealing that inside still burns the passion and fire that this present team have lacked all season.

At time performances so lack-lustre and short of desire they appeared to have been drugged.

But not this night and a 3-0 victory earned by a revitalised Robin Van Persie hat trick and a glorious performance by forty-year old Ryan Giggs. One defying Father Time and surely enough to make any male of a similar age consider yoga. Giggs remaining a footballer light years ahead in both technique and intelligence of the lumbering oak tree masquerading as the twenty-seven million pound Marounne Fellaini. And then today in recognition of sending the Greeks packing, that magnificent Portuguese man-o-war Luis Figo, in his wisdom handed Manchester United, Pepe Guardiola's Bavarian masters.

Cheers Luis.

Amongst the red hordes the words, 'My God' featured high.

Guardiola's preferred playing style refined and mastered in Barcelona now practiced with equal touch, finesse and painstaking accuracy by Robben, Kloos, Ribery and their fellow artisans. Meanwhile, David Moyes has struggled to design a template for his United team that have struggled to pass to a fellow red shirt all season. Like a punch-drunk boxer being battered around the ring and unable to hit back they have staggered, stumbled and constantly fallen.

And guess who is coming to dinner soon?

Before the Munich ties there remains the small matter of Manchester City rocking up next Tuesday at Old Trafford fighting for a second title in three years and always up for wiping the floor with their one-time all-conquering neighbours.

Whether Moyes has enough tactical nous to prevent further humiliation against our blue brothers waits to be seen. His comment after the Etihad 4-1 disaster when he claimed, 'United fans would have to get use to this,' not something you would expect from the so-called prophet labelled the 'Chosen one.'

Not in my eyes.

For I fear another night of embarrassment and howling at the blue moon with this man who appears totally out of his depth. Hopefully, from somewhere he finds the silver bullet that enables him to overcome City and at least ensure Manchester United still have intact that most important asset after the two-legged tie against Bayern Munich.

Pride.

Post note: United lost both and before long Moyes was gone….

C40
KINGDOM FOR A HORSE
(unpublished)

Moscow: Champions League final: Wednesday 21st May 2008: Sir Alex Ferguson stands on the touchline with arms folded in the pouring Russian rain. The game has finished 1-1 after extra time and will now be decided on the lottery of a penalty shootout. Ferguson is thinking of events past and what is to follow...

'So, my legacy comes down to this. These penalty kicks are out of my control. If the boys lose their nerve how will I be judged? If a shot hits a post or the bar, goes wide. If Petr Cech performs a miraculous save, how will I be judged?

Victory will sort many ills. History will judge me alongside the immortals. Two European cups, one more than Sir Matt Busby, but who was loved more by United fans? Busby was known as the father of this football club. Will I be forever associated as the man who built up such trophy laden riches only then to see it all thrown away on a punt?

A gamble to save face? I never needed the money; it was all a question of pride because I don't lie down to anyone. But Magnier and McManus had my measure. What the bloody hell was I thinking? I wrongly believed I was untouchable and infallible, amongst the stars, when in reality I rode blindfolded into a storm. And, from the wreckage the Irish wreaked revenge and so emerged the Glazers. Will I forever be remembered for sacrificing my kingdom for a horse?

After all these years then is this how I will be judged? After everything I've given. The joys and the ecstasy. Have I erred so badly as to be beyond redemption? Here

in Moscow under red skies in the pouring rain the next ten minutes will define this.
Here in Moscow, Abramovichs' backyard against all odds I've taken us once more to the brink of glory.
Here in Moscow……
 Barcelona feels like only five minutes ago.
Nine years previous….
Barcelona: Nou Comp: Champions league final Wednesday 26th May 1999.
The fourth official's board goes up and it's saying only three minutes of extra time. I look at my watch, is that all? A disgrace. We're one down. I always remember Jock Stein telling me to prepare equally for defeat as well as victory.
I think that time has come.
Still the lads keep pushing. Oh, they're tired, so bloody tired but the Bayern players, they're exhausted. Almost out on their feet. So many times this season United have been down and out but from somewhere have found the guts to win. I've installed into them never ever give up. Keep playing your football, focus and concentrate on what we've taught you to do.
Pass the ball and keep it red, be patient, to probe and wait for the chance. Nothing is ever over until the referee blows that whistle. Nothing until I say. Then I'll let you rest.
Then I'll let you breathe. Then I'll let you sleep.
But don't you dare give up whilst the game is live. Don't you dare. So, they run and run until they can run no more.
Our supporters are not giving up because they know their team is capable and suddenly the roar grows even louder as Gary Neville wins a corner down this near side

touchline. I'm watching as if hypnotised. Don't you lot come off this pitch beaten for I won't allow it. Not tonight of all nights. Not tonight here in Barcelona. Our crowning glory. My crowning glory.

I see a green shirted figure race over the halfway line and into the fray. Peter Schmeichel has taken it upon himself to join the fight. Tonight, in his last game for the club the big man is my Captain and should have stopped Mario Basler's first half free kick but that's past now for many times Peter has saved us.
None more than the FA Cup semi-final replay against Arsenal. A fight to the finish, a battle of men with no quarter asked or given by either team or manager. Myself and Arsene have respect but no friendship. We're too alike. Peter's last gasp penalty save from Bergkamp giving us the initiative even with only ten men to go on and win. He's been a great servant for me and will be missed but should have saved Basler's free kick.
He should have saved it….
I watch David Beckham sprint across to take the corner. Remember all you've been taught son. Every breath and every second matters now. David is a cool and calm character and can be difficult off the pitch to handle, but he's as tough as any player I've had. They went for his throat after the 1998 world cup but we looked after him. The press and other supporters but the reds formed a circle and protected him. We did, Manchester United football club. Now he can repay me for everything by putting it onto the head of one of his mates and keeping us in the European cup.
Behind David the crowd is a jumping, desperate, raging and demanding sea of United red. From all corners of the world they've gathered here. This isn't just a football

club it's something almost spiritual. Reared on legends and fed on tales of glory and heroes. 'Nothing is impossible,' I tell my boys. I'm infected too, I've drunk from the well of this amazing football club and now at its helm I'm demanding one more miracle. For ours is a special kind of red.

Blood red.

We've taken a long time to get here, too long and they're still believing even now as the Catalan skies grow even more black there feels no sense of impending doom. For I insist it can still happen and it must happen. In our red world in a single eye blink despair can become delight. For we specialise in miracles and have mastered the art of breaking other team's hearts. Thirty-one years is too long to wait for this club: I've strained every sinew to get here. Now, it all comes down to the beat of a ticking clock speeding endlessly down.

Too fast, much too fast.

In comes the corner and I strain to see Dwight leap at the far post to keep the ball in the six-yard box, but a Bayern defender scrambles it clear. Panic ensues, nothing remains of that legendary Teutonic calm, the Germans have gone and have nothing left.

Time stops still as Ryan Giggs meets the ball on the penalty area edge and with his left foot mishits, only for the ball to land at Teddy Sheringham's feet.

Teddy turns and fires low and true into the Bayern goal. This is madness; my lads have done it again!

They'll be crying down on the Mersey because we have saved ourselves! Oh, they will be seething. Crying and wailing. Years of anger and frustration. They're desperate for us to fail, aye knocked off their fuckin' perches and now screaming at the sour-faced Liverpool moon.

I'll never win the European cup they claimed. They laughed, they mocked and they scoffed.

Well, 1-1, we're still alive and are back from the dead. Bayern have hit our bar, the post but have been unable to finish us off. We still have teeth and have bit deep and now cue this sheer unadulterated madness unfolding around me. How many times can we continue to do this? How many times?

I find myself being embraced by Steve McLaren. I'm on the pitch punching the air. Salvation: I glance to my left and see all my substitutes careering off to join in the celebrations. Any hamstrings and I'll have their bloody heads. The Munich players are on the floor. I look across and my friend and Bayern coach Ottmar Hitzfeld is clearly devastated. But I feel no pity, we'll share a glass later because at this moment I wish him nothing but more agony on the pitch. I wish him nothing but plague and pestilence upon his vanquished Bayern household. They're finished, he knows it. They've nothing left.

'We need to get the player' heads sorted for extra time 'Alex,' says Steve, but I sense something. I look around at the scenes unfolding around the Nou Comp. I feel Teddy's goal is nothing but a mere aperitif. Something else is coming, it's going to happen. I just know it. I can feel it….

'It's not over Steve,' I reply, 'This isn't fuckin' over, you watch. You just bloody watch!' We attack again and win another corner. The Stars in the Catalan heavens have turned red and a shooting star blazes across the jet-black skies. Good evening Sir Matt, happy birthday, took your bloody time!

It's time to end this.
Schmeichel looks across to me seeking permission to go upfield once more, 'You fuckin' stay there' I scream! This is crazy. This is surreal, this is my Manchester United. Never surrendering and never giving up.
Beckham's corner goes into the near post for Sheringham to flick on and then just an explosion of sound!
A thunderous roar the likes I've never known. I see Ole Gunnar Solskjaer fall to his knees and be pounced on by red shirts. Ole has made our dreams come true.
Ole Gunnar Solskjaer has put the ball in the German net from six yards and the Bayern players are lying on the floor like they've been machine gunned. The referee Pierluigi Collina is helping them to their feet but they are reluctant to stand.
The great Lothar Matthaus sits looking into space as though forced to watch his house burn down. Matthaus was magnificent before being substituted. He ran the game, a class apart. But Bayern got cocky, their supporters were celebrating with ten minutes to go.
What were they thinking?
Surely they knew that was akin to pulling a tiger's tale whilst trapped in its cage. We were always going to get them in the end. For they were over confident and you do that against my team and they'll crucify you. They'll nail you to the fuckin' cross and destroy you.
This lot did everything but hammer their own nails in.
In time added on with neither the time to spit on the floor or write your name on a piece of paper left to play this is my moment. This is my impossible dream.
This is how you win a European cup. Nobody has ever done it like this before. No one. Not Stein, Paisley or Clough. Just me, Alex Ferguson. This'll be my epitaph:

this glorious three minutes of wonder here in Barcelona.
My impossible dream comes true.
The final whistle!
The critics and disbelievers can never doubt me now.
Across this grand old cathedral of football daubed red and white are faces etched with looks of incredulity and elation. There are as many tears as smiles.
Here in Barcelona, Manchester United and Alex Ferguson have won the European cup.
Now, what happens next?'......

And the reds go marching on, on, on…….

Printed in Great Britain
by Amazon